Praise for *Our America: A Hispanic History of the United States*

"[Fernández-Armesto] pays rich tribute to the country's Hispanic past, present and future." —*New York Times*, Editors' Choice

"[*Our America*]'s great strength is its optimism grounded in robust, rigorous scholarly enquiry and lyrical, poetic, and engaging prose. . . . I find this book to be indispensable." —Zalfa Feghali, *London School of Economics and Political Science Review of Books*

"[A] valuable contribution to those seeking a broader understanding of U.S. history. Students and politicians alike could benefit from the scholarship of Mr. Fernández-Armesto. . . . We owe him a debt of gratitude for deepening our comprehension of Hispanics in the U.S.— how they came here and how their shared narrative has shaped our nation." —Janet Napolitano, *Wall Street Journal*

"A compelling invitation to explore and imagine the influence of Spain and America from its inception. . . . His lyrical style, attention to detail, . . . and thought-provoking ideas augur well for this story. It is a welcome and most worthwhile addition to American history and historiography." —Roberto Haro, *Somos en Escrito*

"Fernández-Armesto's survey covers . . . an awesome time span that would daunt most mortals but which the author handles with his customary fluency, humour and unremitting scholarship. . . . [A] story that is both entertaining and incisive."
—Henry Kamen, *Times Literary Supplement*

"A well-researched and skillfully constructed history of the United States from the viewpoint of Spanish speakers. . . . [E]loquent and poignant." —Marcela Mendoza,
The Americas: A Quarterly Review of Latin American History

"Fernández-Armesto . . . tells, with extensive depth and customary elegance, the fascinating and little-known Hispanic past of the United States and the country's Hispanic future. The vast majority of history books about this country are too *anglocéntricos*."
—William Chislett, *El Imparcial* (Spain)

"If you think, as I did, that the first permanent European settlement in what is now the United States was Jamestown, then Felipe Fernández-Armesto's *Our America* should be on your reading list."
—Allen Barra, *Dallas Morning News*

"[Fernández-Armesto]'s skill is to move easily between the panoramic and the particular, illustrating his analysis with lively anecdotes."
—David Luhrssen, *Shepherd Express*

"An intellectual in the tradition of Américo Castro and Salvador de Madariaga, Felipe Fernández-Armesto offers a perspective seldom considered—and urgently needed: he looks at the history of the United States from an Iberian viewpoint. Yes, the descendants of the conquistadors, missionaries, and explorers also have a say. With a lucid, engaging style, he seeks to understand the continuity between the Spanish colonization and the fight for justice led by the Chicano movement in the sixties and by immigration advocates today. . . . This is an invitation to look at America in full!"
—Ilan Stavans, general editor of
The Norton Anthology of Latino Literature

"In enviably lyrical prose, Felipe Fernández-Armesto has written a bold and compelling synthesis of our nation's Hispanic past, from the Spanish arrival in the late fifteenth century to the current and contentious debate over immigration reform. Marshaling famous and forgotten individuals and events, he reminds us that there is much more to America's story than simply Massachusetts Pilgrims and Virginia Cavaliers."   —Andrew R. Graybill, director, Clements Center
for Southwest Studies, Southern Methodist University

Also by

FELIPE FERNÁNDEZ-ARMESTO

Conquistadors: A Very Short Introduction
(coauthor with Matthew Restall)

Columbus on Himself

1492: The Year the World Began

The World: A History

Amerigo: The Man Who Gave His Name to America

Pathfinders: A Global History of Exploration

So You Think You're Human:
A Brief History of Humankind

The Americas: A Hemispheric History

Columbus

OUR AMERICA

※

A Hispanic History of the United States

FELIPE FERNÁNDEZ-ARMESTO

W. W. NORTON & COMPANY

NEW YORK LONDON

Since this page cannot legibly accommodate all the copyright notices,
pages 383–84 constitute an extension of the copyright page.

For information about permission to reproduce selections from this book,
write to Permissions, W. W. Norton & Company, Inc.,
500 Fifth Avenue, New York, NY 10110

For information about special discounts for bulk purchases,
please contact W. W. Norton Special Sales
at specialsales@wwnorton.com or 800-233-4830

Manufacturing by Courier Westford
Book design by Barbara Bachman
Production manager: Julia Druskin

Library of Congress Cataloging-in-Publication Data

Fernández-Armesto, Felipe.
Our America : a Hispanic history of the United States / Felipe Fernádez-
Armesto. — First edition.
pages cm
Includes bibliographical references and index.
ISBN 978-0-393-23953-9 (hardcover)
1. Hispanic Americans—History. 2. United States—History. 3. United
States—Civilization—Hispanic influences 4. United States—Ethnic
relations. I. Title.
E184.S75F46 2014
973'.0468—dc23

2013037336

ISBN 978-0-393-34982-5 pbk.

W. W. Norton & Company, Inc.
500 Fifth Avenue, New York, N.Y. 10110
www.wwnorton.com

W. W. Norton & Company Ltd.
Castle House, 75/76 Wells Street, London W1T 3QT

1 2 3 4 5 6 7 8 9 0

Toda la piel de América es nuestra piel.

[ALL AMERICA'S SKIN COVERS US.]

~ *Attributed to Pablo Neruda*

CONTENTS

NOTE ON USAGE

✠

M Y FOCUS IS ON THE MORE THAN FIFTY MILLION US CIT-izens and permanent residents who, like me, list themselves as "His-panic" in official surveys, and their ancestors. I call them "Hispanics" or, in contexts where a Spanish name seems more appropriate, "his-panos." The name corresponds to a form of identity well established in official statistics and widely accepted by people who apply it to them-selves. I use the word "Latino" only when quoting or alluding to the modern academic literature in which it is the favored term for immi-grants to the United States from Latin America or people who share some aspect of culture or tradition of supposedly Latin American ori-gin. I should confess that one reason I avoid it is that it excludes me, as my paternal origins are in Spain; another is that it includes Brazil-ians, who are not part of my remit in this essay. The term "Hispanic" originated in official circles only at the end of the sixties, and initially designated Spanish-speakers. When I use it, it does not entail any language, pigmentation, or other cultural trait: it is simply a self-descriptor. But throughout the book, for reasons of practicality and common sense, I treat the use of Spanish as a sufficient, though not necessary, criterion of inclusion. I call Hispanics' enemies, or those some Hispanics perceived as enemies from time to time, "gringos" in an attempt to capture or invoke a particular point of view; of course I do not consciously use the term, or any other, with a pejorative intention, mindful of the warning of Esmeralda Santiago's "Papi":

> "You should never call an *Americano* a *gringo*. It's a very bad insult."
> "But why?"
> "It just is . . ."[1]

The same goes a fortiori for names applied to Hispanics, such as "greasers" and "dagos." I sometimes use "Chicanos" for Mexican Americans who designate themselves as such, and "indios" for Native Americans in areas formerly belonging to the Spanish monarchy.

As I had different editions of Gonzalo Fernández de Oviedo's *Historia general y natural de las Indias* to hand at different times, I have cited the work by chapter numbers, and have done the same for Richard Henry Dana's *Two Years before the Mast,* because my copy is of an obscure and undated edition. In both works, chapters are short and, as far as I am aware, consistently numbered in all editions.

FOREWORD

BY AMADEO PETITBÒ JUAN

DIRECTOR, FUNDACIÓN RAFAEL DEL PINO

THE IMAGE OF THE UNSETTING SUN HAS STOOD, LONG AND OFTEN, for the enormous size of the Spanish monarchy in the sixteenth to eighteenth centuries. When the great orb shone on Hispanic dominions in Asia, darkness covered the lands of the Crown of Castile in America. The sun's rays reached them after lighting European kingdoms and states that were subject to the Catholic monarch. Vast territories encompassed varied peoples, geographies, and cultures, some of which preceded and survived imperialism, while others emerged and developed within or alongside the framework of the monarchy.

If we focus on Hispanic America, most of which later became a set of independent republics linked by a common language and in cultural fraternity with Spain, we find an apparently anomalous case: a great country, the United States of America. Even though it does not belong to the group of nations that has come to be known as Latin America, the United States shared a common history with most of them, partly because a large portion of its current territory formed part of the dominions of the Spanish crown. We need only recall the frontiers agreed to by Spain and the United States: first, in 1795, under the Treaty of San Lorenzo, also known as Pinckney's Treaty, and then in 1819, under the Transcontinental Treaty, also called the Adams-Onís Treaty after its negotiators. The long period of shared history is not sufficiently known or valued in American and Spanish historiography. Although particular authors have produced works of genuine merit, the scope for further research is enormous.

In the context of the aims of the Rafael del Pino Foundation, which include the preservation of Spain's historical and cultural heritage, the foundation takes an active part in cultural enterprises that highlight all that both nations share, and particularly the role played by Spain in the historical shaping of the United States. In addition, a total of almost three hundred foundation scholars have studied at American universities; currently there are thirteen in the United States. Three ongoing partnership agreements with Harvard University and one with Georgia State University in Atlanta are evidence of our interest in sharing our ideas and sentiments with the United States.

Our sponsorship of Professor Fernández-Armesto's book is therefore not an isolated initiative but part of a broad cultural policy. The book we present is a history of America from a Hispanic perspective. Or perhaps it could better be described as a book on the presence of Spain in the history of America. But it is much more than that, since it also focuses on Hispanic influence in the country's recent past, its present, and even its immediate future. *Our America: A Hispanic History of the United States* will leave no one indifferent. Born and educated in England, now teaching at the University of Notre Dame, and before that at the University of London, Professor Fernández-Armesto invites us to join him on a journey along many paths through the past, present, and future Hispanic dimension of the United States. He starts by taking us back to the time of the discovery and the colonies, and then moves us on to travel through times and places that mark the difficult relationship between the two great powers: albeit one of them, Spain, then in decline with its dominant role forgotten, and the other, America, rising to the peak of its still-active role as a world-shaping and world-reshaping force. The book's closing pages contemplate the future while keeping an eye on the past: *why the United States is—and has to be—a Latin American country.* The author takes a positive approach "is—and has to be—," avoiding the word "problem," the use of which in any intellectual discourse, in the words of the great Hispano-American writer Jorge Luis Borges, "may be an insidious form of question-begging." The book's invariably positive line of argument leads us to a present that is not without difficulty but, above all, to an encouraging future. A past worth remembering; the present embodied by our del Pino Foundation scholars; and a future in which Hispanic influence and the richness of Hispanic culture contribute constructively to the United States: this is the setting for all that the Rafael del Pino Foundation does in partnership with a country that is a fine friend and ally for Spain and the whole Hispanic world: the United States.

INTRODUCTION

"It's like the optical illusion of the tumbling cubes—you know, the pattern of cubes which looks concave to the eye; and then, by a readjustment of your mental focus, you suddenly see them as convex instead. What produces that change? Why, you catch sight of one particular angle in a new light, and from that you get your new mental picture of the whole pattern."

~*Ronald Knox*, *The Three Taps* (1927)

I STARTED THIS BOOK—IN MY HEAD, WHICH IS WHERE I ALWAYS start writing, years before I hit a keyboard—in Colorado Springs. I had gone there to give some talks at the U.S. Air Force Academy. At the time, the academy had a reputation as an evangelical, conservative enclave. Some students had their bibles to hand when they asked me questions. They clearly wanted the world to be a lot simpler than it really is. Generally, however, I thought the academy was an exemplary place of education and that it was comforting to know that the officers of the armed forces of the world's superpower are encouraged in critical intelligence, ethical reflection, and breadth of culture. The teachers I was lucky enough to meet, most of whom were air force officers, with a leavening of lay scholars, were liberal in the best sense of the word: unprejudiced, thoughtful, generous.

I had a long conversation about immigration with one of them. He had—with one limitation—what I would call a proper view of the subject. He realized that the United States needs immigrant labor, and plenty of it. He wanted the country to be welcoming to immigrants and appreciated that the best way to turn them quickly into patriotic citizens or committed residents is to make them feel at home. He had no trace of hostility to any color or creed. He knew that the future of the United States was inescapably plural and that natives had to adapt to change, just as newcomers had to adjust to fit in.

His only scruple was that he thought that "people who come here must learn the native language." I did not think he spoke or meant Ute or Comanche, so I said, "I quite agree. Everyone should learn Spanish." He looked nonplussed for a moment; so I added, "What is the name of this state?" As we were in Colorado, he conceded my point. I could reciprocate by agreeing that everyone in the United States should know English, but not at the expense of forgoing their ancestors' languages. I also insisted that bilingualism is at least twice as good for any community as self-incarceration in a single language.

The encounter made me realize that even well-educated, amiable, open-minded people in the United States do not realize that their country has a Hispanic past, as well as a Hispanic future—or, at least, that if people do realize this fact, they commonly assign it no contemporary relevance or cultural significance.

The 2012 presidential election, in which Hispanic voters in unexpected numbers and in surprising solidarity turned out to support Barack Obama, alerted even the most myopic politicians to Hispanics' current and future strength in numbers. As I check over the text of this book for the last time, tweaking the prose, responding to the publisher's suggestions, thinking better of some assertions and boosting others, I am surrounded by newspaper columns and emanations from airwaves and blogosphere that are abuzz with the importance of the Hispanic vote. In the United States, a "demographic" becomes "the vote" whenever voters in a particular age group or ethnicity or phratry or other psephologically defined tribe evince, in combination, strength of numbers and congruent voting habits. Politicians and power brokers then take notice and court them.

In the 2012 election the winner, according to pundits' consensus, had the backing of 71 percent of voters who class themselves as Hispanic. President Obama's margin of victory in most swing states was so big that he would have won even if Hispanic voters had divided much more nearly equally. But in Florida, Nevada, Colorado, and New Mexico, which are likely to remain among the most fiercely contested states in future elections for many years, he needed the support of the majority of Hispanics to win. He got it. In one respect Hispanic voters decisively bucked a trend: Nevada and Colorado were the only western mountain-region states to support Mr. Obama. The importance of the phenomenon seems bound to grow, partly because Hispanic numbers are growing and partly because Republicans' appeal to Hispanics has declined year-on-year since 2004. Republican strategists are expected to respond by planning Hispanic-friendly policy turns and framing Hispanic-oriented messages.[1] "We have a Latino problem that just cost us a national election," was the response of GOP spokesman Mike Murphy on election night. "We're going to have to have a very adult conversation that might turn into an intra-party fistfight about how we become electable again."[2] Shortly after the election, the Republican scramble for Hispanics' favor began, when governor of Nevada Brian Sandoval announced a fast track to state identity documents for some allegedly illegal immigrants.

NEVERTHELESS, WHILE POLITICS HAVE affected perceptions of Hispanics' role in the present and future, the facts of electoral life seem to have made little difference, so far, to the way most people perceive Hispanics' place in US history.

I recall with pleasure an amusing moment in *The Andy Griffith Show*—perhaps the most-often-aired serial ever broadcast in the United States. When I first stumbled on the show, flicking channels in an attempt to appease exhaustion during an insomniac night in an uncomfortable hotel, I thought the dialogue captured, with greater fidelity than almost any other document of popular culture I then knew, what ordinary people think about the country. In the episode I have in mind, Andy and his friends enroll for an adult education class in US history. They begin by asking when US history began. "As soon," one character suggests, "as the Pilgrim Fathers stepped off that ship." Andy demurs, pointing out that there were English colonists in Virginia before the landing in Massachusetts. His remark provokes someone to say that maybe the story began deep in the history of England. Someone else mentions Columbus, provoking a suggestion that maybe part of the story began in Spain, but the suggestion dwindles in the ether and the course follows the conventional narrative of the unfolding of Anglo-America across the continent from east to west. In another episode, the schoolteacher who becomes Andy's sweetheart asks her class where the United States began. Andy's son pipes up with the instant answer, "Jamestown, ma'am. 1607."

Citizens of the United States have always learned the history of their country as if it unfolded exclusively from east to west. In consequence, most of them think their past has created a community essentially—even necessarily—anglophone, with a culture heavily indebted to the heritage of radical Protestantism and English laws and values. Immigrants with other identities have had to compromise and conform, sacrificing their languages and retaining only vestigially distinctive senses of their peculiarities as "hyphenated" Americans. The heirs of slaves have had to subscribe to the same process. Natives who preceded the colonists have had to surrender and adapt.

Of course, the Andy Griffith version of US history is not wrong. The country, like the stripes in the flag, is woven, in part, of a horizontal weft, stretching across the continent. But no fabric exists without a strong warp crisscrossing at right angles from bottom to top. The Hispanic story of the United States constitutes the warp: a north-south axis along which the United States was made, intersecting with the east-west axis highlighted in conventional perspective. Making the Hispanic contribution conspicuous is like tilting the map sideways and seeing the US from an unusual approach.

History is a muse you glimpse bathing between leaves. The more you shift your point of view, the more is revealed. I do not say this for some postmodern reason, in order to imply that historical reality is nonexistent or inaccessible. On the contrary, I think the truth is out there. But truth cannot be grasped easily or all at once. We build up a picture bit by bit, rather as, circling a sculpture or a building, we compose an overall impression by contemplating each fragment, each aspect at a time. The advantage of a shift of perspective is that it adds to our stock of perceptions and gets us nearer to the truth—the objectivity that lies at the sum total of all possible subjectivities. Fresh perspectives always enhance our vision by challenging our assumptions. Think of the Argentine or Australian maps of the world that put south at the top, or a still life by Paul Cézanne, who, resuming work every morning, would set up his easel in a different spot, in order to place each object he painted in a peculiar perspective of its own. In this book, I adopt only one, Hispanic perspective. So this is not a comprehensive history of the United States, only an essay designed to open a different vista. It does not disclose the whole truth of the subject, but draws attention to an important and still underemployed way of approaching it.

I do, however, try to include the whole country panoptically, and the whole period from 1505 to the present. The justification for trying to scan such a long, broad story in one sideways glance is that piecemeal histories have not so far succeeded in changing the way most people in the United States contemplate their country.

MATERIALS FOR STUDYING THE warp became available in the late nineteenth century, thanks to Hubert Howe Bancroft, a Californian businessman who devoted his retirement and fortune to collecting documents, commissioning professional researchers, and publishing regional histories, bringing into a single conspectus the whole of Pacific-side America west of the Rockies and the Sierra Madre, with some excursions beyond, as far east as the Gulf of Mexico. Bancroft had strong moral sensibilities, conservative inclinations, and an aversion to everything that seemed to him coarse, vulgar, and irreverent. He hated the gold rush, which he thought might have corrupted California forever if honest farmers had not followed the gold diggers. He detested narrow nationalism and saw the mixture of migrants and natives in his state as exemplary—"this intermixture of the best from every nation" whose "effect upon the good-will and advancement of mankind will be felt more and more as the centuries pass by."[3] In fifty years of indefatigable work from 1868 onward, Bancroft's output never included a history focused on the Hispanic contribution to the making of the United States, but he made it possible to see that such a history existed.

Bancroft's successor in teasing the country's Hispanic past out of the archives was Herbert Eugene Bolton. He graduated college in the 1890s—the decade in which the Indian Wars ended and the US Census Bureau declared the frontier closed—just as the United States came to fill the continent from sea to shining sea. Bolton moved west himself, from Pennsylvania, where he did graduate study on free blacks in the antebellum period, back to his home state of Wisconsin to teach school, then across the country in the footsteps of pioneers to professorships in Texas and California. Along the way, he began to question the east-west story of the making of the United States, which he had learned from one of its greatest exponents—his own teacher in Madison, Frederick Jackson Turner. The depth of the evidence of Spanish colonial penetration Bolton saw in the Southwest convinced him that there was more than one story to be told of how the US was made.

In "the old borderlands north of the Río Grande, the imprint of Spain's sway is still deep and clear," Bolton found. "Nor," he noticed, "is this Hispanic cult—or culture—losing its hold. On the contrary, it is growing stronger. In short, the Southwest is as Spanish in color and historical background as New England is Puritan, as New York is Dutch, or as New Orleans is French."[4] He extended the range of the researches Bancroft had commissioned in Mexican and Spanish archives. He adopted a complex, plural vision of the nature of the United States as the confluence of a lot of different pasts—in the colonial era, French, Spanish, and Dutch as well as English—and multiple beginnings. In 1920 he tried to write a history of the colonial period of North America with multiple starting points in Spain, England, the Netherlands, and France.[5] He acknowledged that there were other possible openings or exordia in the Native American and black pasts, though his work never gave them equipollence with those in Europe. He also inaugurated a debate, which is still going on, about whether it makes sense to see the history of the United States as exceptional in its own hemisphere, or whether it is better understood in the context of the history of the Americas as a whole: he changed many scholars' minds on this point, but in popular perceptions the notion seems ineradicable that the United States is marked out as special by the unique features of an unparalleled past.[6]

Bolton wrote with a wide readership in mind, but the reach of his influence outside the academic world was small. Carey McWilliams, on the other hand, was a first-rate popularizer, with a journalist's vocation for communication and a scholar's disposition and grasp. Before he became, in 1955, a long-serving editor of *The Nation*, which is still exemplary in proclaiming liberalism in the United States, he worked in California, dividing his time between his profession as a lawyer—specializing in the advocacy of the underprivileged—and writing reports and commentaries on the glaring social injustices that evidently and deeply touched his heart. He had experienced deprivation himself in his childhood, when his family ranch collapsed. The Depression radicalized him, as he saw workers in desperate straits abandoned or exploited.

From 1939 to 1942 McWilliams worked in the state government's Department of Immigration and Housing, championing immigrant farmworkers and escapees from the Dust Bowl. He raised funds to defend the accused Hispanics victimized in a notoriously corrupt murder trial in Los Angeles in 1942 (see below, p. 269) and defended Japanese-American internees during World War II. He denounced anti-Semitism and McCarthyism. César Chávez, the hero of Chicano farmworkers in the 1960s, claimed to have learned about agribusiness from him. Witch-hunters accused McWilliams of being a Communist for questioning bans on interracial marriages and suggesting that Hispanic children should be allowed to swim in Pomona's public baths.[7] He wrote many influential books. One the world largely ignored, published in 1949, was *North from Mexico*, in which he developed some of Bolton's insights and outlined a case for an alternative history of the United States, constructed along the migration routes of Mexican workers.

McWilliams failed to change public awareness of the Hispanic contribution to the making of the United States. Bolton's legacy, meanwhile, was immeasurably more influential in universities than outside them. He is commonly said to have had more PhD students than any other historian in the history of the world. Those students spread the message and established a tradition, known as the Borderlands school, which has contributed innumerable histories of the regions of the United States that were once part of the Spanish monarchy or the Mexican republic, and which has highlighted the broader influence of the Hispanic past of the United States. The borderlanders have succeeded in supplementing, but not displacing, the traditional myth. Even in academic circles, as we shall see, most Americans still think that Jamestown is the best starting point from which to construct a narrative of the making of the present-day United States; many even think—clearly falsely—that the first permanent European settlement in what is now US territory was English.

There is, of course, an equally mythical Hispanic version of US history, in which the Spanish era appears as a lost civilization truncated by Anglo barbarism, while historians' vision seems hypnotized by the twirl of the caballeros' spurs, enchanted by the dark eyes of sinuous señoritas, dazzled by the flash of swordplay, and disarmed by the piety of missionaries and martyrs. Carey McWilliams was wary of the myth, challenging the mawkish romanticism and fake memories that gilded the Southwest's Spanish past.[8] A representative and surprisingly influential piece in a regional periodical in 1955 denounced Hispanophile mythopoeia for exaggerating the role of Spanish culture in the Southwest "from Helen Hunt Jackson and the Ramona legend to the . . . latest real estate speculator who manufactures

Spanish-sounding place names."[9] I suspect that the Hispanic myth originated as an antidote to the Anglo myth. So in this book I concentrate fire on the latter, and hope that the former will falter in response. Of course, myths should be treasured for the art they inspire, and studied and understood for the sake of their genuine impact on real events. But they can only be fully appreciated as myths if they are distinguished from history.

THIS BOOK IS NOT a study of immigration, because Anglos' understanding of their Hispanic neighbors in the United States has often suffered from representations of the Hispanic presence as a result of immigration into a country with a culture sprung fully formed from its eastern seaboard. Hispanics belong in the entire story of the country—as part of its origins and part of every important episode in its unfolding. Of course, immigration is a big theme in what follows, because it has reshaped the Hispanic presence in the United States—as it has made all communities in the country what they are, regardless of how long they have been around. "Immigrants," as Oscar Handlin, one of the greatest US historians of immigration, pointed out, "were American history." John Higham, a slightly younger and almost equally heroic historian who flourished in the 1950s, studied the equivocations of US responses to immigrants in a classic book that helps make Anglo unease about hispanophone immigrants today intelligible by locating it in historical context. He shared Handlin's perception, which has become US orthodoxy.[10] But the Hispanic United States encompasses more than migrants. Hispanics preceded the United States in what is now national territory. Their presence has been a longer part of the history of the land than that of any other intruders from across the Atlantic, including Anglo-Americans.

Fears grow out of the misperception that immigration is the sole source of Hispanic influence in the United States. Fears and falsehoods gorge one another like serpents sucking their own tails. Two kinds of fear count in the current situation. First, fear of "illegals," which is mainly economic, follows the rhythms of job opportunities:

there are moments, sometimes dangerously sustained, of nativist resentment whenever times are tough, but the fears subside as soon as people realize that immigrants shun shrinking job markets. When economies recover, illegals are welcomed again to do the jobs no one else wants. Cultural fears, secondly, are more insidious than economic ones. Anxieties about the mutability of culture play an understandable part. US unease over the erosion of familiar customs, language, manners, and ways of life is part of a global phenomenon. Even communities with a long investment in multiculturalism, in the Netherlands, for instance, and the United Kingdom, have turned against it in recent years, and politicians have won votes by promising tougher immigration laws, stronger demands for immigrants to "integrate" and "assimilate," and higher standards of cultural adjustment in citizenship tests. Revulsion from multiculturalism—which, admittedly, does not work well but which should surely be praised for working at all—has profoundly affected the United States, where it was never strong and where immigrants have always been expected to plunge their distinctiveness into the "melting pot." In 2005, with courage bordering on recklessness, Samuel Huntington—the Harvard political scientist whose animadversions on Hispanics, to which I shall return at the end of this book, aroused indignation in Europe and Latin America— voiced fears of the dilution or transmogrification of US identity by a wave of Hispanic immigrants. Whether focused on economics or culture, the fears, I want to argue, are irrational. In the chapters that follow, I argue that people in the United States can be unafraid in the face of the changes currently under way.

There are plenty of encouraging historical precedents. Just about every feature of culture that US patriots formerly overvalued or sacralized as essential has turned out to be compatible with other, new or complementary cultures that immigrants have introduced or Anglos' predecessors bequeathed. No particular ethnic model has retained a privileged place in US identity. You can be black and be president. There is music that "sounds American," as Glenn Miller put it, but a lot of it sounds Irish or Latino or Jewish as well. I do not think, for instance, that the pace or direction of immigration will ever attenuate the English tenor and traditions of most US law, but it is easy to imagine a future in which the United States will get its law mainly from the English strand in its history and other aspects of culture from a mixture of contributions from other communities, originating in different parts of the world.

Protestantism has long ceased to be a definingly "American" tradition. Strictly speaking, the founding fathers themselves excluded it by refusing to make an "establishment of religion," though reactionaries fight a rearguard action on its behalf as a supposed source of such secular features of culture as individualism, capitalism, and even democracy (though as we shall see [below, p. 336], Protestantism really has little or nothing to do with any of these). Catholics have long outnumbered any Protestant church in the population. They were already the largest single denomination by the middle of the nineteenth century, growing to about 20 percent of the population by the time of World War II. About a quarter of US citizens today are Catholics. In the last four decades the Catholic population has grown by nearly 75 percent. Now there are four times as many Catholics, according to declarations made in the census, as adherents of the next biggest communion—that of the Southern Baptists. It is no longer (if it ever was) un-American to be Catholic.

The English language still has a powerful hold on minds searching for unifying principles. In this land of immigrants, most non-Spanish speakers still tell pollsters that the country must have a single language to remain united (though historical precedents suggest the opposite: most successful states, including many of the most powerful and longest enduring, for most of history, have combined political unity with bilingualism or linguistic plurality). The status of English could and probably will change. The English of the United States has already borrowed many peculiarities of its grammar and lexicon from other languages, especially Spanish and Yiddish. Spanish is already de facto the second language of the United States and de jure the second language of parts of it (although for reasons we shall encounter, I doubt whether Spanish will ever be as privileged in the United States as, say, French is in Canada). The idiom of the fictional dialogues by the acclaimed US writer of Dominican birth, Junot Díaz, captures modern American hybridity. Most of the Spanish words in his macaronic lexicon are about sex. In "Ysrael," his first short story, published in 1995, *tigres* scrawl *chocha* and *toto* on the walls and *chingan* the *chicas*. It is as if Samuel Pepys, who chose Spanish, along with French and Latin, to conceal his diary's dirty thoughts from his wife and servants, were reincarnated as a street urchin, and Díaz's profanities, like Gibbon's footnotes, were clad in the decent "obscurity of a learned language." Yet the impression should be resisted. Spanish is not arcane or esoteric in the United States. As my Air Force Academy host came to acknowledge, it is a native language of the country, with a longer history as such than English. A genuinely US identity can survive in a bilingual and multicultural future.

THE PURPOSE OF THIS book, in short, is to show that there are other US histories than the standard Anglo narrative: in particular, a Spanish history, rolling from south to north and intersecting with the story of the Anglo frontier, provides me with a narrative yarn, and I thread other histories across and through it. I rotate the usual picture, so that instead of looking at the making of the United States from the east, we see what it looks like from the south, with Anglo-America injected or intruded into a Hispanic-accented account. The effect, I hope, is that, instead of the history of blacks, Native Americans, and later migrants becoming add-ons to an anglocentric story, they become equipollent strands in a complex fabric.

Today's plural America looks, in these perspectives, like a product of the whole of America's past, not a threat to traditional US identity. There was, we learn, no single frontier, no single language, or tradition, or identity, no manifest destiny, no culture that deserves to be hegemonic or that predominates or ought to predominate by virtue of US historic experience.

The very diversity of Americans' origins helps to explain why Americans typically are so invested in symbols of unity—the language, the law, the flag, the historical myths, the "American Dream." *E pluri-*

bus unum: the founding fathers meant the slogan to apply to a multiplicity of states, but now the multiplicity is of ethnicities and identities and tongues and colors, and the process of constructing unity continues in a cultural rather than a political sense. Ironically, the United States is now so rainbow-hued that pluralism is the most effective common value. Americans can hold together only by being at ease with their own diversity. In these circumstances, US people are bound to reconsider their history and see it as originating in numerous places. Plymouth Rock may never be submerged by the rising tide of pluralism, but it will be less prominent.

Because I frankly adopt a single perspective, I offer what follows only as an essay on the history of the United States, not a comprehensive study, with the aim of stimulating thought rather than accumulating knowledge. Part One covers the colonial era. Chapters One and Two tell the story of the first European colonies in what is now US territory east of the Rockies: Spanish establishments in Puerto Rico, Florida, and parts of what we now think of as the Southwest. In Chapter Three I turn to the English or (as they became) British establishments and their early intersections with those of Spain. Chapter Four is about early colonization in California and the ensuing showdown with Anglo-America, culminating in the Mexican War. The next two chapters make up Part Two, which deals with the decisive episodes of the nineteenth century that made the Hispanic story of the United States seem—for a while—trivial, marginal, or over: the subordination of the Hispanic population and the expansion of Anglo-America into the West. In Part Three I turn to what I call Hispanic countercolonization since the late nineteenth century and its transformative—and, I argue, salutary—effects. Each chapter is named for a myth, because myths impel history. Material conditions and exigencies shape it—bodies, biota, elements, economies—but the events they shape start in the minds that imagine them. In America, especially, the stuff of which history is made are dreams.

PART ONE

ORIGINAL SINS

*The First Hispanic
Colonization of What Is
Now US Territory,
c. 1505~1846*

CHAPTER ONE

THE FOUNTAIN OF YOUTH

The First Colonies in What Was to Be the United States, c. 1505~1763

America is a young country with an old mentality. It has enjoyed the advantages of a child carefully brought up and thoroughly indoctrinated; it has been a wise child. But a wise child, an old head on young shoulders, always has a comic and an unpromising side.

~*George Santayana,* Winds of Doctrine (1913)

THE FIRST EUROPEANS TO SETTLE IN WHAT IS NOW THE TERRI-tory of the United States of America were three pigs and some goats.[1] The year was 1505. The place was Puerto Rico.

When I was teaching at Tufts University, in Massachusetts, not far from the legendary Plymouth Rock where, according to a long-standing misconception, US history is commonly supposed to have "begun," a vacancy occurred for a professor of history in the colonial period of what is now the United States. The best postdoctoral specialists in the period applied. We had the cream of the country to choose from. I asked all the candidates the same question. It was rather a sneaky question, but not unfair in the circumstances: "Where, in what is now US territory, was the first enduring European colony, still occupied today, established?" Surely it was reasonable for a prospective or actual professor of the colonial period of the United States to know the answer. None of the young people who passed hopefully before our panel committed the folly of pointing in the direction of Plymouth Rock. "Jamestown, Virginia," was the unthinking answer of most candidates, reflecting the assumption that English colonists forged what became the United States, and built it from east to west. Others, more aware of the possibility of a trap, said, "It must be somewhere in Florida, or maybe the Southwest," and nominated San Agustín, Florida, or Santa Fe, New Mexico. These answers, though not strictly correct, were sensible. Europeans have been in continuous occupation at San Agustín since Spaniards fought Frenchmen for it in 1567. Santa Fe and El Paso were in Spanish hands from 1598—a decade before the colonization of Jamestown began—though Santa Fe was briefly evacuated during a seventeenth-century Indian revolt. The correct answer to the question about the location of the first permanent European colony in what is now US territory is, however, Puerto Rico, founded over a hundred years before Jamestown.

Yet nobody thinks of Puerto Rico as the place where US history began, partly because the island did not become US territory until 1902, when the republic had been in existence for fully a century and a quarter, if one counts from the Declaration of Independence, and the country already had a character and constitution to which Puerto Ricans had made no contribution. Obviously these are valid scruples. They account for why, in one of Stephen Sondheim's versions of his lyrics for *West Side Story*, he wrote that "nobody" in the United States knows that Puerto Rico is "in America."[2]

But in part, Americans—including Puerto Ricans, sometimes— ignore or deliberately exclude Puerto Rico because of prejudice: prejudice that the United States is a country made by white Anglo-Saxon Protestants, constructed by anglophone colonists, where

concepts of liberty and law are defined by traditions that originated in England; where the English language is the basis of whatever cultural unity can be contrived among all the ethnicities that
make up the population; and where you become "American"—or,
more accurately, where you qualify to be a citizen of the United
States—by subscribing to a canonical version of the history of the
country that begins among English colonists on the east coast of
the continent.

None of those prejudices is unquestionable. All are founded on
shaky historical assumptions. No country has an unchanging essence.
No community has an unchanging identity. What it means to be
English or Chinese or Spanish or Indonesian or American changes all
the time. There was never a time when most Americans, or most people in what is now the United States, were white English Protestants.
The making of the country has been a collective effort—sometimes
collaborative, sometimes conflictive—of all the ethnic and religious
minorities who inhabit it. Native American "Indians" have been contributing for longer than Anglos. By the end of the colonial period, in
much of the rural south, blacks counted for more in terms of numbers
and perhaps effort than white English people. Over 40 percent of the
population of Georgia and the Carolinas were black when the Declaration of Independence was signed. Without the input of other communities of European origin, the United States today would be
unrecognizable. Without the migrants who have joined from Asia,
especially in recent times, the future character and dynamic of the
history of the United States would be very different and, probably, less
successful in conventional terms—in terms, that is, of wealth and
power—than it would otherwise be. I can imagine a US history text-
book of the not-too-far-distant future beginning not with the arrival
of Puritans in Massachusetts, or with English adventurers in Jamestown, or even with French and Spanish contenders in Florida, or conquistadores at El Paso or in New Mexico, but with three pigs and
some goats in Puerto Rico. What might such a rewriting of the country's past look like?

—

COLUMBUS CALLED THE ISLAND San Juan Bautista, in honor of the patron saint of the heir to the Spanish throne at the time. "Boriquen" was the nearest he could get to the way the natives said the name of the place where he landed in November 1493. The assonance with the Spanish word for rich, *rico,* turned out to be fortuitous: the island had gold.[3] So San Juan de Puerto Rico was a suitable designation and, eventually, after the relocation of the main city on Puerto Rico Bay in 1521, Puerto Rico became the island's enduring name.

Columbus was searching for what he could recognize as civilization—somewhere he could engage in sophisticated, potentially profitable trade and, if possible, find evidence of the supposed proximity of the rich, advanced lands of east Asia, such as China or India— some proof that he had delivered on his promise to his backers to open a new route to the Indies. It was disappointing to him to find that the buildings were all of straw and wood, but comforting to be able to assert that they were cunningly and solidly constructed. They were also empty, even the tall beach house that Columbus supposed belonged to the local ruler as a sort of pleasure resort, although it was presumably, at least in part, a watchtower. The fleet's physician guessed why the natives fled at the Spaniards' approach. They lived in fear of cannibal raiders from neighboring communities or nearby islands. The encounter between native and newcomer began in misunderstanding and suspicion. Each suspected the other of cannibalism. As far as the prospects for colonization in Puerto Rico were concerned, the natives' behavior seemed auspicious. Their timidity was a short-term source of annoyance, as it meant that at first the Spaniards could not get at them. In the long term, however, it suggested that they would be easily cowed, bloodlessly conquered, handily domesticated, and profitably exploited.

Other Spaniards did not share the discoverer's distress at the apparent inaccessibility of China. On the contrary, the failure of Columbus to deliver on the terms of his contracts with his financial backers and with the monarchs who legitimized his enterprise meant the lapse of his rights to the exclusive exploitation of his discoveries.

From 1498 the routes he had pioneered were flung open to interlopers. Puerto Rico, an easily conquerable island with plenty of native gold, was ideally equipped to excite cupidity in Spain. The environment, though tropical and unfamiliar to Spaniards, had congenial aspects, demonstrated by the profusion of fruit trees—"like those of Valencia," Columbus said in a transparently promotional choice of language. One of the opportunists who sailed in Columbus's wake was his former partner, Vicente Yáñez Pinzón, who obtained a patent from the king and queen as governor-designate of the island, with the right to conquer it. His ambitions bedeviled and delayed settlement, because Columbus's heirs disputed his claims. On August 8, 1505, however, he took the first step toward founding a colony. He released those pioneering pigs and goats.[4] It was the usual procedure for preparing new islands for settlement. The plan was that the animals' progeny would multiply and provide food for the colonists who would arrive in a year or two. But the lawsuits began and the colonists did not come.

After nearly three years of haggling, with the rivals' claims still unresolved, a way forward emerged. Juan Ponce de León, a Castilian gentleman of obscure origins, had made a favorable impression as governor of the town and province of Higüey in Hispaniola, the first island Spaniards subjugated and settled in the New World. The governor of Hispaniola chose him to make a preliminary incursion into San Juan, with temporary authority to gather gold and find a site for a colony. The expedition sailed on July 21, 1508, with forty-two men, including a ship's crew only eight strong: not enough manpower to hold a whole island in subjection or establish a settlement, though the ship's carpenter would be able, if the opportunity arose, to supervise the building of a stockade on land. Juan Ponce's search for a habitable site was unsuccessful, but he did gather significant samples of gold— according to his accounts, more than 800 pesos (in modern terms, of a little over 450 grams, or about a pound each). Flushed with gold and optimism, he went to Hispaniola in 1509 to bid for a contract with the crown to rule the island himself.

Three circumstances delayed the resumption of his efforts. First, the Columbus family still had an outstanding claim, though that of

Vicente Yáñez de Pinzón had lapsed. Second, the pigs and goats had failed to deliver their potential: there were insufficient food sources—at least, insufficient for Spanish tastes and appetites—on the island. Finally, during Juan Ponce's spell in charge of the island, the crown would not authorize the exploitation of indigenous labor. The last problem was a frequent source of grief to conquistadores and investors in many parts of early America. Without pliable labor, no colony could succeed. But the Spanish monarchs regarded the natives of the New World as their subjects, whom it was their duty to protect, and potential converts, whom they had to encourage in Christianity and treat with charity. Colonial entrepreneurs had to find a way around the monarchs' scruples—ignoring them in some cases or, in others, supplementing or supplanting native labor with imported slaves.

Apart from importing labor, two strategies were available. First, indios could be classed as subject to enslavement, either as captives in morally justifiable warfare—waged, for instance, in defense against aggression or to recover usurped property—or as infringers of natural law by virtue of cannibalism, human sacrifice, supposed sexual perversions, or rebellion "against their natural lords." Alternatively, by means of a legal device known as encomienda, which the crown authorized in Hispaniola in 1503, the more or less informal arrangements by which natives contracted to serve Spaniards could, in effect, be imposed by gubernatorial decree.[5] Most governors did not wait for royal authorization to divide native labor services among their followers. In Juan Ponce's case, however, compliance with royal policy was essential: he needed royal patronage to secure his rights against competitors.[6] Juan Ponce returned to his island without formal rights as governor, but with a governor's effective authority for the time being to distribute land and exploit mining rights. His freedom to exploit the natives remained highly circumscribed. He could buy provisions from them, for fair recompense, only if they had a ready surplus and "not against their will."[7] He doubted whether he would be able to honor his obligation to protect the natives from depredations: there were Spaniards on Hispaniola keen to enslave them, and natives on other islands anxious to eat them. To protect his wards, Juan Ponce tried to have canoes on neighboring islands destroyed, but the governor of Hispaniola refused to cooperate in so radical a measure. The terms on which Juan Ponce was authorized for mining, moreover, were hardly generous. After the deduction of the usual royal tax of one-fifth of all proceeds, he had to split the remaining profit fifty-fifty with the crown. This left insufficient funds, he claimed, to cover the costs of employing men and dogs, providing their rations of salted pork and fish, wheaten bread, oil, and vinegar, almost all of which had to be imported.

Still, to a remarkable extent, Juan Ponce's colony overcame the disadvantages that afflicted it. He found, at first, that the natives, or some of them at least, were remarkably cooperative. This is one of the unremarked paradoxes of Spanish conquest in the New World. In many places, it was not really conquest at all, but a negotiated process in which native communities, for reasons of their own, admitted Spaniards to privileged and sometimes ruling positions. To understand why and how such a surprising turn of events was possible, we have to make a brief excursion into what one might call the anthropology of conquest.

Two ASSUMPTIONS HAVE WARPED previous accounts of the establishment of Spanish rule in the Americas: first, that conquests are necessarily violent and conflictive episodes. "War," as Thomas Hardy said, "makes rattling good history, but peace is poor reading." Therefore, our history books have concentrated on the blood and guts of the subject—the massacres, the atrocities, the pitched battles, the protracted sieges. And of course all these things happened frequently and ferociously in the New World when Europeans intruded. But for every serious passage of arms there were scores, perhaps hundreds, of cases in which natives came to an accommodation with the newcomers after little or no bloodshed. In Mexico, for instance, our traditional accounts are full of the sanguinary horrors of the fall of Cholula, where Hernán Cortés, by his own account, authorized the massacre of thousands of townspeople, or of Tenochtitlan, which he razed to the ground, or of the conquest of Michoacán, where the conquistador

Nuño de Guzmán committed so many cruelties, according to the chief chronicler of the events, "that he was the principal cause of the aversion of the natives to the soft yoke of the gospel."[8] But the conquistadores did not have to fight for the allegiance or alliance of literally hundreds of cities or towns, formerly tributaries of the Aztecs.

The conquistadores themselves, or the priests who wrote their own explanations of what happened, tended to attribute successes to a miracle of Providence, or to Spanish prowess, or to technical or moral superiority. Some ascribed their success to the folly, superstition, or fatalism of the natives, who, undermined by prophecies of their own doom, supposedly resigned themselves to the rule of beings they mistook for gods. In reality, however, none of these explanations had much merit. The workings of Providence lie beyond a historian's brief and beyond the reach of evidence. In battle, the technical advantages Europeans enjoyed in the Americas did not last long. Their adversaries readily acquired and adapted to horses, which were not, in any case, suited to most of the terrains Spaniards conquered. The available guns were slow, inaccurate matchlocks reliant on supplies of volatile powder and scarce shot, of little or no use except for purposes of display in most of the environments in which conquistadores labored. Moreover, Spanish armor was generally an encumbrance in the New World, quickly discarded. Steel swords and bolts were deadlier than most natives' weapons, but insufficient for victory against the sort of odds conquistadores commonly faced. Spaniards enjoyed a huge advantage in nautical technology, but, after getting them to the New World in the first place, it played little part in warfare, except in relatively rare instances of lake and river wars. Nor, of the celebrated trinity of guns, germs, and steel, did germs make a decisive difference in most conquests, since almost everywhere Spaniards relied absolutely on native allies to do most of the fighting. The ravages of the new diseases from Europe, to which natives of the Americas were unimmunized, affected the allies as much as or, since they were in close contact with the sources of infection, more than the enemy.[9]

Natives did not usually mistake the newcomers for gods and, if they did, were quickly disabused by the all-too-human behavior the intruders evinced. Conquistadores were not, on the whole, superior to any other class of persons, including natives, except perhaps in their own estimation. Stories of their exceptional heroism and valor derive mainly from their own accounts, which they wrote, typically, in an attempt to secure rewards from the crown for their services in the conquest and which, therefore, project an exaggerated and often incredible image of their authors' merits. In Puerto Rico, a tradition that began with Gonzalo Fernández de Oviedo, the chief chronicler of Spaniards' observations of ethnography and natural history in the early years of the conquest, asserted that the natives regarded the Spaniards as "children of the sun," immortal and invulnerable, until they tried an experiment. They offered to carry a Spaniard over a river, pitching him in and holding him under until his mortality was beyond doubt. In case of divine trickery, they repeatedly checked up on the corpse, "until he smelled bad."[10] Such tales of awestruck natives and divinized Spaniards come from the accounts of conquistadores, who were themselves trying to understand the strangely favorable way in which many indigenous people responded to them. Conquistador literary output, moreover, was under the influence of delusive literary models: the lives of saints and the fiction of romantic chivalry, in both of which realism played little part. The deeds of the conquistadores in their own works, and in the historical tradition that derives from them, resemble those of modern comic-strip heroes endowed with special powers.

The conquests of what became Spanish territory in what is now the United States engendered many such stories. In Puerto Rico, the most egregious tale was of the conquistador Diego de Salazar, whose most famous escapade might have been written by Hollywood screenwriters, though its real source, prior to its appearance in the chronicle of Gonzalo Fernández de Oviedo, was almost certainly Salazar's own *probanza de méritos*—his account of his services for presentation to the king in solicitation of rewards. If the document were believable, we should have to acknowledge that he crept unseen into the heart of a hostile village to rescue a woefully disheartened captive conquistador. While the natives were feasting in preparation for the ritual sacrifice of their prey, whom in obedience to their custom they proposed to torture to death in agony prolonged for the pleasure of gods and spirits, Salazar released his comrade. Single-handed, he led him out of the midst of the foe, fighting off three hundred enemy warriors, fatally wounding their chief, and escaping, bloodied but unbowed.[11] As if this feat were insufficient, he returned to the enemy camp in answer to a summons from the moribund chief. His companion begged him on bended knees to refuse the request, but Diego demurred: he would rather return and die than flee in fear. Far from exacting revenge, the affronted chief begged to be allowed to take Salazar's name: the exchange of names was, supposedly, a way of signifying respect and cementing friendship. Salazar assented and went away laden with gifts of food, jewels, and slaves. Thereafter, "I fear you as if you were Salazar" became a proverbial testimonial among the natives.[12]

The romantic and rhetorical flourishes make the story incredible. The dénouement echoes many fictions of chivalry—indeed, Fernández de Oviedo himself had written such a work of fiction before taking up a chronicler's vocation. The chivalric theme is even more prominent in his story of a black conquistador known as Mejía, whose job was to guard a friendly native chieftainess. She refused to flee when Carib raiders—anthropophagous natives from some nearby island—arrived, but Mejía would not leave her side in the face of impossible odds. He was bristling with the enemies' poisoned arrows when he expired—not, however, before he had transfixed their leader with a single lance thrust and dispatched two other assailants, wounding many more.[13] The story is a typical fantasy: if Fernández de Oviedo did not make it up, Mejía's heirs probably did.

So why did so many native communities ally with or, as in the case of Puerto Rico, initially submit to the Spaniards? Unless we acknowledge that native peoples retained their initiative in the face of would-be conquerors from Europe, and made rational decisions, consistent with their own cultures and traditions, about how to react, we shall never understand the origins of the modern Americas. Generally speaking, wherever Spaniards were favorably received, they established their empire. Where they were not, it commonly took generations of fight-ing to subdue resistance or, in many places, to reach a stalemate. In some places, the difference was simply a matter of calculation on the natives' part. All indigenous peoples had traditional hatreds and con-flicts of their own with neighbors. They made use of the Spaniards for their own purposes in the service of their internecine wars. That does not, however, explain why in so many cases they deferred to the new-comers and assigned them places of command in war, or authority afterwards.

The solution to the problem lies in what I call the stranger-effect—the propensity some cultures have to receive the stranger with excep-tional honor. In our modern Western societies, the propensity is hard to understand, since our attitude to strangers is like that of the peoples who resisted the Spaniards. We mistrust them. We reject them. We call them "illegals." We impose on them bureaucratic or fiscal burdens. If we admit them, we make them unwelcome and typically assign them low status and demeaning work. In other times, however, and in other parts of the world, people have not, in these respects, behaved like us. Sacred rules of hospitality oblige people in some cultures to greet strangers with their best gifts and goods and women and even actual deference. When Spaniards found themselves treated this way in parts of the Americas, they felt godlike—and with some reason: the anthropologist Mary W. Helms has collected many instances of cul-tures in which the value of visitors from afar increases with the dis-tance they seem to have traveled, because they bring with them the aura of the divine horizon.[14] This does not necessarily mean that peo-ple mistake them for gods, but it does explain why their persons are regarded as special, even sacred. Though the notion is remote from modern Western sensibilities, I think the most hardened, secular-minded Westerner can understand it, if he or she thinks of how we add value to goods according to the distance they traverse. In my local grocer's shop—allowing for relatively modest differences in produc-tion and delivery costs—domestic Parmesan commands a much lower price than the kind imported from Italy, not because it is worse, but because it is familiar. The exoticism of the foreign product imparts prestige. So it is, in many cultures, with people. In Christendom in the past, pilgrims profited from a similar effect, acquiring prestige with their neighbors, on returning home, in rough proportion to the remoteness of the shrines they visited.[15]

To defer to the stranger—given an appropriate cultural context—is often a highly commendable, rationally defensible response. The stranger is useful as an arbiter or judge because he or she is uninvolved in existing factional and dynastic conflicts and can bring an objective eye to matters of dispute. For the same reasons, strangers make first-class bodyguards or close counselors for existing rulers—which is how many European intruders (and even runaway black slaves, who sometimes ascended to positions of power in indigenous society without any of the advantages commonly said to be decisive in the case of European conquistadores) began to acquire eminence in American and Asian polities in the early modern period. The stranger is often sexually attractive, perhaps for evolutionary reasons or perhaps for sheer novelty. In the Caribbean, Gonzalo Fernández de Oviedo thought native women "were very chaste with their own men, but gave themselves freely to Spaniards," in what sounds like an act of sexual hospitality instanced in many other cultures.[16] In any case, the stranger typically represents an excellent choice of marriage partner for powerful or ruling families by virtue of arriving untainted by any previous associations with local rivalries. To this day all over the world, where monarchies still exist, heirs typically marry foreigners or, increasingly nowadays, social outsiders, for this very reason.

The proliferation of stories of stranger-kings in many parts of the world—stories, that is, of individuals whom polities have entrusted with kingship after arrival from afar or return from long and distant exile—demonstrates the value of strangers as rulers. Even in Europe, many royal dynasties have traced their origins to stranger-founders, and legends multiply the instances. Such cases are very frequent in Southeast Asia and parts of the Americas and Africa.[17] That touch of the divine horizon, moreover, makes the arriviste from afar a good candidate for sanctity. Many conquistadores in the New World really were holy men, friars who arrived with little or no military support but commanded their hosts with surprising, if sometimes precarious, success. Others were treated as if they were holy men (see below, p. 36).

ALTHOUGH OUR SOURCES FOR the events that unfolded when Juan Ponce landed in Puerto Rico are exiguous, it is apparent that he benefited from the stranger-effect or something very like it. A chief whom the chronicler calls Agüeibana "took great delight" in Juan Ponce's company and showed him the whereabouts of rivers of gold.[18] The chronicler put a warning into the mouth of the cacique's mother: her son must heed the Spaniards if he did not want to die at their hands. The story sounds like a romantic flourish, but intimidation may have played a part in securing an apparently warm welcome for the invaders. Some natives, it seems, were willing to work on the Spaniards' behalf: the evidence is that Juan Ponce had lands sown with cassava, the native source of starch, as well as with wheat, to offer for sale to intending colonists. The beginnings of colonization were not delayed by native resistance, but by the old dispute with the Columbus family. By June 1510, however, the crown had acceded to one of Juan Ponce's most urgent requests: henceforth, ships from Spain would be allowed to call at Puerto Rico, so supplies would always be obtainable and the island would have first pick of intending settlers from Spain. The following month, Juan Ponce had received his confirmation in the office of governor and could proceed to the foundation of a town.

It was a decisive moment in the inception of every Spanish colony. When two Englishmen meet on a savage frontier, they found a club. When two Spaniards meet in similar circumstances, they found a city. The moment was also worthy, surely, of celebration in any history of the United States: the founding of the first European city on what is now US territory. Caparra, however, did not last. It prefigured the history of America as a land of ghost towns and overambitious settlements. The site proved unhealthy for Spanish occupants, and various relocations were attempted before the present site of what came to be known as San Juan de Puerto Rico was founded in 1521. Meanwhile, also with native help, Juan Ponce proceeded to pan for gold. The first smelting took place in November 1510. Between then and his death in 1521 Juan Ponce oversaw the smelting of nearly 22,000 pesos of gold, nearly ten tons in weight, according to official reports. Presumably the real figure was higher, owing to peculation, tax evasion, and fraud.

The new governor's main achievement so far had been to keep peace with the natives—owing less, perhaps, to his own benevolence than to awareness of the fragility of his position and his need to preserve the favor of the crown. Columbus's son, Diego, continued to agitate at court against Juan Ponce and, asserting his rights as viceroy in Hispaniola, had sent agents of his own to Puerto Rico in an attempt to wrest power from his rival. Eventually, in November 1511, Diego Colón prevailed. Royal instructions to him and his agents said that Juan Ponce had killed no indios and ordered his successors to follow the same humanitarian course;[19] yet within a few months native insurgencies convulsed the island. What went wrong?

The sources conflict and historians have never established a consensus. The key to getting the sequence of events right lies, however, in the archival documents, rather than in the rambling, patchwork chronicles. A reasonable reconstruction of the history identifies the arrival of Diego Colón's agents as a turning point. They claimed that violence had broken out under Juan Ponce before their arrival, alleging that native conspirators had murdered another of Diego Colón's men, Cristóbal de Sotomayor. They used the story to justify the raids they launched against native communities for slaves.[20] Without a state of war, slaving was illegal: under Spanish law only captives taken in the course of a just war could be legitimately enslaved, and the monarchs were scrupulous in enforcing the rule. So the agents' claim looks self-interested. At court in Spain, prevailing opinion backed a rival story: Sotomayor's assailants had been Carib raiders from an unidentified island, not natives of Puerto Rico.

Instead of relying on informal, ad hoc arrangements for the exploitation of native labor by agreement with individual chiefs, as Juan Ponce seems chiefly to have done, his supplanters instituted a new system of forced labor, modeled on the encomienda of Hispaniola. They assigned groups of natives to particular Spanish colonists, who had the right to take tribute from their indios in the form of labor and the obligation of providing Christian proselytization. The newcomers' reasons for innovating are unrecorded. In part, no doubt, they were simply implementing arrangements familiar from their experiences in Hispaniola. In part, they were introducing a labor regime Juan Ponce might have favored if he had been able to get away with it. In part, perhaps, they were responding to necessity. Native labor was not only hard to mobilize: it was declining in numbers. Though reliable figures are unavailable for the period of Juan Ponce's rule, we can fairly assume that—as on almost every frontier of colonization in the early modern world—natives succumbed in large numbers to European diseases, against which they had no inherited immunity.

The combination of corvées and slaving *razzie*, with the abandonment of the former policies of coexistence on the Spaniards' part, seems to have provoked what the Spaniards called revolts among adversely affected communities, though strictly speaking the native peoples had not renounced their sovereignty and owed no allegiance to Spain. The natives' own divisions, and the fact that some regions remained exempt from the effects of the new regime, made the insurrections containable. Juan Ponce took part in suppressing the so-called rebels, if reports of his enslaving sixty-four captives can be believed.

The new regime's priority was to get him out of the way. The best scheme was to get him a promotion that would rid them of his presence: a promise of unfettered authority as governor in a new conquest. In March 1513, Juan Ponce sailed northward in search of a reputedly gold-rich island called Bimini. He might expect better luck there than in Puerto Rico, for now he had a commission directly from the crown, which no rival official could revoke. The news of his departure "has pleased me much," the king wrote. "May it please our Lord God to carry him to Bimini and grant him a good voyage."[21] In some ways the voyage was propitious. Juan Ponce laid claim to Florida, which he seems to have regarded as an island, and reported the existence of the Gulf Stream, which would speed the passage home of Spanish ships from the Caribbean from then onward. He never ceased, however, to complain that Diego Colón's men were unlawfully enslaving peaceful indios, while violence and rebellion continued to spread. While Juan Ponce was away, the king reversed his policy for governing Puerto Rico, reinstating many of the subordinate officials who had formerly worked with Juan Ponce, pardoning the natives whom Colón's men had incriminated, and banning further enslavements even in cases of war.

To reinstate Juan Ponce in person, however, was more problematic, since Diego Colón had established his right to appoint the governor of Puerto Rico. Instead, therefore, the king divided responsibilities on the island. On October 27, 1514, leaving the governorship in the hands of Colón's nominees, he appointed Juan Ponce to a new office as "captain" with military but not civil responsibilities and with the express purpose of restoring peace, "so that the indios in rebellion may be pacified more readily and with less harm and fewer deaths than has been the case hitherto, and so as to establish such order that they shall not rebel henceforth."[22] As a prospective reward, the king also granted Juan Ponce a new contract to conquer and govern "the islands of Florida and Bimini." Gonzalo Fernández de Oviedo, in another of his romantic and chivalric elaborations, claimed that one of Bimini's attractions was "the Fountain of Eternal Youth." Maybe Juan Ponce was susceptible to such a picturesque legend, which was certainly circulating at the time. In December 1514, a resident chronicler at the royal court in Spain wrote to the pope to say that everyone at court except himself believed that the Fountain of Youth lay 325 leagues from Hispaniola on an island he called Boyuca or Ananeo.[23] There is no direct evidence to link Juan Ponce with any similar belief, but it seems appropriate that a quest for youth should inspire the first attempt to found a colony on what was to become the continental United States of America. Self-perception as denizens of a "young country" is part of the equipage of the people who call themselves Americans. Constant self-reinvention, renewal, and rebirth have been features of US history—through the dilatations of the frontier, the long-sustained demographic vitality, the cult of innovation, and, in latter days, the youth-fetishism that sells irrational amounts of plastic surgery, Botox, and collagen.

Presumably, if any of Fernández de Oviedo's stories about warfare in Puerto Rico are true, some, at least, of the fighting to which they relate occurred during the operations Juan Ponce undertook on his return from Florida, when, as the chronicler said, Juan Ponce was "always in the vanguard" and indefatigable in leading the Spanish effort. His account, probably written within five years of the events it narrates and certainly within ten, alleges that the native army was 11,000 strong. All of them fled after one of them was killed. Generally, according to Fernández de Oviedo, the Spaniards who conquered Puerto Rico suffered from lame limbs and strange, tropical sicknesses, but they rallied "because they had no other help than God and their own strong arms."[24] He devoted several pages of his report to the career of a fighting dog called Becerillo, who earned one-and-a-half times an arquebusier's pay, and was responsible for inflicting a third of the casualties sustained by the enemy. *Si non é vero, é ben trovato.* The author's writerly touches make a good story far too good to be true. On one occasion, Fernández de Oviedo assures us, the dog spared an old Indian woman who pleaded successfully for her life on the grounds that she was carrying an official message between the lines. Instead of tearing her limb from limb, which was his usual practice, Becerillo merely lifted his leg. His clemency inspired Juan Ponce to let the woman live, as he did not wish to appear less merciful than a dog.[25]

AFTER THE PACIFICATION OF Puerto Rico, Juan Ponce continued to feel the call to Florida. In November 1520, he wrote to the king's chaplain, the future pope Adrian of Utrecht, to explain that the death of his wife had delayed his return there. He was resolved, however, to return and spend all he had "so that Christ's name be exalted."[26] By the time he set sail for his next conquest, in February 1521, never to return, the island he left behind was in a state of utter, headlong transformation. Four circumstances, in particular, turned Puerto Rico into a world Juan Ponce would barely have recognized.

First, the native population was in a state of irretrievable decline. The absolute numbers involved cannot be calculated, neither those of the population at contact, nor of the losses that followed: in the absence of sources, historical demographers have produced "numbers from nowhere."[27] Their estimates range from 30,000 to 600,000. The upper range can be dismissed as fantastic: the productivity of the island before the arrival of edible biota of European and African origin could not have sustained so many people. Thirty thousand, on the other hand, may be slightly too cautious an estimate. But an abrupt collapse can be reliably inferred by analogy: wherever Europeans went in the New World, they took smallpox and other diseases to which unimmunized natives succumbed in terrible numbers. "The breath of a Spaniard," according to proverbial wisdom, was fatal. The available data are consistent with catastrophe. When Diego Colón's men distributed the labor services of some native communities in 1511, they parceled out about 5,500 people: no one knows the extent of the catastrophe the figure represents. But when the first census occurred in 1531, only 1,148 were left. The conflict between rival regimes in the early years of Spanish colonization was among the consequences: the increasingly desperate efforts of Colón's party to exploit native labor by selective enslavement and coercion reflects the problems falling population posed. Surviving natives tended to withdraw, where they could, into mountainous terrain beyond Spaniards' reach and beyond the remit of later censuses. The last census in which natives were separately enumerated took place in 1797, when 2,312 were counted, but these were exceptional *ladinos*—hispanized, town-dwelling artisans, almost all of whom were in the capital.

The decline maddened Spanish administrators, who blamed the indios for dying uncontrollably: the policy of the crown was to keep them alive not only or even primarily for humanitarian reasons, but because the colony needed them. This was the source of the biggest difference between the Spanish and later English experience of colonialism in the New World. With few exceptions, Spain occupied areas of relatively dense population in tropical or semitropical environments, where the natives' contribution to survival and prosperity was fundamental. The English acquired some underpopulated tropical islands and enclaves, where imported slaves did the work, but focused their settlements in relatively temperate areas, where they could practice their own traditional style of agriculture, and where, once colonial farmers had arrived, the natives, who were more of a hindrance than a help, could be exterminated or expelled. Spaniards, by contrast, struggled to keep the native populations intact, but were helpless in the face of deadly and elusive microbes.

Demographic disaster led directly to the second reason for the transformation of Puerto Rico. In the 1520s African slaves began to arrive in large numbers to replace the lost native labor. The census of 1531 counted 2,264. Without a further huge influx over the next two or three decades the colony would probably have perished, as the lure of newly developed, hugely richer opportunities for colonization in Mexico and Peru drained Puerto Rico and other older colonies of entrepreneurs and preempted the arrival of new settlers. Meanwhile, a third circumstance conspired to transform Juan Ponce's island: the gold was running out. New forms of exploitation were essential to create the wealth that would link the island to the growth of the long-range trade that the vast Spanish empire facilitated.

Fortunately for the colonists, the new economy could take shape in a transformed environment. Although colonization wrought unfavorable mutations in the disease environment, the overall effects of ecological change were positive, as new food plants and edible or otherwise exploitable animals arrived with the colonists from Europe and Africa. For the long-term future of the island, sugar was the most important new arrival. Over the entire period of Spain's preponderance in Puerto Rico, from the sixteenth century to the beginning of the twentieth, explosive growth in global demand for sugar gradually turned the island into the home of a vast, tentacular monoculture. Although sugar rapidly became dominant, other new elements in the ecology also made major economic contributions. Ranching was a suitable activity in a region of declining population, and Puerto Rico became, in the sixteenth and seventeenth centuries, a major source of cowhides for the Spanish empire's leather industries. Ginger, although production in volume terms was always small, was an important commodity because of its relatively high value per unit of bulk. Until the nineteenth century, its production was something of a Puerto Rican specialty. Rice, finally, was important for domestic consumption, alongside European wheat, especially for the sustenance of the African slaves on whom the colony relied for labor.

As in other lands where sugar and cattle predominated in a tropical climate, further modifications of the disease environment ensued. Malaria and yellow fever, in particular, contributed to the control of population, which, according to official figures, never surpassed a few thousand in the entire island in the seventeenth century. Many influences made life on the island precarious in the first two centuries of colonial rule: the ravages of European corsairs, the visitations of Carib raiders, the competition of more prosperous colonies elsewhere. But in the eighteenth century, the long-term benefits of ecological change kicked in. Food production soared with the multiplication and acclimatization of more African foodstuffs and with the abundance of slaves. Slave families, which had been notoriously infertile, became increasingly philoprogenitive. And the population became increasingly indifferent to increasingly familiar tropical fevers. The total numbers disclosed in censuses rose in the course of the century from 6,000 to 44,000.[28] The environmental innovations that favored this modest explosion were part of a global pattern, as killer diseases worldwide evolved and receded from previous niches, and ecological exchanges boosted the sources of food.

As a result, Puerto Rico became, in a sense, a frontier zone between Spanish America and the British, who coveted the island with growing cupidity. It was an objective of English, Dutch, and French pirates at intervals from the 1590s but only became a target of British imperialism towards the middle of the eighteenth century. In 1748 an English prisoner on the island thought his countrymen could turn it into a "paradise on Earth."[29] During the wars of the 1750s and 1760s—usually called the Seven Years' War—British merchants and ministers debated whether to concentrate on Puerto Rico or Florida as the most desirable potential acquisition from Spain as part of the price of peace. In 1763, when the opportunity arose, they chose Florida, chiefly, perhaps, because its forts commanded access to the Gulf Stream.

Maybe if Puerto Rico had become part of Anglo-America at so early a date, it might have joined what historians conventionally treat as the mainstream of US history. But that seems unlikely. No part of the British Caribbean joined the rebels of 1776, nor did the other colonies Britain had recently acquired in Canada. Spain, in any case, would probably have reacquired Puerto Rico in the Revolutionary War, just as she reacquired Florida. The warp of US history never stretched north from Puerto Rico to the mainland until the United States wrested the island from Spanish hands in the war of 1898–1902. Still, if the events of 1763 made little difference to Puerto Rico, they were decisive for the relationship of Florida to the rest of what became the United States. The region, which had undefined borders stretching across Georgia to the Carolinas, became the scene of bitter competition and fluctuating fortunes between Britain and Spain, and remains a borderland between Anglo-America and Hispanic America. From the point of view of a history of the United States that starts in the south and is slanted towards a Hispanic perspective, Florida is the most representative state of the Union: 85 percent of under-fives speak a language other than English at home. Miami is celebrated as the Union's biggest Spanish-speaking city. If the future of the United States continues to be increasingly hispanophone and pluralistic, Florida may replace Massachusetts and Virginia as the place people typically think of as the birthing bed of America.

JUAN PONCE DE LEÓN died on his last expedition to Florida without leaving any imprint on the country. But he aroused the interest of his countrymen in controlling the coast that commanded the Gulf Stream. In 1521 explorers reconnoitered at least as far as the Carolinas. The next expedition, under Lucas Vázquez de Ayllón, a royally appointed judge on Hispaniola whose sense of bureaucratic security seems to have been insufficient to deter him from adventure, landed on the Georgia coast in 1526 and founded a town dedicated to San Miguel and the Virgin of Guadalupe, but abandoned it when it proved uninhabitable owing to disease, the hostility of the natives, and the difficulty of maintaining communications with Hispaniola. A further effort led a reconnaissance force to Tampa Bay in March 1528, with the intention of crossing the peninsula to a rendezvous with the fleet. Distracted by natives' tales of gold, the men missed their objective and, depleted by disease, hunger, and skirmishes, settled to building rafts to make their escape. The endeavor was heroic. They felled trees for planks, killed deer for hides, plucked horses' manes and pounded vegetable fibers for cord, forged nails from armor, and stripped the clothes off their own backs for sails. Then most of them perished, wrecked or foundered on their makeshift craft. Of the three hundred men of the expedition, eighty-six survived to try to march overland to Mexico. In the end, after eight years of struggle, four made it.

As long as no rival European power preempted Spain in Florida, the failure to establish a colony did not matter much. But the enviable success of the conquistadores of Peru in the 1530s ignited new enthusiasm for the exploration of remoter regions of the Americas and reinforced the assumption that more rich civilizations might lurk unknown in secret hinterlands. Heading to Florida in 1539, Hernando de Soto, an overconfident and, in his own opinion, underrewarded veteran of the conquests of Central America and Peru, led the most ambitious and best-equipped expedition ever mounted by Spaniards in America: over 600 men, more than 200 horses, and a formidable and burdensome array of guns and armor. The stranger-effect, however, was unattainable in most of the North American southeast. Soto encountered a rare exception in the company of a chieftainess he called the "Lady of Cofitachequi," perhaps at the old mounds near Camden, South Carolina. From her "litter covered in delicate white linen" and her canopied canoe, she gave the Spaniards clothing and hung a string of river pearls around Soto's neck. She had Spanish axes and trade beads and a rosary, which convinced Soto that he was, as he said with a soldier's contempt for a bureaucrat, "where the lawyer Lucas Vázquez de Ayllón came to his ruin."[30]

In other places, natives offered battle almost everywhere the invaders ventured: the warfare was indecisive and the toll of casualties dispiriting. Nowhere could the invaders find enough sources of food or wealth to justify settlement. They wandered for three years, and though the surviving records are insufficient to reconstruct their itineraries exactly, they explored, at least, much of what are now Florida, Georgia, Alabama, Arkansas, Mississippi, Louisiana, and Texas. Their leader's demonic energy drove them on, but Soto died of fever in May 1542. The survivors headed overland for home, but were unable to cross the deserts that obtruded. So they built brigs, using the same expedients as their doomed predecessors of 1528. They were luckier, encountering better sailing conditions. They reached Mexico after fifty days of painful, dangerous coastal navigation, pursued for most of the way by hostile war canoes, under hails of arrows. By the time they reached safety, they had lost well over half their number across the entire course of the expedition.

After a long sequence of deterrent disasters, appetites for conquering Florida faded, but experience had shown that the region had two attractions beyond its strategic appeal: abundant deer hides and large numbers of potential, albeit apparently intractable, converts to Christianity. Missionaries might succeed in establishing a threshold where warriors had failed. A mission in 1549 ended with the martyrdom of its leader. Hope, however, continued to triumph over experience. To understand Spanish persistence, one must appreciate how little people knew of the geography of the western hemisphere. Columbus's old delusions—a narrow Earth, a short route to China—defied the evidence. In 1557, when officials chose Santa Elena, in what is now South Carolina, as the probable site of Spain's first Florida colony, they mistakenly thought that it was near Lucas Vázquez de Ayllón's "land of Chicora"—named after a captive of the explorers of the 1521 expedition—which was somewhere in the Carolinas.[31] The viceroy of New Spain, Luis de Velasco, thought the colony would be close enough to Zacatecas in Mexico to be supplied by cattle drives,[32] but really it was about 1,800 miles away, with the Mississippi in between. Pedro Menéndez de Avilés, who in 1565 finally succeeded in founding an enduring colony in Florida, hoped that the Chesapeake might lead directly to the Pacific.

Meanwhile, the threat of a preemptive strike at Florida by a rival power continued to obsess Spanish policy makers. In the late 1550s French pirates operating from Florida havens halved Spanish revenues from the New World.[33] In 1559, while Tristán de Luna y Arellano—an old but unaccomplished hand at American exploration—was establishing a Gulf base and crossing Florida, King Philip II wrote to New Spain with news of the danger of a French invasion. Another Spanish colonizing venture in 1561 was unable to find a habitable berth on the Atlantic coast and unwilling to settle at Pensacola, which seemed the most promising site. So the Florida coast remained unguarded, open for buccaneers and filibusters to lie in wait and prey on Spanish shipping. The situation became intolerable for Spain in 1565, when Huguenot interlopers founded a colony several hundred strong at what they called Fort Caroline, near what is now the St. Johns River.

A prudent response might have been to leave the heretics to starve and sicken. But the chance that the colony might succeed or, if it failed, inspire successors, just as the Spanish failures had induced emulators, led the king and his counselors to take immediate and decisive countermeasures. More than a punitive expedition was needed: the entire previous course of Spanish policy in the Americas had to be reversed. Hitherto, the crown had only authorized colonies that had some prospect of being self-sustaining. Florida, where there were few or no hospitable Indians and scant chance of growing enough food to keep a large garrison alive, was a new kind of venture. The Spanish authorities knew that they would only be able to sustain it by supplying it themselves, by sea.

In contrast, therefore, to the modest beginnings of Puerto Rico, Florida's birth was prodigious, with a long and painful labor, a violent parturition, and a loud noise. The appointed leader of the expedition of 1565 was Pedro Menéndez de Avilés, who had a solid record of success in chasing down pirates. The expedition comprised 2,646 persons—soldiers, sailors, colonists, priests. The plans, which would never be fully realized, included visionary schemes for fortifying a series of strongholds along the coast. He planted unworkable garrisons along a route he imagined might lead overland to Mexico.

On August 28 Menéndez landed near the St. Johns River on what is now known as Florida's "First Coast." After the saint whose feast day it was, he called the place San Agustín, went through the usual rites for founding a town, and dispersed, captured, or killed the entire French establishment in a few days of ruthless fighting, massacring 300 Huguenots at Fort Caroline to "serve God our Lord, as well as Your Majesty, and that we should be thus left more free from this wicked sect."[34] Success went to his head. He promised the king "that in the future Florida will be of little expense, and will pay Your Majesty much money, and will be of more value to Spain than New Spain or even Peru, and it may be said that this country is but a suburb of Spain, for it does not take more than forty days' sailing to come here, and usually as many more to return."[35]

It was a cruelly overoptimistic assessment. Jesuits who visited in 1568 found the garrison of San Agustín pallid with exhaustion and hunger.[36] In 1571 the Jesuit mission in Chesapeake Bay, founded the previous year at the northern limit of Spanish penetration, came to grief when a native rabble-rouser who called himself "Don Luis de Velasco," a crypto-pagan convert of the 1561 expedition, instigated a massacre. By 1574, of the posts Menéndez founded, only San Agustín and Santa Elena still functioned.

Menéndez did find some friendly natives. He needed to. The Spaniards could not feed themselves. They brought wheat seed, together with vine cuttings, 200 calves, 400 pigs, 400 sheep, and unspecified numbers of goats and chickens; in 1573, however, "herbs, fish and other scum and vermin" sustained them when rations were short. Corn bread and fish, foodstuffs copied from the indigenous diet, were their mainstays.[37] When Menéndez reached Ays country, in what is now Martin County, the chief "received the Spaniards with much kindness, kissing them on the mouth, which . . . was their greatest sign of friendship."[38] In Guale, in northern Georgia, the chief the Spaniards found on their arrival in 1566 embraced baptism without demur. Owing, presumably, to the stranger-effect, for the rest of the century and beyond, Spanish legitimation became for local chiefs a desideratum so powerful that they fought each other for it, despite the fact that Spaniards could rarely enforce compliance on their subjects on so distant a frontier.[39]

From the 1590s onward, Franciscans established missions on the Georgia coast and inland in Timucua and Apalachee. But indio compliance was unreliable and always contingent on payola in the form of doles of European goods or material help against other native peoples. In the interior, the Spanish empire came to rely on unfortified and largely ungarrisoned missions, which were viable as long as no one disputed them in arms. Even then, they tended to be economically precarious and feeble as agents of Christianization. One of the Jesuits who launched the Santa Elena mission summed up the difficulties in a letter to Menéndez in 1570. Seasonal migrations interfered with evangelization, so that "in order to obtain fruit in the blind and sad souls of these provinces, it is necessary first of all to order the Indians to come together and live in towns and cultivate the earth." But

> it must be done rightly, as our Lord commands, neither by compelling them nor with a mailed hand. And this for two reasons: the first that they have been accustomed to live in [the present] manner for thousands of years, and to take them out of it is like death to them; the second, that even were they willing, the poverty of the soil and its rapid exhaustion will not admit of it. . . . Unless this is done, although the religious remain among them for fifty years, they will have no more fruit than we in our four years among them, which is none at all, nor even a hope, nor the semblance of it.[40]

Still, the Franciscans who took over from the Jesuits made huge investments of effort and manpower. By 1675 they had nine missions at intervals on the Florida coast from San Agustín northward almost as far as modern Savannah, while twenty-six more stretched inland to beyond the Apalachicola River. Most had a few dozen indios. There were 150 at Santa Catalina, the largest and northernmost. The westernmost missions, however, were rebellious and unsustainable. Such security as they enjoyed ended in the late seventeenth century, when French and English adventurers began infiltrating Georgia and western Florida respectively, from the Mississippi and Carolina.

In 1670 a treaty fixed the frontier with Anglo-America a little south of Charleston. English slavers, however, never respected it. Between 1680 and 1706 most Georgia missions collapsed, albeit temporarily, as a result of English incursions, culminating in 1704 in the raid led by James Moore, former governor of Charleston, who destroyed missions and burned the missionaries at the stake, enslaving 4,000 women and children, and killing most men. "I never hear," Moore reported, "of a stouter or a braver thing done."[41] The Franciscan provincial likened the English to "hungry wolves" who slaughtered Indians until "the grass turned red with the blood of the poor."[42]

MEANWHILE, CONSIDERED AS A secular undertaking, the colony never turned a profit. From the late sixteenth century, Florida was a drain on imperial finances. The Council of the Indies resisted repeated temptations to disband the colony because of the advisability of retaining the harbor of San Agustín against French, English, and Dutch pirates. In 1606, when the population was 500, and all but five adult males were maintained at the crown's expense,[43] the council decided the outlay was unjustifiable. The decision to leave, however, provoked the Franciscans to protest at the danger withdrawal would pose to the souls of converted Indians. The king submitted. Over the seventeenth century the crown spent nearly 7 million pesos in Florida on subsidies to missions and the salaries and subsistence of the professional soldiers who, in the absence of ordinary colonists, defended the outpost.[44]

This level of expenditure just about kept the colony going, but did not make it secure. In 1673 the governor of Cuba—evincing from his own remote frontier a metropolitan sophisticate's contempt for an even remoter region—complained that "it is hard to get anyone to go to San Agustín because of the horror with which Florida is painted. Only hoodlums and the mischievous go there from Cuba." In 1702, anticipating English attack, the governor applied for urgent help from Madrid: 150 extra men, 28 cannon, 400 other guns, 400 pikes or lances, a thousand grenades, and a large subsidy to repair and improve the seaward defenses. No response was forthcoming until the English attack was under way. Even then, all Florida got were 6 cannon, 250 rusty small arms, 200 pikes, and the requested grenades. The reinforcements demanded were authorized, but by 1704 only twenty men had assembled. They had to be chained to prevent them from deserting before embarkation.[45]

The *residencia*—the regular examination, at the end of an official's term of office, into the probity of his conduct—of Joseph de Zúñiga y Cerda, retiring governor of Florida, in 1707, brings the stresses and pleasures of frontier government to life. The form of a *residencia* was always the same, modeled on Roman law. The judge commissioned with the task would formulate a series of questions about the outgoing official's behavior, addressing them in turn to whoever could be found to testify from among the staff and citizens with whom the *residenciado* had dealings. At Zúñiga's *residencia,* most of the thirty-three questions the investigator posed were routine: inquiries into the governor's pecuniary scruples, obedience to orders, impartiality in justice, deference to law, care of the disadvantaged, respect for the Church, concern for the natives. Other questions were specific to the problems of Florida: defense against the English, regulation of contraband. Some were specific to Zúñiga's personality: was it true that he abused his office to obtain sexual favors? Did he seduce women, cuckold citizens, father bastards? The prominence of questions on these matters reflected the frequency of complaints and, therefore, presumably, a real flaw in the governor's moral character. He was the Don Juan of Florida, comforting grass widows whose husbands were away on active service. His lax attitude to the control of drinking, dancing, and adultery mirrored his own conduct. He fomented and embodied a culture of impropriety.

His administrative peccadillos were modest by comparison. The *residencia* strained to find wrongdoing. Most of the instances for which he was cited were trivial by the standards of the time. Instead of scourging, imprisoning, or executing a black slave who killed an

Indian, he fined the culprit and earmarked the money for masses for the victim. Instead of imprisoning a soldier who whipped and chained his errant daughter, the governor removed the girl to a foster home. He failed to keep up with supply and repair for the Fort of San Marcos to the required standard. His only major, repeated transgression was illicit trading with the English. As always on the colonial frontier, contraband was part of the colony's lifeblood, and Zúñiga, like almost every other governor, had to compromise on the rigor of the law to keep his people supplied. A combination of winds, currents, and regulations made by self-interested profiteers in the bureaucracy meant that all goods had to be shipped from Havana via New Spain. The cost was unbearable. In 1701 he complained that Florida was starving, with soldiers reduced to begging in competition with cripples, widows, and orphans. If he waited for official supply ships—his defenders claimed—the shipments would typically be intolerably delayed and, when they arrived, "putrefied with cockroaches."[46]

A generation later, in 1735, charges against another governor, Francisco del Moral Sánchez, demonstrate similar problems. Moral was less popular than Zúñiga and had made enemies of the Franciscan missionaries who predominated among his detractors. Quarrels between Spanish and Creole priests—the former despised the latter while the latter resented the former—caught him up and frustrated his efforts to arbitrate. Among the more or less trivial accusations his enemies leveled, the charge of encouraging and profiting from English contraband stood out. Only English goods, claimed the Franciscans, were on sale in San Agustín. English merchants swaggered around the town, spreading Protestant heresies. Moral overreacted to the criticism, suspecting a conspiracy, arresting and imprisoning prominent citizens. The crown intervened to replace him, not so much because of the merits of the case against him as because colonial government had to rely on and conciliate local collaborators. Moral's case exposed the usual syndrome: the intractability of the colony's problems of supply, the impossibility of firm government, the bunker politics of a tiny, cramped, emulous corner of the empire, the way isolation and impotence bred paranoia and conflict.[47]

When at last a governor arrived who was determined to ban contraband, the policy proved his undoing. In 1756 Governor Alonso Fernández de Heredia exposed a previously tolerated scam in which vessels used fishing licenses as cover for trading ventures in Charleston, where they sold Spanish tobacco and sugar for British consumer goods that would command a high premium in Florida. In a show of force he used sixty soldiers to seize nearly 4,500 pesos' worth of illegal furniture and household goods, and dragged from sanctuary malefactors who took refuge with the Franciscans.[48] He pleased no one. Back in Spain, the Council of the Indies was dissatisfied with the severity of the penalties he imposed. The Church was outraged at the violation of sanctuary. Colonists resented the threat to their prosperity and even their survival. Fishing licenses were revoked. The smugglers found other loopholes or brazenly continued to defy the law.

DESPITE THE REALITIES OF life on the frontier, Madrid and Mexico City continued with fantastic decision making shaped by delusively beautiful maps, mercantilist assumptions, and insistent fears of foreign encroachment on the indefensibly vast monarchy. The policy of restricting foreign trade was defensive in inspiration and ruinous in effect. Closed ports impoverished the North American colonies and prevented the development of shipping and shipbuilding—a grave deficiency that meant that England's poor and marginal colonies could begin to close the wealth gap with Spain's. Channeling goods through privileged ports did not prevent contraband or keep foreign raiders from Spanish coasts. But it did impede the empire's exports and magnify the costs of frontier life. In 1700 the parish priest of San Agustín complained that soap and sugar quintupled in price between Havana or Veracruz and Florida because of the roundabout routes vessels were obliged to follow.[49] Colonies drifted from allegiance to Spain, as economic necessity tugged them into relations with rivals. For English and, until defeat in the Seven Years' War, French leaders in North America, the continent was a land of opportunity, stimulating investment and inviting expansion. For Spain, it was a loss leader:

a land of disappointment, valuable only as a buffer to protect the rich and populous heartlands of the empire farther south. By 1745 English Carolina had over 20,000 European inhabitants—ten times the number of Spaniards in Florida.[50] By 1760, including the population of the new English colony of Georgia, the disparity had grown: nearly 45,000 in the English establishments contrasted with only some 3,000 in Florida. Huge numbers of slaves, always much more numerous than the whites, boosted the enemy colonies' size and productivity. If Florida failed to attract English ambitions of conquest in the late eighteenth century, it was more because of the reticence of the British government, sated with more North American territory than it could defend or exploit, than because of Spanish strength.

Indio allegiance remained slippery. In some ways indios showed a remarkable partiality for Spanish ways, even beyond the reach of the missions. In the 1740s a visiting Jesuit found to his surprise that people at the mouth of the Miami River in Florida spoke Spanish, which trade had spread in their direction.[51] In the 1770s William Bartram, the deft botanical artist and plant hunter who was irrepressible in seeking species to catalog, noticed that Creeks and Seminoles "manifest a predilection for the Spanish customs" and language.[52] In general, however, Native Americans' sympathies were conditional on rewards, and only dependency could guarantee submission. There were never enough goods in Spanish warehouses to make the natives dependent or permanently well disposed. If governors and commanders gave supplies away to the Indians, their own followers resented the waste of resources.

Spanish reluctance to buy loyalty with muskets and rum let in English and French interlopers. In 1733 the English colonizer of Georgia, James Oglethorpe, took the Uchize chief, Chamachichi, to London, where society feted the noble savage and the king decorated him.[53] In June 1734 the garrison of Apalachee ran out of supplies with which to appease the truculent Creeks and keep the hostile Pequots at bay. The English were happy to oblige the Indians with weapons to turn against Spain, and to pay for the scalps of any tribes that declined to forswear their former allies. In response, the governor had only promises to offer. In October 1736 he prevailed on the English to

abjure, by treaty, "outlaws and bandits who are the shape of Humankind, who might . . . molest the provinces of both kings and with
impunity destroy the innocent peasants and planters"[54]; many English
officials found natives distasteful allies, but English "men on the spot"
preferred to follow their own counsel and to see Spain as their principal enemy. By 1739 only nine villages in Florida adhered to the Spanish cause. The governor claimed he could rely on only 354 natives.

For the English the policy was costly in rum, muskets, and bales of
cloth, and yielded, in practice, little military advantage, as the natives
were more interested in the prosecution of their own quarrels—the
Choctaws against the Chalaques, the Uziche against the Talapuses—
than in the enlargement of the British empire. Gradually, the English
investment in buying Indian cooperation dwindled. In 1745, on orders
from Madrid, and in response to native overtures, Governor Manuel
de Montiano reestablished trade with the Uziche in western Florida.
"We must procure articles to carry on our trade, regaling the Indians
with as many presents as, I am informed, they are accustomed to
receive from the English and French."[55] He could never assemble
enough goods to satisfy their demands or secure their loyalty. In a
pattern often repeated in the later history of Native American relations with "white" empires, self-seeking native factions would defy
their own leaders, infringe treaties, and abuse weapons the Spaniards
gave them to make war at will. Still, by the time the Seven Years' War
broke out in 1756, almost all the natives of Florida were, with varying
degrees of enthusiasm, allied or submissive to Spain.

In 1763, at the end of the war, Spain handed Florida to Britain—
just as the reorganization of the garrison made it formidable: the
Conde de Revillagigedo, viceroy of New Spain, had persuaded the
crown to boost subsidies and rotate the garrisons in frontier zones, so
that despair at ever being relieved no longer drove men to desertion.[56]
It was not, as we shall see, the end of Spanish Florida, but it was the
moment when, for the first time, parts of Spanish America and
Anglo-America fused, presaging the whole history of the formation
of the United States as a plural state with an Anglo and Hispanic
condominium as its foundation.

CHAPTER TWO

THE CITIES OF CÍBOLA

The Colonial Midwest from the Mississippi to the Rockies, c. 1598–1798

———

I pursued my journey to within sight of the city of Cíbola. . . . It has the appearance of a very beautiful town, . . . bigger than the city of Mexico. At times I was tempted to go to it, because I knew that I ventured only life, which I had offered to God the day I commenced the journey. At the end I feared [to do so], considering my danger and that if I died, I would not be able to make a report of this country, which to me appears the greatest and best of the discoveries.

~*Esteban de Dorantes* (1539)

T HE HISTORY OF EXPLORATION HAS SOME OF THE WORLD'S BEST stories, many of them made up by explorers whose accounts no one could put to the test. Few are more intriguing or sensational than the tale of Alvar Núñez Cabeza de Vaca, one of the most extraordinary Spanish pioneers in the Americas. He was cupidinous and ambitious, but his head was full of bookish theory he picked up in Spain. In particular, he followed Dominican critics of Spanish neglect and maltreatment of native peoples in conquered lands. When he campaigned on the River Paraná in the 1540s, he virtually banned violence, distributed gifts to the natives, and tried to win them over with what he called love. But his policy owed almost as much to experience as to dogma or fantasy. He had, by his own account, lived among Indians for years, and loved and was loved among them. That experience happened in Texas. Despite his eccentricities, he is an ideal guide to introduce the Hispanic history of the central lands of the United States, between the Mississippi and the Rockies.

His American career began when he was a royal nominee in the ill-starred reconnaissance of Florida in 1528. Castaway on the Texas coast in the debacle of the expedition, he led a party of survivors—two fellow Spaniards and a resourceful black slave, Esteban de Dorantes, known as Estebanico—on a seven-year odyssey, via enslavement by hostile natives and adoration by friendly ones, to safety in New Spain. On arrival, he was clad in skins, long-bearded, and with waist-length hair. Not only did he look like a holy man: he also behaved like one. To the astonishment of the Spanish slavers who met him on the frontier, over a thousand native followers accompanied him. His narrative of his adventures is unsurpassable as a gripping story, and no historian of the episode can escape its spell. It was a remarkable achievement to reach Mexico at all, picking a path across potentially lethal country amid potentially murderous enemies. To have emerged as the head of what seems to have been an extraordinary, almost messianic, mass movement of indigenous people was a staggering outcome. How did he do it?

Alvar Nuñez's explanation was providential. God procured his survival by a miracle and endowed him with strange graces—like a Siegfried with a supply of dragon's blood or a Samson with an abundance of curls—in order to help bring the natives he met to Christianity. In particular, God gave him powers of healing. At first, our hero relied on the rudimentary medical knowledge of one of his Spanish companions to swap cures for kindnesses along the road. One night, however, the little expedition's resident physician cried off, and Cabeza de Vaca was left to handle one of the most difficult cases the party had encountered: the patient, according to local opinion, was already dead. Alvar Núñez made the sign of the cross over the body, and imitated native physicians by blowing breath over it. In the first of his many supposed miracles, the corpse revived, ate, strolled, and chatted. Other, less advanced victims of ailments, whom Alvar Núñez treated later that day, "had become well and were without fever and very happy." For the autobiographer, the miracles became evidence of validation by a higher authority, like the battlefield deeds of prowess asserted by conquistadores in the statements of merits with which they plied the crown in search of offices and titles.

On the face of it, the stories are incredible. Alvar Núñez and his companions relied on more than miracles. They were also war leaders, and their followers were not just pilgrim bands but hell-bent marauders, determined, as Alvar Núñez confessed, "to take us wherever there were many people, and . . . wherever we arrived to steal and loot what the others had, because such was the custom." Such passages also make it clear that Alvar Núñez exaggerated his agency: he was at the mercy and whim of his native entourage. The strange route his party took to Mexico's Pacific coast, wiggling and wavering across southern Texas, was the result of native priorities. Naturally, his account did not emphasize his role as the natives' dupe or his part in war unauthorized by crown or church.[1] Still, much of the story remains perplexing. Above all, we want to know how and why Alvar Núñez got the chance to parade his charisma as a native figurehead. Why did the natives need him as the poster boy for their inspired wanderings? Would they not be equally effective in war and migration without him?

When they got to the frontier of effective Spanish power in New Spain, in what is now Sonora, members of Alvar Núñez's entourage refused to believe that he and the Spaniards they met could be fellow countrymen. Cabeza de Vaca put into their mouths words that he no doubt modified, but which—in their general sense—have the ring of truth. "We came from where the sun rose, and they [the Spanish slavers] from where it set; . . . we cured the sick, and they killed those who were well; . . . we came naked and barefoot, and they went about dressed and on horses and with lances; and . . . we did not covet anything but rather, everything we later returned and remained with nothing, and . . . the others had no other objective but to steal everything they found and did not give anything to anyone."[2]

These lines need to be interpreted skeptically. They relate to an agenda the writer shared with his friends among the friars, who campaigned to keep lay Spaniards out of Indian lands. But they also point to an important truth: Alvar Núñez was credible as a holy man because he was unidentifiable as anything else. Along his road, he was passed from one community to the next as a trophy in a complex culture of gift exchange, in which the natives waged ritual warfare on one another, exchanging tribute and spoils according to what seem to have been rules intelligible to themselves but mysterious to Alvar Núñez. He never understood that his value to the natives arose from their own culture, rather than from any merits of his own.

Still, he was as strange to his hosts as they were to him. His acceptance among them is further proof of the efficacy of the stranger-effect— the propensity of some cultures to honor the stranger, sometimes to the point of confiding authority to him—which, as we have seen, best accounts for the extraordinary success of Spaniards wherever they found a welcome among native hosts. Even in hospitable traditions, of course, the stranger is marginal—literally marginal, as he approaches a potential host community across its frontiers. He is dangerous, and though one can respond to danger by harnessing it, it is safer to destroy it. Most of Alvar Núñez's fellow castaways died in captivity or, after enforced adscription into host communities, remained on sufferance and at risk. More interesting, however, are the instances like Alvar Núñez's own, of collaboration between strangers and host communities, such as many Spanish conquistadores experienced. Because, as we have seen, the stranger is unimplicated in existing factions and networks, he can arbitrate with objectivity, marry with impartiality, confront the esoteric with esoteric wisdom, and perform sacred rituals without fear or favor. So he often becomes holy man or king or judge. He brings to these roles the magic of distance. Alvar Núñez followed many other conquistadores bamboozled by the reverence they received: he assumed that the natives mistook him for divine, and wasted much effort trying to disabuse them with his stories of Christ. But his reception was not the result of the awe owed to a god. On the contrary, it meant that the natives knew Alvar Núñez and his companions were men, whose exotic origins deserved special respect.

The stranger-effect, however, has its limits. The most harrowing moment in the story that began with Alvar Núñez's odyssey came in 1539, three years after the party's return to Mexico, when the black slave, Estebanico, returned as a Spanish scout to the lands of his former triumphs and became a celebrity again, showered with women and turquoise. But he pressed ahead, northward, into unknown territory, across northern Sonora. There or thereabouts—the exact location remains unknown—a different kind of culture responded differently to the stranger, and he died "as full of arrows as St Sebastian."[3] Before his death, he left a report garbled by delirium and inflated by the hopes of those who heard it. Cíbola, he claimed, was one of seven great cities in the North American interior. It was bigger than Tenochtitlan. Its temples, in rumors spread by Chinese whispers, were smothered in emeralds.[4] The news seemed to Fray Marcos de Niza, the Franciscan missionary who recorded it, "the greatest thing in the world."[5] The report so captivated him that he convinced himself that he had seen Cíbola in the distance, luring him like a mirage. The effect can be seen in the map made in Catalonia by Joan Martínez nearly forty years later: a richly gilded compass points straight from Chihuahua and Sinaloa into a colorful region of domed, spired, and turreted cities that did not exist.

In April 1540 Francisco Vázquez de Coronado led an expedition of two hundred horsemen in search of them, ahead of a support column of a thousand slaves and servants, driving pack mules and herds of livestock for food. Cíbola was said to lie beyond mountains, so they simply headed upstream until they reached the watershed of the Mogollon Rim, the towering, narrow edge of the escarpment the Colorado plateau thrusts eastward. From there they followed the creeks and rivers downstream. With his supplies lagging far behind, Coronado led his men into extremes of hunger in the highlands. Some of them died, poisoned by greenery they chewed on the trail. After two months they reached a populated region. The indios they called Pueblo, because of their well-built settlements, were sedentary farmers. They were "good people," the Spaniards reported, "more devoted to agriculture than war,"[6] but their material culture fell well short of the reputed marvels of Cíbola. They possessed no emeralds, only turquoise in small amounts.

The Great Plains were close. At the Pueblo settlement of Hawihuh, now a spectral coil of ruined stonework on the Zuñi reservation in New Mexico, Coronado first heard of what he called "the country of the cows"—the American bison.[7] He first saw a buffalo tattooed or painted on the body of a member of an embassy that brought buffalo-hide shields, robes, and headdresses from people who lived near the edge of the grasslands. Following the emissaries to their hometown of Tziquite, Coronado acquired a charismatic guide who "talked with the devil in a pitcher of water."[8] This guide could speak a smattering of Nahuatl, or perhaps he just belonged to the people later called Comanches, whose language had common roots with the Aztecs'. Lured by talk of a state with canoes of forty oars and prows of gold,[9] Coronado pressed north to a supposedly rich, urban culture called Quivirá. Never out of sight of the buffalo, he rode on "plains so vast that in my travels I did not reach their end, although I marched over them for more than three hundred leagues."[10]

The Spaniards' reports reveal a region where prairie fades to desert, and where life depended on the herds of bison. The natives ate nothing else. They dressed in buffalo hides tied with thongs of buffalo leather. They slept in buffalo-skin tents and wore moccasins of the same material on their feet. They impressed the visitors with their fearless and friendly greetings, but their table manners embodied Spanish ideas of savagery. They swallowed raw meat, "half-chewed, like birds"; they drank fresh blood from vessels made of buffalo guts. They drank with relish the half-digested contents of buffaloes' stomachs. For explorers seeking what they hoped they would recognize as a great civilization, the disappointment was intense.

After five weeks of fruitless searching in "lands as level as the sea," Coronado decided that his guides were trying to lose him. But Indi-

ans he met continued to wave him northward when asked for Quivirá. He took a bold decision in the best conquistador tradition.
Sending most of his force and all the camp followers home, he headed
north by the compass with only thirty horsemen. They lived off buffalo, heaping mounds of buffalo dung as they went to serve as markers
of the way home.

They finally found Quivirá in what is now Cow Creek, Rice
County, Kansas, on the edge of a zone of relatively long grasses, which
thickened as the prairie descended to low altitudes. The vaunted "cities" were turf-lodge settlements of the "raccoon-eyed," tattoo-faced
Kirikiri, who farmed patches of plain with difficulty in villages that
had gradually spread west along the Arkansas River. Coronado transformed their world: he brought horses into it. With horse and spear
he was able to kill five hundred buffalo in a fortnight. Though natives
on foot could achieve multiple kills in pits, the horsemen's prowess as
hunters was of a different order. It was a revelation of the future—a
future still surprisingly distant, for it was more than a century before
the horse became the universal companion of man on the plains.

MEMORIES OF ALVAR NÚÑEZ'S and Coronado's reports echoed in
Mexico. In 1561, Alonso de Zorita recalled their findings when he
wrote a memorandum proposing to return to "the Tierra Nueva to
which Francisco Vázquez Coronado went, and to Nuevo México."[11]
He was a judge in the Audiencia of New Spain—the court of last
resort, save only for appeal to the king in Spain—and a deeply committed defender of native rights and advocate of serious evangelization. His mentor was the official "protector" of the indios, Bartolomé
de Las Casas, who was then approaching death in disillusionment in
a college in Valladolid, issuing ever-fiercer denunciations of the injustice of Spanish treatment of the natives of the New World. In his day,
however, he had been an influential figure, shaping royal policy, and, as
Bishop of Chiapas in what is now southern Mexico, dictating missionary strategy in the field. Zorita was one of many officials in state
and church whose views Las Casas had helped to mold, and his insis-

tence on his Christian motives for wanting to go to New Mexico was entirely sincere. He had Franciscans who wanted to accompany him. But the crown wanted him in Mexico, doing his job. There was no chance of his getting permission to go so far afield. The viceroy of New Spain considered the land useless and was anxious about the attenuation of precious Spanish manpower that an extension of the frontier implied. The king of Spain refused to spend a mite from the royal treasury to conquer and settle New Mexico. If the land were to join the Spanish monarchy, private enterprise would have to conquer and colonize it.

Indeed, it seems odd that anyone should have wanted to risk lives and endure suffering for the sake of New Mexico. The existing empire surely encompassed enough remote, inaccessible, and inhospitable places to satisfy the most extreme wanderlust. By the time of Zorita's plan, one might have thought that it was obvious that the cities of Cíbola did not exist, but the rumors continued to rattle inside susceptible heads. The sort of people who colonize one distant frontier often remain evasive and restless wherever they are, and are, to the rest of us, surprisingly ready to move on to the next. At the same time as people in New Spain were agitating for the conquest of New Mexico, there were others in Peru—an even more distant province of the Spanish monarchy—who were yearning for transpacific conquests in islands so vaguely reported that in some cases when the colonists set sail, they were unable to find them.

In any case, other motives were accumulating for trying to extend the frontiers of Spanish settlement beyond the deserts of northern New Spain. As always when faced with the apparent irrationalities of conquistadores, one must remember how they were literally venturing into the unknown, with little genuine notion of the geography of the regions they penetrated. They knew that a narrow peninsula lay to their south. It was possible, therefore, that North America or parts of it were equally narrow and that an even shorter route to the Pacific and the wealth of the Orient might lie to their north. Ignorant of the size of the hemisphere, they hoped that only a short distance might separate the proposed new colonies from those of Florida, which, as we have seen, needed constant resupplies of food and munitions to survive, but which were vital to guard the sea route back to Spain. They had no reason to suppose that the prospects of finding precious metals or previously unknown civilizations diminished the farther north they went. In any event, they had three solid pieces of knowledge, as well as all these more or less vaporous speculations, to encourage further efforts: first, exploitable, fertile land beckoned, which could sustain a settler population. Second, the would-be conquistadores knew there were souls to evangelize beyond the desert. Finally, those souls were inside bodies whose labor could be exploited: although the pueblos Coronado and Alvar Núñez reported were not rich in gold, they were the dwellings of people Spaniards felt they could work with—urban people, numerous and sedentary, with productive agriculture. From the point of view of the crown, the clergy, and the bureaucrats, to leave the natives outside the protection of the monarchy, at the mercy of slavers, was worse than a crime: it was a mistake. Slave raids impaired productivity for the sake of short-term gains. Collaborative methods of mobilizing labor or collecting tribute served evangelization and colonization better. Where the stranger-effect produced too little spontaneous or peaceful indigenous cooperation, the Spaniards could usually find willing partners in coercion among the incumbent elites or their rivals. With these quislings and collaborators they shared power and wealth.

The frontier of Spanish settlement was, moreover, already moving rapidly northward, as mining prospectors set up ever-remoter camps in the area of what is now northeast Mexico, then known as Nuevo León. Slavers, who were often also miners, raided with impunity beyond the frontier into the southerly pueblos, causing outrage among officials of Zorita's stamp and anxiety among the religious. In 1580 Franciscans who had been reading the accounts of Alvar Núñez and Coronado renewed the project, making the journey in the company of lay Spaniards whose motives were less pure. It would have been foolhardy for the friars to go alone. They acquired the services of Francisco Sánchez Chamuscado and his companions in the hard-knuckled, hard-drinking mining towns of northern New Spain—not an environment in which religion and morals flourished. The laymen of the expedition spent most of their time prospecting for mines and extorting tribute from indios. When they returned to New Spain, the friars stayed behind. A follow-up expedition in search of them a couple of years later learned that they had died at the hands of their congregations.

Officials heard and dismissed many more applications to settle New Mexico in the 1580s. One of the unsuccessful applicants was Gaspar Castaño de Sosa, an official from the northern frontier disgruntled with a life in charge of unruly miners and unproductive mines, who eventually abandoned caution and legality to launch a colonizing venture on his own initiative. He probably reckoned that like Cortés, whose conquest of Mexico started as an illegal venture, he would get away with it if only he was successful. His opportunity arose in the summer of 1590, when his immediate superior was arrested on charges of slaving—which were valid—and of judaizing, which were routine on the frontier, where heretics and apostates gathered with other fugitives and renegades. Gaspar Castaño was also accused more than once of being a crypto-Jew. If the charges were true, they would constitute another reason for him to practice further evasion.

It is a tribute to the reputation of New Mexico—or perhaps an indictment of the miseries of life by the mines of Almadén, from where he set off—that he was able to recruit two hundred potential colonists. A mixture of intimidation and the stranger-effect secured them a welcome in most of the pueblos they visited. The prospects seemed good. But Gaspar Castaño surrendered to the force that came from Mexico to arrest him for launching an unauthorized expedition. He genuinely intended to found a settlement and to maintain good relations with the pueblos, but the viceroy, exasperated at his powerlessness to restrain enthusiasm for northern conquests, evidently thought the expedition was a pretext for more slave raids. Apologizing to the people of the pueblos for the intrusion, he had Castaño hauled off in chains and expelled to the Philippines. Castaño's fate did not deter Francisco de Leyva, who took advantage of his appointment as commander of a small force commissioned to punish hostile indios on the northern frontier to scour the plains for precious metals or signs of civilization;

the members of his party fell out with one another; mutineers killed him; and natives exterminated the rest. The only survivor was a native recruit from Durango called Jusepe, whose narrative is the only evidence of what happened. Evidently, clamor for new conquests was uncontainable. The only way to stop more extravagances of Castaño's or Leyva's type was to grant official sanction to another expedition.

The successful applicant was Juan de Oñate. From the viceroy's point of view, he seemed more reliable than the desperadoes who preceded him—an insider in the colonial world, a rich man, born in New Spain, with no taint of heresy or discontent. In 1595 he received his commission with the title of *adelantado*, a common designation for extemporized frontier leaders, and the right to distribute native tribute and labor among his followers. Enervating bureaucratic delays postponed departure for three years. His undertaking was a private initiative, a business venture. The king's instructions were unequivocal. "This discovery and pacification"—according to the Spanish monarchy's official newspeak, conquests were "pacifications"—"is to be accomplished without spending or pledging any money from my treasury."[12]

As he set off on the "uncertain, unknown road to that New Mexico," to deliver his promise of conquering "a New World, greater than New Spain,"[13] Oñate had about 130 Spaniards, with a long train of camp followers, thousands of livestock, and eighty-three wagonloads of equipment. Captain Luis de Velasco's baggage contained linen handkerchiefs, Cordovan boots and shoes, fancy hats, six suits (two satin, one silk, and one of "blue Italian velvet . . . trimmed with wide gold passementerie"), and green silk stockings with gold-laced blue garters.[14] As usual, official Spanish records omit the biggest fighting force: the Native American auxiliaries who always made up the major contingent.

The best guide to what happened—not because of unblemished accuracy but because his account perfectly captures the spirit of the enterprise—is Gaspar Pérez de Villagrá, who in 1610 wrote his version in an effort to obtain rewards from the crown for his part in the conquest. Perhaps to make him more conspicuous among the many complaints suppliants addressed to the king, he wrote in heroic verse, loud with classical and chivalric allusions. His epic actually began with the same words as the *Æneid*—"Arms and the man I sing"—and a Homeric litany of the names of the chief participants in the expedition. He makes Oñate address his men, who were for the most part the dregs and scum of the monarchy, desperadoes bound for New Mexico as refugees from their own previous failures, as "Valiant noblemen, cavaliers of Christ!"[15]

Villagrá's classical and romantic rhetoric was not the result of his idiosyncrasies or evidence of aberrant psychology. It was entirely typical of the way conquistadores thought and wrote about themselves. Imagine what it was like to undergo the hardships of exploration and war on remote frontiers, in unexperienced, hostile environments, surrounded and outnumbered by people whose culture seemed baffling and threatening, thousands of miles from home, with no hope of help. Many conquistadores literally went mad—like Lope de Aguirre on the Amazon in the 1560s, who murdered his comrades and recast himself as pope and emperor. The standard response was to reimagine oneself as a fictional character, or to try to understand one's predicament in terms of one's reading. Villagrá read the classics for erudition and the chivalric romances for pleasure. Soldiers mired in the trenches of World War I adopted a similar strategy of mental escape, reclothing the horrors of war in the romantic language of poetry.[16] Only five years before Villagrá published his work, Cervantes had released the first volume of the adventures of Don Quixote. Most modern readers have made the mistake of assuming that Cervantes was deriding a vanishing world of knight-errantry. But satire has no bite unless it targets current customs. Real-life Quixotes were at large on the frontiers of the Spanish monarchy—men like Pedro de Quirós, who in 1605 crossed the Pacific, mistaking the little island he called La Austrialia del Espíritu Santo for a fabled "Great Southern Continent" and celebrating by dubbing his men, including the ship's boys and cooks, "Knights of the Holy Spirit." The Spanish empire could never have happened if the men who forged it had faced without artifice the reality they endured.

Although the main purpose of Villagrá's work has to be teased from amid thousands of lines of narrative, it is obvious that like many conquistadores of literary inclinations, he spent much of his time exchanging grumbles with old comrades who felt insufficiently recompensed for their sacrifices in royal service. The privatization of conquest opened a gap in perceptions between rank-and-file participants, who thought of themselves as doing the monarchy's work, and royal officials, who regarded them as self-seeking adventurers. Villagrá overcompensated, extolling "the deeds and prowess of those valorous Spaniards."[17] He and his fellow conquistadores, he noted, provided their own equipment, spent their fortunes, experienced extremes of suffering, performed great marvels, and achieved "great prodigies in lands and nations never seen before, labors and adventures never previously told, unheard-of tasks, and sufferings that pursued us and assailed us because of inconstant fortunes and evil spirits."[18] When they had accomplished their tasks, "their own could not recognize them, so broken, aged, wearied, and afflicted were they, so old, ill, wretched, and miserable. And if, as their last recourse, your Majesty, they ask to be strengthened and helped by a crust that you might order to be vouchsafed to them without stint from the great store you command, with an open and generous hand, they are no different from those other poor folk, the lost sons, grandsons, and great-grandsons of those brave men who served you in the first conquests in this New World."[19]

"In military service," Villagrá opined, addressing the king directly, "no work seems hard nor time lost in suffering if the fruit of it is proportionate to what is right for those gallant hearts who served your Majesty in the wars,"[20] for "as you well know, great king, there is no man who, after suffering such heavy hardships and miseries, does not want some pay and recompense for his many services and labors. For their memorable endurance, I beg and beseech you, with hands folded in prayer, that you keep in mind, most clement Monarch, the memory of these unfortunates, whose heroic valor merits, uplifted, perpetual glory and triumphant renown."[21]

Villagrá's personal sense of grievance derived in part from a particular episode on which his poem dwelt. During an exceptionally tense phase of the conquest, when mutiny and native hostility threatened the expedition, the friars quieted the natives by praying successfully for rain. The celebrations included a week of feasting, jousting, bull-fights, a reenactment (of a kind traditional throughout the Spanish monarchy) of Reconquest battles, and "a happy comedy, very well acted."[22] This fact is well attested from other sources. Amid the privations, horrors, bloodshed, and atrocities of conquest, the Spaniards really did amuse themselves with amateur theatricals. Pantomime and motley make excellent disguises for unpalatable realities. The mutineers were pardoned, but some of them took flight and Villagrá was ordered to pursue them. When he caught them, he admitted, he summarily beheaded two of them, an abuse of authority for which royal officials later tried him and, although he was pardoned, held him in permanent distrust. On his way back to camp, hostile indios captured him as he struggled across mountainous terrain in bitter weather. He escaped, but was caught in a snowstorm and trapped in one of the pits the enemy dug for their own defense. Abandoning his horse and all his equipment except a sword, a dagger, and his faithful dog, he climbed out and reversed his boots as he plodded across the snow. After many days of deprivation and thirst, he saw no remedy except to sacrifice his suffering dog to his own hunger. The dying animal licked his master's wounds along with his own, inducing in Villagrá a terrible remorse and annihilating his appetite. In what was no doubt a romanticized dénouement, a search party rescued him just as the pursuing indios were catching up.

As well as special pleading on his own behalf and that of his comrades, Villagrá wrote with two further purposes: to justify the conquest and to promote colonization. The opening phase of his poem is the most puzzling part of it: a fanciful reconstruction of a mythic episode of a remote past when, Villagrá imagines, the supposed ancestors of the Aztecs leave New Mexico to conquer and settle old Mexico. He describes their army as a chivalric cavalcade, paralleling the conquistadores. Even by Villagrá's standards, the excursion seems fantastic and unintelligible unless one knows that according to the theory of just war approved by the Spanish crown (a theory first formulated by Saint

Augustine more than a thousand years before and elaborated by Saint Thomas Aquinas in the thirteenth century), one way of legitimizing conflict was to represent it as an attempt to recover lost land. For Villagrá the conquest of New Mexico was a reconquest—a reappropriation of the heartlands of the people of New Spain. The parallels between the Aztec army and Oñate's conquistadores were perfectly conscious and carefully contrived.

In some ways, Villagrá's poem was a promotional brochure, intended to represent New Mexico as a suitable land for settlement. But the effort to balance this purpose with the need to emphasize the conquerors' sufferings led the author into many conflicts of perception or representation, especially in depicting the natives. On the one hand, according to Villagrá, the pueblos evinced order and beauty, with many-windowed buildings up to seven stories high, and throngs of attractively busty women in brightly woven shawls. Arts and crafts throve in an economy of specialized activities: agriculture, fishing, painting, handiwork, manufacture of cotton cloth. The inhabitants were comfortingly fair of form and feature in a world still full of imaginary demons and monsters whom explorers continually expected to find enfleshed. They were intelligent, ingenious, sober, and adaptable, "extremely good workers" with a talent for agriculture. They readily adopted crops the Spaniards introduced, which the writer listed as "wheat, grapes, lettuce, cabbage, peas, chick-peas, cumin, carrots, turnips, garlic, onions, artichokes, radishes, and cucumbers," as well as Spanish livestock, including chickens, sheep, cattle, and goats, with which to supplement turkeys from central Mexico and abundant rivers full of fish. Society seemed orderly and reproduced elements of a familiar hierarchy, with women subordinate to men.[23]

Even Villagrá's accounts of battle display knightly foes who weep for each other and noble native womenfolk who sacrifice themselves for love, explicitly like Dido, or for honor, expressly like Lucretia. The author emphasizes discord among even the most inveterate of the Spaniards' opponents, and exonerates the peaceful faction from guilt for the war. One of the native guides, Mompil, commands respect as, with an arrow in the dust, he draws a map of "our New Mexico . . . like the very sagacious pilot he was . . . as if he had been well educated in our mathematics," while the Spaniards watched spellbound, "without moving an eyelid, as all together listened to the gallant barbarian." Villagrá's chivalric imagination turned a native squaw into a damsel of romance, when the wife of one of Mompil's colleagues arrived at the camp, "a furious but noble barbarian, frantic with love and urged by love," looking for her husband, nursing her baby at her breast, and carrying offerings of a fawn, rabbits, and a hare. The Spaniards' commander ordered her husband to be released "because this barbarian lady, wholly noble, deserves a courtly response." But, like Theseus abandoning Ariadne, says the poet, her husband fled the camp. Despite the loss of a valuable guide, the Spaniards allowed the woman to follow him.[24]

On the other hand, Villagrá recorded scandalous deficiencies among the natives. They were "superstitious sorcerers and hopeless idolaters." They had "neither kings nor laws" and he saw no malefactors punished in public.[25] These were not disinterested observations. Scourges and gallows were essential apparatus of civilized life. A society without a system of crime and punishment was a sign of a people ignorant of natural law and therefore bereft of its protection, fair game for conquest and subjection. Idolatry and sorcery were prima facie evidence of crimes against natural law, which stripped those guilty of them of legal protections and rendered them liable to war and enslavement. The unresolved contradictions of Villagrá's picture of the pueblos were typical of the Spanish monarchy, where favorable and unfavorable views of native peoples jostled according to the shifting agendas of the writers, the jurists, the crown, the public, and the conquistadores themselves.

For the conquerors of New Mexico, sufferings began even before they arrived at their destination. They celebrated Holy Thursday at San Elizario on the Río Grande with self-inflicted suffering, as the general, soldiers, and friars joined in a bloody rite of penitential self-flagellation to make themselves worthy of God's grace.[26] The trek north, straight across the desert from Santa Bárbara in Chihuahua, had taken fifty days of despair "through the broken scrublands of nomads and graceless savages." For five or six days along the notorious

Jornada del Muerto, the Dead Man's March, they had nothing to eat, according to Villagrá, but wayside roots, amid briars that tore their leather cuirasses and sand dunes that burned and blinded them, "with our wretched eyes boiling and burning in their sockets under our hard helms."[27] They marched on shoeless, swollen feet, driving their horses across crags. They had to abandon twenty-two wagons.

On April 30, 1598, they celebrated their arrival at the Río Grande with a formal act of possession of the land on behalf of the king, a sermon, a salute, a rite of blessing of the flag, and the performance of a play. The local indios made signs of peace by raising fingers as if in blessing, and as the expedition advanced, some natives greeted them with food, though other pueblos were empty of people, who had either fled in fear or died of diseases previous Spanish visitors had brought. On July 4, 1598, where the Chama River joins the Río Grande, Oñate founded a city he called San Juan de los Caballeros, the first European foundation in the central lands. So perhaps the fourth of July makes a suitable date on which to celebrate the beginnings of the Hispanic as well as the Anglo United States. By the end of August they had an irrigation ditch to supply the place. About 1,500 collaborative Indians built a church. On September 9, the day after its consecration, many chiefs of the region submitted to a ceremony of vassalage, though they presumably did not know what it meant to the Spaniards. The expedition's notary made a detailed inventory of pueblos assigned to each of the two Franciscan missionaries present: evidently, Mompil or other native informants had supplied a good map.

One pueblo, however, was resentful and resistant. At Acoma, toward the end of the year, the massacre of a Spanish party provided what Villagrá called "the first sacrifice of martyrdom to be offered in this Church of New Mexico,"[28] though this seems unfair to the Franciscans who had lost their lives on previous expeditions. After Fray Alonso Martínez had explained Saint Augustine's theory of just war, the governor, satisfied at meeting the conditions the saint had specified, ordered "war with fire and sword proclaimed against the fastness of Acoma." Vicente Zaldívar, the brother of one of the martyrs, led the punitive sortie. His orders were "to restrain the men from impieties, treat natives well, give the Acomans every opportunity to make peace by surrendering those guilty of the massacre," and in that case to allow only friars to enter the town to preach, "since it was for this alone that they had come from such distant lands."²⁹ Zaldívar faced Indians who wore captured armor and spent the night in "huge dances and carousals, shouting, hissing," and taunting the Spaniards, waving swords, displaying mail. They threatened to kill native collaborators, but the conquistadores and their native allies inflicted total defeat on the defenders. The Spaniards—so they claimed—rounded up the Acoman women and children to save them from native auxiliaries. As usual, however, chivalrous behavior alternated with atrocities. As so often in the conquest of the New World, the conquistadores resorted to terror to inhibit resistance. Oñate ordered the mutilation of enemy warriors. The Spaniards chopped a foot off each of twenty-four of them. (The crown later punished Oñate and Zaldívar for this excess by confiscating all their holdings and banishing them.) Terror, however, was not mere cruelty. It was a psychologically intelligible response to fear on the part of men aware of how tenuous their position was and how little power they would have to repel widespread native revanche.

Illusions still underpinned the enterprise. When he first met natives, Oñate asked about Cíbola. Everyone at the time underestimated the size of North America. The English at Roanoke and Jamestown thought a short trek would take them to the Pacific. The viceroy of New Spain thought the distance from the Chesapeake to New Mexico "is not thought to be too great."³⁰ The New Mexico and Florida colonies sent vain expeditions in each other's direction, ever refusing to admit that the distances were effectively untraversable. Oñate believed that the commerce of the "Great South Sea" would enrich his colony. Repeated efforts to find a road to the Pacific failed until, in 1605, Oñate made his way to the tip of the Gulf of California, inscribing a record of his achievement over a native petroglyph at El Morro on his way home: "Through here the Adelantado Don Juan de Oñate passed having achieved the discovery of the South Sea."³¹ The journey generated unreliable news of mirabilia—commonplaces of travelers' tall stories. Oñate claimed to have seen or at least heard of monstrous races who never existed outside the pages of Pliny's *Natural History* and other classical sources of conjectural ethnography. He had found the Nasamones, he claimed, who dangled ears so enormous that they could wrap themselves in their folds, and people who, for want of other orifices, took nourishment by inhalation through their noses. "This conquest," reported the viceroy, who resented the waste of manpower on an unpromising frontier, "is turning into a fairy story."[32] He was wrong. Conquistador imaginations had already turned it into a fairy story, with all the combination of fantasy and fear typical of the genre.

FOR THE FIRST FEW generations of the history of Spanish New Mexico, it was not the numbers of natives that threatened the colony's survival, but the lack of them. Invasions of microbes always preceded Spanish invaders. Some pueblos were already ghost towns when the first Spanish army marched into what is now New Mexico in 1598. Spaniards' need for native manpower was probably the main reason for the relocation of the capital to Santa Fe, in more populous country, in 1610. The newly arrived governor, Pedro de Peralta, hoped, no doubt, to break the Oñate family's hold on the colony, in line with the crown's policy of preventing the creation of hereditary aristocracies that might rival or usurp royal power. In any case, however, Spanish settlement was bound to be drawn to areas of densest native population. Peralta immediately found his job dominated by the need to arbitrate between clerical and lay demands on indios' time. He tried to appease the friars and please the crown by instituting draconian punishments for abuse of native labor, but he could satisfy no one and, at least in the friars' opinion, abused natives himself, as he drove on the work of building the new city on a grand scale, around a plaza big enough to exercise a thousand soldiers—another of many cases of fantasy dominating town planning on Spanish frontiers. In 1613 the Franciscan provincial, Fray Isidro Ordoñez, carried out what was in effect a coup d'état: he arrested the governor, seized his powers, and held him in chains until the king should appoint a more compliant successor.

The monarchy relied on the Franciscans to keep indios alive. Over the course of the seventeenth century, the crown spent 2,390,000 pesos in New Mexico, of which 1,340,000 were subsidies to missions. The Franciscans virtually monopolized the enterprise. At first, the results were encouraging. In 1630 Alonso de Benavides, the greatest of the apostles of the region, claimed 86,000 baptisms during a single summer's campaign by the mission he served, based at Santa Clara. He was aware, however, of daunting problems. "Since the land is very remote and isolated," he reported, "and the difficulties of the long journeys require more than a year of travel, the friars, although there are many who wish to dedicate themselves to those conversions, find themselves unable to do so because of their poverty. Hence only those go there who are sent by the Catholic king at his own expense, for the cost is so excessive that only his royal zeal can afford it."[33]

In the longer term, however, the indios seemed to respond to every kind of treatment, from brutal to benign, in the same ways: they died and they bred less. Disease, more than the effects of war, wiped out half the surviving population over the next hundred years. Pueblo numbers decreased from 60,000 in 1598 to 40,000 in 1638 and 17,000 in 1680. During a famine in 1669, a priest saw "a great many indios perished of hunger, lying dead along the roads, in the ravines, and in their huts." They were reduced to "soaking and toasting" hides for food. Famine made nomad raiders more exigent, driving them to ever more desperate depredations.[34]

The scale of baptisms suggests a second source of problems. Franciscan evangelization had, according to critics in other religious orders, always tended to be shallow or perfunctory—hurried on with messianic zeal as if the world were about to end, as indeed some friars thought it was. Imperfect converts to Christianity made imperfect subjects of the monarchy. Yet friars did not generally want soldiers in or near their missions, only invoking their aid when their converts were under attack from unevangelized tribes, or when the indios rebelled. One of the consequences of the stranger-effect was that it wore off after a while, so that native allegiance came to depend on the monarchy's effectiveness in guaranteeing peace and providing protection, conditions undermined because of the ravages of European diseases and the raids of unevangelized indios attracted to the spoils of the missions by their very economic success. Gradually the clergy of New Mexico caught up with Counter-Reformation standards of Christian observance, which demanded more than ritual compliance: sacramental life, serious catechesis, dogmatic awareness, veneration for universal cults at least as intense as for local devotions to neighborhood saints or Virgins or Christs of particular advocations. To the friars' disappointment, indigenous Catholicism was, perhaps, more concerned with survival in this world than salvation in the next. The natives' devotional practices were dappled with local customs that seemed like apostasy to zealous pastors: dances, oracular consultations, shamanistic performances, magical healings. Rather than the universal cults of the Church, local devotions perpetuated the memory of shrines and sacred places stained with the blood and lubricity of pagan rituals.

As in Europe, where the godly waged fierce campaigns of extirpation against popular religion, so in New Mexico and other parts of Spanish America the ecclesiastical authorities became increasingly impatient with the shortcomings of their congregations. Secular officials, on the other hand, were less fastidious and generally preferred to leave the status quo undisturbed. They tended to resent the friars' autonomy and the way they guarded access to the indios' tribute and labor. In the third quarter of the seventeenth century, while the friars launched a campaign of persecution of popular religion, the secular authorities did their best to undermine the friars' authority. From 1670 a series of terrible droughts, which the friars' prayers could not temper, induced widespread hardship and alienated many mission dwellers.

A series of conflicts culminated in 1675, when the governor, having acquiesced in the arrest and scourging of some shamans and the execution of others, decided to release most of the survivors. He seems to have acted out of fear of provoking an uprising. But he was sowing the wind. The released men became the kernel of an insurrectionist cell, which organized a remarkably widespread movement, uniting an unprecedentedly large number of pueblos in a ferocious and destructive series of attacks on missions and lay Spanish outposts in 1680. The Spaniards evacuated almost the entire area they had formerly occupied, broadcasting as they fled ferocious tales of martyrdoms, iconoclasm, and gratuitous atrocities committed against the Spanish dead.

The inhabitants of some pueblos, however, hated each other more than the Spaniards. Testimony Spanish investigators gathered when the rebellion was over includes a lot of back-covering and blame-scattering by witnesses fearful of reprisals, but the overall picture of insuperable divisions among the indios is irresistible. Some pueblos never wavered in their loyalty to the friars or the king. One of the leaders of the revolt allegedly murdered his own son-in-law to prevent his defection. Some of the incoming regime's orders—to uproot Spanish crops and desecrate Christian symbols—provoked noncompliance or active dissent. The Spaniards' departure, in any case, did not release rains or dispel disease. After the first Spanish attempt at reoccupation largely failed in 1681–82, a decade of Pueblo self-rule gradually split the rebels' ranks and restored the pro-Spanish constituency. In 1692, many communities submitted bloodlessly. The returning Spaniards and their native allies subjected the rest to ruthless reprisals, which they justified with a lot of religious rhetoric, dignifying massacres as battles, claiming battlefield apparitions of the Blessed Virgin, invoking the memories of the reconquest of Spain from the Moors and the conquest of Mexico from the Aztecs. It took four years to repress all resistance, but thereafter the Pueblo never rebelled again.[35] There were some whose distaste for Spanish rule made them flee to Kansas, where they built a tiny simulacrum of a pueblo, only a few households strong. The Spaniards pursued them. In 1706 Juan de Ulibarri rounded them up and, at their little stronghold near the Arkansas River, invested a friendly Apache chief as Spain's governor of what was then the remotest frontier of the monarchy.

FOR THE SETTLERS WHO trickled back into New Mexico, however, life was never really secure nor, in most cases, prosperous or even comfortable. There were no more than a thousand of them. They were among the most marginal denizens of the Spanish monarchy, never prized, rarely pondered in Madrid or even in Mexico City. The colonists' mental worlds were even wilder—more fantastic, more undomesticable—than the land they settled. The conquistadores' stories showed how they escaped from bloodshed and hardship into fantastic imaginings: battlefield visions, epic legends, romantic playacting, religious exaltation, chivalric language; though after the conquest the sources that take us inside colonial minds dried to a trickle, enough literature has survived to show that the mix remained the same: the same imaginative strategies helped sufferers cope with the misery and insecurity of frontier life. A mid-eighteenth-century confrontation in New Mexico between a realist and a fantasist opens a window into their world.

Miguel de Quintana was one of the reconquerors who arrived in 1693. Formerly a resident of Mexico City, he was evidently a poor man, unprivileged and unremarkable in more competitive environments, for he was prepared to make almost any sacrifice for the sake of modest preferment and a small competence. He described himself, rhetorically perhaps, in a bid for his persecutors' sympathies, as "a weak, poor man, forced from my necessity to seek for bread for my children," who numbered seven. Setting up home in just about the remotest town in the region, Villa Nueva de Santa Cruz de la Cañada, founded in 1695, he served the local council and church as a scribe. His reward was a small grant of land and seed money of 300 pesos to establish a smallholding. He worked it himself, at least in part, for a surviving lawsuit he initiated complained of a neighbor's indio servant who stole his two horses, which "were my feet and hands for carrying a little provender and firewood and for getting around to do my work."[36]

Quintana was remarkably pious, a Franciscan tertiary who wrote dialogues for church performance. All was well as long as he maintained his privileged relationship, as church scribe, with the parish priest. He formed what was evidently a close friendship with Fray Juan de Tagle, who, until his death, was something of a patron and encouraged him in mental prayer and mystical practices. In one of the first signs that something was amiss in Quintana's mental world, Tagle appeared to him in a vision recorded in 1732, "as he was at his death, in his habit, with his hands tucked into his sleeves, and his face displaying extreme affliction." The visionary remained friends, albeit much less warmly, with Tagle's successor, Fray Manuel de Sopeña, who like Tagle approved of Quintana's increasingly bizarre literary output. For years the scribe produced devotional verses in apparent confidence of his own sanctity. It seemed to him that a heavenly voice dictated the writings, even goaded him into submitting them for the priest's approval. "Believe, Miguel," said the voice, "that the priest will not demur over these compositions."[37] Even when he realized that the heterodox flavor of his output troubled the priest, he did not abate the flow of verse and even expected—so he said—to get sugar and chocolate as a reward.[38]

This sort of thing may formerly have been all very well in New Mexico, but it was in the nature of frontier missions that, periodically, new clergy arrive to jolt the remote provinces into awareness of current devotional fashions. Mysticism always invites inquisitorial scrutiny: not even Saint Teresa of Ávila escaped without serious investigation. For mysticism is, so to speak, the Protestantism of Catholicism—a hotline to God that enables the devout to bypass the clergy. Quintana's mysticism was essentially oral: his visions were of the dead, not of God. He never claimed the sublime mystical rapture of self-identification with God. The messages he got from his voice were mundane—advice to be faithful, patient, humble, penitent, and appreciative of the graces that accompany poverty and misfortune. But the Church had become increasingly wary of mystics in the course of the late seventeenth century, after a spate of fraudulent visionaries and manipulative charismatics. In 1734, when the new Franciscan provincial, Fray Joseph Yrigoien, heard about Miguel Quintana's revelations, he instantly grew suspicious. He demanded that Sopeña disgorge the evidence and scoured it for heresy. He did not find much. Miguel's only serious error occurred in a single line of his output, in which his voice had assured him that his verses came from God: "Believe, Miguel, with living faith, that the God of Heaven alone has given you, as a poor and humble man, all the verses you have composed."[39] Quintana never appreciated his danger. Even in his recantation he was defensive rather than abject, as a good penitent should be. He explained in his that he wrote his poetry in adoration of God, and that, like King David, he had been unable to keep silent without feeling the pain of his silence in his bones.[40] He survived, but his career as New Mexico's first writer was snuffed out. Frontiers, in theory, breed an individualistic and dissenting spirit. They can also repress it and starve it of inspiration.

NEW MEXICO SEEMED POOR to everyone but the hunting and foraging nomads who surrounded it and dodged in and out of it. Contact with the Spanish monarchy transformed the peoples beyond the frontier more thoroughly, perhaps, than Rome transformed the Germans or China the Jurchen or Manchus before the great invasions. Horses revolutionized their economies and way of life. Loot disturbed society and redistributed power. War chiefs and leaders of mounted bands contested the power of shamans and hereditary chiefs. In some cases, like that of the Comanche, who dominated the southern plains from eastern New Mexico to southern Kansas, societies became militarized—dedicated to and organized for war, united under war leaders, and motivated by visions of empire over the plains, where it was easy to shunt mounted armies back and forth, exacting tribute from the inhabitants. In other cases, among the peoples known as Apache, whose lands fringed those of the Comanche to the south, the effect of Spanish payola and loot was fissile, loosening the traditional bonds of kinship and hierarchy, creating a new warrior class, and releasing ad hoc war bands to hurtle and zoom into sedentarists' territory to raid for booty or seize loot by intimidation. Unlike the sedentary peoples, they were unconquerable, because, in the case of the Apache, you could not pin them down, and in the case of the Comanche, they had an economy and way of life—the former based on bison and the latter on horses—well adapted to the control of vast spaces with little manpower. Spanish policy wavered between strategies: playing them off against each other, as the Byzantine Empire did with its barbaric neighbors in the Middle Ages; trying to attract them into the empire by evangelizing them in both Christianity and sedentarism; intimidating them with punitive expeditions; or seeking to exterminate or expel them, as the Anglo settlers did. The problems became acute after the pacification of the pueblos and the recovery of their demographic growth and economic viability in the late seventeenth century: Apaches and Comanches became increasingly alert to the prospect of pickings, and increasingly troublesome to the colony. They were, moreover, ideal allies for a new enemy who, at about the same time, began infiltrating Spain's frontiers from the Mississippi valley: the French. The ensuing conflicts obliged Spain to extend her empire across Texas and Arizona into the plains, just as barbarian incursions compelled ancient Rome to engage in an endless and unsatisfactory search for stable, defensible frontiers.

The career of Juan Sabeata offers an approach to the story. He was a mission runaway, probably born in Rio Conchos, Nueva Vizcaya, in a region that became a major Spanish silver-mining colony in the 1630s. He lived in his youth at the Parral mission, from where he fled at an unrecorded date, toward the middle of the seventeenth century. The reasons for his flight, and his subsequent, uneasy relationship with Spaniards, are undocumented, but the context is clear. Sabeata belonged to a people the Spaniards called Julimes, part of a class of linguistically related, sedentary, agrarian peoples known as Jumanos, whose name was a corruption of the Spanish word for "human," signifying the Spaniards' sense of kinship with them in contrast to the bestial nomads. The Jumanos lived along and around the middle Rio Grande, with settlements stretching as far as the Colorado, but their main center, by the late sixteenth century, was at La Junta de los Rios, south of El Paso.

In some ways, the arrival of Spaniards favored them. They adopted horses quickly, acquiring a military advantage over their neighbors and launching raids for buffalo pelts into the plains. Wherever Spaniards went, trade opportunities multiplied and trade routes lengthened, which suited people like the Jumanos, who had a large agricultural surplus to dispose of. But ever-fewer people shared the growing prosperity. For protracted periods from the 1620s to the 1660s droughts exacerbated the effects of disease. Meanwhile, competition for buffalo products increased as other native groups became adept in horseman-ship. So the Jumanos generally adopted a wary attitude towards the Spanish monarchy: they kept out of Spaniards' way as much as possi-ble, but collaborated whenever a trading profit, a military advantage, or a lucrative raiding opportunity beckoned.

Sabeata, with his background in mission life, knew how to appeal to Spanish sensibilities. In 1683 he led a mission to El Paso and told the governor that the Jumanos had won a battle against Apache inter-lopers thanks to an apparition of the Virgin and the sign of the cross. They therefore wanted missionaries to join them, and if Spanish sol-diers were available too, so much the better. Wherever the friars went in Jumano country, women came out to kiss the hems of their habits, and native leaders sought to perpetuate their visit. For two years, the Jumanos were able to pursue their war against the Apache with Span-ish help. But, increasingly aware of how their hosts were manipulating them, the Spaniards withdrew in 1685. Other Jumano groups then made similar arrangements with French allies—or "new Spaniards," as they called them—from what is now eastern Texas. Spanish coloniza-tion of Texas from the 1690s was a response to French attempts to secure the region watered by the lower Mississippi. While Spaniards and Frenchmen distracted one another in mutual fighting, Apache exploited the power vacuum and largely expelled the Jumanos, or con-fined them to a few centers, by the second decade of the eighteenth century. When the Spanish monarchy resumed efforts to absorb the region, the Apache were the main incumbent power with whom the Spaniards had to deal.[41]

TEXAS WAS AN ALMOST impossible outpost, separated from New Mexico by the breakwater that divided the valleys of the Mississippi and the Rio Grande, and, for the most part, hard of access from the Gulf coast. There were only two possible methods of colonization: military settlement, with expensive soldiery housed in remote garrisons with little prospect of putting down roots, or missionary activity, which was fragile, vulnerable, and useless for purposes of defense. The first missions turned away the troops sent to protect them but could not survive without them. In the 1720s they tried to create a barrier against the French by evangelizing Caddos of Texas, but the natives demurred on the grounds that "holy water kills them." Franciscans found the natives more responsive to French gifts of guns and liquor than to the blandishments of Christianity. Between 1718 and 1722 Spaniards set up ten missions and four forts manned by a total of 250 men. It was like trying to brand a herd of buffalo. In 1727 a royal inspector found "no Indians in the missions."[42]

From the French perspective, exploitation of the Mississippi valley also demanded frontier security, and the vast, undomesticable region to the west was almost as problematic as it was for Spain. The Franco-Spanish frontier was deep, undefined, and permeable in both directions. No individual illustrates that fact better than the French trader and entrepreneur Louis Juchereau de Saint-Denis. In 1714 he arrived in New Mexico with wagonloads of French contraband, which he hoped to sell at a profit to Spanish settlers. Instead of allowing him to trade, his hosts took him captive, but he adjusted to circumstances, married locally, and became a Spanish agent, helping to establish missions in Texas.[43] He lived equivocally, running illicit trading operations from French to Spanish territory, and for many years running France's Texan outpost at Cadodaquious on the Red River. Were his sympathies French or Spanish? Toward the end of his life, in 1743, he sought permission to leave French territory to die in his wife's homeland, but his superiors refused him.

If Cadodaquious was France's remotest toehold, the story of the Spanish frontier forts at Los Adaes, a little to the west of the Red River in what is now Louisiana, shows the intractability of the frontier to Spanish imperialism. Built to pinion the French intruders, the first fort, at San Miguel, was the subject of many Spanish dispatches and orders, but never of sufficient investment or effort to make it viable. A force of seven Frenchmen overwhelmed it in 1719. The disparity of power was evident: there was only one soldier in the

Spanish garrison, and he did not know the monarchies were at war.[44] Spain responded with an expeditionary force led by a self-proclaimed knight-errant, the Marqués de San Miguel de Aguayo, who raised an army of five hundred at his own expense. The French withdrew, but chiefly because their king had made peace with Philip V. Aguayo built an impressive new stockade at Nuestra Señora de Los Adaes, with a garrison initially a hundred strong, as part of an extensive program of restoring the presidios and missions of eastern Texas. But, having endured mosquitoes, chiggers, and floods, he was assailed by ice and bitter cold on the long march back to Mexico. Only fifty of his four thousand horses survived the expedition. The frontier was so far from its own hinterland that occupation was impossible without French forbearance—which could generally be relied on because French merchants appreciated Spanish custom. Spaniards in turn relied on supplies from French New Orleans. By the mid-eighteenth century, foreign goods in Los Adaes greatly outnumbered those produced within the Spanish empire. A kind of modus vivendi had emerged. The French and Spanish empires stretched such feeble fingertips towards each other's territory that neither felt either permanently threatened or constantly secure. From time to time violence seemed the only source of relief from the tension.

IN 1763 FRANCE'S WITHDRAWAL from continental North America relieved Texas and New Mexico of their role and burden as buffers against the French. Meanwhile, however, the Spanish monarchy had another rival empire to contend with—not French or English but Comanche. Comanche raiders were first mentioned in New Mexico in 1704. Within two generations they became the most formidable polity on the North American plains, "a nation so bellicose and so indomitable that it rules all those of the interior country," according to a Franciscan observer.[45] Vast flatlands nourish huge, volatile imperialisms. Think of the Huns or Mongols in the steppes of Eurasia or the medieval empire of Mali in the African Sahel. Comparable developments in the Americas were impossible before Spaniards introduced horses, and thereafter remained odd by comparison with those in other grasslands: in contrast to the pastoralists of Eurasia and Africa, the peoples of the American prairies and pampa were hunters, relying on vast herds of buffalo or, in South America, guanaco. Even so, imperial states emerged among peoples able to mobilize with sufficient unity and energy to exact tribute from other grassland dwellers and tyrannize neighboring sedentarists.

By the eighteenth century, horse-borne hunting made the South American pampa and North American prairie desirable places to live. Intrusions of farmers and city dwellers on the edges enhanced the new economic opportunities offered by horses, cattle, and sheep. Pastoralism and mining enabled peoples of the pampa in what is today Argentina to open new trade with Chile and to absorb lessons in large-scale chieftaincy from the Araucanos, the impressive warriors of the South American southwest, who maintained effective independence beyond the frontiers of the Spanish empire. By the mid-eighteenth century, chieftains on the Negro and Colorado rivers, such as Cacapol, the "Attila of the pampa," and his son Cangapol "the Brave," could turn the elective position of war chief into hereditary rule. They could organize lucrative trade in furs, assemble harems of a size to mark their status, impress a Jesuit visitor as "monarchs over all the rest,"[46] raise thousands of warriors, and threaten the city of Buenos Aires.

A similar transformation began to affect the North American prairie. Huge kills of buffalo for their hides generated a trading surplus, which in turn introduced maize to Native American hunters' diets, whiskey to their religious rites, and guns to their armories. As the horses multiplied, the plains became a source of supply for the white colonies on the edges of the region. Even before white men disputed control of them, the prairies became an arena of competition between ever-growing numbers of immigrant Native American peoples—many driven, as much as drawn, from east of the Missouri River by the pressure of white empire building. Those with agricultural traditions edged toward or into nomadism. All tended to become herders of horses as well as hunters of buffalo, which forced them into unstable contact with one another on shared trails and pastures. The Sioux, converts to nomadism, were a potentially imperial or at least domineering people who became the terror of a settled Native American world still intact on the Upper Missouri River. By 1790 there were 25,000 Sioux.

Even when they had adopted a horse-borne way of life and an economy reliant on the slaughter of bison, the Sioux kept an interest in their traditional forest economy. When their conquests covered the plains, they extended them into new forests farther west, where deer hunting still conferred special prestige. The Black Hills in North Dakota were their "meat store," seized from Kiowa, Cheyenne, and Crow. Meanwhile, trade exposed the region to killer diseases of European origin. Smallpox epidemics facilitated the Sioux's conquest of the Arikara and Omaha peoples the way that diseases had prepared the way for white imperialism among unimmunized peoples.[47] The Sioux adopted the values of imperial society, rewarding skill in battle above other qualities and tying social status to the possession and distribution of booty. The white man did not introduce imperialism to the plains: he arrived as a competitor with a Sioux empire that was already taking shape there.

To the south of the lands that the Sioux would come to dominate, the exceptional potential of the Comanche was apparent by the mid-eighteenth century. Their heartland was central. They could accumulate wealth by raiding the Spanish empire, and use it to buy guns from the French. Millions of horses and bison were at their disposal. By the 1740s they were entirely mounted, with 120,000 horses in their corrals. They organized for mobility in units of about 250 people, called *rancherías*, each with dual leadership—a war chief to supervise military operations and an older leader, called a *paraibo*, who was responsible for logistics and for the labor of women and children— supported by a council of elders. Their success in culling and extorting food is obvious from the way their population exploded, from 15,000 in 1750 to 45,000 by 1780, probably three times as many as all the other native peoples of the southern plains in combination.[48] Their dominion covered the valleys of the Arkansas, Cimarron, Canadian, and Red rivers, and the plains of northern Texas beyond the Spanish frontier. Their raids reached as far south as Guadalajara. A martial ethos dominated Comanche culture, with status proportionate to prowess. The entire nation gathered on a war footing when a majority of *paraibos*, who met periodically or in response to an emergency or opportunity, so decided. Spaniards had no doubt that the Comanche were an imperial people like themselves. A play performed in New Mexico in 1780 put these words into a Comanche mouth:

> *From east to west, from south*
> *Northwards, across the plains*
> *Clear notes from trumpet's mouth*
> *Proclaim where my steel reigns.*
> *I battle every nation*
> *With valour, daring, zest*
> *And so ardent is the passion*
> *That heaves within my breast*
> *That my banner ever flows*
> *Like the wind that does not rest*
> *Taking tribute from my foes.*[49]

The rise of the Comanche wrecked Spanish efforts to turn the plains into a secure and relatively untroublesome zone. In the seventeenth century Spain targeted the Ute as the most promising potential surrogates in the plains, bringing a Ute embassy to Santa Fe to pledge friendship in 1675.[50] In 1714 and 1719 they invaded Colorado to try to force recalcitrant tribes into quiescence, but French agents were at work, inciting resistance among plains sedentarists—Pawnee and Wichita—supplying arms in exchange for slaves raided from the Spaniards' Ute and Pueblo allies and subjects. In 1720 the governor of New Mexico sent a forty-strong task force into Nebraska to try to detach the Pawnee from the French, but their hosts almost wiped out the visitors. A Pawnee painting on hide depicts the scene: the Spaniards in their tricorne hats, huddled in a square beside their tents, while their attackers in livid paint, armed with delicate, curling bows and accompanied by French agents, circle menacingly.[51]

The growth in Comanche power in the 1730s and 1740s cemented the friendship between the Spaniards and the Ute. Meanwhile, squeezed between the Comanche and the French, Spaniards and Pueblos huddled for defense. A policy Spaniards called "attraction" brought increasing numbers of Apache communities into settlements under Spanish protection. The results can be admired, for instance, in a decorative plan of the settlement of San Juan Bautista on the Río Grande in 1754, where through the neat files of colonnaded streets processions of indios and Spaniards thread, with their traditional arms and music, to meet the mission folk in the main square and erect celebratory crosses in each of its corners. A party of religious sisters and children from the mission schools join the party.

THE CHIMERA OF SECURITY led to renewed Spanish interest in Arizona from the 1730s. The indefatigable Jesuit missionary Eusebio Kino had founded a series of missions there in the 1690s, among the Pimas people, in the course of his attempt to propel Christendom northward from Sonora. But the missions were fragile and isolated, without support from the secular authorities in Sonora or New Mexico. When the first priests died, there was no one to replace them at Bac and Guevavi until 1732. They did introduce ranching—Kino took a herd of twenty cattle with him and they multiplied prodigiously— and the notion, at least, of allegiance to the Spanish monarchy. Reoccupation, however, was hardly trouble-free when Spaniards returned, not least because this time soldiers accompanied the missionaries and the usual tensions between laymen and clergy ensued over exploitation of the indios. In 1750 the authorities in Sonora imposed their own choice of local native governor in defiance of the Jesuits' wishes: Luis Oacpicaguigua of Sáric, who used the same talents of persuasion to incite most of the people of his governorship into revolt. Late in 1751 they killed over a hundred Spaniards, including two Jesuits, and many native adherents to the Spanish side. Don Luis's targets included churches at Guevavi, Tubac, and Bac—the principal missions still functioning or revived since Kino's day. He surrendered in 1752, but resentful shamans, such as Hawani Mo'o of Gila River, who attacked Bac in 1756, continued to cause trouble.[52] Spain responded by pumping more resources of men and money into the unproductive colony. Fortifying frontiers in America was like setting spiders to catch flies. Every escalation made the effort harder to sustain.

A surprisingly successful expedient, practiced with increasing intensity in the 1740s, was to ransom captives from the Comanches and settle them to farm and defend northern New Mexico. As most of them had been seized from plains tribes, whose habit was hunting, they seemed unpromising material for the role, but surprisingly large numbers stayed put and played their part in frontier security. They numbered perhaps 10 percent of the population of New Mexico by the mid-eighteenth century. Nevertheless, the long, exposed border was always open to attack from the Great Plains. The northern flank of the road that led from Arizona across New Mexico and Texas could be pierced with ease. According to a report on the frontier drawn up in 1766, the road was useful for restraining natives, as a "ship at anchor in mid-Atlantic" would be for controlling pirates.[53] In 1757 Spaniards fortified the San Sabá River to strengthen the road and defend such Apache communities as they had successfully persuaded into Christianity, sedentarism, and submission. At the same time, the Franciscans of the nearby mission refused a garrison, only to be massacred by Comanche invaders within a year. Spanish efforts to exact revenge foundered in the face of well-organized Comanche defenses backed by thousands of muskets given by the French merchants who arrived in increasing numbers along the Arkansas River or from the Missouri. The balance of firepower increasingly favored the Comanches. In 1759, when Spain mounted another invasion attempt of Comanche territory, Wichita and Comanche gunfire turned the force back at a Wichita village on the Red River, where a French flag flew over well-manned defense works. The Spaniards clung to their fort of San Sabá, rebuilding it in stone, but their presence was tenuous, and by 1769 they suspended the effort and abandoned the fort.

By then, however, the Spanish and Comanche empires had established a balance of mutual respect. An informal Comanche-Spanish alliance against unsedentarized Apaches, who were intractable foes of both empires, gradually took shape. The very success of the alliance was its undoing. Apaches sought refuge from the merciless war in settlements Spaniards called *establecimientos de paz*. With every diminution of the Apache threat, the amity between Spaniards and Comanches cooled. The Comanche chief, Cuerno Verde, was, in any case, more wary of Spain than of unruly but unambitious tribes, and greedier for Spanish tribute than that of poor indios. In 1779 Juan de Anza, a soldier who had been responsible for exploring the mule-train route to California, launched a daring raid on the chief's camp, killed him in battle, and carried off the Comanche hoard: 104 mule-loads of booty.

The impact was immediate and lasted for a generation. More native communities joined the monarchy peacefully. Hopis descended from their cliff-top fortresses. The Arizona frontier benefited from the release of resources. In 1784, 800 men were available for an expedition against Gila Apaches and claimed to have killed sixty-eight and captured seventeen of them. Defending the frontier, however, was like stoppering a dike. In another campaign in the same direction the following year, 350 men captured twenty-seven horses—but they lost over fifty. Though Apache heads "crowned the palisades" of Arizpe in Sonora, this was evidence that the Apache retained the initiative and remained dangerous.[54] Cheyenne and Arapaho horsemen, moreover, whom the Comanche could not control, kept problems of security alive.

OVER THE COURSE OF the eighteenth century, the defense of Spanish North America became ever more costly and complex. Miners' incursions aroused native hostility. Missions gave way to forts as the most numerous and conspicuous outposts of the Spanish empire. Efforts redoubled to harness native peoples to the monarchy and deploy them in its defense. But some communities always remained intractable, unblandished by the gospel, unimpressed by Spanish strategies for unity and security against rival invaders. Hostile Apaches and raiders from the plains became adept on horseback and expert in the use of firearms. As they gathered booty and trade goods, war chiefs challenged the traditional structures of society, gathered followers, and turned them into mobile bands. Spaniards and Indians traded atrocities: beheading on the one side, scalping on the other. Manpower shortages made officials withdraw garrisons and organize militias. In 1766 the Marqués de Rubí suppressed the garrison of El Paso, despite its exposure to Apache raids, on the grounds that the population was big enough to defend itself. He also ordered the abandonment of San Sabá, on the grounds that it was indefensible. Munitions were in short supply on the frontier and it was hard to get them into citizens' hands. When Rubí reached Santa Fe, on his tour of inspection he found the defenders relied on bows and arrows. The city was still little more, beyond the main square, than a straggling line of adobe dwellings along the river. At Los Adaes, the garrison of sixty-one men had two muskets between them, though security was good in the area since the withdrawal of French forces from Louisiana a few years before.[55]

Rubí's tour of inspection signified a new, vigorous policy in Madrid. Early modern empires, until the late eighteenth century, succeeded best by benign neglect and masterly inactivity, leaving incumbent elites to manage local and regional affairs. But the Enlightenment awakened statesmen to the responsibilities of government and the opportunities of power. Interventionist policies in the British Empire in North America drove colonists to revolt. The Spanish monarchy was more successful both in initiating schemes of interference in colonial affairs, and in defeating or controlling the unrest that followed. In 1772 new regulations announced a bold series of measures: the refortification of the frontier, the settlement of the hinterland behind a cordon of forts, the removal of nomadic Indians to settled townships, the militarization of frontier society, the prosecution of war against hostiles from beyond the border.

Rather like Chinese debates about how to deal with nomads—teetering between trying to "civilize" barbarians according to Confucian principles and trying to force them into submission—Spanish inclinations oscillated between contradictory points of view. Rubí and the governors he influenced favored ending the Indian problem by war. Others favored a strategy of attracting the barbarian. In 1778 Bernardo de Gálvez argued that through trade "the king would keep them very contented for ten years with what he now spends in one year making war upon them."[56] Though Gálvez also favored keeping them busy with their internecine wars, he thought the best solution for Indians lay in buying off their hostility as cheaply as possible, reducing them to reliance on Spanish food aid and liquor, "creating for them a new necessity that will oblige them to recognize their dependence on us."[57] In the long run many native societies came to depend on Spanish goods and payola. Food, clothes, copper kettles, and axes bought peace. Protection from enslavement was a bonus, when and if it could be delivered, though every time Spaniards ransomed a captive from the Comanche they enriched a potentially hostile warlord.

In 1786 a peace treaty established coexistence between the Spanish and Comanche empires, with a frontier on the Arkansas River and mutual trading privileges. Meanwhile, the Spanish cordon of forts had expanded to include Tucson. Security enhanced communications and stimulated settlement. In 1765 the number of Spaniards residing in New Mexico was only 9,600. By the end of the century there were 20,000. In Arizona, settlers trickled in behind a new curtain of garrisons. In the 1780s and 1790s pack-mule trains ambled from Tucson to San Antonio, though an effort to extend the system to California did not last. A campaign in 1788 under Manuel de Echegaray with 400 men reached Zuñi country and captured 125 Apache. At last the new policy Rubí inaugurated was showing results.[58]

There were problems to which the Spanish monarchy never found answers. Though the French threat receded in 1763, new dangers from Russian and British expansion were growing. The vastness of the American interior, which the first conquistadores, to their cost, had so drastically underestimated, proved intractable to settlement with the resources available. It was impossible to recruit reliable settlers from Europe in anything like sufficient numbers, which was the main reason why the French were willing to renounce what they called Louisiana. In 1804, a report on the value of frontier outposts would deplore the dearth of public works, settlers, and imported goods.[59] Missions were costly, dwindling assets. By 1781 the mission of San Juan Bautista—something of a flagship among Texan missions—which had baptized 1,434 Indians up to 1761, and typically held 300 native residents at a time, was down to a total of 169 indios, with only 63 natives under instruction. Church-state tensions were always interfering with the efficiency of the empire and disturbing its peace. The microbial world, mutable and deadly, was beyond human control as new diseases colonized new eco-niches. In the late 1770s and early 1780s a virulent and unfamiliar strain of smallpox killed thousands of people along the frontier. Spain abandoned the project of keeping open a land corridor to California. Spaniards "never did more than nibble around the margins" of the plains.[60]

The successes Spaniards achieved in the central lands are more remarkable than the failures they suffered. By 1760 the Spanish population of Texas was still under 1,200, nearly half of whom lived in San Antonio. San Antonio was the most impressive success, founded in 1731 with colonists from the Canary Islands, procured with heavy subsidies from the crown. But peace with the local Apaches guaranteed the colonists' freedom to farm. By 1790 the town had grown to house about 1,500 Spaniards and there were some 4,000 in the whole province. Even Arizona was thriving in parts: the Tubac garrison had 1,000 head of cattle and 5,000 sheep. High yields of corn and a good output of blankets attested to the productivity of some of the missions. As we shall see, Spanish power in the late eighteenth century was reaching beyond the Rockies with the colonization of much of California, which, despite the problems of access via Arizona, was approachable by land and sea from the south.

In 1796 a Spanish agent planted Spain's flag among the Mandan natives of the Upper Missouri. Spain's dominion in the Americas was at its height. But there was still a touch of fantasy about it, worthy of the fairy-tale quality Governor Velasco had denounced in the projects of the conquistadores of New Mexico in 1598. The successful agent in Mandan country was a Welsh refugee from Britain, John Evans, whose motive for immersing himself in the dangers and discomforts of the American interior was his personal quest to find traces of the legendary exploits of Prince Madoc, a supposititious medieval Welsh prince who had, according to story, fled across the western ocean to escape English persecution six hundred years before. Mandans, he presumed, must be the people of Madoc.[61] If, as Evans fervently expected, he could prove that they spoke Welsh, he would add not only to the dominions of Spain but also to the glory of Wales. The interior of what is now the United States has always shimmered with impossible visions—the cities of Cíbola, Amazons, Nasamones. Evans was a worthy successor to Juan de Oñate and Gaspar Pérez de Villagrá.

CHAPTER THREE

THE PURSUIT OF KING ARTHUR

The Shadow of Anglo-America, c. 1607–1784

And who in time knows whither we may vent
The treasure of our tongue? To what strange shores
This gain of our best glory shall be sent,
T' enrich unknowing nations with our stores?
What worlds in th' yet unformed Occident
May come refin'd with th' accents that are ours?

~Samuel Daniel, "Musophilus,"
Poetical Essays (1599)

Exactly as I would speak of my nearest personal friends or enemies, or my most familiar neighbors, he spoke of Sir Bedivere, Sir
Bors de Ganis, Sir Launcelot of the Lake, Sir Galahad, and all the
other great names of the Table Round—and how old, old, unspeak-
ably old and faded and dry and musty and ancient he came to look
as he went on! Presently he turned to me and said, just as one
might speak of the weather, or any other common matter—"You
know about transmigration of souls; do you know about transpo-
sition of epochs—and bodies?"

~Mark Twain, A Connecticut Yankee in King Arthur's Court (1889)

Invoking an old joke, George Santayana, the Spaniard of Harvard who spent many years as a professor of philosophy there, used to say, "One Englishman, an idiot; two Englishmen, a sporting event; three Englishmen, an empire." He then revised the saying: it took only one Englishman to conquer an empire.[1] In the eyes of the world the English (and, by extension, the British) are indeed a fearsome people, all too generous in bestowing the benefits of their guidance. They create empires with ease and abandon them with profligacy.

They acquired, in a sense, a continental dynastic empire in the twelfth century, which they lost in the thirteenth; conquered another in the fourteenth, which they lost in the fifteenth; settled a third in the seventeenth, which they lost in the eighteenth; and created another still in the nineteenth before losing it in the twentieth. God knows what they will do next. Some recent foreign investment figures suggest that the world may be in for another spell of British imperialism, in the business sense, with British-based companies preserving British influence in the global economy.

Meanwhile, although British influence has declined, its residue is everywhere, and its leavings lie on beaches from which British power has withdrawn. You feel the force of the legacy when, for example, you evince surprise that in the middle of Singapore there is still room for a cricket green in the shadow of an English cathedral; or meet young Copper Inuit who talk English and play soccer; or hear the language of Hansard in the legislature in Harare; or travel to Melbourne—a journey from England so long that you could expect to land somewhere close to the moon—and emerge in a land of fish-and-chip shops, where lawyers wear wigs.

The cultural legacy—the mild but deep impress of what people now call "soft power" or of "business imperialism" or of the reach of missions and merchants and migrants—extends even beyond the old limits of empire. You find congregations in Patagonia who still sing hymns in Welsh; or, in neighboring Chile, a passable simulacrum of an

English preparatory school; or, a little to the south, Anglican Fue-
gians. Some of the most inventive productions of Shakespeare are
played in Japan.[2] A similar effect of surprise at the reach of British
influence ensues when you reflect that in 1988 there were 103 new
productions of Shakespeare in Germany, more than of any German
playwright;[3] or that Mozambique has joined the commonwealth; or
that two Spanish suburbs that I know of are built in imitation of
English housing estates; or that the French—or some of them—like
rugby football, which seems to me the most astonishing cultural transmission of all.

Even the most inveterate historic enemies of England are susceptible to British cultural influence. It may be that in relation to their
numbers, apart from the ancient Greeks and Jews, the British have
achieved the greatest impact of any people on the rest of the world.

For a Hispanic-focused history of the United States to ignore the
presence and projection of Britain in America would therefore be as
misguided as those conventional anglocentric histories I have
denounced for sidelining Spain. So at intervals, in this chapter and
again in Chapter Six, we have to turn to look at the origins and unfolding of the story of Anglo-America, advancing from east to west, while
the Hispanic United States spread from south to north. To understand how the histories of two Americas intersected, we have to identify and examine key episodes of both processes. Conflict and
complementarity often happen together. The Hispanic US and the
Anglo US are only intelligible together.

PEOPLE WHO ARE THE descendants of the victims or subjects of
British preponderance—whether in the formal sense of subjugation
by the British Empire or of informal control or domination by business imperialism—tend to be equivocal about the effects. They often
denounce atrocities and demand apologies but relish elements of the
legacy. People in India lament the suppression of their native industries in the interests of British industrialization, but worship cricket
and garner prizes for the literary use of English. Africans rage against

the empire for encouraging slavery in the seventeenth and eighteenth centuries, but acknowledge Britain's leading role in suppressing it.

It is not surprising, therefore, that, despite the brevity and paucity of some of their ancestors' experience as British subjects, people in the United States have an equivocal attitude to the relationship of their country's history to Britain's imperial past. They are proprietary about the English language, mythopoeic about some British political and religious traditions, and starry-eyed about common law; yet they are fiercely proud of the revolution that freed them from Britain's monarchy and aristocracy and loud in their condemnation of imperialism in general—at least, of other people's imperialism.

The rhetoric, however, is delusive. In part, people in the United States have conflictive sentiments about the British Empire because they are equivocal about their own past and present imperialism. Candidates for naturalization in the United States have to take an exam in which they have to answer a lot of silly questions about the history and politics of the country. One of the silliest is, "What form of government does the US have?" The language of the question is influenced, perhaps, by a famous story about Benjamin Franklin, who, replying to a lady who asked him, as he emerged from America's first constitutional convention, what form of government he had chosen, said, "A republic, madam, if you have the will to keep it."[4] In the citizenship test, the correct response—so designated by the unimaginative bureaucrats who write the officially approved answers—is, "a republic." An equally good designation for the form of government of the United States would be, "an empire."

The founding fathers were unafraid of the word. Alexander Hamilton hoped the young republic would be "the embryo of a great empire." Thomas Jefferson envisaged an "empire of liberty." The country grew by conquest, mainly at Native American, Mexican, and Canadian expense. When those conquests spanned the continent, they spilled into the oceans. Hawaii, the Philippines and other Pacific islands, Puerto Rico, Guantánamo, and the Panama Canal Zone were all seized between 1898 and 1903. Meanwhile, the empire practiced genocide—it would be evasive to suppress the word when referring to relentless campaigns of violence, deprivation, forced migration, and cultural and economic subversion—on Native Americans. The imperial republic victimized other subject communities, especially blacks and Hispanics. It espoused a universalist program of values—which is perhaps a defining feature of imperial behavior—and sought, and still seeks, to promote and impose those values on others. The United States made its last permanent territorial acquisitions in 1917, with the purchase of the Danish Virgin Islands, and has uttered anti-imperial rhetoric ever since. But it has gone on bombing and invading countries where people defy its will or impede its interests. To adapt a saying: if it looks like an empire, walks like an empire, and quacks like an empire, it's an empire.

Many US citizens, including some historians, are in denial. They hate to apply the word "empire" to their own country, because of connotations of evil and because of the strength of the tradition of US anti-imperial rhetoric. A reasonable and persuasive judgment would be that all states, including those we call empires, are, at best, morally equivocal, but that some are worse than others. The United States is, or at least has been, an empire, and has been responsible for many of the characteristic iniquities of empires, but that does not disqualify "America" from doing and having done a great deal of good for the world—modeling democracy, for instance; fighting totalitarianism; patronizing arts; nurturing research.

The US empire, in short, was like the Spanish empire and the Mexican empire and Mexican imperial republic that succeeded Spain in North America, mixing mercies and malignity. For Mexicans also behaved imperially, much as Spaniards did previously and gringos simultaneously: subjugating, exploiting, victimizing, and sometimes massacring Native Americans, suppressing regional autonomies from time to time, arbitrarily subjecting peripheral regions to the center, repressing autonomists and secessionists, and suppressing or trying to suppress their rebellions. Mexico experienced a similar conflict, which, from one side, resembled resistance to empire, between "federalist" centralizers and advocates of devolution to the states.

Vast stretches of what are now the US West and Southwest have, therefore, a long history as terrains of competition between rival empires: first, as every schoolboy knows, between the Spanish, British, and French in the seventeenth and eighteenth centuries; then, also, as we have already seen, between intrusive and indigenous empires—Spain's and that of the Comanche in the eighteenth century, or the US and the Sioux in the nineteenth; and finally between the postimperial states that launched imperial trajectories of their own as they continued the history of colonialism in their own backyards: Mexico and the US.

Unlike most nineteenth-century empires, however, that of the United States in continental North America and, ultimately, in Hawaii, self-converted into part of "the nation." The majority of inhabitants came to think of themselves as "Americans," albeit in some cases modified by regional feeling or by pride of ancestry, signified by the hyphenated identities that distinguish Italian-Americans, Irish-Americans, and so on. The case most comparable to that of the United States is China's. Both empires have been astonishingly effective in spreading, among their constituent peoples, common allegiance and customs and uniform notions of themselves. In the case of the United States, this was probably, in part at least, the result of the country's explosive economic success in the nineteenth and twentieth centuries. It was also partly due, no doubt, to some of the genuinely benign effects of federal rule, which did make people believe reasonably in the rhetoric of the land of the free.

I think it is fair to say that China is the only other surviving empire (or surviving state with an imperial past) that can match the United States in this respect. Mexico cannot, despite the ferocity of typical Mexican nationalist rhetoric. Most people in the US South, say, are reconciled to the republic that conquered their forerunners and ancestors in a way that descendants of Yucatec rebels, for instance, who still think of the state that rules them as alien, cannot share; indigenous identities in Mexico, in my experience and judgment, are more like alternatives to being "Mexican," whereas self-professed members of Native American tribes tend to be happy with self-identification and allegiance, first and foremost, with the United States. It is not easy to think of oneself as a Lakota or Navajo without being self-consciously part of the US, but you can be a Maya or Yaqui without feeling or even formally being Mexican.

Yet people's experience of the process of becoming part of the United States did not always seem entirely benign at the time. As the United States grew, natives and neighbors were not alone in feeling afflicted. The nineteenth-century republic was an empire for many of its own frontiersmen, too. Its self-perceived victims included its own colonists. In 1884, Martin Maginnis, observer at the US Congress for the territory of Montana, called the territorial system "the most infamous system of colonial government that was ever seen on the face of the globe. . . . The colonies of your Republic," he continued, were "situated 3,000 miles away from Washington by land, as the thirteen colonies were situated 3,000 miles away from London by water." It was an exaggeration, as far as Montana was concerned, but the experience of the thirteen colonies informed the standard language by which the US empire's citizen-subjects lambasted Congress in the nineteenth century. The territories endured "taxation without representation." The federal government was as intrusive on their autonomy as George III's had been on that of British North America before the revolution. A Dakota newspaper in 1877 made the same point, "heartily disgusted with our dependent condition, with being snubbed at every turn . . . with having all our interest subjected to the whims and corrupt acts of persons in power that we feel very much as the thirteen colonies felt." Maginnis's exaggerations continued—but they contained an irritating kernel of truth. "And it is a strange thing that the fathers of our Republic . . . established a colonial government as much worse than that which they revolted against as one form of government can be from another."[5]

Carpetbaggers exacerbated the ill feeling of the frontier colonists. Federal fiscal impositions for defense heaped them with grievances. After forcible reintegration into the empire in the war of 1861–65, the Deep South was treated, in some ways, as the British Empire treated zones of what the British called "indirect rule"—left to local elites to exploit, while suffering economic oppression, impoverishment, stagnation, and the denial of democratic opportunities for huge sections of the population. In the lexicon of US political euphemisms, the federal government called this "Reconstruction." Although according to US law and rhetoric, new states joined the Union on an equal footing with the original thirteen, in effect they were colonies before then, as surely as Ireland was before it joined the United Kingdom, or Algeria, say, despite the legal fiction that made it part of metropolitan France. Imperialism is not the whole story of the United States, but it is part of the story, and needs emphasizing now to counter its former neglect.

Unless US citizens acknowledge and understand their country's imperial past, they will not be able to understand its present or future. Much of the recent and current Hispanic resettlement of parts of the United States is a consequence of empire, just as much as the presence in France, say, of millions of migrants of Maghribi origins, or in Britain of emigrants from the Indian subcontinent, or in Holland of people from Indonesia, Surinam, and the Netherlands Antilles. Countercolonization follows colonization, and the waves of migrants always flow back like returning tides.

IN CONSEQUENCE OF THEIR equivocal recall of Britain's influence on the western hemisphere, Americans do not like—or, for most of the recent past, have not liked—to think of the United States as originating in imperialism. The standard myth has sidelined not only the role of Spaniards in founding America but also of English imperialists.

The "Pilgrim Fathers," therefore, in their supposed innocence of and opposition to empire, have become the mythic progenitors of the United States—almost as improbably as Solomon was of Ethiopia or Aeneas of Rome or his suppositious brother, Brut, of Britain. But almost everything most Americans think about the Plymouth colonists of 1620 is false. The truth is more credible. The first colonists in Massachusetts, exchanging accusations of "bestial, yea, diabolical affectations," were as divided and conflicted as people usually are when fate flings them together. Their leaders did not seek liberty, except for themselves: they aspired to godly dictatorship. Their motives for seeking life in America, according to their own accounts, were not primarily religious but economic and social. Their tyranny has extended to modern American imaginations, occluding the truth about the prismatic origins of the United States, which are black as well as white, Catholic as well as Protestant, and Native American, Spanish, Irish, French, and Dutch—to say nothing of numerically small but culturally important contributions from elsewhere—as well as Anglo-Saxon. Yet the Pilgrims, as part of the reality as well as the myth of the United States, need to figure in a Hispanic history of the country, just as Juan Ponce's or Oñate's colonies should in a history written from a conventional perspective.

The "Pilgrims" were not, of course, pilgrims, but migrants, like the wetbacks from across the Rio Grande who are their real successors today. Their project did not originate in England, but in Holland, and they nearly sailed under Dutch political auspices. Most of them were members of a self-exiled community in Leiden of radical rejecters of woolly minded Anglicanism. They did not leave England because the Church persecuted them but chiefly because the Church disgusted them. When they abandoned Leiden, they did not do so for religious scruples either, but because of "the hardness of the place," the erosion of their community in an alien culture, and the poverty—"a dry crust and watery eyes"—that obliged them to apprentice their children in harsh trades. Above all, they fled, once again, from their own disgust—this time with the disappointingly lax morals and religious tolerance of the Dutch. The recruits who joined them from England tended to mercenary motives and lukewarm spirituality. Their motives were not generically different from those of their Spanish predecessors in the South and Southwest, and their mind-sets did not prefigure democracy or liberty or any other of today's commonly dear US values any more than those of their counterparts.

The *Mayflower* did not head for New England, where the voyagers made landfall by a navigational error. They were aiming for a more southerly berth. Bad weather hemmed them in and forced them to start their colony at Plymouth instead of at the economically promising mouth of the Hudson. Like the settlers of New Mexico, they blundered into the unknown, confronting in ignorance a geography of illusion. Like Spanish colonists relying on the stranger-effect, the Plymouth settlers depended, at first, on the charity of the natives—that much of the standard account is true—and they returned some of the hospitality after their first harvest; most of the traditional myth of the first Thanksgiving, however, is fanciful.

It is also true that the Pilgrims were industrious and, ultimately, successful farmers, but the real economic vocation of their colony was commercial from the first. The investors who kept it going through its long struggle towards profitability demanded beaver pelts—the black gold of this English El Dorado. The notion that the colonists were democrats and republicans who launched American liberties when they signed the Mayflower Compact is nonsense: the forty-one leaders and cronies who subscribed the document were perpetrating a coup—arrogating to themselves the right to make and unmake laws for the colony, and appealing to "our dread Sovereign Lord King" to legitimize their power. Their politics were intensely local, rooted in petty power struggles; many of them were decayed gentry, social climbers, or failed businessmen, attracted more by hopes of getting rich quickly in the fur trade than by the prospect of toiling over a plow. In the long run, commerce, not farming, would be the basis of New England's economy. Some of the land the colonists grabbed might have compared favorably with salt-marsh grazing land in Europe.[6] On the whole, however, the rock-ribbed soil of New England is unattractive for farming, and the real future of the colony was as a base for expansion outward, toward a richer hinterland and seaborne trades.

IN THEIR DAY, in any case, the Plymouth colonists were marginal types. Anglo-America was really founded in imitation of the Spanish empire. You can see the project taking shape in Elizabeth I's most famous portrait—the so-called Armada portrait—in which her fingers extend acquisitively over Spanish-ruled parts of the Americas as she rests her right hand on a globe. The imperialist propagandists of her reign, Richard Hakluyt and Humphrey Gilbert, argued tirelessly for an English empire to emulate and ultimately, perhaps, even to rival and replace Spain's. Toward 1577, the Welshman John Dee, physician, astrologer, and Renaissance magus, who flitted between the courts of Elizabeth I of England and the Holy Roman Emperor Rudolf II, was working on a book in celebration of the maritime vocation of what he called, presciently, "the British Empire," although the union of England and Scotland was not yet a foregone conclusion. The surviving frontispiece hints at what the work—now mostly lost—was like. The queen stands in the prow of a ship named *Europa*, perhaps because Dee saw Elizabeth as the potential liberator of Europe from the Spanish yoke. The queen's hand reaches to grasp a laurel crown held out by Opportunity—a damsel atop a tower, like Rapunzel in the fairy tale—with invitingly loose hair, waiting to be grasped. On the seashore Britannia kneels, praying for a navy. Rays from the divine tetragram impel the ship. Sun, moon, and stars cast benign influences. Saint Michael the serpent-slayer descends, sword in hand, with hostile intent, toward the Spaniards who occupy the New World.[7]

Dee's was one of many works of lobbying and propaganda designed to coax Britannia into attempting to rule the waves, and, in particular, to challenge Spanish preponderance by exploiting England's privileged access to the north Atlantic. The propagandists invented, or compiled from others' inventions, an imaginary history of English navigation in boreal seas, which allegedly gave England a prior claim to disputed northern lands and routes. They attributed to King Arthur the conquest of Iceland, Greenland, Lapland, Russia, and the North Pole.[8] Spaniards were not the only invaders of America to be aroused by fantasies and drawn by myths. The invocation of King Arthur was designed to appeal to Elizabeth I in person, as her dynasty, the House of Tudor, justified its usurpation of the English crown by appealing to supposed prophecies of Merlin, King Arthur's fabulous court wizard. No one should be surprised at the role of legend in the making of America. Myths are motors of history. Facts that happen are often powerless to affect behavior. People act on the basis of the falsehoods they believe.

The English strategy of imitating Spain was doomed to frustration. The English tend to be self-congratulatory about their maritime traditions. They still tend to date their empire from Elizabeth's reign, whereas really the failures of England at sea are conspicuous and curious features of the history of the age. They represent Elizabeth's reign as their epoch of national greatness, whereas really, by the standards of the rest of western Europe—of Spain or Italy or even France or the Netherlands—England was a realm of lightly gilded savagery and serious underachievement. England had all the prerequisites for maritime empire: easy access to the sea, a seafaring tradition, the direct experience of imperialism in Ireland. In the previous century, moreover, the English had lost their continental empire—the provinces of France controlled by the English crown. This might have released energy for seaward expansion. Yet despite these advantages, England's empire remained unlaunched until the seventeenth century. The problem is a dog-in-the-night problem: why did this bitch not bark?

A great deal of English energy was expended exploring ice-bound culs-de-sac. The White Sea to the north of Russia and the straits that lead to Hudson's Bay—two major theaters of English endeavor in the sixteenth-century search for northern routes to Asia—were navigable for only two or three months a year. This was not enough time for ships to get in and out and still engage in further exploration. Beyond these waters, the only way to make progress was to accept the constraints of the enclosing ice and to drift, trapped, with the current. But this was a long business for which ships at the time were ill equipped, having neither the space nor the means to keep supplies fresh for long. In view of the problems, it is not surprising that the effects of English efforts were modest.

Meanwhile, England had scant energy to spare for colonizing other accessible parts of the Americas. English colonies promoted by Sir Walter Raleigh at Roanoke Island between 1585 and 1587 failed, just as Spanish Jesuits' attempt to establish a mission in the same region, at the mouth of the Chesapeake, failed fifteen years earlier as a result of indigenous suspicions and the newcomers' overextension and isolation on the edge of an unmanageably vast frontier. Natives, provoked by the colonists' rapacity and violence, wiped out the first

English settlement; the settlers of the second disappeared without a trace and were never located. From 1602 to 1607 private English venturers on reconnaissance missions sought suitable sites for potential colonies along the coasts of New England, experimenting with three different transatlantic routes: they might follow Cabot's to Newfoundland before dropping south—but even in the most favorable season this counted on unreliable winds and faced adverse currents; or they might follow Columbus, by what became the preferred route, taking the northeast trades to the Caribbean before using the current to head north; they even tried to cross the North Atlantic directly in the face of the wind.

Not until 1607 did an enduring English colony take shape at Jamestown, Virginia. Success was more a matter of luck than of judgment. In the work of Robert Johnson, the Virginia Company's official promotional copywriter, self-deception misrepresented the dismal swampland and laborious forest as "Nova Britannia," "offering most excellent fruits, . . . a good land and, if the Lord love us, he will bring our people to it and give it us for a possession . . . most sweet and wholesome, much warmer than England, and very agreeable to our natures."[9]

Among all the awkward facts Johnson minimized, one was particularly irksome. This Eden had its own Adam. The colonists classified the natives as suited them, first as ideally exploitable, then, almost in the same breath, as brutish victims unworthy of human treatment. Virginia, Johnson continued, "is inhabited with wild and savage people . . . like herds of deer in a forest. They have no law but nature . . . yet . . . they are generally very loving and gentle and do entertain and relieve our people with great kindness. . . . And as for supplanting the savages, we have no such intent . . . unless as unbridled beasts they procure it to themselves."

Evidently the English enjoyed in Virginia some of the same touches of the stranger-effect that greeted Spaniards in New Mexico and Puritans in Massachusetts, and responded with some of the same equivocations about the natives. Of course, in English perceptions, the "Indians" would seem to want to "procure" the land to themselves: it was, after all, their land. To an unprejudiced eye, however, they were by no means "brutish." On the contrary, they had the rudiments Europeans reckoned as essential to civilization—built dwellings and towns, an organized polity, fear of law, and a venerable, though "barbarous," monarch whom divinity hedged, as William Strachey, one of the colony's early chroniclers, observed:

> The great emperor at this time amongst them we commonly call Powhatan . . . the greatness and bounds of whose empire by reason of his powerfulness, and ambition in his youth, hath larger limits than ever had any of his predecessors. . . . He is a goodly old man, not yet shrinking, though well beaten with many cold and stormy winters. . . . And sure it is to be wondered at, how such a barbarous and uncivill prince should take unto him . . . a form and ostentation of such majesty as he expresseth, which oftentimes strikes awe and sufficient wonder into our own people, . . . yet I am persuaded there is an infused kind of divineness, and extraordinary (appointed that it shall be so by the king of kings) to such who are his immediate instruments on earth.[10]

Obviously, if the English believed Powhatan was a true sovereign chosen by God, they had no business seizing his land. Their plan for doing just that followed Spanish precedents. The government's instructions of 1609, addressed to the governor, Sir Thomas Gates, were larded with cant, but you can feel the rough edge under the slick language:

> If you find it convenient, we think it reasonable you first remove [from the natives] . . . their . . . priests by a surprise of them all and detaining them prisoners, for they are so wrapped up in the fog and misery of their iniquity and so terrified with their continual tyranny, chained under the bond of death unto the devil, that while they live among them to poison and infect their minds, you shall never make any great progress in this glorious

work. . . . And in case of necessity or conveniency, we pronounce it not cruelty nor breach of charity to deal sharply with them and proceed even unto death.[11]

As for the Indians' leader, "if you find it not best to make him your prisoner, yet you must make him your tributary." The model for this program is plain: Cortés and Pizarro, according to standard accounts of the conquests of the Aztecs and Incas, had devised it. The English resolved to follow it.

The English had no serious plans to make the colony productive. Like Oñate's followers, they still expected to find great riches, lost civilizations, or a route to the Pacific not far off. Unsurprisingly, therefore, the first colonists of English Virginia proved to be a feckless lot who depended on their precarious and sometimes coercive friendship with the locals for food. "The Indians," they admitted, "did daily relieve us with . . . such corn and flesh as they could spare," assuring the English that "we know that you cannot live if you lack our harvest and that relief we bring you."[12]

There was, however, one man of energy and vision among the colonists. Captain John Smith was, in part, a fantasist who lied his way into esteem and wrote self-aggrandizing romances in praise of his own adventures. Contemporary satirists lampooned him as "Captain Jones," a Munchausen who fantasized equally about his sentimental conquests of women and his physical conquests over men. He was also the first American tough guy: a self-important tyrant whose real personality—bloody, bold, and resolute—has been coated with sugar crust by a cloying Disney myth. He claimed to be able to charm goods and girls out of the Indians, and to awe them with his knowledge of astronomy, in imitation, perhaps, of a story Columbus had told about himself, allegedly tricking the natives of Jamaica by predicting an eclipse.[13]

Smith modeled himself—consciously, I think—on Cortés and Pizarro. An engraving adorning a book he commissioned in praise of himself shows him capturing a native chief, as Cortés had captured Moctezuma and Pizarro had captured Atahualpa. When the natives' generosity flagged, Smith tried to terrorize them into supplying the colony. "Some," said one of his many critics among his companions, "he hunted up and down the Isle, some he so terrified with whipping, beating and imprisonment . . . it brought them in such fear and obedience, as his very name would sufficiently affright them." English readers' mental picture of Spanish conquests derived from the engravings of Theodore de Bry and other illustrators of Spanish cruelties, including scourging, tortures, incarcerations, and scenes of Spanish terror tactics of every kind. If Smith had set out to reenact them, he could not have done so more faithfully. He tried similar tactics on the colonists, threatening to starve into submission or death anyone who disobeyed him, "for the labors of thirty or forty honest men," he declared, "shall not be consumed to maintain a hundred and fifty idle varlets."[14] The words are an indication of the feebleness of the colony in its early days.

Most of Smith's abundant energy went on keeping the colony alive. But he also conducted some modest exploratory forays. In 1607 he traveled up the James River to the falls beyond the lodge of the Powhatan ruler. He was unable to discharge what he later claimed were his secret instructions "not to return without a lump of gold, a certainty of the South Sea or one of the lost colony of Sir Walter Raleigh," but he did acquire an Indian map and the information that the interior of the country was mountainous.[15] The following year he explored Chesapeake Bay as far as the Susquehannock and, pursuing Indian reports of a "shining big sea water" in the interior, followed the Potomac to beyond the present site of Washington, DC.

When an accident disabled Smith and forced him to return to England, his fellow colonists rejoiced. So did the Native Americans. "The Savages no sooner understood Smith was gone, but they all revolted, and did spoil and murder all they encountered."[16] The colony felt bereft of security, labor, and food, forced to hand over their weapons in exchange for food to "the Savages, whose bloody fingers were so imbrued in our bloods, that what by their cruelty, our governor's indiscretion and the loss of our ships, of five hundred within six months after there remained not many more than sixty most miserable poor creatures. It were too vile to say what we endured."[17] Famine and pestilence joined the natives' killing spree. The survivors were too few and weak to keep the gates and walls of the settlement in repair.

Smith's terror campaign had been a temporary expedient. The colony seemed doomed by its own unviability, in an unhealthy place, surrounded by alienated natives. But the colony, imperiled by following one Spanish model, recovered by imitating another. An enterprising heavy smoker saved the day. John Rolfe was the real but relatively undersung hero of the making of English America. Without his Spanish-style taste in women and weed it is reasonable to ask—and, I think, easy to answer—whether the Virginia colony would have survived. For Rolfe was the real-life, married lover of Pocahontas, Powhatan's daughter, and the first planter of Spanish tobacco in the colony. He arrived in Virginia in 1611, after a voyage worthy of Sinbad, in which he was cast away and his first wife and daughter perished. He found the colony starving, with the population down to a pitiful sixty souls, with no strategy for survival, no means of retrieving native amity, and no hope of forging a viable economic future.

In contrast with Smith, whose legendary romance with Pocahontas probably originated in one of the captain's typical tall tales, Rolfe realized that the essence of Spanish success in colonization lay not in terror but in harnessing the collaboration of native elites. Though the stranger-effect manifests itself in many ways—sometimes enduing the stranger with sanctity, sometimes with power, sometimes with use—one of its commonest displays is sexual: the stranger evinces exotic magnetism, especially for elites in search of marriage partners unencumbered by involvement in existing webs of kindred and faction. That is why royal families often look abroad for marriage partners. It is also why Spanish conquistadores were able so often to solemnize or even initiate their political alliances with native dynasties by marrying chiefs' daughters or taking them in concubinage. Rolfe stressed disinterested motives for his marriage—to curb his own lust, and to convert his wife to Christianity. In a way, he also protested his love for a girl, "to whom my hartie and best thoughts are, and have a long time bin so intangled, and inthralled in so intricate a laborinth."

He was at least equally candid, however, in acknowledging that his decision was "for the good of this plantation, for the honour of our countrie."[18] The renewed alliance with Powhatan's people outlasted Pocahontas's life and endured until Rolfe died in 1622.

Meanwhile, dissatisfied with the unpleasant weed the Virginian natives smoked, John Rolfe thought of transplanting Spanish tobacco from the Caribbean. No one knows how he got the idea or where he procured the seeds, which were strictly controlled by Spanish authorities anxious to preserve the monopoly of their own plantations. But whatever the origins of the scheme, it worked. Rolfe planted his first crop in 1611. By 1617, 20,000 pounds of tobacco were harvested. The smoking habit ensnared European customers and made Virginia viable, at least for colonists with enough land and capital to make a profit from it. Throughout the summer of 1622, an observer saw little activity among the colonists "but securing themselves and planting tobacco. It passes there as current Silver, and by the oft turning and winding it, some grow rich, but many poore."[19] That year the output was 60,000 pounds, despite the recurrence of war with the natives. By 1627 Virginia produced half a million pounds of tobacco. By 1669 the total had risen to 15 million pounds.

Tobacco saved the colony, but the climate still killed incoming colonists. Of 15,000 arrivals from 1607 to 1622, there were only 2,000 survivors. Most migrants to Virginia died without surviving issue until the second half of the seventeenth century, and life expectancy remained low. Few colonists saw the better side of fifty. The population did not begin to increase naturally until some fifty years after the first settlement. Increased rates of white immigration accompanied the breakthrough: they tripled in the period from about 1650 to 1670. This success, dearly bought as it was, inspired the extension of Anglo-America southward into the Carolinas and Georgia.

From Virginia southward, most English North American colonies were in torrid lowlands that could be adapted to the same sort of economy—planting cash crops with imported slave labor. The failure of early antislavery statutes in Georgia showed that paratropical America could not pay without it. There were blacks in Virginia before the first mention of a shipment in 1619, when a Dutch man o' war "sold us twenty and odd Negroes."[20] Among or alongside lists of white servants in the next couple of decades, black slaves appear in the records, often without a name and without a date of arrival—important omissions because they distinguished slaves from servants, whose term of bondage was fixed. Numbers remained small until the 1660s because of the steady supply of poor migrants from England, who cost something under half the price of an African slave.

The exploitation of poor whites was cost-effective because mortality rates among newcomers of every kind remained high: investing in four servants rather than two slaves spread the risk. Forty-five thousand laborers arrived between 1650 and 1674, when there were probably fewer than 3,000 slaves. Thereafter, the proportions began to be reversed. Reliance on large-scale, capital-intensive enterprises created huge disparities of wealth. Latifundias grew up, more reminiscent of the Mediterranean or Brazil than of England or New England. As early as 1700, half of one county in Virginia was owned by the richest 5 percent of settlers. Anglo-America was patterned from the first not solely or even chiefly on England, but on what we now call Latin America.

North of the Chesapeake the environment was less hostile for European settlers, though the extremes of a continental climate still took early settlers by lethal surprise: half the Plymouth colonists died in the first winter. At first they relied on the stranger-effect to keep themselves fed. From early in the 1630s, however, New England colonies could feed themselves and natural increase kept the population growing. Without valuable cash products, however, except for the furs procured mainly from trade with Native Americans, the region was of little appeal to immigrants. Only 21,000 came in the whole of the seventeenth century, and the numbers diminished, with only a third of the total arriving after 1640. Except in the Connecticut River valley and as domestic servants, slaves were largely unsuited to the climate and unaffordable to the economy. Farmer-settlers worked wonders with rocky soils, which were duly abandoned, to be replaced by mills or returned to forest, as newer, better farmland opened up farther west.

Mountain barriers and the boundaries of rival states cut the maritime colonies off from the interior. They were best equipped for a seaborne venturers' economy. The impoverished hinterland drove work and wealth creation seaward, to the cod- and whale-fisheries and long-range trade. In a sense, these were the wages of success: early in the eighteenth century, New England's population outgrew its capacity to grow food. A trading vocation replaced the farming vocation with which the founding fathers had arrived. Although New England remained oriented towards the sea, its wealth was essential to the burgeoning of British North America, attracting people and capital from Europe and providing investment for new enterprises.

So there were two Anglo-Americas, one in the south, where the economy, demographics, and way of life resembled those of the Caribbean and peri-Caribbean regions; another in New England, New York, Pennsylvania, and the neighboring states, where independent farmers and traders predominated. It made little difference, however, to the Native Americans. Everywhere, wars thinned their numbers. Disease winnowed them. In what became the United States, preconquest levels of demographic buoyancy have never really returned among native peoples, outside the formerly Spanish Southwest. English colonies, relying on the labor of indentured servants and slaves, could afford to exterminate or expel their natives. The English, in their own perceptions, were "the new Israel," facing the "uncircumcised," to be smitten hip and thigh, as the old Israel smote Moab and Philistia. Indifferent, on the whole, to clerical discipline, English colonists rarely endured Spanish-style agonies of conscience about the justice of their presence in America or the morality of their wars. People who left their land unexploited or unenclosed deserved, on English principles, to lose it. The line of the fence and the scar of the plow were signs of true tenure. In British areas of expansion, moreover, most Native Americans were too poor in goods Europeans coveted to be worth exploiting for tribute. It was more economical to dispossess them and replace them with white farmers or black slaves.

Pennsylvania was the only colony where this reasoning was modified. Here, moral and material considerations combined to favor a policy of friendly collaboration with the original inhabitants. Thanks to the Quaker founder's high morality, dispossessed Native Americans received supposedly just prices for their land and were encouraged to stay on the frontier as buffers against hostile tribes or rival European empires. This equilibrium of "love and consent" was doomed to collapse in the eighteenth century as the pressure of white population grew and overspilled the limits of the state the founder had conceived.

As in the Spanish dominions, where the representatives of the crown tried to restrain settlers' cupidity towards the natives, throughout British North America native peoples were a source of conflict between frontiersmen and the' authorities, who wanted to prevent frontier conquests that might disperse the white population. From the point of view of most colonial subjects, Native Americans were mere impediments to land grabbing. Genocide was the best means of dealing with them. In 1637 an explicit attempt to wipe out an entire people—the New England Pequot—was half finished in a massacre on Mystic River, where, the governor reported, the victims could be seen "frying in the fire and the streams of blood quenching the same." The tribe's very name was proscribed. In defiance of official policy, a settler malcontent, Nathaniel Bacon, launched war in Virginia in 1675 with the explicit aim of destroying all "Indians," friendly and hostile alike. This was a characteristic outrage in the late seventeenth century, a period of increasing tension that, as we have seen, also provoked violent clashes in Spanish-settled areas in New Mexico and Florida between growing colonies and threatened natives. In terms of the sacrifice of life on both sides, the worst such episode was King Philip's War in New England in 1675–76. An Algonquin chief managed to put together an uncharacteristically big Native American coalition, which threatened to reverse the direction of extermination. The white presence was, for a few months, genuinely in peril, until quisling tribes from the interior were drafted in on the colonists' side to restore the balance in the white man's favor. The crown renewed efforts to modify frontier policy in the eighteenth century, when competition with France increased the value of Native American friendship and compliance. Every victory against the French, however, and every accession of security, increased friction on the frontiers of Native American lands.

FOR ALL THESE REASONS—BECAUSE, in sum, of the intractability of the available environments and the scarcity, cost, or recalcitrance of labor—English efforts on the Atlantic seaboard were slow to prosper. French efforts to create colonies on the Atlantic coast north of the Chesapeake were equally modest, while Spain never bothered with lands so superficially unattractive. Because no colony in the region made productive probes into the interior, as we saw in Chapter One, the first encounters of Anglo-America and Spanish America occurred in the Carolinas and Georgia.

In those areas the Spanish missions recovered and the garrisons redoubled after the devastating raids of English slavers in the late seventeenth and early eighteenth centuries. Most indios ended up regarding Spain as the lesser evil. As the balance of power in the region swung in favor of Spain, however, the English felt increasingly the need to establish a buffer zone in Georgia against Spanish counterattacks. Furthermore, demand was growing, in Britain and in British colonies farther north in America, for tropical and semitropical products, especially tobacco, sugar, rice, cotton, and hardwoods. In 1727 the English crown declared Georgia a British colony—including in the terms of the charter virtually no territory occupied by British subjects, but a great deal of land where Spain had missions, forts, and settlements. For a generation the region teetered and tilted between the contending powers. The British showed as much resilience in founding colonies as the Spaniards did in destroying them. In 1743, however, the British managed to repulse a Spanish attack on the tiny outpost of Frederica off the Georgia coast, and although a treaty in 1748 restored the area to Spain, the occupiers never abandoned it.

Stalemate had set in. In 1750 the British authorities warned their subjects in Georgia to refrain from further incursions against Spanish territory or subjects, in order to "avoid giving the least ground for such complaint as may, in any wise, interrupt the good Harmony . . .

between the two Crowns."[21] Not for the last time, however, the ambition or irresponsibility of "men on the spot" forced reluctant politicians into conflict. In 1755 a band of unruly colonists, expelled from
the British Georgia colony, proclaimed a colony of their own on Spanish territory at what they called New Hanover—"an Asylum by Persons who fly thither, to shelter themselves from Justice." Britain
ordered them out, but the fugitives "did only make a show or appearance of so doing, and immediately returned."[22]

Even then, peace between Spain and Britain might have survived,
as Britain was at war with France from 1756 and anxious for Spain's
neutrality—thanks to which, in part, by 1760 Britain was uniformly
victorious, dealing lethal blows to French ambitions in both India and
Canada. The very success, however, of Britain's war effort made it
impossible for Spain to remain aloof. Historians have often puzzled
over the reasons that induced King Carlos III, against his evident
interests, to join the French side in a war France had already lost. His
decision is usually represented as a noble and selfless act of loyalty to
the compact that bound the two main lines of the Bourbon dynasty
together. But on grounds of pure realpolitik, the king had no choice. It
suited Spain to maintain a three-way split in North America, so as
always to be able to play off the British against the French. If, as
seemed likely, British victories continued and France were altogether
expelled from the continent, Spain's diplomatic freedom would be
compromised. Spanish ministers, moreover, had no confidence in
long-term British goodwill. Ricardo Wall, formerly Spain's ambassador in London, who as minister for foreign affairs in the Spanish government had done his best to maintain peace, told a British
representative frankly of his suspicions: Britain's aim was "to ruin the
French power, in order the more easily to crush Spain."[23]

In the event, Spain could neither shore up France's position nor
protect her own. Further British victories at the expense of both allies
in 1762–63 meant that Britain dictated the terms of peace. Britain got
Canada from France and Florida from Spain. The forfeiture was only
temporary, as Spain reconquered the territory in the next decade, but
part of the effect was to seal the fate of Georgia as part of

Anglo-America. All Spain's effort and success in defending the Georgia frontier over the previous half century counted for nothing. The rest of France's continental dominions in North America, of which France had already despaired, were divided between Britain and Spain, with a boundary at the Mississippi. It was a damnable inheritance for Spain—a vast, underpopulated domain behind an indefensible border.

France's attempt to create an American land empire had failed, chiefly because the French, despite the density of their home population, were reluctant emigrants in the eighteenth century. Prior to French withdrawal in 1763, what they called Louisiana—encompassing most of the Mississippi valley—was little more than an outline on the map. In 1746, it had only 3,300 settlers, mostly concentrated around New Orleans, while South Carolina alone, in a poorer region with a less congenial environment, had 20,000. France had tried and failed to get colonists to settle, but Frenchmen were unenthusiastic about the place. They preferred the comforts of home. A few frontiersmen rattled around the great open spaces. A few forts clung to the rim on borders shared with the British. A few modest towns speckled the river routes that fed the trade of the only substantial city, New Orleans. But Spain needed the collaboration of the existing population, both French and native, to make the land a useful and enduring part of the monarchy. When Antonio de Ulloa arrived to govern New Orleans, he left the French officeholders and laws in place and let the Bourbon flag float over his headquarters alongside that of Spain.

Ulloa was already a hero of Spanish imperialism who, as a young man, had demonstrated his genius during the great scientific expedition the Academy of Paris organized in the 1730s to measure the length of a degree of longitude on the surface of the earth at the equator. He remained an ornament of the Enlightenment—dedicating scientific knowledge to the solution of practical, technical problems, using astronomy to speed navigation, meteorology to improve agriculture, and metallurgy to increase the output of mines. He had returned to the New World as governor of a region of Peru that produced mercury and silver, on which the Spanish monarchy depended. His policy in Louisiana was rather like that of China in today's Hong Kong—

one country, two systems. He brought only a handful of Spanish soldiers, relying on the collaboration of the French residents to keep the peace. He maintained the existing structures of authority, transmitting his orders via the French incumbents. He allowed trade with Caribbean colonies that remained in French hands—a remarkable concession, as Spain's empire was founded on commercial protectionism.

Conciliation did not work. The merchants of New Orleans, fearful of Spanish mercantilism, and aware that their trade with British North America was contrary to Spanish aims and interests, drove Ulloa out of the city in October 1768 and begged the French to return. Instead, a new governor arrived with 2,000 men to overawe the 6,000 citizens, make bloody examples of the ringleaders of the revolt, and impose Spanish bureaucrats, language, and laws. At the same time, the Spanish government encouraged the liberal terms of trade that made the merchants prosper. New vigor animated the remotest reaches of the territory, as John Evans, the Spanish king's Welsh renegade representative, who rejected Englishness, swore the Mandan to allegiance on the Upper Missouri, while Spanish surveyors began to build up a detailed picture of parts of the North American Midwest. Gradually, Louisiana showed an economic yield under Spanish rule. When Spanish troops arrived, the systems of supply for New Orleans and Saint Louis were so poor and production so exiguous that the food supply failed. Local peace, however, and integration into a wide network of trade enormously enhanced the prosperity of the cities. The settler population of Spanish Louisiana more than doubled from the 20,000 people the Spaniards found when they took over from the French. Cotton exports amounted to 200,000 pounds sterling in 1791, rising to 18 million in 1800. At the time, Etienne de Boré's plantation, six miles above New Orleans, produced 5 million pounds of sugar, 200,000 gallons of rum, and 250,000 gallons of molasses annually.[24]

WITH THE COLLAPSE OF French efforts in Louisiana, the British and Spanish empires in North America really began to intersect inseparably. Simultaneously, the formerly distant but highly permeable frontier with British North America drew closer, extended farther, and became ever more porous. British North America had formerly been a small undertaking, evoking, in Madrid, little menace and, in London, marginal interest. Now, suddenly, it was a big empire in which people in the mother country were willing to invest emotion and money.

Until the middle of the eighteenth century British settlements were sparse and dispersed, clinging to the rim of the continent. After a hundred years of colonization, the total white population was less than a quarter of a million. Utopian projectors, feudally minded proprietors, and religious fanatics with otherworldly priorities had dominated the leadership of many communities and hampered economic success. In the early years, most colonists tended to be evasive about their economic motives. Economic self-betterment had been the explicit aim only of those desperate enough to sign away their liberty and labor for the term of an indenture in order to buy a passage from home and a few tools and clothes with which to start an independent life when their bond was paid. In the eighteenth century, however, the colonial horizon broadened and the prospects of a good life in America became better defined. The mood of migrants changed and their numbers exploded. By the end of the revolutionary war, the total population was probably near two and a half million.

This astonishing increase—by a factor of ten within three generations—had no precedent or parallel elsewhere in the New World. It was an accelerating process, most of which was crammed into the last third of the entire short period. Between the middle of the century and the outbreak of the revolution, the number of annual foundations of towns in New England trebled, as, roughly, did the populations of Georgia and South Carolina. In the 1760s the population of New York rose by nearly 40 percent and that of Virginia more than doubled. Emigrants from England were almost all young men, of the sort society had always willfully wasted in war. From western Scotland whole families went to America, eroding the demographic base at home and contributing to the creation of a stable and settled tenor of life in the colonies.[25]

In America the results included the burgeoning world and dilating frontier described with astonishment by writers in the generation before the Revolutionary War. From about 1760 a rush of settlers scaled the previously impassable west wall of the Appalachians to found "a new land of Canaan" between the Susquehanna and the Ohio. Michel-Guillaume Jean de Crèvecoeur, who, uncertain whether he wanted to be British or French, ended by becoming one of the architects of American identity, imagined himself joining a mass of migrants heading out from Connecticut to the wilds of Pennsylvania, where he found "a prodigious number of houses rearing up, fields cultivating, that great extent of industry opened up to a bold and indefatigable people."[26] On the day the land office opened at Fort Pitt in 1769, 2,790 claims were staked. Ten thousand families were living on this frontier by 1771. By 1785, there were about 50,000 Anglo colonists west of Pittsburgh. The most adventurous imaginations were overstimulated by what they saw. George Washington dreamed in the 1760s of laying "with very little money the foundation of a noble estate" on the Ohio. Washington bought specious titles to over 30,000 acres in the Ohio Valley. Government policy prevented him from realizing the value of his investment. He hoped to recruit three hundred families. In 1774 he failed to interest any potential colonists in his scheme. He was disappointed, and had to make do instead, after an interval, with the presidency of a fledgling democracy.[27] If Ohio was a land of smallholders, in which Washington's dreams of a latifundia were impracticable, slave labor could fuel colonization inland from Britain's possessions in the semitropical south. In both directions, Spain barred the way.

The beginnings of British colonization of the North American interior paralleled similar landward turns among other formerly seaboard-bound European empires in the eighteenth century. Portugal acquired her Novas Conquistas inland from Goa in India, and vastly increased her commitment in Minas Gerais and Amazonia. Holland took control of much of Java. All these empires were becoming more like that of Spain, which had ruled vast hinterlands as well as coastal toeholds since the sixteenth century. In most cases, however, the move inland was not an imperial initiative, but a spontaneous ebullition among ordinary colonists. The British authorities were equivocal about it, anxious to keep peace with the natives whose lands the colonists were, in effect, stealing, and concerned to avoid provoking Spain. In 1763 they issued a decree against further erosion of Indian lands. Adventurous colonists never intended to obey it. Washington regarded it as "a temporary expedient to quiet the Indians," doomed to "fall, of course, when the Indians consent to our occupying the lands."[28] Colonists' avidity for Indian land and the home government's unwillingness to dispossess more natives were among the major, unremarked causes of the revolution. In 1773, the home government refused to countenance settlement of the lower Ohio, "which cannot be reconciled with the spirit and intent of the king's instructions."

Colonial opinion, however, was solidly in favor of expansion. George Croghan, the settlers' agent and propagandist, countered that "the emigration is surprising. I am told that there can't be less than 60,000 souls settled between Pittsburg and the mouth of the Ohio—so that the policy of the people in England in delaying the grant of the new colony, in order to prevent emigration, answers not their purpose, as it does not prevent the settling of the country."[29] Benjamin Franklin was among the propagandists who painted an improbable picture of overpopulation in the existing northeastern colonies if the landward turn were halted. The idea that migration was unstoppable had increasing evidence to support it. The usual inference was that it had to be legitimized in order to be controlled. Migrants who jeopardized peace with the Indians could be regulated and pacified only by official recognition. A notion akin to that of what would later be called "Manifest Destiny" was already in the air. The westward course of empire, according to a widespread assumption, was one of the grooves in which history inevitably ran. Jonathan Carver, who was prominent in the fur trade on the Mississippi under the pretext of exploring a route to the Pacific, assured his readers in 1770 that "as the seat of empire from time immemorial has been gradually progressive towards the west, there is no doubt but that, at some future period, mighty kingdoms will emerge from these wildernesses, and stately palaces and solemn temples supplant the Indian huts."³⁰ The interior, one must remember, was still full of hippogriffs. Its extent was unknown. Optimism filled speculative maps with rivers and lakes that made communications easy and fertile zones that would feed great populations. The disappointment, when exploration became detailed enough to reveal the truth, was still in the offing.

IN A FURTHER RESPECT, British North America and Spanish America were growing more alike. Colonies laboriously created, carefully built in the image of Europe, gradually grew away from home. Creole sentiments and values began to emerge almost as soon as colonies were established. Some settlers came to escape their mother countries. Others, determined to remold the frontier in the image of home, were nonetheless seduced by the novelties of the New World, turning their backs on the ocean as they struck inland and seeking a new identity. In some ways the New World tended to drift away from the old almost as soon as the shores were linked, slipping as if from newly tied moorings. Internal economic systems developed, followed by new loyalties, and finally by political independence.

By the eighteenth century, creolism—it might fairly be said—was a strong Spanish-American ideology. In 1747 the enlightened French naturalist Georges-Louis, Count de Buffon, lost patience with utopian depictions of the New World, which, it must be admitted, owed a great deal to the promotional purposes of empires. He sketched out an alternative America, an ugly world of harsh climates, dwarfish beasts, stunted plants, ugly women, and degenerate men. His views sparked fiercely patriotic reactions in the New World. Creole science responded to European scholars' contempt for America by arguing that American nature was superior to that of the Old World: according to some claims, even the sky was more benign, and the influences of the stars were more favorable in the western hemisphere. The creole elite of Peru affected Inca dress and collected Inca artifacts. In Mexico, interest in Native American antiquities was boosted by discoveries in the late eighteenth century, including the "Maya Pompeii"—the ruins of

Palenque in 1773—and the uncovering of the Aztec "calendar stone" under the paving of the main square of Mexico City in 1790. The ruins of Xochicalco—the most complete surviving city from Aztec times—began to be systematically described at about the same time.

These movements in Hispanic America had parallels in British colonies. Until independence in 1776, most of the leaders of the colonies that became the United States still thought of themselves as Englishmen, but the sense of being American was beginning to take shape. Gradually, elites in British North America identified with fellow colonists.[31] In Thomas Jefferson's mind, the rights of true-born Englishmen came to include the right to renounce English identity: Americans were founding a new society, independent of Britain, just as their Saxon forebears had founded a new society when they went to Britain in the fifth century, independent of their native Germany. This was the reason for Jefferson's frustrated efforts to have Hengist and Horsa, the supposed founders of Anglo-Saxon England, adorn the seal of the United States.[32] At Monticello, Jefferson's estate in Virginia, his domestic museum was rich in American specimens and Native American artifacts. Painted buffalo hides hung in his hall. "Savage" carvings from Tennessee lined the atrium, rather as a Renaissance Italian palace might exhibit Roman inscriptions and statues. The portraits Jefferson collected included supposed makers of America—the explorers Columbus and Amerigo Vespucci hung alongside heroes of the American Revolution, such as George Washington and the Marquis de Lafayette. After the Revolutionary War, Crèvecoeur, who had once believed that American freedom was an overseas version of England's "national genius," revised his opinion: Americans were "neither Europeans nor the descendants of Europeans" but "a new race of men." Joel Barlow, the first epic poet of independent America, hailed them as "call'd from slavish chains, a bolder race."

New Englanders in their own way, by sea, drifted apart from the "mother country," just as the landward-driving settlers and investors in Ohio edged away by land. For the ocean led to the world. Ever-improving maritime technology was always—slowly, by little step-by-step advances, or by sudden leaps, such as the introduction of a method for determining longitude in the late eighteenth century—opening more of the globe to commerce. Gradually, in the course of the century, it became a marked disadvantage for a trading people to be limited by the regulations of empire. New England's quarrels with Britain focused increasingly on issues of barriers to trade and the freedom of the seas, and disputes over the definition of contraband. The great symbolic acts of resistance that preceded the Revolutionary War happened offshore and made these issues explicit in acts of civil disobedience: the Boston Tea Party in 1774 and the seizure of the small British warship *Gaspée* in Narragansett Bay, Rhode Island, in 1772: "God damn your blood!" screamed the respectable merchants who boarded and burned this piracy-control vessel. The Native American disguises worn at the Boston tea party were in part, perhaps, creole uniforms, like the Inca headdresses in which Peruvian gentlemen of entirely Spanish ancestry liked to have themselves painted in the late eighteenth century.

Meanwhile, under the stress of war with France in the 1750s and 1760s and in the flush of victory that followed the collapse of France's American empire in 1763, Britain's attitude to America became more centralizing and interventionist. The British colonies had their own institutions and "liberties" that got in the way of some of the most crucial functions of government, especially the housing of troops and the levying of taxes. An era of increasingly vigorous government from Britain was designed to make the colonial administration more uniform, to exploit fiscally the colonies' growing wealth and security, and to organize defense on modern and efficient and, therefore, more centralized lines. These measures incurred the resentment of colonists anxious to retain the privileges and liberties that they had secured during the long period in which the home government had taken little interest in their affairs. The new demands of the prerevolutionary years came not so much from the colonists as from a Britain anxious to exact efficiency from its empire. The threat to the colonies' comfortable habits of effective self-rule and cheap government provoked confrontation.

It became increasingly obvious, moreover, in the early 1770s that British rule threatened two vital colonial interests. In 1772 a British judge declared slavery illegal on English soil, in a judgment that caused much premature anticipation among black people in America. Vermont rapidly adopted the ruling into its own laws, but it was unwelcome in the slave-dependent economies of much of British America. It seemed only a matter of time before colonial slave-owners clashed with an elite in Britain that increasingly favored abolishing both the slave trade and slavery itself. Moreover, the British government was determined to attempt to keep the peace on the "Indian" frontier, and to preserve Native American buffer states between the British and Spanish empires in the interior of North America. This was precisely the region to which American colonists were looking for expansion.

A period of increasing interventionism from Europe and increasing friction with colonial elites was broadly paralleled in the Spanish monarchy, where "reformist" governments in the same period took increasingly burdensome measures in a similar spirit: reasserting bureaucratic controls, reorganizing imperial defense, eliminating traditional colonial customs, maximizing the power and fiscal reach of the crown. Spanish administrators were as intrusive and troublesome in Spanish colonies as governors were in those of Britain. In both empires, the home governments tried to ease local bigwigs out of influential offices and replace them with creatures of the home government. In both empires the results included growing, and potentially revolutionary, resentments. For both empires the Americas housed some of the remotest, most difficult-to-govern provinces, with the most marked peculiarities of interest. In both empires home governments encouraged militarization—mobilization and training for defense. These measures were in rational response to the problems of security in vast territories with ill-defined frontiers, but the effect was to create potential reservoirs of armed revolutionaries.

The Seven Years' War, or French and Indian War, as Americans call it, which began in 1756 and ended in 1763, removed the French threat to the colonists' security. With the British conquest of Canada and the

French abandonment of Louisiana, the colonies were now free to challenge their rulers in England. By imposing high costs on imperial defense, the war encouraged Britain to seek new ways of taxing America, with all the familiar consequences. It trained American fighters in the skills they would need if they were ever to challenge British forces. The experience of military collaboration between American militias and British regulars initiated or exposed cultural differences: the brutalities of regular army discipline repelled the militias, while colonial resistance to stationing troops in private houses, which was the usual practice elsewhere in the British Empire, seemed to the army to represent "neglect of humanity" and "depravity of nature." The colonists saw themselves as "true-born Englishmen" but were shocked to find that their perception was not shared by their fellow countrymen from across the Atlantic. Mutual alienation led to violence.[33]

The uprising in thirteen of the English mainland colonies in the 1770s used to be pictured as a peculiarly English affair—the inevitable outcome of long-standing traditions of freedom that colonists took with them as a heritage from deep in the English past. On the contrary, current scholarship tells us, it was an ad hoc solution to short-term problems, a typical convulsion of a colonial world that was full of rebellions and colonial conspiracies in the late eighteenth century: against the British government in the north of Ireland, against Spain in Colombia and Peru, against Portugal in Minas Gerais. The war was in one sense an English civil war, pitting self-styled "free-born Englishmen" against an intrusive government, recycling the rhetoric of seventeenth-century conflicts in Britain itself in which "the commonwealth" had fought the crown. At another level, it was an American civil war, in which at least 20 percent of the white population, and most of the black people and Native Americans, sided with the British. Increasingly, it also became an international conflict. After the first two years' campaigns, when the raw American forces proved surprisingly effective, France in 1778 joined by Spain in 1779 saw the opportunity to inflict a defeat on the British. Usually the British won eighteenth-century wars by buying the alliance of other powers on the continent of Europe. This time, no such allies were available. The colonies that now began to call themselves the United States of America were the main beneficiaries.

Spain did not intervene on the rebels' behalf without much soul-searching. In some ways, the decision was like that to intervene against Britain in favor of France in 1762—a marginal choice, undertaken in awareness of the drawbacks, on the basis of a nicely balanced calculation. Spanish ministers knew that independence would not arrest the growth of the thirteen colonies' wealth and power. Nor would it remove the sources of conflict that had already accumulated along the border. They were aware that in the long run an independent United States would be at least as formidable a foe as Britain, with more reason to covet Spanish territory. Without exception, they felt revulsion at supporting rebels against their king: it was a perversion of the natural order, an almost pathological depravity, for subjects to abjure allegiance. Spanish decision makers were conscious, too, that they had their own actual and potential rebels, whom a patriot victory in the Revolutionary War would encourage, and whom elements in the United States would actively support. On the other hand, in the short term the case for intervention was decisive. It was worth taking risks to weaken the principal foe. The influential minister the Conde de Aranda pointed to a British map of 1775, which united a vast amount of intelligence about Central America, and predicted that the British would try to seize the region, splitting Spanish America in two for piecemeal conquest.[34] Extrusion of Britain from Spain's North American borderlands would remove many causes of future friction. The chance to recover Florida was compelling, as the security of Spain's Caribbean possessions depended on control of the coast that commanded the Gulf Stream. A further incentive was the prospect of weakening Britain's hold over Mediterranean shipping lanes and recovering Minorca and Gibraltar from their British occupiers.

US historians are still only beginning to appreciate the extent of Spain's help in the Revolutionary War. French help was critical to American success. Without it, patriot victory against Britain would have been unthinkable, though an unthinking, infantile tradition of US historical writing continues to represent independence as entirely homespun bunting. Spanish help, in turn, was critical to French success. In 1776, France's foreign minister, the comte de Vergennes, argued candidly that a Spanish alliance was essential: "[I]t is a fact that his French Majesty cannot struggle long on equal terms with the English and that a prolonged war . . . could entertain the ruin of his navy and even of his finances."[35] Without Spanish subsidies, the French war chest would have run out of cash. Without backup from the Spanish fleet, the French navy would have had no freedom of maneuver and, in particular, could not have mustered the ships to blockade Yorktown. Even before intervening directly, Spain resolved, as one of her chief ministers said, "to do everything in our power to help the colonists."[36] Financial aid was critical. Spain paid many of the war expenses not only of the French contingents but to an even deeper degree of the patriot army, too, bankrolling garrisons on the Ohio and the costs of the siege of Yorktown. Spanish matériel cascaded into rebel hands, most of it free of charge.[37] Once committed to the war, Spain fielded more soldiers in support of the rebels than the patriots could muster on their own account. Most Spanish operations were designed to suit Spain's specific war aims in Florida and Louisiana, but expeditions went as far afield as Illinois and Michigan to relieve pressure on the patriots.

The decisive reason for Britain's defeat was not, perhaps, the combination of her enemies so much as her lack of allies of her own. Her commitment, moreover, was always equivocal, with a good deal of the political nation at home sympathizing with the Americans. The polymath John Huddleston Wynne argued in his *General History of the British Empire in America* in 1770 that "a country of manufactures without materials; a trading nation without commodities . . . and a maritime power without either naval stores or sufficient material for shipbuilding could not long subsist as an independent state without her colonies."[38] William Pitt, however, who had presided as prime minister over Britain's victories in the Seven Years' War, favored concessions to the colonies. So did his colleague William Petty, who was to become prime minister before the Revolutionary War was over. Petty advocated independence for the colonies loudly and consistently from 1777 onwards. Edward Gibbon, perhaps England's leading man of letters in his day, whose work on the fall of the Roman Empire was, in part, a surrogate history of Britain's imperial shortcomings, and Adam Smith, the economist whose theories would dominate the modern world, both regretted the government's recourse to war against the colonists and welcomed US independence. In the very year of the Declaration of Independence, Smith summed up the case for withdrawal from the colonies: the empire was economically unproductive, "an empire of customers . . . unfit for a nation of shopkeepers," and that it was not worth a war. It was "not very probable," he predicted, "that they will ever voluntarily submit to us; and we ought to consider that the blood which must be shed in forcing them to do so is, every drop of it, blood either of those who are, or of those whom we wish to have for our fellow-citizens. They are very weak who flatter themselves that, in the state to which things have come, our colonies will be easily conquered by force alone."[39]

He thought an independent America would be better for British trade than an enforced imperial system. He turned out to be right: British trade with the former colonies increased after the war.

When the war was over, Spain seemed to have achieved all her war aims. The British threat had receded from her frontiers. On the map of North America, Spanish success looked formidable. Spain had replaced France in most of the Louisiana territory, restricted Britain on the west coast, pacified or seduced into submission most of the Native Americans on the northern frontier, regained Florida from Britain, and—at the cost of installing a potentially even more formidable foe in the form of the fledgling USA—expelled Britain from most of the mainland of the New World, from Canada to Belize. Meanwhile, as we shall see in the next chapter, she had established effective occupation of California. Yet no informed observer in Spain or Spanish America felt secure. Within little more than a generation the empire would be in ruins. Our next task is to see how it happened and what it meant for the future of the United States.

CHAPTER FOUR

THE REALM OF QUEEN CALAFIA

The Foundation of California and the Showdown with Anglo-America, c. 1766~1846

Know that at the right hand of the Indies there exists an island called California, very close to one side of the Terrestrial Paradise; and it was peopled by black women, without any men existing there, for they lived in the manner of the Amazons. They were beautiful and robust of body, of intense courage, and great strength. Their island was the strongest in all the world, with its steep outcrops and rocky shores. Their weapons were all of gold, and so were the harnesses of the wild beasts they customarily tamed by riding them, for in the entire island there was no metal but gold.

~*Garcí Rodríguez de Montalvo,*
Las sergas de Esplandián (1510)

HE HAD THE SCENES OF HIS TRIUMPH CARVED ON TRUNKS of red cedar, and set them up behind his house. That was the traditional way Chief Skowl's people—the Haida—kept records and cast spells in their island homeland off the Alaskan coast. They raised columns of carved and painted wood. They piled them on top of one another to mark the graves of chiefs and shamans or line the entrances

of important buildings. Some of these so-called totem poles com-
memorated rituals. Some narrated events. Some served to express
contempt for enemies.

An image of a majestic eagle, with wings outspread, surmounts
Chief Skowl's "ridicule" pole, erected early in the second half of the
nineteenth century. The eagle was the chief's personal emblem. Below
it, as if in subjection, appears the image of the foe the chief wanted to
lampoon: a priest with braided hair and well-combed beard, raising
a finger more in reproof than in blessing. A glum angel, wrapped in
his own wings, stares out from under the priest's feet. Other figures
of priests and another rampant eagle decorate the lower portions of
the composition. It is a monument to indigenous resistance to what
we might call evangelical imperialism—a symbol of the rejection of
the intruders' religion and claims to authority. The garb and coiffure
of the priests on his totem pole mark them unmistakably as Orthodox.
The empire Chief Skowl rejected was Russian.[1]

The pole is a reminder of the enduring Russian presence on the
Pacific coast of what is now the United States. In the case of Alaska,
Russia ruled, at least superficially and along parts of the coast, until
1867, when the US government, under the shadow of looming Canadian independence, made the best bargain in the country's history
and bought the vast and, as it turned out, rich region, twice the size of
Texas, for two cents an acre. By then, Russia's American empire had
dwindled to feebleness, but it had begun, like other European empires
in the Americas, with expectations that blended into fantasy. In the
mid-eighteenth century Russia had barely colonized its own hinterland in Siberia: there were only about 300,000 peasants scratching
the surface of the entire vast region. Yet promoters in Moscow wrote
of going on from there to a vast program of further expansion: to
seize a share of the furs of North America, grab unrevealed mineral
wealth, challenge the Spanish monarchy for supremacy in Pacific-side
America, girdle the earth with shipping lanes, and reach across the
entire length of the Pacific to found an Antarctic empire.

Spain took the threat seriously. In the late 1760s José de Gálvez, the
official sent from Madrid to impose reforms on the government in New
Spain, decided to preempt Russian pretensions by securing the reput-

edly fine harbors that indented the coast of Upper California. The area had been strangely neglected. When Spanish navigators first discerned California in the 1540s, they named it after the mythical realm of Queen Calafia, a character in a pulp-fiction romance of chivalry popular at the time, as if abstracting the region from reality. California remained so imperfectly explored that it continued to appear as an island on maps into the eighteenth century. Yet the coast was vital for the strategic interests of the Spanish monarchy. Just as the Florida shore guarded the Gulf Stream and the route from the Caribbean to Spain, so California guarded the route back to Mexico for shipping from the Philippines, which had to follow a wide arc through the North Pacific, before turning south along the Pacific coast of North America in order to take advantage of the pattern of currents. Spain could neglect Upper California only for as long as no rival threatened it.

The need to act came at the worst possible moment as far as available manpower was concerned. In 1766 the Spanish monarchy had decreed the expulsion of the Society of Jesus: the act was part of a connected series of predatory, secularist, and anticlerical initiatives undertaken by governments over much of Catholic Europe, intended to shift power and wealth away from the Church into royal hands. At the time, Baja California was virtually a Jesuit republic. The expulsion, which took effect in 1767, deprived the monarchy of its most determined frontiersmen. Anticlericalism as well as common sense dictated the next focus of policy: military colonies. The practical realities of conflicting demands on military personnel made it inevitable, however, that the monarchy would also turn to the Jesuits' regular understudies: the Franciscans. In 1768 Gálvez announced, probably insincerely, in language that echoed most expressions of the purpose of the empire, that "the prompt conversion of many gentiles," as well as "the extension of the king's domains," demanded the colonization of Upper California.[2]

Junípero Serra arrived to head the Franciscan effort in that same year, mortifying his flesh with undergarments of bristles or wire and a program of unsparing self-flagellation. His brief was not only to occupy the former Jesuit missions but to extend Spain's reach northward at least as far as Monterrey, to counter the Russian threat and keep the great natural harbors of California out of the hands of other powers. A march of 250 miles led him to San Diego. Naval and military expeditions took an agonizingly long time to find Monterrey but located an even better harbor farther north at San Francisco in the process. So both had to be occupied.

The natives responded to the Franciscans with indifference in some places, violence in others. The enterprise seemed doomed—and almost perished for want of commitment in New Spain. Yet Serra followed the "call of so many thousands of pagans who are waiting in California on the threshold of holy baptism, . . . on a road the principal end of which was the greatest honor and glory of God."[3] Serra's determination was extremely heroic, or perhaps extremely foolhardy. Lay explorers helped, especially Juan de Anza, who developed land routes to New Spain and mapped the interior as far as the Rockies and Utah Lake, and naval commanders, especially Juan Francisco de Bodega y Quadra, who charted the coast of Pacific North America and made it safe for Spanish shipping. Within a few years of Serra's first efforts, California began to look viable.

Anza led the first lay colony overland from Arizona in 1775. The thirty families were driven by poverty and drawn by royal doles, which included a seven-ply leather coat for every man and—as H. E. Bolton put it—"all inventions known at the time from frying-pans to blank books." Spanish administrators seemed keen to urge on the work of settlement. In 1777 Governor Felipe de Neve wrote to Viceroy Antonio María Bucareli on the Rio Porciúncula that "no other service could have so much importance as to encourage sowing, planting, and raising of cattle . . . as well as to aid settlers, giving them all possible assistance applicable to agriculture and the raising of cattle."[4]

The governor's zeal, however, was more the result of apprehension at the danger of Russian or British incursions than enthusiasm for possessing California. His purpose was to feed the presidios at relatively low cost. By the early 1780s, a string of economically precarious missions and forts threaded from San Diego to San Francisco, where an annual ship was the only contact with the rest of the Spanish monarchy. The colony converted the environment as well as its inhabitants, wrenching the people out of nomadism, producing new crops—wheat, grapes, citrus, olives—from the soil. In 1783 the missions produced 22,000 tons of grain, a total that rose to 37,500 in 1790, and 75,000 by 1800. By the time the secular authorities seized it in 1834, Serra's model mission of San Gabriel had 163,578 vines, 2,333 fruit trees. Serra also founded veritable industries. San Gabriel had looms and forges and made woodwork, bricks, wheels, carts, plows, yokes, tiles, soap, candles, earthenware, adobe, and leather shoes and belts. The productivity of the mission economy could be measured by the contribution of $134 San Gabriel made to the cost of the Spanish commitment to the war for the independence of the United States. (The eleven families living in the newly founded town of Los Angeles raised $15.)

Ranching on mission land grew even more spectacularly. The Franciscans had only 427 head of cattle in 1775. Between 1783 and 1790 their holdings in horses, mules, and cattle grew from 4,900 to 22,000; other livestock increased from 7,000 to 26,000. By 1805 they had at least 95,000 head all told. San Gabriel alone counted 12,980 cattle and loaned out a further 4,443 cattle to lay colonists, along with 2,938 horses and 6,548 sheep. In 1821 the mission had 149,730 cattle, 19,830 horses, 2,011 mules.[5] In terms of head of kine per mission resident, the total represented 1.3 per person in 1785, and 7.3 in 1820.

The friars also exploited the potential for trading furs with Yankee merchants, who made laborious voyages around the South American cone to take advantage of the opportunity in the 1790s. William Shaler of Connecticut, who visited in 1804 on a trading venture from China, drove satisfactory bargains by advancing supplies for the missions against delivery of furs. His journal revealed how "for several years past, the American trading ships have frequented this coast in search of furs, for which they have left in the country about $25,000 in specie and merchandise. . . . The missionaries are the principal monopolizers of the fur trade, but this intercourse has enabled the inhabitants to take part in it."[6]

Even more remarkable than their economic success was the missions' record in boosting their own populations. They survived the terrible demographic disaster that ensued in California as in all the other places where European intrusions exposed Native Americans to unaccustomed diseases. Indios achieved unprecedented prosperity under Franciscan tutelage, with the advantages of the new food sources—animals and crops—that the Franciscans introduced and the extra muscle power of the mules, oxen, and horses that arrived from New Spain. The effect, however, as a Franciscan complained, was that "as soon as we bring them round to a Christian and community way of life, . . . they fatten, sicken, and die." But because the missions spread, attracted indios, and privileged the active population, who were least likely to succumb to disease, the overall numbers of mission denizens grew. When Serra died, there were 4,650 indios in the missions. In 1790, mission indios numbered 7,500. The total rose to 13,500 in 1800. By 1821, when Mexico succeeded the Spanish monarchy in taking responsibility for California, there were, on average, over 1,000 Indians in each of the twenty missions.[7] By the same date, the colonial population had risen to over 3,000.

The missionary enterprise achieved these transformations amid the usual conflicts between the friars and the lay authorities. Soldiers' outrages made the friars' work harder, provoking a hostile alliance among formerly divided local tribes. Felipe de Neve, governor of California from 1779 to 1782, was indifferent to piety, steeped in the anticlericalism of the Enlightenment, and jealous of the friars' successes. He was at odds with Serra from the first,[8] taunting him with the threat of secularization of mission lands, and reminding the friars that their missions were revocable royal grants, conceived as temporary and destined to revert to civil jurisdiction when their work was done. In other words, the friars' reward would be deprivation. Neve challenged the Franciscans' right to confirm baptized indios and accused the friars of disobedience, immeasurable pride, and unspeakable artifice. He ignored missions in his plans for future colonization.

He also cast doubt on the efficacy of the conversions. All evangelization involves compromise with the neophytes' cultures and traditions. The friars tended to be suitably strict where sex was concerned, locking up nubile mission girls at night,[9] but were more indulgent about what they considered to be indifferent traditions, including dancing and traditional healing.[10] Hugo Reid, a Scot who settled in

Los Angeles in 1832 and profited locally from secularization of church property by the Mexican government, thought the indios of San Gabriel "have at present two religions—one of custom and another of faith. Hell . . . is for whites, not for Indians, or else their fathers would have known it. The Devil, however, has become a great personage in their sight; he is called Zizu and makes his appearance on all occasions. Nevertheless, he is only a bugbear and connected with the Christian faith; he makes no part of their own."[11]

That judgment was self-interested and insensitive to the supple variety of Catholic devotion. Certainly, however, the friars had to struggle continually against Native intractability or indifference. When San Gabriel was founded, indios "made themselves so scarce," according to one of Serra's helpers, that over a few months "one hardly saw a single indio." The locals, he reported, "moved to another site far away from us." In 1775 Fernando Rivera y Moncada, captain of Baja California, reported a rebellion at the mission of San Diego de Alcalá in which Fray Luis Jaume was martyred, because the indios "wanted to live as they did before."[12] In October 1785 the green-eyed sorceress Toypurina launched a rebellion at San Gabriel, because, she declared, "I hate the padres and all of you, for living here on my native soil . . . for trespassing on the land of my fathers." When Natives took up arms in several California missions in 1824, their shamans relied on amulets and talismans to prevail against the Spaniards.[13]

The alternative course for failed or flinching rebels was to run away from the missions. A typical missionary's evidence was, "Let the more intelligent Indians be asked why they run away and they will reply: '. . . Naturally we want our liberty and want to go hunt for women.'" But the testimony of recaptured runaways from Dolores near San Francisco in 1797 concentrates on hunger and fear of excessive punishment as reasons for flight.[14] In 1801 Fray Fermín Lasuén explained how malcontents would claim to be "hungry" and ask to go to the mountains for a week to hunt. The hunger was rather for a way of life than for food, which was usually available in abundance in the missions. "I said to them with some annoyance," the friar continued, "'Why, you make me think that if one were to give you a young bull, a sheep, a bushel of grain every day you would still be yearning for your mountains and your beaches.' The brightest of the Indians who were listening to me said, smiling and half-ashamed of himself, 'What you say is true, Father.'"[15]

The friars' only recourse was to flogging or chaining, sometimes applied in frustration or despair. Serra acknowledged, "I am willing to admit that in the infliction of the punishment . . . there may have been inequalities and excesses on the part of some fathers." Fray Esteban Tapis of the Santa Bárbara mission explained that the lash or the stocks were used to punish sexual misconduct or a second offense of running away, while shackles were applied for a further offense, for "such are the chastisements which we inflict, in keeping with the judgment with which parents punish their own beloved children."[16] In 1806 a mission indio, Julio César, recalled a further hazard from the caprice of lay supervisors who inflicted punishments without reference to the priests: "We were at the mercy of the administrator, who ordered us to be flogged whenever and however he took a notion."[17]

Mission life was, in its way, as hard for the friars as for the indios. The Franciscans, wrenched from their familiar environments and ways of life, facing superhuman demands in hostile surroundings, struggled to contain common temptations with excesses of discipline. César spoke of how Fray José María Zalvidea "struggled constantly with the devil. . . . He constantly flogged himself, wore haircloth, drove nails into his feet."[18] From time to time missionaries succumbed to problems of sexual incontinence, drink, and spasms of lunacy.

Lay settlements were even harder to establish than missions. When Serra died in 1784, there were, perhaps, nearly a thousand lay colonists in and around the presidios, keeping the wilderness, paganism, and rival empires—British and Russian—at bay. It was hard to scrape communities together. Upper California continued to make progress in the 1790s: Los Angeles had 140 citizens in 1791 and 315 by 1800, but in the middle of the decade, a priest expressed disappointment that "the towns founded twenty years ago have made little progress. The residents are a group of laggards."[19]

The frontiers that Upper California superseded were themselves underpopulated and reliant on migrants. Escapees from acceptance worlds elsewhere—the outcasts of Spanish colonies, which were themselves refuges for the empire's desperadoes, dregs, and undesirables—came to populate them. People who because of poverty or a criminal past or lack of education or mixed or doubtful parentage were disadvantaged in the competition for status and wealth could attain respectability and even power on the newest edges of empire. A priest in 1757 noticed that "there is hardly a true Spaniard in Sonora," where *castizos*—progeny of a parent with traceable Spanish ancestry— with up to a quarter of Indian blood were classed as Spaniards and could serve as priests. Precarious, hard-won status was precious and the newly minted Spaniards regarded neighbors of more richly mixed blood "with contempt."[20]

Half-breeds sought their own escape by living in indio communities, where their own status was relatively high, but the colony needed them to boost the population of settler towns and from the 1780s tried to force them back into the company and tyranny of the *castizos*. Missionaries were ordered to discourage marriages that might further attenuate European bloodstock. In San Antonio, Texas, freed blacks, whom the authorities encouraged to supplement the meager population descended from the Canarian founding families, were a major part of the population. Indios constituted 10 percent according to the official census of 1790. By then, intermarriage made whites and non-whites indistinguishable. Antonio Salazar de Zacatecas, the master mason of San Antonio mission from 1789 to 1794, appears in various documents as indio, mestizo, and Spaniard.[21] In New Mexico, according to the governor's report to the Cortes of Cádiz in 1811, indios were "Spaniards in all things."[22]

Upper California, therefore, was bound to be an ethnically mixed society, where social and racial distinctions would be mutually severed. One-third of men and one-quarter of women who founded San José and San Francisco in 1777 called themselves *españoles,* but no one inquired too closely into what the name meant. Twenty-five of the original forty-six settlers of Los Angles were blacks or children of blacks. In San José in 1814 all *gente de razón*—the main test for which was not skill in reasoning but wearing European-style dress—were "considered Spaniards."[23] Indios formed the only other class in the town. In other words, the appearances of civilized life, of which European attire was the critical signifier, counted towards status, whereas parentage and the color of one's skin did not. "Although it is well known that not all are genuine Spaniards," wrote a priest in Santa Bárbara in 1813, "if they were told to the contrary they would consider it an affront." Bernardo de Gálvez explained the frontier ethos to persnickety visitors: "What does it matter to His Majesty if one who serves him well is black or white, if the color of his face is negated by the nobility of his heart?" According to Richard Henry Dana, the Harvard man who crewed, allegedly for his health, on a trading venture to California in 1834, "the least drop of Spanish blood, if it be only of quadroon or octoroon," qualified a Californian "to call himself Español, and to hold property, if he can get any."[24]

Even as the California colony took shape, it became apparent that Spain would have to renounce any hope of occupying territory farther north along the coast. No manpower was available. In the 1780s Spanish naval forces kept British, Russian, and American interlopers at bay and erected forts as far away as what is now British Columbia, but the effort hardly seemed worthwhile. In 1789 the French Revolution threatened the peace of Europe and the security of its monarchies. In the 1790s, in a series of conventions, Spain in effect agreed with Britain to refrain from asserting rights in northerly latitudes. When war broke out in Europe in 1792, it hobbled the Spanish monarchy and relegated Pacific-side North America to a low level of priority. In 1795 both sides abandoned a contentious site at Nootka, off the Vancouver coast, and agreed to postpone the resolution of the boundary dispute. In effect, however, Spain abandoned Oregon from that moment onward.

US INDEPENDENCE, MEANWHILE, WAS a threat disguised as an opportunity. Expansion was among the revolutionaries' main motives for breaking with Britain. Territorial conflicts with Spain were current or imminent, even while the rulers of the new republic were expressing their gratitude for Spanish help in their struggle.

The northern limits of Florida had never been definitively settled. Spain, moreover, had not agreed to acknowledge the east bank of the Mississippi as part of the United States. The question of freedom of navigation on the Mississippi was vital for the US economy. Since the 1760s English officials had contemplated fantastic schemes for engineering works to divert the flow of the river into their territory, or for conquering New Orleans, as if that could be done more easily or more cheaply. For the rulers of the young republic, there was no hope of a river of their own to rival the Mississippi, as the whole of the Gulf coast was in Spanish hands. The prospect of war to seize the Floridas, at least, and control or share the use of the great river, was already in Thomas Jefferson's mind, even while Congress was fighting for independence and dependent on Spanish help. John Jay, the ill-chosen US minister in Madrid during the Revolutionary War, was certain that

the Americans, almost to a man, believed that God Almighty had made that river a highway for the people of the upper country to go to the sea by; that the general [Washington], many officers, and others of distinction and influence in America were deeply interested in it; that it would rapidly settle; and that the inhabitants would not be readily convinced of the justice of being obliged either to live without foreign commodities or lose the surplus of their productions; or be obliged to transport both over rugged mountains and through an immense wilderness to and from the sea, when they daily saw a fine river flowing before their doors and offering to save them all that trouble and expense, and that without injury to Spain.[25]

In 1790, as secretary of state, Jefferson issued his representative in Madrid with instructions that were unashamedly aggressive. More than half the territory of the United States, he stressed, was in the Mississippi basin, "where 200,000 people, of whom 40,000 can bear arms, are impatient of Spanish delays. . . . If we cannot by argument force Spain to a conclusion, we must either lose this western people, who will seek other alliances, or we must, as we shall, wrest what we want from her."[26] He proposed to offer protection of Spain's trade via the Mississippi in exchange for New Orleans and Florida—a suggestion the Spanish court would have found insulting.

To secure the Mississippi, Jefferson contemplated a diplomatic revolution—a reversal of the pattern of alliances that had won independence for his country. The end of the War of Independence ought to have made Spain and Britain natural allies. But British opinion adjusted quickly and was already well disposed towards independent America. Britain proposed an anti-Spanish alliance and attack on Santa Fe, the effective capital of Spanish North America. Jefferson was tempted to accede, but he did not trust the British and was anxious to avoid a war that might give Louisiana to Britain. He hoped, he said, to see "the New World fattening on the follies of the old."[27] In 1796 the demagogue Aaron Burr, who was to become Jefferson's vice president and archrival, had threatened to "revolutionize and take possession . . . in its entirety"[28] of South America. He told a British envoy that he would bust the Union, break the Spanish monarchy, and found an empire in Spanish North America. Arrested early in 1807 while leading an unimpressive armed expedition to stage a coup in New Orleans, he narrowly escaped conviction for treason and left an example of adventurism in Spanish America that drew many imitators. Evidently, in the long run hostility between Spain and the United States was predictable.

Alternatively, the Spanish hold on western Louisiana might be eroded by attrition and the constant infiltration of migrants across the Mississippi. Jefferson realized that US immigrants could be "the means of delivering to us peaceably what may otherwise cost us a war."[29] Spain's dilemma was intractable. According to Vicente Manuel de Zéspedes, governor of the Floridas in the 1780s, Spain needed "a living wall of industrious citizens,"[30] but subsidies intended for colonists had to be diverted to feed troops. Immigrants from the United States, even Protestants, could secure a welcome, partly because the influx was unstoppable, partly because the land needed settlers. Spain needed colonists for the region, and the United States was the only big source of them. Daniel Boone, Spanish citizen and a commissioner for the king to the natives of Louisiana, was among the settlers who took advantage of the opportunity, while Spanish authorities speculated on the prospects of getting Irish priests to reeducate immigrants' children.[31]

Spanish officials knew the risks of accepting settlers from the United States. Manuel Gayoso de Lemos, governor of Louisiana, predicted in 1798 that the intruders "will establish their own customs, laws, and religion. They will form independent states, aggregating themselves to the Federal Union, which will not refuse to recognize them, and progressively they will go as far as the Pacific Ocean."[32] More concisely, from Chihuahua the commander of Spanish forces, Nemesio de Salcedo, summed up the American arrivals as "crows to pick out our eyes."[33]

On the other hand, the chances of converting migrants to the Catholic religion and Spanish allegiance did not seem altogether bleak. There were secessionists on the US fringe whom Spain hoped to seduce. Kentucky almost joined the Spanish monarchy. In 1788, James Wilkinson, one of the most prominent generals in the US forces and a leading figure in Kentucky, conspired to secure the territory's secession from Virginia and adscription to Spain. His claim that "I have given my time, my property, and every exertion of my faculties to promote the interests of the Spanish monarchy"[34] was not far from true. In 1796 the chief justice of Kentucky arranged a bribe of $10,000 for Wilkinson, and subsidies of $200,000 to finance a coup and proclaim an independent Kentucky, allied with Spain, with a boundary from the mouth of the Yazoo River to the Tombigbee. Wilkinson later became a fellow conspirator with Burr, whom he eventually betrayed. His treasons escaped detection, or at least prosecution, until after his death in 1821 in Mexico, where, like many US malcontents, he was trying to negotiate a land grant from the government. Though his attempt to shift Kentucky into the Spanish monarchy failed, it demonstrated that some Americans saw advantages for local elites in submission to a power more distant than Washington, DC.[35]

NATIVE AMERICANS, TOO, WERE inclined to show partiality for the Spanish monarchy, which tried to protect them from enslavement, expropriation, and massacre. In some areas, Spain's links with indios were ingrained as a result of long mutual contact and interdependence. In the 1740s, a visiting Jesuit found that people at the mouth of the Miami River in Florida spoke Spanish. Trade spread the use of Spanish deep into the interior.[36] In the 1770s William Bartram noticed that Creeks and Seminoles "manifest a predilection for the Spanish customs" and language.[37] If they were beyond the reach of Spanish power, Native Americans tended to prefer to remain attached to Britain rather than trust the Anglo colonists. They generally realized that Spain would befriend them, the United States betray them. In June 1784, Alexander McGillivray, the Creek chief whose father was a Scots trader, signed a treaty with Spain, promising that "the Crown of Spain will gain and secure a powerful barrier . . . against the ambitious and encroaching Americans."[38] In the south, indio chiefs became adept at playing the United States and Spain against each other. In 1794 Washington summed up their guile: "The old counsellors among the Indians will profess to be at peace, and continue to receive their annuity, while their young men continue their depredations, and the others will say that they cannot restrain them."[39]

On the new republic's northern frontier, meanwhile, indio resistance was effective at first, under Little Turtle, the Miami chief who had already demonstrated his excellence as a general in fighting the French. Anthony Wayne's summer campaign of 1795 switched the Indians who signed the peace—Ottawas, Pottawattamies, Wyandots, Delawares, Shawnees, Miamis, Chippewas, Kickapoos, Weas, Eel Rivers—to the status of "children" rather than "brothers," which was the term British negotiators had preferred. Wayne took the frontier to Lake Erie. To keep peace there cost the United States about $30,000 a year in subsidies to Native tribes, a little more than the cost of the war—but the expense made further settlement practicable.

DESPITE THESE FAVORABLE AUGURIES in America, developments in Europe put the Spanish monarchy under intolerable pressure. In conflict between Britain and France, Spain was caught between hammer and anvil. On the one hand, the French republic appeared invincible, fighting off the combined might of European monarchies, trampling the edges of Spanish territory, and demonstrating a frightening appetite for expansion at the expense of other neighboring states. On the other, Britain remained invulnerable to French attack and a threat at sea to all other colonial powers. Faced with the dilemma of which side to opt for, Spain vacillated and oscillated. It was essential to keep other potential enemies appeased. So, in October 1795, Spain signed the Treaty of San Lorenzo with the United States, fixing the boundary of Florida at 31 degrees north and conceding to the Republic the navigation rights along the Mississippi that Jefferson craved. It was a fatal move. The evidence of Spain's weakness implanted in French minds the possibility of regaining Louisiana.

The progress of the war in Europe left Spain increasingly exposed. By 1802 she was alone and friendless. Napoleon, who had seized supreme power in France in a coup d'état four years previously, bludgeoned the rest of Europe into submission and made peace with Britain. He was always a curious mixture of visionary and opportunist: his vices now conspired to alert him to the possibility of founding a new empire for France in America. Spain could not resist his demand for the return of Louisiana. Indeed, in one respect, the opportunity seemed a godsend: it would give Spain a buffer against US ambitions of expansion. Henceforth, Spanish ministers reasoned, France would resume the burden of colonizing the North American interior and keeping the United States at bay.

They did not reckon with Napoleon's mercurial ambitions and the mutable state of European politics. Within half a year of resuming sovereignty in Louisiana, Napoleon realized that the problems of the territory were insoluble, and that imbroglios in the western hemisphere would impede his freedom to act in Europe. His troops, moreover, suffered a humiliating rebuff in their attempt to recover France's former colony of Saint-Domingue from rebellious slaves. The sale of Louisiana to the United States was formalized in 1804. "I am so disgusted," wrote José Vidal, a Spanish captain, with the "ambitious, restless, lawless, conniving, changeable" Americans, "that I can hardly wait

to leave them behind me." Spain opened Texas to the king's "unfortunate vassals" from Louisiana, "who prefer his rule to any other."⁴⁰

FOR A FEW YEARS, Louisiana satiated US lust for expansion, or at
least absorbed US dynamism. Individual US citizens attempted the
dismemberment of the Spanish empire for the benefit of their country
or themselves, but with, at most, covert connivance rather than official
approval from the government. In 1807, however, a new phase of the
European war began, when Napoleon contrived a coup d'état in Spain.
Taking advantage of his status as an ally, he infiltrated large numbers
of soldiers into the country on the pretext of invading Portugal. He
then abused his place as an arbitrator in an internal dispute within the
Spanish royal family to lure the king, Carlos IV, and his heir, the
Infante Fernando, onto French soil, where he imprisoned them and
demanded their abdications. He nominated his own brother, Joseph,
to the vacant throne.

He had expected to rely on the support of a progressive elite in the
country, known as the *afrancesados*—the Frenchified—who, saturated
in readings of the French *philosophes*, were willing to support a regime
that promised uncompromising reform. Spanish law and government
had grown up over the centuries in a traditional, organic, irrational
fashion, and might benefit from streamlining, by force if necessary,
along the rational, practical principles of the Enlightenment. Even
some of the *afrancesados*, however, recoiled from the crudeness of
Napoleon's attempted takeover. Every other powerful constituency in
the country—the church, the army, the local and provincial elites, the
urban patriciates—united against the French. Defying expectations
that arose from the long sequence of French victories against all com-
ers since 1792, the Spanish army proved surprisingly effective in resistance, as did urban mobs and rural guerrilla bands. With the leading
figures of the royal family imprisoned in France, juntas of local nota-
bles assumed power and gradually established a pattern of collaboration in resistance from which emerged a national government of
gigantic pretensions but modest effectiveness.

In Spanish America, almost no one supported Napoleon's coup. Joseph Bonaparte declared that independence for the colonies was "in the natural order"[41] of things. His opponents proclaimed (but could not deliver) equality for representatives of the colonies in the institutions of a single transatlantic nation. The juntas that sprang into life in the Americas could not share the unifying experience that galvanized their counterparts in Spain. They had virtually no one to oppose except one another. From 1809 onward, juntas proliferated, all declaring, in effect, independence of each other, and expressing increasingly a widespread unwillingness to surrender power back into the hands of peninsular officials. The creole spirit—the American "patriotism" described in the last chapter—which preceded and nourished the independence movement in what became the United States, now inspired local power seekers to take over institutions of government in Spanish America too. In 1810 a series of civil wars began, pitting patriots against loyalists, juntas against one another, and eventually—when Spain had expelled the French occupiers—Spanish armies of reconquest against the *independentista* forces.

West Florida was among the first would-be republics to declare independence. The rebellion started, like all the rest, with a junta professedly loyal to the former infante, now generally recognized as King Fernando VII. Because Fernando was still in French custody and unable to exercise any power, he was a safe choice as figurehead, but as the French war effort in Spain faltered and the king's prospects of liberation improved, local interests in the colonies began to view him apprehensively. In September 1810 malcontents in West Florida took over and proclaimed a republic. Some were opportunists whose aim was to increase their own local power. Some were in the pocket or pay of the US government and invited annexation even as they extolled independence. The self-appointed governor, Fulwar Skipwith, tried a double game—braying for union with the United States while negotiating rewards of power and wealth for the perpetrators of the revolution. His efforts lasted ninety days. Without recognizing the new republic, US president James Madison seized the territory on the grounds that it belonged to the United States anyway. Spanish forces contained rebellions in East Florida and Texas, at the cost of terrible devastation that halved the settler population of Texas.

It was increasingly obvious that Spain could not contend simultaneously with threats from the monarchy's own rebels from within and the United States from without. By 1817 dispatches from the northern frontier had an unmistakable air of desperation. The governor of Texas complained that his troops were "absolutely unclothed" except in San Antonio and among a few elite units, whose coats and breeches were tattered and rotting. "Sometimes," he continued, "I cannot get together a party of twenty-five men to . . . escort convoys or execute any other mission, because I cannot trust that many individuals to return."[42] In 1819 a treaty fixed the frontier between Spain and the United States at the Sabine River. The United States renounced claims to Texas. Spain resigned East Florida. Local resistance to the US takeover continued until July 1821, when the last redoubt, Pensacola, was handed over as Spanish officials wept.

By then Spanish revanche had become impossible. For a while, when veteran Spanish armies arrived fresh from their victories over the French, it had looked as if their triumph was inevitable, so deep were the divisions among the creole patriots and so large the number of loyalists who rallied to the empire's side. But the Spanish counterinvasion concentrated, for strategic reasons, on the tropical heartlands of the empire, where yellow fever and malaria devastated the newcomers. The disease environment of the Americas, which had enfeebled defenders and favored invaders when Europeans first arrived exuding unfamiliar microbes, now operated in reverse. Invading armies buckled before diseases that hardly troubled their naturally immunized opponents. The South American republics that today hail Simón Bolívar as their national hero should dethrone him in favor of *Aedes aegypti*, the yellow fever–bearing mosquito. The latter killed far more Spanish soldiers than the former.[43] By the 1820s it was virtually impossible to raise troops in Spain to replace the victims or to get the army to support the continuation of the war. In 1828 Spain conceded defeat and left the *independentistas* to retrieve what they could from the wreckage of the wars.

AN OLD SPANISH GYPSY curse is, "May you have lawsuits and win them," because the costs of victory in litigation are morally and, often, financially ruinous. "May you have wars and win them" would be an even more effective curse. The republics that emerged from the wars of 1810–28 were broken vessels—impoverished, depopulated, ungovernable. Their societies were highly militarized and their armed forces highly politicized, a combination that condemned much of formerly Spanish America to long and painful histories of military government. The United States never endured this legacy, because the Revolutionary War was, by most standards, remarkably undestructive (see below, p. 348). French and Spanish intervention took up much of the strain and cost of war that, in Spanish America, fell on the colonies. For the former British colonies the War of Independence was the first of many in a remarkable series from which Americans emerged in credit. The consolidated debts owed by the state and federal governments at the end of the war amounted to a nominal $75 million—notoriously the starting point of a national debt that has never stopped growing. The combined value, however, of confiscations and informal appropriations from loyalists, Natives, and the crown greatly exceeded costs. The United States began life with an economic advantage over other states in the hemisphere. In political terms, the legacy of colonialism and revolutionary wars, in this respect, diverged in Anglo-America and Spanish America.

A further difference between the United States and the Hispanic republics soon became apparent. Continental Hispanic America was fissile. The process of fragmentation that began with the formation of juntas continued after independence, as the newly minted states split. Virtually every *audiencia* became the kernel of a new republic. In Paraguay and Uruguay the wars of independence were as much about secession from what became Argentina as from Spain. The viceroyalty of La Plata split between Bolivia and Argentina. In what is now Colombia, every region, every city pronounced its own independence of all the others along with—or rather than—independence from

Spain. It was, for most local leaderships, even more vexing to be ruled close-up from Bogotá than from decently distant Madrid. Gran Colombia emerged from the wars of the early nineteenth century, but its unity was unsustainable. In convulsive, violent, and widely separated phases over the next three generations, it split into what are now Ecuador, Colombia, and Venezuela (with Panama seceding later). Fission befell the Central American Union. Though the fact escapes attention in the United States, similar friability threatened to make British colonies crumble. What became the Canadian colonies would not join those that became the United States. Nor would those of the Caribbean. The thirteen sustained a tense alliance not because they were happily united, but because they faced compelling external threats and reassuring opportunities. They had plenty of room for expansion at outsiders' expense. They also benefited from being more compact than the Spanish colonies, while relatively easy communications united them. They lay mainly on a common seacoast linked by a single current, with harbors well protected by windward positions. Thanks to these advantages, the differences that separated centralists (misleadingly known as "Federalists" in US jargon) and devolutionists (almost equally misleadingly known as federalists in Latin American parlance) erupted into secessions and war late in North America; but they were the products of the same influences—vast geographical range, differences of environment, chasms of culture, and the introspection of provincial elites—that shattered Spanish America.

The nominally "united" states, though potentially as fissile as other American republics, held together until the 1860s, thanks to a series of contingencies and opportunities. Secession crises that recurred at intervals from the 1790s onwards focused on a bewildering range of grievances: the definition of sedition; centrally regulated tariffs that supposedly favored the North; foreign policies that supposedly favored the South; the powers of federal judges; the boundaries between various states and territories; the remit of slavery. Whenever fracture threatened, circumstances supervened: war or rumors of war, the acquisition of new territories, power brokers' deals. Texas, which seceded from the United States within a generation of joining the

Union, was almost as restive under the Stars and Stripes as under the Mexican tricolor. Threats of secession still come glibly to the lips of some Texan politicians. The long period of deferred fracture proved to be critical: the United States could take advantage of the friability of neighbors to the south.

The breakup that threatened independent Mexico therefore becomes intelligible if viewed in pan-American context. In some ways it is surprising that the collapse did not detach more territory. The first time I went to Mexico for research, I arrived late in Mérida and switched on the large television that was the unique and surprising amenity of my repulsive garret in a sordid hotel. The Miss Yucatán beauty contest was in progress, and the pundits' commentary took the form of a sort of erotic-aesthetic secessionism, praising the attractions of Yucatec womanhood over those of "Mexicans." Yucatán, or parts of it, have repeatedly come near to secession. During the period of supremacy of the Cruzob (literally, "people of the cross") in Quintana Roo in the late nineteenth and early twentieth centuries, the region was home, in effect, to an independent Maya theocracy. Meanwhile, filibusters repeatedly intervened to detach bits of the rest of the homeland from the state. The northern provinces of Upper California, New Mexico, Arizona, and Texas were only ever lightly tacked onto Mexico. Much of the region was so remote and isolated in the early years of Mexican independence that local elites had little need to assert sovereignty. Their power was unassailable. Texas, however, was structurally troublesome—close enough to the heartland for the alternations of power in Mexico City to make a difference to the local balance, but too far away to be easily coerced into submission to centralism.

As the Viceroyalty of New Spain self-transformed into independent Mexico, it lost its southernmost provinces to the Central American Republic, which in turn lasted for a while before crumbling into small states. Mexico was itself an unwieldy giant, struggling against secessionists inside its own borders. In the 1820s and 1830s, as we shall see (below, p. 142), Mexican governments wavered between centralist and devolutionist policies, partly in an attempt to hold the country together, and partly because devolution tended to appeal to politicians, unless and until they took control of the federal government—when they suddenly discovered the merits of central- ization. Mexico, moreover, had inherited one of the intractable prob- lems that had bedeviled the Spanish empire: the long, indefensible frontier with the United States. In 1822 Mexico's first ambassador to Washington reported that "the haughtiness of the Republicans does not permit them to look upon us as equals. . . . Their conceit extends . . . to the belief that their capital will be that of all the Americas."[44]

THE ALTERNATIVE AMERICA—THE CREATION of Spanish mis- sionaries and colonists in what is now the United States—was already in ruins as a result of the cost of the independence wars in blood and wealth and infrastructure. Independent Mexico contrived in some ways to make the ruin worse. The most radical change Mexico imposed on its northernmost provinces was the despoliation and abolition of the mis- sions. Cupidity, anticlericalism, and misplaced idealism all played parts in the decision. Children of the Enlightenment composed Mexico's first ruling generation. Members of the elite genuinely believed that the land would be more productive in lay hands and that liberation from the friars would turn indios into citizens. A few years before seculariza- tion, Juan Bandíni in Upper California combined typical complaints: missionaries, he said, "have appropriated nearly all this territory. . . . The mission system is the most appropriate to retard Indians' mental devel- opment."[45] For Mexican decision makers who lived a long way from the frontier, the image of the indio came from the pages of Enlightenment texts, with their convictions of the nobility of the savage and the univer- sality of liberty, equality, and fraternity. At about the same time, José Antonio de la Guerra's daughter recalled that José María de Echeandía, when he arrived from Mexico City to govern Upper California in 1828, proposed to teach citizenship and liberty to neophytes. "My father counseled . . . that he should try to curb the Indians because many of them were treacherous and any day might rise up and kill the whites."[46] De la Guerra, the patriarch of Santa Barbara, had made his home in

California since 1778: his advice was that of an old hand, experienced in the frontier but uneducated in the Enlightenment.

Indios were, on the whole, skeptical of the secularists' charity. When Commissioner Juan Bautista Alvarado arrived in San Miguel (north of San Luis Obispo) to enforce secularization in 1831, he "vividly pictured the advantages of freedom to the Indians." According to the account of one of the friars, he invited those who wished to remain under the padres to separate "from those preferring freedom." They nearly all went to the padre at once. Those who havered followed. Commissioners reported similar incidents at San Luis and San Antonio.[47] In practice, the secularizers never got around to fulfilling their promises to distribute most of the missions' land among Native residents. Rich ranchers took over and the indios fled or died or became peons. At San Gabriel, a Native woman called Victoria benefited indirectly: her husband was the Scots immigrant Hugo Reid, who carved the big ranch of Santa Anita from the spoils of the mission.[48]

Secularization was, of course, the culmination of a long process that had begun with the selective liquidation of missions under Spanish rule, especially in Texas, where most missions were wound up in the 1790s, as Christianity took hold. The encroachment of secular ownership continued informally under the independence regime, when ranchers eroded mission lands at the edges or appropriated the lands of tame Apaches at knockdown sales.[49] The achievements of the missions, which look so creditable from today's distance, seemed less impressive at the time. By the 1820s they were all in decline in terms of numbers of neophytes:[50] in a sense, this was a measure of the missions' success in creating Native Christianity. In Texas in 1792, for instance, the Franciscan provincial reported that the mission of San Valero had accomplished its task. All the indios were Christians, and "no pagans remain within 150 miles."[51] The mission could be wound up.

The dwindling of missions cast an image of decline, which, according to a report on conditions in Arizona in 1828, most of the northern territories shared. No settler in Arizona had more than twenty-five livestock, which had to be corralled and guarded because of the depredations of hostile indios. The cultivated area had shrunk since the coming of independence. The Mexican commander back in Arizpe, Sonora, understood that Tucson was in danger of abandonment, needing a commander who "would rather sleep with his gun than his wife."[52] Panicky rumors of mission rebellions alarmed the Mexican authorities in 1824, when an incident—apparently a rumor that the priest at Santa Inéz in northern California was going to crack down on collective indulgence in psychotropic substances and other traditional rites—provoked violence at three or four Californian missions.[53] But the priests who filed reports seem to have exaggerated the extent of the problems in their anxiety to blame the insensitivity and indiscipline of the Spanish troops who suppressed the rebels.

In Arizona and California between 1831 and 1845, the extinction of the missions affected at least 15,000 indios, who lost their way of life, and maybe 100,000 cattle, who found new masters.[54] A report of 1843 summed up the results: churches in disrepair, fields overgrown with mesquite and scrub, orchards barren. Broncos grazed the hills. The formerly large and prosperous communities that the missions sustained had dwindled to handfuls.[55]

PARTLY IN CONSEQUENCE OF the withering or extinction of the missions, Mexico's need for lay colonists in the northern territories was even greater than Spain's had been. The Spanish empire was, in a sense, a victim of its own success. It outgrew its capacity for recruiting colonists. French Louisiana was therefore a fatal acquisition. It had been unsustainable as a French colony because of its unattractiveness to French settlers. Its largely empty vastness multiplied the problems of recruitment that already afflicted the northern reaches of New Spain. Those problems, as was acknowledged in Madrid, demanded "the most urgent circumspection as well as the greatest prudence."[56] The numbers of potential settlers who combined the requisite qualities of industry, reliability, and loyalty to the monarchy and the church were unpromising. When the United States acquired former French Louisiana by purchase, Texas became a frontier zone, facing an aggressive and expanding power.

The Spanish authorities in the region responded by trying to keep out US intruders. They refused settlers, imprisoned traders, confiscated goods, and fought off filibusters. In 1800 they dispersed a band of adventurers under Philip Nolan, whose many efforts to trade in Texas had been rebuffed because of his attempts to incite rebellion. They tracked Lewis and Clark but could not capture them. In 1807 they did capture the follow-up expedition of Zebulon Pike, whose mission was to explore the Red River to its source, but who overshot his mark and was rescued from exhaustion and starvation when he fell into Spanish hands on the upper Rio Grande in Colorado. In 1812 a filibuster army, 3,000 strong, took advantage of the chaos of the wars in which Spain was embroiled to attack San Antonio, and from 1819, James Long, nephew by marriage of the notorious General Wilkinson, made repeated attempts to seize parcels of territory. It was as if the conquistador spirit had revived, albeit unsuccessfully, among adventurers from the United States.

In 1819 the Spanish authorities, whose hold in New Spain was weakening alarmingly, rejected a proposal for introducing US settlers in Texas. The projector was Moses Austin, a Spanish citizen and entrepreneur of Yankee birth, who had been among the residents of the Louisiana territory before its transfer to the United States. As the empire collapsed, the governor of Texas relented, as long as the only beneficiaries were "honest, industrious farmers and mechanics," and Catholics bound by oath of allegiance to Spain.[57] Austin's death put an end to the scheme, though his son, Stephen, would revive it a few years later.

When Mexico became independent, the urgency of securing that frontier seemed magnified, but so did the risks of confiding in colonists from the United States. In December 1821 the newly independent government decided in favor of relaxing discrimination. "If we do not take the opportunity to people Texas," reported the commission charged with investigating the question, "day by day the strength of the United States will grow until it will annex Texas, Coahuila, Saltillo, and Nuevo León as the Goths, Visigoths and other tribes assailed the Roman Empire."[58] Three months previously, even before the new policy was officially unveiled, William Becknell, a horse trader in New

Mexico, discovered how the impact of Mexican independence eased US penetration: US trade was now welcome. Beaver pelts were available in exchange for consumer goods imported via New Orleans more cheaply than Mexican merchants could supply them. From 1825 to the 1840s, Ceran Saint Vrain, allegedly an aristocratic refugee from the French Revolution, and Charles Bent (a US Army officer whose brothers-in-law included Kit Carson and a Cheyenne chief, White Thunder) dominated the trade in partnership, with the help of Cheyenne protectors and mediators. The wars for Texas independence, together with Comanche opposition and visitations of cholera among the Arapahoes and Cheyennes who supplied the partners with buffalo pelts, brought their business to an end—but not before Saint Vrain and Bent had joined the leading US fifth columnists in Texas and New Mexico.[59]

José María Tornel y Mendívil, a Mexican official with a centralist agenda, blamed the state government of Texas and Coahuila for "truly astounding prodigality" in granting contracts to colonial entrepreneurs. "We made a present of Texas to the Americans of the North, sometimes freely granting them our territory and sometimes giving it to Mexicans without resources or wealth for the ostensible purpose of colonizing it. With a few honorable exceptions the real object of the Mexicans in obtaining these grants was to sell at the lowest price and to the citizens of the United States the land thus acquired." The speculators were "like the asps of the fable. After we took them to our bosom, they destroyed us."[60] Texas became home to "an Anglo-American colony rather than a Mexican population." Between the lines of his narrative of the events that led to war, the blame falls on the devolved system of government, which, according to Tornel, had two consequences fatal to the unity of Mexico. First, it encouraged foreign colonists, for whom it was "natural" to "strengthen their common ties . . . in order to turn their combined strength against the country who had taken them to her motherly bosom." Second, by remitting taxation and turning a blind eye to contraband, the state government laid a light hand upon the foreigners, such as was sure to provoke, in time, a violent reaction:

The colonists enjoyed a privilege which gradually developed in them the habit of not contributing in any way to the support of our national burdens. . . . It was useless for the Americans residing in Texas to proclaim their independence, for they were independent in fact and it was even advantageous for them to claim that they were a part of the Mexican nation in order to enjoy the benefits conferred by the laws. . . . But it was evident that the moment the Mexicans awoke from their lethargy and attempted to consolidate their dominions by means of those measures to which all nations resort in similar cases, they would meet with a decided opposition which would not hesitate to resort to arms.[61]

The case of the Galveston Bay and Texas Land Company demonstrates the scope for speculators and the dangers to the Mexican state. The company bought up land grants illegally to the tune of over $140,000 and sold worthless title on to hundreds of victims. They needed Texas to be independent to legitimate their title and realize the profits they sought.

The colonization policy was indeed injurious to the integrity of Mexico because it transformed Texas into a region of shallow loyalties and disparate culture. It is doubtful, however, whether most colonists were really committed to the role of fifth columnists on behalf of Texan independence or US annexation. Many of them had equally shallow loyalties to the United States. They were, in a sense, escapees from that country, and many of them were recent arrivals. Many were or became Catholics. Many put down roots in Mexico and sincerely adopted Mexican nationality. Some married locally. Stephen Austin, the first and most conspicuous of the colonizers, seems genuinely to have wanted a working relationship with the Mexican state, and to have believed that he would enjoy more freedom, and more autonomy, in a land ruled from Mexico City than from Washington.

Conversely, not all native Mexicans were averse to secession. Frustrated devolutionists saw the gringos as allies against Mexican centralism. Some were deeply implicated in gringo land ventures as partners or go-betweens. José Antonio Mexía accumulated 243,540 Texan acres in his own name.[62] One of the Mexicans who tried to make the settlement policy work to Mexico's advantage was Martín de León, patriarch and patrician of Béxar and the San Antonio valley. In April 1824 he applied for a grant to bring colonists to the Guadalupe Valley. Initially, most of his proposed colonists were his relatives. Gradually he had to cast his net ever wider, embracing, with some success, Irish Catholics, but eventually having to welcome several migrants from the United States into his fold. Gringo ventures surrounded his colony. Martín de León's own son-in-law, José-María Jesús Carbajal, made a fortune surveying land grants. One of León's sons was jailed by both sides in turn—a measure of the oscillations of loyalties, the ambiguities of allegiance, and the exigencies of partisanship characteristic of most civil wars.[63]

By 1834, when rival surveys differed over the extent of settlement in Texas, there were at least 17,000 immigrants from the United States, including the 2,000 slaves the colonists brought with them. They outnumbered indios and dwarfed the officially designated Mexican citizenry, which was only 3,500 or 4,000 strong. Mexicans nourished hopes of acculturating the newcomers, encouraging them in local marriages and demanding their adherence, at least nominally, to Catholicism. But a priest was "a rare show" in settler-dominated areas, where men eluded the law by contracting "provisional marriages" unsolemnized by the Church. From 1829, when Mexico inaugurated a more vigorous policy to enforce compliance and sent priests to make honest women of the provisional wives and baptize their offspring, settlers reacted with mingled anger and derision. To Henry Smith, who later fought for Texan independence, the spectacle of "brides on the floor, . . . while the marriage rites are performing, with their bosoms open and little children sucking at the breast, and others in a situation really too delicate to mention, appeared . . . more like a burlesque on marriage than a marriage in fact."[64]

From 1831 to 1834, Mexico's centralist government suspended the settlement policy, but immigrants from the United States continued to be the "illegal aliens" of their day. And profiteers bought up land grants

in the expectation that the policy would change. In California, meanwhile, a few Yankee infiltrators settled as the Spanish empire waned.
Abel Stearns of Massachusetts, who set up shop in Los Angeles in
1819, was one of the pioneers: a smuggler who became an administrator of customs, acquired an estate of 200,000 acres, and married into
one of the most respected Spanish families. He later took over the
export-import business of the San Gabriel Mission and handled rancheros' trade, in exchange for a commission on hides.[65] In 1824 Mexico
opened California to immigrants and in 1828 guaranteed naturalization for Catholics of two years' residence and good conduct. This liberal policy bred vipers. In 1831 Alexander Forbes, a Scot in Mexico
who dreamed of securing California for the British Empire, wrote to
Abel Stearns, characterizing the province as "by all accounts . . . worthy
of more wise and more enterprising masters than those to whose rule
it is subjected. . . . How many Countrymen of mine who are jostling
one another for room at home might live happily in those fertile but
uncultivated fields!"[66] Not long after, Richard Henry Dana, whose
account of his life "before the mast" became an American classic, sailed
around Cape Horn to California, allegedly for the sake of his health.
He echoed the sentiments on behalf of his own fellow countrymen:
"In the hands of an enterprising people, what a country this might
be!"[67] According to the secessionist conspirator Stephen Smith, "We
only want the flag of the U.S. and a good lot of Yankees and you would
soon see the immense lot of natural riches of the country developed,
and her commerce in a flourishing condition."[68] Mexico's governor in
California, Pío Pico, foresaw the consequences: "We find ourselves
threatened by hordes of Yankee immigrants who have already begun to
flock into our country and whose progress we cannot resist."[69]

Dana observed the nature of penetration by US immigrants: "In
Monterey there are a number of English and Americans (English or
Ingles all are called who speak the English language) who have married Californians, become united to the Roman Church, and acquired
considerable property. Having more industry, frugality, and enterprise
than the natives, they soon get nearly all the trade into their hands.
They usually keep shops, in which they retail the goods purchased in

larger quantities from our vessels, and also send a good deal into the interior, taking hides in pay, which they again barter with our ships."[70]

There were still only about 1,300 of those immigrants, amounting to perhaps 10 percent of the settler population. Their economic influence, however, was out of all proportion to their numbers. The trade of California was already largely in Yankee hands. Richard Henry Dana explained that heavy import duties "keep all merchants but those of heavy capital from engaging in the trade."[71] The firm that owned his ship had carried "nearly two thirds of all the articles imported into the country from round Cape Horn, for the last six years." Yet such was the amount of liquid wealth in the country, in the form of silver bullion and tradable hides, that peddlers and storekeepers could add substantial markups to the cost of imported luxuries and still make handsome profits.

Dana's report conveys a vivid impression of economic life. California made a "very disagreeable" first impression on him. A shipmate thought Santa Barbara a strange city "and no Christian one, neither."[72] But when they got to Monterrey, the signs of prosperity were more encouraging: "The Mexican flag was flying from the little square Presidio, and the drums and trumpets of the soldiers, who were out on parade, sounded over the water, and gave great life to the scene. Every one was delighted with the appearance of things. We felt as though we had got into a Christian (which in the sailor's vocabulary means civilized) country."[73]

Dana described how shoppers and spectators put on their best clothes to clamber aboard—men, women, and children, ferried from shore in the ship's boats, "if it were only to buy a paper of pins." The cargo included spirits by the cask, "teas, coffee, sugars, spices, raisins, molasses, hardware, crockery-ware, tin-ware, cutlery, clothing of all kinds, boots and shoes from Lynn, calicoes and cotton from Lowell, crapes, silks; also, shawls, scarfs, necklaces, jewelry, and combs for the women; furniture; and . . . everything . . . from Chinese fireworks to English cart-wheels,—of which we had a dozen pairs with their iron tires on."[74]

Dana's explanation for the thriving market in imports was that "the Californians are an idle, thriftless people, and can make nothing for themselves." He was amazed that in a country full of grapes they were willing to pay inflated prices for "bad wine made in Boston" and that in a land full of cattle people bought "shoes (as like as not made of their own hides, which have been carried twice round Cape Horn)." Goods generally added 300 percent in value between Boston and Monterrey. The real explanation for the differential was not, of course, the character deficiencies of Californians, but the reality of an economy awash with cash, and a society without traditional social distinctions, where consumption largely defined status.

Even in California, where US immigrants were relatively few, the shifting balance of population and wealth in favor of Anglo-America was an ineluctable trend. But Texas was by far the main destination for US settlers. Most Mexicans who visited the region felt repelled by inhospitable wastes and untamable natives. On US imaginations, however, it exercised strange fascination. Land hunger was probably a major motive, as the far west was not yet accessible and available land on the existing frontier of the United States was in short supply. In 1820 the amount of land changing hands collapsed from five million acres to one million.[75] The crisis coincided with the moment when the former Spanish frontier opened to immigrants. As always among migrants, escapees from crime, debt, and unsatisfactory marriage were among those who took the opportunity. Stephen Austin, the most effective promoter of US settlement in Texas, acknowledged in 1828 that "the majority of the immigrants to Texas owe debts in the country from whence they came."[76]

TEXAS SECESSIONISTS ALLEGED MANY causes of discontent: the remoteness of Mexican appeal courts; the distinctiveness of the environment and economic needs of Texas; and tenuously alleged shortcomings of governance they condemned, rather illogically, as simultaneously tyrannous and anarchic.[77] The chief cause of conflict between settlers and the Mexican government was black slavery. Mexico freed its slaves in the liberal glow of independence. Laws of 1821 decreed that slaves automatically became free when they stepped on

Mexican soil.[78] Stephen Austin, despite his aversion to slavery, based his economic plans on cotton and realized that slave labor was the only hope of making his enterprise pay. He negotiated exemption for the colonists he brought into the country, but Texans of US origin, who were overwhelmingly in favor of slavery and dependent on slave labor for their businesses, lived in constant fear that antislavery laws would be enforced. In 1829 the Mexican authorities reaffirmed their commitment to emancipation. When centralizing governments took office, secession from Mexico became slave-owners' best hope of survival. The protection of slavery was among the most urgent economic reasons for rebellion. Tornel was rhetorical, but not wrong, in claiming that "the land speculators of Texas have tried to convert it into a mart of human flesh where the slaves of the south might be sold and others from Africa might be introduced, since it is not possible to do it directly through the United States."[79] The common opinion of the time, moreover, was that the economic future of the eastern half of the state would depend on cotton—a labor-intensive crop to harvest, almost wholly reliant at the time, wherever it grew in the United States, on slaves. When war broke out, John Quincy Adams was in no doubt that "in this war, the flag of liberty will be that of Mexico, and ours, I blush to say, the flag of slavery."[80] Divisions between the cultures of slave-owners and abolitionists, which helped to provoke the war of Texan independence, remained bitter until well into the twentieth century.[81]

In any case, metropolitan Mexicans never confronted the problems of Texas with candor. From Mexico City it looked as if the trouble in the province originated among native secessionists and opportunists. The place seemed contemptible. Antonio López de Santa Anna, five times president of Mexico in the 1830s and 1840s, was simply uttering a commonplace when he compared the role of Texas in the Mexican polity to Siberia's in that of Russia. The idea that Texas could be a viable republic on its own seemed risible. Vicente Filasola, who was to play a prominent role in the wars for control of Texas, reported its lack of attractions: "I have . . . seen its immense, unpopulated areas, its sandy wastes, and its barren lands where there is not, nor can there be, any considerable population. The few who lived there before the land was devastated could scarcely be distinguished from the native nomads. . . . Texas does not possess, nor will it possess for a long time, the necessary resources to constitute itself either an independent entity under a federal government or an organized province of our republic under the present political system."[82]

With attitudes like that, it is not surprising that Mexicans responded with indifference to developments in Texas and fought, when the time came, without much enthusiasm or commitment.

THE RHYTHMS OF REBELLION in Mexico's northern provinces matched the oscillations of policy in Mexico City as centralists and devolutionists struggled for supremacy. A series of revolts in California between 1828 and 1831 in response to an effective and interfering Mexican government convinced Richard Dana that "revolutions are matters of frequent occurrence in California. They are got up by men who are at the foot of the ladder and in desperate circumstances, just as a new political organization may be started by such men in our own country. The only object, of course, is the loaves and fishes; and instead of caucusing, paragraphing, libelling, feasting, promising, and lying, they take muskets and bayonets, and, seizing upon the presidio and custom-house, divide the spoils, and declare a new dynasty."[83]

Like all the best jokes, Dana's lampoon enshrined a good deal of truth. But even cultures dedicated to violence need pretexts, and in remote parts of Mexico fear of centralization was the trigger for most rebellions. A further shift in favor of centralizing policies in Mexico in 1833 provoked unsuccessful rebellions in Zacatecas and Yucatán. In California, the crisis subsided in 1836, when the particularist leader, Juan Bautista Alvarado, became governor.

In Texas the rebellions that smoldered and spluttered between 1826 and 1832 were potentially more serious because their instigators were US immigrants and because the US president, Andrew Jackson, had a personal ambition to annex the territory. The first rebellion, in 1826, started when Haden Edwards, a US planter with a large government territorial concession around Nacogdoches, began turning neighbors off land he claimed was his. When the authorities revoked his grant, he declared his tract of territory to be an independent republic. Stephen Austin's militia joined in suppressing the revolt, partly because Austin still hoped to hold Mexico together, and partly because Austin's lands, which bordered those of Edwards, seemed threatened by the upstart's depredations; in 1832, at Anahuac, near Galveston, government agents provoked another secessionist insurrection by impeding smugglers of slaves and—in a prophetic reverse simulacrum of current outrage over Mexican "illegals" in the United States—trying to exclude unauthorized US immigrants.

Jackson's agent in Texas, Sam Houston, became convinced that annexation "is desired by nineteen twentieths of the population of this province. . . . I may," he informed Jackson, "make Texas my abiding-place. In adopting this course I will never forget the country of my birth."[84] Jackson's hope was, at first, to pressure Mexico into ceding Texas in return for cash. There was little real chance of the scheme coming to fruition, and in any case Houston seems to have convinced the president that Texas could be more cheaply delivered by an insurrection. In 1833, Jackson ordered his envoys to break off negotiations for the purchase of Texas on the grounds that US colonists were about "to hold a convention in Cochuita and declare their independence, after which it will be useless to treat with Mexico for Texas."[85]

In practice, Houston was not able to rally support for secession as fast as he hoped. Devolved powers, either for Texas on its own or as part of a relatively autonomous state of Coahuila, were enough to satisfy most dissidents, including Stephen Austin, who raised troops against the rebels in 1826 and 1832, but who felt that the best future for Texas would be as a state within a loosely federated Mexico. In 1834, however, the authorities imprisoned him for favoring this moderate solution, and he turned to independence as the only way forward. By driving moderates into extremists' arms, the Mexican government tilted the chances of a successful rebellion in favor of the insurrectionists. In October 1835 Mexico took another lurch towards centralization, with the suppression of state legislatures, while the authorities began an attempt to disarm separatist militias. In Texas the separatists resisted, boosted by the arrival of thousands of new recruits from the United States.

In February of the following year, a Mexican army arrived to suppress the rebellion, while the separatists' convention formulated a constitution for "a free, sovereign, and independent republic."[86] The regular army's initial successes caused panic in the convention, but Houston, with about 900 men, launched a counterattack so daring that it took the enemy by surprise, while the army was asleep or dispersed for foraging. Houston's forces captured 730 men, including the Mexican commander, who also happened to be the head of state, President Antonio López de Santa Anna. The rebels lost only nine dead. One of the US recruits wrote home:

> To see a mere handful of raw, undisciplined volunteers, just taken from their ploughs and thrown together . . . to meet the trained bands of the hero of so many victories; to see them with trailed arms marching to within some sixty or seventy yards of such an army, at least double in number, intrenched [*sic*] too behind a breastwork impregnable to small arms, and protected by a long brass nine-pounder . . . was no ordinary occurrence. Yet such was their conduct . . . that it was not more than from fifteen to twenty minutes from our first fire until a complete rout of the enemy was effected; and such slaughter on the one side, and such almost miraculous preservation on the other, have never been heard of since the invention of gunpowder.[87]

Allowing for the exaggerations of rhetoric (the Mexicans had a small numerical superiority but nothing like two to one), this was a pretty accurate summary of the Battle of San Jacinto. Aaron Burr, dying in disgrace on Staten Island, felt vindicated: "You see? I was right! . . . What was treason in me thirty years ago is patriotism now!"[88] In some ways, San Jacinto recalls one of the most famous battles in the history of the world, where, at Marathon in 490 B.C., a small attacking force similarly advanced in daylight across a long stretch of open ground, without sacrifice of surprise, to rout a larger army, with an outcome that seemed to defy probability and has never been satisfactorily explained. As at Marathon, which reputedly saved Greece from Persian conquest, with vast and enduring consequences for the history of the world, the Battle of San Jacinto had disproportionate effects. In the long run, it made the loss of Mexico's northern provinces predictable, and their annexation by the United States probable. It demonstrated that the balance of power in the hemisphere had shifted decisively into Anglo hands and seemed to preordain US hemispheric hegemony.

The immediate outcome ensured temporary military security for the Texan Republic and supreme power for Houston. Mexico did not, however, recognize Texan independence, and Jackson's enthusiasm for welcoming Texas into the Union waned. "Prudence," he decided, "seems to dictate that we should stand aloof, and maintain our present attitude, if not until Mexico herself, or one of the great foreign powers, shall recognize the independence of the new government, at least until the lapse of time, or the course of events, shall have proved . . . the ability of that country to maintain . . . separate sovereignty."[89]

Most of the Union, moreover, was opposed to the incorporation of another slave state. But the conditions Jackson laid down did eventually materialize. France and Britain engaged in a race for the commercial advantages of recognizing Texas: France did so in 1839, Britain the following year. Fear of British and French influence stimulated US opinion in favor of annexation. Mexican threats to declare war incited aggression rather than fear. Annexationists won the elections of 1844, and Texas joined the union in December 1845—tainted, wrote John Quincy Adams in his diary, "with two deadly crimes, the leprous contamination of slavery, and robbery of Mexico."[90] The US government offered unacceptably humiliating terms for prolonging peace: the cession of Texas, New Mexico, and California for a pecuniary consideration. A border incident in April 1846 ignited the inevitable war between Mexico and the United States.

THE WAR FOR TEXAS unfolded in an atmosphere infected by what people then called "anthropology": the effort to array humankind in order of rank, with the various races in their places, like parti-colored condiments in Mrs. Beaton's or Fanny Farmer's kitchen. Racism was not a backwoods indulgence but the scientific certainty of the day, embraced, in various measures and with different degrees of critical commitment, by thinkers across the political waterfront and in every clique and sect of religion and philosophy.

Stephen Austin, for instance, was in conspicuous ways an embodiment of the survival of the Enlightenment in the United States in the early nineteenth century: an opponent of clerisy and tyranny, though he accepted slavery rather unenthusiastically. Before he became "Father of Texas" by espousing the cause of secession, he had accumulated a long record of service to the Mexican state. He adopted much Spanish tradition, including the Catholic religion, and sought honorable coexistence with native, Hispanic Texans. He only joined the independence movement after the Mexican authorities spurned his efforts to achieve a compromise between secessionists, autonomists, and federalists. But he saw—or claimed to see—the war between Texas and Mexico as "a war of barbarism and of despotic principles, waged by the mongrel Spanish-Indian and Negro race against civilization and the Anglo-American race."[91]

Even Henry Stuart Foote, despite his occluded reputation in the standard liberal version of US history, was by no means a standard reactionary. He was a Mississippian who became governor of his state and a tenacious defender of slavery. But he was also a master of political compromise, who twice became a refugee from the South in pursuit of a rational accommodation between conflictive states within the Union. When he came to the end of his term as governor in Mississippi in 1854, he withdrew to California to escape the agitation for secession. He returned to serve the Confederacy when the break came, but bent his influence towards a policy of peacemaking and fled to federal territory before the war was over. He was, however, an adept of the rhetoric of hatred who enjoyed taunting political enemies, if they happened to be Jewish, with coarse anti-Semitism. Under his classically educated veneer a roughneck lurked: he pulled a gun on an adversary in a famous incident during a debate on slavery in the US

Senate. His vision of a uniformly white, preponderantly Anglo-Saxon, culturally Protestant America was, for him, beyond compromise. His opinion of Mexicans in the United States, uttered in 1841 as the tensions mounted that led to the Mexican War, was that "extermination may yet become necessary for the repose of this continent."[92]

Francis Parkman, on the other hand, was a model Yankee. He had befriended priests in Rome, but recoiled from Catholicism in disgust. He lived with Sioux for a while, in what might fairly be called anthropological fieldwork *avant la lettre*, but rejected their habits as bestial or demonic and their way of life as savage, worthless, and expendable. He tried to understand cultures alien to him, but his prejudices, religious and patriotic, interfered with the attempt. His first impression of Hispanics, when he saw some in Missouri in 1846, reflected opinions he had formed before his encounter: the "dark-skinned, slavish-looking Spaniards" were "squalid, mean, and miserable, . . . gazing stupidly out from beneath their broad hats."[93] Those slavish looks were in the eye of the beholder. The epithets were comprehensive. According to the prevailing anthropology of the age, people's pigmentation was pale in direct proportion to intelligence, industry, and moral value. Painters and illustrators who communicated views of the Hispanic southwest to Yankee readers emphasized the same image, locating idle, swarthy, woebegone, and rickety men (while conceding beauty and élan to the women) outside ramshackle adobes, amid rough-hewn landscapes that seemed to be waiting for a civilizing touch.

In the eyes of Anglo critics, Mexicans suffered from the notion that they were typical human hybrids—half-breeds in whom whatever virtues might have existed residually in Spanish blood were tainted or extinguished by breeding with Indians. This was a potentially fatal compromise, since the science of the time, such as it was, linked interbreeding with degeneracy, with mulish infertility, and with impurity. Thomas J. Farnham, the pioneer of the Oregon Trail, who thought no American soil exploitable unless "the bones of Indians" enriched it, was prepared to concede some semblance of outward normalcy to the Mexicans he met in California: "Looking at the mere exterior of these men," he wrote in the early 1850s, "the observer would most probably come to the conclusion that they were some-what humanized." Really, however, they were "in every way a poor apology of European extraction . . . an imbecile and pusillanimous race of men, and unfit to control the destinies of that beautiful coun-try." Darwin had not yet pronounced, but Farnham anticipated him by condemning Mexicans to extinction as unfit for survival in a compet-itive world. Mixed races, he opined, "must fade away" and "the old Saxon blood must stride the continent . . . and in their own unaided might erect the altar of civil and religious freedom on the plains of California."[94] In June 1846, the Californio Creole Salvador Vallejo was outraged to find himself at the mercy of captors who called men "of the purest blood of Europe" greasers.

Racism, of course, was not just an Anglo vice. Mexicans themselves were not exempt from sentiments towards Indians as contemptuous as those of Anglos for Hispanics.[95] Fray Gerónimo Boscana, a Fran-ciscan missionary at San Juan Capistrano in the 1820s, thought that "the Indians of California may be compared to a species of monkey, for in naught do they express interest, except in imitating the actions of others, and particularly in copying the ways of the *razón* or white men, whom they respect as being much superior to themselves; but in doing so they are careful to select vice in preference to virtue. This is the result, undoubtedly, of their corrupt and natural disposition." He found them all shifty-eyed, ungrateful, and untruthful.[96] Even at their best, missionaries were paternalistic. Indios were children rather than brethren: imperfect or immature in judgment, needful of instruction, properly subject to chastisement. The reports of anticlericals and sec-ularizers interested in appropriating mission lands have to be read critically when they denounce missions as no better than slave colo-nies or death camps; but vices of exploitation, oppression, and insen-sitivity to suffering almost always arise when humans fail to feel common humanity.

JOHN O'SULLIVAN COINED THE term "Manifest Destiny" in the context of an attempt to justify the war against Mexico. Amid a lot of rhetoric about Providence, democracy, and the "natural" right of the United States to expand at other people's expense, the publicist relied ultimately on the argument—in a modern academic's summary—that "Mexicans were not capable of 'imagining' the concept of natural rights and peoplehood." His associate, Caleb Cushing, explained that "race is the key" to understanding Mexico's failures: a land of Indians and half-breeds was doomed.[97]

Moralists condemned the war. Thoreau vowed to go to prison rather than support the costs by paying his taxes. But superior numbers and superior credit were bound to win—as, with rather more difficulty than the US commanders initially expected, they did. Lieutenant Napoleon Dana reported the atrocities and barbarities to his young wife. He witnessed "a war of extermination, . . . the sight of ghastly wounds, the agony of death, . . . the groans of the expiring and the cries of excruciating pain, the smell of blood and putrid human flesh and the polluted atmosphere, and a woman on the field of battle, with a babe in her lap, unable to weep but wringing her hands and combing the hair of her husband's mangled corpse and kissing his bloody lips."[98]

He vowed never to see war again (though he lost his resolve as memory of the horror faded). The war was won and lost in Mexico. In New Mexico, Mexican resistance collapsed and the garrison fled. California, however, proved more resolute. At Los Angeles and San Pascual, the Californios—fighting on their own behalf rather than that of the government in Mexico City—defeated the insurgents and US invaders. But when large US contingents arrived, the major cities and strongholds could not hold out indefinitely and by the end of 1846 they were almost all in US hands. Even before the final collapse of Mexico in 1848, the oppression and expropriation of Mexicans began in the lands the United States was to absorb.

PART TWO

THE EMPIRE OF EDEN

*The Expansion of Anglo-America
and the Hispanic Retreat,
c. 1846~1898*

CHAPTER FIVE

THE CURSE OF ZORRO

The Great Expropriation, c. 1846–1887

———

All the census-takers in the world could not make me believe that I was a foreigner in a land that my ancestors found.

~Pedro Vallejo (1893)

Beneath the broad-brimmed Mexican hat, and long, uncombed hair, the bushy beard and greasy shirt, intellect, humanity, and heart may be concealed, or hellish hate and loathsome lust.

~Herbert Howe Bancroft, Essays and Miscellany (1890)

What have not these devils done to our country ever since they came here? . . . Where now are our extensive ranchos—our large herds of cattle? They have managed to rob us of our lands through clever laws that we of California cannot understand; they have stolen from our people thousands and thousands of cattle!

~David Belasco, The Girl of the Golden West (1911)

ONE OF BORGES'S DISTURBINGLY COMIC CHARACTERS DEVOTES his life to the "original" work of copying word for word a chapter of *Don Quixote*. María Amparo Ruíz de Burton did not quite prefigure him, though one of her contributions to English-speaking culture in the late nineteenth-century United States was to provide a popular abridged, culturally adjusted version of the Don's adventures for US playgoers. She was a paradoxical character—the Doña Marina of California who, barely out of girlhood, married one of its Yankee conquerors. Like the original Doña Marina, Cortés's Native American mistress and interpreter whose diplomacy put together the alliance that beat the Aztecs, she was therefore a practitioner of that most provocative form of collaboration: sleeping with the enemy. She deserted her native language by deploying English in her literary career—a further kind of treason for Spanish-speakers in the United States, who have to struggle to make their voices heard and their works respected in their native tongue.

Yet at the same time she was a heroine of Hispanic resistance, both in her life and in her works. Her family ranch was a target, like those of so many of her fellow Californios, for the shysters and squatters who wrecked and pillaged the property of the incumbent elite after California's annexation by the United States. Her most famous novel, *The Squatter and the Don,* was barely concealed autobiography, deftly denouncing the iniquities of legal procedure in the United States and the hypocrisy of the courts. Equally dyed in her own experiences, her earlier work *Who Would Have Thought It?* is about an aristocratic Mexican girl who fails to win acceptance in Yankee society because of her dark skin, her Spanish name, and the assumption—albeit false in her case—that these are the properties of a half-breed. Like *The Squatter and the Don*, the book is a fictional parachronicle of "how we have been despoiled, we conquered people."

In Texas the despoliation began with the birth pains of the independent republic and the arrival of hordes of predatory recruits to the secessionist cause. In revenge for atrocities committed against gringo prisoners during the war, secessionists massacred or dispersed the innocent inhabitants of Goliad and razed the town—formerly a community of a thousand people—to the ground. Mexicans were victimized regardless of their conduct during the conflicts. In Victoria families who had fought for the new republic later recalled how they "were driven from their homes, their treasures, their cattle and horses and their lands, by an army of reckless, war-crazy people."[1] Fernando de León, who had tried to practice neutrality or perhaps, rather, to play both sides in the war, was forced into exile, not before, according to his petition of restitution, he had been "deprived of a large amount of property, consisting of clothing, furniture, plate and jewelry by men professing to be patriot volunteers . . . who won their chief laurels by taking the ear rings and jewelry from the persons of helpless females belonging to your petitioner's family."[2] In San Antonio, Edward Dwyer, the richest local Anglo fixer, complained in 1836 that citizens were not yet "sufficiently scared" to sell their land cheaply, and hoped for a garrison of "two or three hundred of our troops" to help his plans for extortion. In the 1840s he abused his authority as mayor and commissioner for supposedly fraudulent land claims to dispossess Mexican families. Juan Seguín, a Texan partisan who had fought heroically at San Jacinto, struggled to defend citizens "exposed to the assaults of foreigners, who, on the pretext that they were Mexican, treated them worse than brutes." Along with at least two hundred other families, Seguín's had fled to Mexico by 1842. By then, thirteen buyers from the United States had acquired 1,368,574 acres from 358 Mexicans.[3] The notion that US rule always broke up latifundias and introduced morally superior smallholders is risible.

With the Mexican-American War the ethos of revenge intensified and the scale of expropriations increased. Napoleon Dana quickly realized that for the Texas militias the war was one "of extermination,"[4] or, as we might now say, genocide. The easiest way to appropriate Mexicans' land was to kill them off under cover of war and create an atmosphere of terror that would send refugees fleeing in panic. The treaty that ended the war guaranteed existing residents of the occupied territories "all the rights of citizens of the United States according to the Constitution," including, in particular, "free enjoyment of their liberty and property" and, together with the treaty that rounded off the Gadsden Purchase ten years later, confirmed "land grants located and duly recorded in the archives of Mexico."[5] But men on the spot never intended to honor those parts of the treaties. Texas claimed that the terms did not bind its courts or legislature. The state set up its own commissioners to adjudicate disputed land, with results predictably frustrating to Mexicans' claims. "Popular tribunals," self-elected or appointed by interested parties, administered discriminatory "justice," sometimes reinforced by lynchings.

Regular courts were hardly more reliable, as officials brought in from the United States monopolized authority. Mexican testimony counted for less generally than that of a gringo and was often discounted altogether on racial grounds. R. C. Barry, Tuolumne's county judge during the racial violence known as the "Sonoran Difficulties" of 1850, assumed that greaser oaths could not be respected. An antivagrancy law of 1850 was actually called "Greaser Law" in the official text. An Anglo lady in Victoria, interviewed for the *New York Times* in 1856, was unfortunately representative in thinking that "[w]hite folks and Mexicans were never meant to live together anyhow and the Mexicans had no business here."[6]

The new administrations reclassed as "foreigners" former subjects of the Spanish empire, many of whom were the descendants of many generations of residents. Some of them, with varying degrees of justification, were classified as "Indians"—which involved being stripped of the most basic rights, including the right to testify in court. Law enforcement too was concentrated in Anglo hands. Texas had virtually no sheriffs or marshals of Mexican antecedents.

Legislatures were stacked against natives of the occupied territories. In Texas, though the legislative convention rejected a proposal for the formal disenfranchisement of anyone classifiable as Mexican, gerrymandering ensured that Mexicans were unrepresented in the state legislature and underrepresented in local institutions, even where they formed a majority of the population. In San Antonio, for instance, most aldermen were Mexicans under the republic, but in the first council after unification with the United States, their numbers dwindled to seventeen, as against eighty-two Anglos.[7] In California in the first legislative convention in 1849, out of forty-eight delegates there were only eight native Californios to represent over 80 percent of the citizens.[8]

California's Land Law of 1851 imposed on landowners a demand for all titles to be justified by documentation in the sort of detail that did not exist in former times. Senator William Gwin, who drafted the law, later admitted that his plan was to encourage homesteaders to force old claimants off their land.[9] Early grants had understandably indeterminate boundaries, vaguely qualified by the words "más o menos."[10] Rancho San Antonio, for instance, which belonged to the Lugo family of Buenos Aires, was defined as "marked by a bullock's head or bluff, a place where two roads crossed, a spot between the hills at the head of a running water, a spring surrounded by little willows, a brush hut on the banks of the San Gabriel river, a clump of trees on the same stream, a large sycamore, a ditch of running water, and an elder tree blazed in several place with a hatchet."[11] Prejudiced courts and land-claims commissions refused to acknowledge the validity of such imprecise language. Teodoro Arrellanes was dispossessed of Rancho El Rincón, which his family had enjoyed for over nineteen years of continuous occupancy, on the grounds of "vague boundaries," such as were inherent in the ranching life.[12]

A great many grants were deemed suspect on the grounds that they were formalized only in the final years of the Spanish monarchy or the Mexican state, hurriedly drawn up in emergency conditions in order to forestall disputes. In the dying years of Mexico's northernmost provinces, from 1837 to 1846, the last governor, Manuel Armijo, granted away most of what was to become the state of Colorado and more than half the 31 million acres covered by Spanish and Mexican land grants in New Mexico.[13] In California, the last governor, Pío

Pico, was equally eager to make the most of his dying opportunities to distribute land, or at least to give existing colonists scrip with which to defend their rights after the impending gringo conquest. He lost his own ranches in subsequent litigation but remained, in gringo eyes, "the gentleman always."[14] The haste and scale of grant makers' activities left plenty of scope for lawyers to haggle and quibble.

Probably about 20–25 percent of ranchero land was lost to quasi-judicial depredations in California under the vigilance of the Land Commission of 1852–56.[15] The most notorious case was that of Don Manuel Domínguez, a mestizo, whose estate of 75,000 acres had been established by a grant of the Spanish crown in 1784.[16] In typical maneuvers, the US authorities swindled him out of his land by imposing burdensome requirements to defend his rights in prejudiced courts against vexatious litigation,[17] though he retained 24,000 acres in Southern California, where land laws inhibited sales and discouraged depredations.[18] In Texas Henry Kinney convinced the owner of El Chiltipín, an immense ranch near Corpus Christi, to give the property to him in trust as a means of thwarting predators. Kinney then sued the rightful owners for trespass. Mifflin Kennedy, who eventually acquired the ranch after the parties had exhausted each other in the ensuing lawsuits, reputedly fenced in his Mexican neighbor's property without authorization or compensation "because he needed water."[19] The case of the land belonging to Juan José Ballí and his heirs was before the courts for fifty years. The estate ended up in Anglo hands as part of the immense King ranch—reputedly one of the biggest in the world—between Corpus Christi and Brownsville. By alienating large amounts of land to lawyers, the Cavazos family got the courts to endorse their ownership of the rump of their estate near Brownsville, but meanwhile a speculator had laid out the town on part of it. Lawyers appropriated it and sold it to the speculator for a fraction of its value.[20] Fernando de León, the biggest landowner in the San Antonio valley, was reduced to poverty as courts fixed judgments against him and sheriff's sales turned his properties into the prey of the invaders. Vexatious litigation stripped his brothers and nephews of their ranches. The colonists who had taken part in the lawful settlements of the

1820s were equally at risk. Noah Smithwick, one of the first settlers on the de León family grant, who remained loyal to his old friends, denounced "land sharks who victimized those who through ignorance of the law had not exactly complied with the requirements."[21]

Litigation rarely benefits anyone except lawyers. Former subjects of Mexico were at lawyers' mercy because of their own ignorance of US law and because the courts and commissions would not admit a presumption in favor of incumbent landowners: every title had to be contested. In California, according to the leading historian of the tenure disputes, "of the fifty or so attorneys who specialized in claim law in the 1850s most were shysters."[22] One of the honest ones, Henry W. Halleck, realized that the politicians colluded with the land commissioners for squatter votes. After José María Sánchez died in 1852, lawyers gradually fleeced his widow of herds, land, and $70,000 of gold dust over thirteen years.[23] Delos Ashley, the lawyer whom the city of Monterrey employed to defend its lands, overcharged his client and took the land for himself in lieu of payment.[24] Don Julio Verdugo took a mortgage in an attempt to hold on to his estate in 1861. By 1871 the family had 200 acres left out of more than 50,000. The ranchero Peralta family fell into the hands of double-dealing lawyer Horace Carpentier, who swindled them out of $3 million of real estate by substituting a mortgage for a lease.[25] Vicente Peralta, the head of the family, went mad, and the dynasty dwindled into poverty.

The saga of the Berreysa family of San José was even more harrowing. After most of one generation of the family had been wiped out— captured and arbitrarily shot by invading forces during the Mexican War—James Jakes swindled them by persuading them to squat on their own land and seizing the vacated claim.[26] Nemasio Berreysa was lynched on a false charge of a murder in a dispute over the family's mercury mine, seized by Anglos using forged grants. Lawyers absconded with the documents in the case. Two of his brothers were victims of further lynchings, probably instigated by the purloiners of the mine. Others went mad. In 1876 surviving family members threw themselves on the charity of the San José town government. In Texas, even Stephen Powers of Brownsville, who had a reputation for fairness, managed to acquire scores of thousands of acres of formerly Mexican land, including that of some of his clients, for himself. He did so while helping to build up the holdings of other clients, including Richard King and Mifflin Kennedy, founders of the most notorious rancher empires to be built up from expropriated lands. Powers, it was said, was so eloquent that he could persuade landholders "that they had never really owned their land."[27]

Californio landowners lost even more to squatters than to shysters. Some of them had ranchlands so vast that it was impossible to guard them against interlopers: in California at the time of the US takeover, two hundred families owned nearly 14 million acres. Farming settlers hated "Spanish cows"—the alien-seeming cattle that took up disproportionate space.[28] Typically, they proposed humiliating settlements to the owners of land they seized, offering a farmer's share to the incumbent families, who were invariably ranchers used to working vast ranges. If the offer was refused, they squatted across access to wood and water and killed ranchero family members who crossed their pickets. According to their victims, they "burned crops, shot stray cattle, chased off *vaqueros*, tore down or occupied outlying buildings, blocked off gates," and fenced off routes.[29] Squatters on the Peralta estate "blocked off the very doorways" of the house. Salvador Vallejo won his case against squatters before the Land Commission, but by that time the settlers had already taken all but an eight-mile strip of his claim. They moved onto what remained under cover of an appeal and drove him off by burning his crops. In 1851 Colonel John Bartlett, a disinterested member of the Boundary Commission, reproved squatters' "shameful and brutal conduct. . . . It is no uncommon thing for a party of these men to encamp and turn their animals into a field of corn, on which the helpless ranchero and his family are probably depending for their chief support. They will enter a house, pistol in hand, demanding whatever it affords; frequently they help themselves, without the ceremony of paying . . . and commit other outrages which make one who has any national pride blush to hear recited."[30] By 1853 there were squatters in every ranch within a day's march of San Francisco Bay.[31] The long-term impoverishment of

Californios and Mexicans was glaring. In 1850, 61 percent of them owned land worth more than $100. By 1860 the figure had fallen to 29 percent, and it continued to fall.[32]

THE CALIFORNIA GOLD RUSH exacerbated hatreds even as it turned the state, as the US president's special agent observed, "as if by magic" into "one of great wealth and power."[33] Gold fever started when sawmill workers in the Sacramento valley found gold in their stream early in 1848. By August of that year prospectors were picking gold in lumps out of rivers and open holes in the rocks "as fast as you can pick the kernels out of a lot of well cracked shellbarks."[34] The hordes of migrants who came looking for gold in 1849—reputedly 100,000 of them entering a state with a total population of less than a third of that number—did not always recognize the people they encountered on the road as belonging to the same moral community as themselves.[35] In June at Cieneguilla, south of Altar, Arizona, thirty raiders tortured the priest to death and robbed and raped their way through the town on their way to the gold fields. A month later, a party of Texans at Santa Cruz terrorized the inhabitants and refused to comply with the law that obliged them to return retrieved cattle for the lawful premium. They responded to admonitions by throwing the entrails of one of the beasts at the alcalde and holding him at knifepoint.

Eighteen-forty-niners came from Mexico, too, in large numbers and from farther afield in Hispanic America, especially Peru and Chile. By 1850 newly arrived Mexicans probably outnumbered the 15,000 remaining Californios.[36] Antonio Coronel, an effective mediator between Anglos and Californios, who became mayor of Los Angeles a few years later, thought that "the reason for most of the antipathy against the Spanish race was that the greater portion was composed of Sonorans who were men accustomed to prospecting and who consequently achieved quicker, richer results—such as the *californios* had already attained by having arrived first and acquiring understanding of this same art."[37] The gold fields became "a sort of Siberian work camp" colonized by emptying the jails of Sinaloa and Sonora.

Thomas Butler King, the US president's personal agent in California, complained that Mexican miners took gold dust worth $20 million out of the country, and that it belonged to the United States by purchase. Technically, it was true that his government had paid $15 million for territory seized from Mexico, but that did not deprive miners of their right to the fruits of their labor. "If not excluded by law," King continued, "they will return and recommence the work of plunder."[38]

As soon as California joined the Union in 1850, the legislature demanded the exclusion of miners of foreign birth, even if they were naturalized US citizens.[39] From May 1850, a series of Foreign Miners' Tax laws imposed punitive levies "with the aim," the Sonoran press claimed, "of depriving foreigners of the discoveries they have made, so that those in power can take advantage of the situation." Gringos invaded the claims even of those who paid the tax. They tore up permits.[40] An army lieutenant on the Colorado River had orders "to make all the Sonorans passing out of California with gold pay a duty . . . and for my trouble to put the whole of it in my pocket." Thomas Jefferson Green, the proposer of the tax laws, who also proposed further campaigns for the total conquest of Mexico, vowed that he "could maintain a better stomach at the killing of a Mexican" than at the crushing of a louse. The levies drove most miners away; intimidation and violence expelled others. The exodus harmed the economy by leeching demand that gringo entrepreneurs could exploit. According to General Riley, who commanded US forces in the gold field, "Americans by their superior intelligence and shrewdness in business generally contrived to turn to their own benefit the earnings of Mexicans, Chileans and Peruvians." Tradesmen, in their own interests, called for the laws to be repealed.[41]

Californios, meanwhile, seemed doomed to extinction. They got no credit for not being Mexican. Francisco Ramírez's Los Angeles newspaper, *El clamor público*, voiced their resentments in the 1850s. Responding to an assemblyman who accused him of treason, Ramírez explained that he was describing the sufferings of Californios "who see their fathers and brothers tortured in the presence of innocent children" by extortionists and robbers. He favored Americanization

as Californios' best means of defense of "our own, our native land."[42]
From 1856, he even campaigned for Republican presidential candidate J. C. Frémont, who had led US troops into California during the
Mexican War and had ordered many arbitrary shootings and judicial murders.[43] Don Pablo de la Guerra professed himself an adoptive Yankee, albeit a deficient and unwilling one because he preferred
Spanish, "the language of God, which I understand tolerably as I
intend to become a saint one of these days and to speak with him."
He derided English: "the idiom of birds, I do not know . . . as I have
neither beak nor wings, things . . . I believe inherent to every Yankee."
His colleague, Andrés Pico, was one of only two Californios who persevered in the state legislature after 1852, when Antonio María de
la Guerra—scion of one of the sometime-richest, longest-established
Californio dynasties—abandoned politics because of the expense of
the office and the intractability of the task.[44]

The cultural life of the Californios withered. From 1850, Sunday
observance laws multiplied, filleting Catholic gaiety out of the Lord's
Day. The last Holy Week festival in Santa Barbara took place in 1854.
In Los Angeles, the last Spanish-style horse race—formerly the pride
of the Californio elite—was in 1858. In 1861 bullfighting was outlawed and the fandango subjected to licensing and fees. In 1855, when
the Know-Nothing Party, whose platform was the repression of
Catholicism, captured the state governorship and many other major
offices, the legislature refused to have documents translated into Spanish and threatened to impose a temperance law.[45] Between 1862 and
1864, floods and bovine plagues almost finished off the last Californio
ranchers. Vicente Lugo lost his entire herd of 48,000 head of cattle.
Once, practically all ranches worth over $10,000 were in Californio
hands. By 1870 the old inhabitants held barely one quarter of them.[46]

IN THE REMOTER REGIONS of Arizona and New Mexico, expropriation was slower but equally thorough. In Arizona speculators moved
in to buy up cheaply the rights of harassed residents who fled leaving
vacant lots, many of which appeared as the property of newcomers

from the United States on real estate registers that Anglo lawyers and bureaucrats compiled without reference to the rights of previous occupants. Tubac—formerly a modestly surviving town on the Santa Cruz River—was completely deserted when gringos occupied it in September 1856. When the Court of Private Land Claims finally settled the ensuing disputes in the early twentieth century, only eight preconquest grants were upheld, all of them by then transferred to Anglo hands.[47] Phocion R. Way, the early railway travelogue writer, who arrived in Arizona from Cincinnati in 1858, observed of Tucson that "there are about 40 Americans residing here who monopolize all business and rule the place. The Mexicans fear them, acknowledge them as a superior race, and submit without a murmur."[48] Within a few years, most of the businesses in the area were in Anglo hands, with the former Mexican businessmen reduced, typically, to the status of peddlers or artisans. Phelps Dodge, the notoriously predatory mining company that had aggressively acquired a lot of Arizona copper, drove out a group of Mexican families by engrossing the water on which their farms depended. By the 1880s all the big ranchers in Arizona were Anglos. Over 80 percent of land grants in New Mexico went to Anglos.[49] From 1866, the law firm of Murphy and Co. in Santa Fe organized a massive despoliation of hispano farmers, forging deeds, and selling land they did not own. In 1870 Fred Walsen—known as *el Fred* to the locals—opened a store in Los Leones, Colorado, and transformed the plaza into an Anglo-American town, complete with a local chapter of the Elks. He ran it from "his new house of proper American brick with bay window, scrollwork porch, and picket fence." He found the Hispanic population "always opposed to any change that bears the appearance of improvement." The plaza's name changed to Walsenburg.[50]

IN THE RELATIVELY FEW densely populated spots, Hispanic culture was surprisingly resilient in the face of legal, perilegal, and downright illegal onslaughts. It was hard for parts of Texas, for instance, to become Anglo country. Even in Corpus Christi, a settlement founded after the gringo conquest, the prevailing culture was hispanophone and Catholic, as Maria von Blücher found out. She was one of the socially eminent but financially indigent immigrants the place attracted from Europe in the immediate aftermath of the Mexican War. Spanish was the only language her children learned to speak well in infancy. She could not find a Protestant minister to baptize them until 1870. In 1855 she recorded an incident that demonstrated the culture of the city—the wedding of Don Álvaro Pérez's fifteen-year-old daughter. *Le tout* Corpus Christi was there, with Maria and her husband in the roles of *madrina* and *padrino*. By custom, thenceforth they addressed the couple's parents as *compadre* and *comadre*, and the couple as *ahijado* and *ahijada*.[51]

Still, in most places US immigrants were too numerous and too hostile to be absorbed peacefully, and the huge disparity in numbers that opened between natives and newcomers doomed the prospects of armed resistance to the US takeovers of property and subversion of culture. But resistance was continuous at the guerrilla level—small warfare or the social banditry of outlaws that swim like fish in the sea of popular support.[52] Eusebio Chacón, the New Mexican writer who abjured the language and even the influence of English literature in the 1890s, created a social bandit–hero in one of the first novels of magical realism, *El hijo de la tempestad*. The hero commits vicious crimes, but behaves chivalrously towards a female captive and claims plausibly to be the enemy of wicked politicians who corrupted the country. There is much debate over who, if anyone, was the prototype of Zorro, the fictional masked freedom fighter invented in 1919 by the pulp novelist Johnston McCulley. The original Zorro, protagonist of a short story, *The Curse of Capistrano*, operated as a Hispanic Robin Hood in Mexican California, but he was so popular that his creator and many imitators reinvented him over and over again, gradually transforming him into a unique hero, at once a foe of the United States and an all-American hero who battled bad gringos in defense of poor Californios. His image spawned Anglo imitators, the Lone Ranger and Batman, who shared his profile: a noble individual, a refugee from his own world of social privilege and exploitative wealth, masked both as a gesture of sympathy with the faceless masses and as a device to preserve his anonymity. A similar transformation from outlaw to hero befell O. Henry's character the Cisco Kid, who began life in 1907 as a ruthless Tex-Mex desperado in a short story. By the time he was a radio series protagonist in the 1940s, he was still an outlaw, but now an admirable *caballero* fighting injustice. The marks of Zorro—liminality, disguise, invincibility, loneliness, self-effacement except when in costume—distinguish just about every American hero, though Clark Kent had to remove his spectacles rather than don his mask in order to act in character. It is delightfully ironic that this all-American tradition may have started with a hero of anti-US resistance.

Zorro's most commonly asserted prototype was Joaquín Murrieta, whose very existence some scholars doubt, but "the point," as one of them says, "is not whether he existed but the fact that Anglos and californios alike thought he did."[53] Murrieta took to banditry in 1851, after dismissal as a "foreigner" from jobs as a worker in gringo-run mines and farms. His career as an outlaw was not entirely discriminating: fellow Mexicans were among his victims, but the annoyance he caused the US authorities endeared him to gringophobes. He died in 1853; the evidence of his existence—his whiskey-pickled head, which earned $1,000 in bounty for the Rangers who killed him—vanished in the San Francisco earthquake of 1906. Legend transformed him hemisphere-wide into a hero of Hispanic resistance to US imperialism, celebrated in folk ballads along the border. The *Corrido de Joaquín Murrieta* uses him as a mouthpiece for resistance rhetoric, political and cultural alike:

> *De México es California*
> *Porque Dios lo quiso*
> *Y en mi sarape cosido*
> *Traigo fe de bautismo.*

> *California is Mexico's own*
> *For that was God's true will.*

My baptismal writ is still
Here, in my poncho sewn.[54]

In the 1960s, the Chicano activist Rodolfo "Corky" Gonzales made Murrieta a vicarious mouthpiece for Hispanic sentiment (see below, p. 295). Pablo Neruda's line, "I call the rage of my countrymen just and I sing of Joaquín Murrieta," elevated him to the status of a hero for the hemisphere.[55] It is to me a delicious irony that a great line of American superheroes, with their lone trajectories, their alienating experiences, the disguises that place them outside society, and the astonishing dexterity with which they stun evildoers, goes back to a prototype who was a legend of anti-US resistance. American superheroes, though sometimes enlisted on the side of "law and order," all operate on the edges of strict legality. In Murrieta's day, crime and resistance shaded into each other. Between 1854 and 1865, 16 to 20 percent of the inmates of San Quentin Penitentiary were Spanish-speakers. The same headgear, the broad sombrero, identified Mexicans as Mexicans and bandits as bandits.

Texas had a professional gendarmerie, the Texas Rangers, to repress resistance. The Rangers adopted the gunslingers' ethos of "shoot to kill" and administered their justice with frank partiality. In 1958 Américo Paredes, the great Texan poet, scholar, and humanitarian, characterized them, with only a little exaggeration, as "Americans, armed and mounted, looking for Mexicans to kill."[56] To counter the Rangers, Texas had its own real-life Zorro, Nepumoceno Cortina. Born in 1824, he spent his infancy under Mexican rule, his adolescence in independent Texas, and barely had time to grow to manhood before the land became part of the United States. So, although all three regimes accused him of disloyalty and lack of "national" feeling, his shifting identity seems to reflect the uncertainties of his times. In some ways, his profile matches the romance of the *bandolero* or the literary image of a Latin Robin Hood.

He loved every underdog, and the defining moment of his drift into outlawry came when he shot a sheriff whom he saw abusing a prisoner. As a scion of one of the dispossessed native families of the

Brownsville area, he haunted the town's café. On a July day in 1859 he intervened in an attempt to stop the Anglo sheriff from giving a savage beating to one of the Cortina family's former employees. After remonstrating unsuccessfully, he shot the sheriff in the arm and whisked away the victim of the assault. Cortina gathered a band of malcontents together, about eighty strong, and returned in September to seize the town and proclaim a rebellion "to chastise the villainy of our enemies . . . who have connived . . . to persecute and rob us without any cause and for no other crime on our part than that of being of Mexican origin."[57] He attracted a formidable number of partisans—reputedly over a thousand within the first three months of his campaigns, but perhaps no more than 150 for most of his active career. He fought off local militia and Texas Rangers, hoisted the Mexican flag over his camp, and for a while held off the US Army, but a heavy defeat at the army's hands at the end of the year forced him into hiding. Admirers and enemies alike, however, suspected that he continued to control the cross-border rustlers' business, or at least to play a major role in it.

Cortina was the hero and villain of that resistance along the Rio Grande, in the vicinity of Brownsville on the US side of the river, and in its Mexican sister town of Matamoros. Historians still contest his role. He took up arms, he said, "to defend the Mexican name." But is he best classified as a revolutionary, a patriot, a guerrilla, a terrorist, a "social bandit," or a bandit pure and simple? He could be capricious in initiating bloodshed and arbitrary in calling it off. Like many of the best pirates and bandits, he was a master of chivalrous gestures. In October 1859, for instance, having seized a supply-laden ship, he entertained the captain at a courteous repast and released him with the assurance that "he had no quarrel with any Americans" beyond the few criminals he claimed to have targeted for punishment. But his mercurial politics gave him a reputation of self-seeking and unreliability among the elites of Washington, Austin, and Mexico City.[58]

Cortina was largely illiterate and relied on professional amanuenses to write his many proclamations. Their elaborate rhetoric, with overblown imagery of honor, freedom, and nobility, obscured his real thinking. His unwavering fidelity, however, was unmistakably to his own phratry of native Texan landowners. His most consistent complaints were against expropriations by "a multitude of lawyers, a secret conclave . . . despoiling the Mexicans of their lands, . . . a perfidious inquisitorial lodge to persecute and rob us without any cause." The language he used suggests that his scribe was anticlerical, but Cortina had no ideology. For him the struggle was personal. He proscribed his own worst enemy, his former partner Adolphus Glavecke, whom he blamed for the loss of some of his cattle. Glavecke had also stripped assets from a ranch he managed as trustee for the estate of one of Cortina's aunts. "Our personal enemies," Cortina declared, "shall not possess our land until they have fattened it with their own gore."[59]

His resentment, however personal, resonated with fellow countrymen, who swarmed to join his band of outlaws, protected him against the authorities, and adopted him as a hero. "The whole Mexican population on both sides of the border are in favor of him," as Rip Ford, a Texas Ranger who stalked him without success, confessed.[60] When Cortina defeated the local militia, it was impossible to find new recruits to oppose him because, as a Mexican captain observed, the locals "would not fight against" him.[61] When he launched his war on gringo usurpers in 1859, his supporters, according to gringo petitioners for help from the federal government, included "persons who have hitherto been regarded as good people."[62] Some of them were prosperous enough to subscribe $6,000 for equipping his forces. But most of the few score who joined him came to him out of peonage, degradation, hunger, and despair.

By the end of 1859 Cortina's profile had hardened. To the editor of the local gringo press, he was an "arch-murderer and robber" whose case against the United States was "balderdash and impudence." To Mexicans generally, meanwhile, he had become, perhaps as much by adoption as ambition, a leader of national or racial resistance. His propaganda still stressed the wickedness of the predators and shysters who had robbed the old landowners and the iniquity of the unpunished crimes gringos were allowed to commit against native *tejanos*, but now he claimed all "Mexican inhabitants of the State of Texas" as his constituency.[63] In Corpus Christi all Mexicans were under suspicion of sympathy with his revolt and had to surrender their weapons.[64] Part of the fear he inspired in the gringos arose from his program or threat of freeing slaves. Sam Houston, newly elected governor of Texas, tried conciliation. He promised laws "executed alike to all citizens of whatever tongue, and none need fear prejudice," an amnesty for Cortina's men, and a hearing of Mexicans' grievances.[65] Cortina, soundly evaluating the overtures, rejected them, withdrew into upland fastnesses to elude increasing pressure from the Rangers, and took to guerrilla warfare, generally escaping the expeditions the Rangers, the US Army, and the Mexican forces sent against him.

Cortina was fortunate to be operating in conditions favorable for peripheral warlords, as conflict between conservatives and liberals in Mexico and federalists and secessionists in the United States gave him opportunities to play off the opposing sides. He emerged with the outbreak of the American Civil War, but his attack on the town of Zapata failed and he reverted to cross-border banditry, mainly rustling for his own profit, which he continued with some success and much braggadocio. By 1863 he had carved a niche for himself in the midst of a five-sided struggle, between the Confederacy and the Union on the north bank of the river and, on the south, between the supporters of Benito Juárez and Emperor Maximilian for supremacy in Mexico. Cortina played a dangerous game, consistent only in opposing the Confederacy. He tacked between nominal support for Juárez and for Maximilian, gradually accumulating honors, military rank, and money from both. His assurances of loyalty to the Union were equally insincere: easy to make while the power of the federal government was at bay. He was lucky, when the civil wars ended on both banks of the Rio Grande, to be on the winning sides. He was too deeply implicated in Mexican politics to stake his future by returning to social banditry in Texas.

He was touted as a potential governor, a former poacher (that is, suitable to be a gamekeeper), with a special talent to turn against outlaws. For a while he prospered as a Mexican frontier garrison commander with the rank of general, continuing his campaign of vengeance against the gringos' outrages by raiding and rustling vast numbers of their cattle. After relinquishing his command, he continued in the same vein as mayor of Matamoros. Charged with his crimes, he defended himself with convincing counteraccusations of "a vast deposit of animals stolen from Mexico," burnings, murders, and other "acts against defenseless Mexicans." Cortina revived the old charge of "inestimable loss of lands sustained by Mexican families . . . after the Treaty of Guadalupe, . . . among whom my own family is included."[66] Eventually, diplomatic pressure from the United States made successive Mexican governments try to curtail his activities, and Porfirio Díaz recalled him to Mexico City and disciplined him with a brief bout of imprisonment in 1875. Cortina continued to direct his rustling operations from afar. They ended only when old age and infirmity compelled him to embrace a retirement the authorities had never been able to enforce.

Uncharacteristically large-scale resistance broke out anew in the El Paso region in 1877 in defense of traditional, communal rights of access to the local salt pans, which an eighteenth-century grant of the Spanish monarchy had guaranteed to local inhabitants. When a gringo entrepreneur staked a claim to the salt, local juntas mobilized the population over a radius of some hundred miles. Mustering a force of about 500 men, they captured the claimant, forced a renunciation from him at gunpoint, excluded officers of the state and federal governments from their communities, and drove off an attempt by Texas Rangers to suppress the rebellion in the town of San Elizario.[67]

Violent resistance, however, could never score more than local and temporary victories against the might of the state and the vast resources the United States could draw on. The only long-term hopes for the defense of Hispanic rights lay in political action, which became an increasingly credible option as the Hispanic population increased. Vigilantes in New Mexico in 1888–92 demonstrated this fact. The Gorras Blancas, as they called themselves, dressed in white capes and masks, the garb of Catholic penitents, to cut the barbed-wire fences that marked where ranchers and railway companies had seized natives' land. Like other social bandits, they relied on the support of the population to protect them from official harassment and castigation. Their campaigns never included violence, save against property. They eventually transformed into a political party, Pueblo Unido, which won seats in the Territorial Legislature and, in 1890, in Congress.[68]

SURPRISINGLY, IN SOME WAYS, despite the flow of refugees out of former Mexican territory, the making of the United States by northward migration from Mexico continued and increased. It was as if, having resisted the attractions of the far interior while it was still part of their country, Mexicans suddenly discovered them after the land was lost. Partly, no doubt, this was because of the increasing buoyancy of Mexico's own population, which generated surplus manpower for export, and partly because the inflow of gringo migrants to New Mexico, Arizona, and Colorado—to say nothing of the frontiers of Utah, Nevada, and Oregon, where no settlers penetrated under Spanish or Mexican rule—created a critical mass of population and a critical pace of activity. In California the 1849 gold rush was paramount among the influences that drew Mexican immigrants. In Colorado the Pike's Peak gold rush of 1858 played a similar role.[69]

By then, the upper Rio Grande was already attracting large numbers of would-be farmers, mostly from the United States. The population of not more than 20,000 at the beginning of the nineteenth century rose to about 60,000 by 1850. In the following decade settlements speckled the San Luis Valley and the fringes of the Sangre de Cristo and Manzano ranges.[70] The first productive gold mine in the Rocky Mountains seems to have been worked by Mexican prospectors in 1857. The discovery drew scores of thousands of migrants towards Pike's Peak over the next three or four years. Perhaps as many as 40,000 people flowed and ebbed, while, "seeing no gold lying on the ground," as the *Missouri Republican* satirically observed in May 1859, "they succumbed to humbug" and moved on to even more improbable utopias or back to former lives of frustration and retrospection. But gold was available, and before it was exhausted, it justified itself. It built Denver. Speculative cities pullulated. William Byers, one of Denver's outstanding pioneers, imported a printing press for his publishing venture, the *Rocky Mountain News*, "because," he explained, "we wished to collect and send forth reliable information, because we wished to help mould and organize the new population, and because we thought it would pay."[71]

Residents created the institutions of government on their own initiative: they founded claims clubs, people's courts, and, in 1860, the "Provisional Government of Denver, Auraria and Highland City." They could not, however, assert authority over or tax independent mining communities, which elected their own magistrates. Until 1861, when the Civil War spurred the US Congress into organizing government for Colorado, Nevada, and Dakota, this sort of political home cooking produced the recipes for all the institutions of the territory. In October 1860 Mount Vernon District, west of Denver, declared itself subject only to the federal government and wrote its own constitution. South Platte District, today part of the Pike and San Isabel National Park, elected its own representative to Congress. The United Mining District at the headwaters of the Arkansas River elected a legislative committee. Intense migration went on meanwhile. Five thousand immigrants arrived in Colorado in 1860, when "a single train . . . extended from the mountains to the Missouri"; gold production that year was worth over $3 million.[72]

Many of the migrants were part of the continuing northward drift of frontier folk from Mexico via New Mexico. From 1863 William Gilpin, the first US governor of Colorado, began driving off those who had settled to farm and ranch along the Culebra and Costilla rivers in the northwest of the territory: he had acquired cheaply a specious claim to the land. But hispanos kept coming. By 1870, 90 percent of the 6,400 residents of Las Animas and Huerfano counties were Spanish-speakers who built settlements they called *plazas* and *corrilleras*—dwellings huddled for help and protection. The accompanying tensions were apparent in an incident in Trinidad, the main town of Las Animas, on Christmas Day 1867, when some gringos tried to spring an imprisoned fellow countryman who had shot a hispano resident: Sheriff Gutiérrez had to protect them from a lynch mob until US troops arrived to impose peace on the violently divided community.[73] Penetration of the region by railways in the 1870s exacerbated the disadvantages of the hispano minority, whom the *Missouri Examiner* characterized as "ignorant and debased to a shameful degree."[74] Susan B. Anthony, the crusading suffragette, visited Colorado in 1877, prepared to make an exception of the state on the grounds that "Mexican greasers" were incorrigible. "Have you converted all those Mexicans?" she asked later suffrage campaigners in the state.[75]

At least until the railroad arrived, Colorado was still a precarious experiment, as liable to bust as to boom. In the first half of the 1860s gold production plummeted to $1.7 million while population fell from 34,277 in 1860 to 27,931 in 1866. Drought took its toll in 1863, followed by floods the following year. In 1866 a visitor to Gilpin County recorded "a period of doubt," signaled by "deserted mills, idle wheels, empty shafts." The abandoned shafts in Central City and Blackhawk were "thick as prairie-dog holes"[76]; Denver almost collapsed in the same period, losing a third of its people and becoming, according to a Union Pacific Railroad official, "too dead to bury,"[77] though it recovered over the following few years.

Cheyenne and Arapaho raids contributed to the instability in Colorado. The indios had suffered to breaking point from white immigrants' diseases and depredations. George Bent, William Bent's half-Cheyenne son, revisited his mother's people in 1863 as a refugee from the Civil War. "As I rode past each village," he reported, "I saw war dances going on in each one, and every lodge was full of plunder taken from captured freight wagons and emigrant trains."[78] In 1864 the *Rocky Mountain News* called for a "few months of active extermination of the Red Devils." The hour produced the man. The Methodist preacher and ex-Union colonel John Chivington, who had been instrumental in turning Confederate invaders out of Colorado, advised that "to kill them . . . is the only way" to deal with the Natives. In 1864 he led militia in the massacre of a large band of Cheyenne and Arapaho under collaborative chiefs who had already submitted to the US Army. It was a deliberate provocation, designed to unleash a war of extermination. In 1867 most surviving Cheyenne were forcibly removed to Oklahoma. Denver citizens confronted a party of senators who had come to investigate reports of massacres and atrocities, with screams of "exterminate them!"[79] The following year the Utes surrendered most of their territory, which previous enforced treaties had already depleted.

With the elimination of the indio threat, improved smelting technology made recovery of production levels possible in the mines. During the 1870s mineral output in the territory increased sixfold, to over $23 million. Silver was discovered: production began in 1877 at Leadville, which had 31 restaurants, 35 brothels, 115 gambling houses, and 120 saloons within about a year.[80] Many of Leadville's miners came from Mexico, but the town also had quarters for Irish, Germans, Cornish, and blacks, reflecting the shift in the balance of the population as a result of improved communications with the rest of the United States and with the ever-less-distant transatlantic highways of migration.[81] The coming of railroads in the 1870s provided a further boost to the economy—cutting freight costs and stimulating a huge increase in demand for cattle to feed the workers—as well as in population, which rose from under 40,000 to nearly 200,000 in the course of the decade. William Jackson Palmer, the railway entrepreneur, founded Colorado Springs in 1871. This "little London," as journalists called it, was the antithesis of a Hispanic town: in conformity with the founder's Quaker principles, residents had to be teetotal. Franklin Hall, the first chief justice of Colorado's Supreme Court, published illustrated brochures for Europeans and gringos "to be favorably impressed with the country and induced to emigrate hither, bringing capital, science, labor, and all the elements that are essential in building up a new state."[82] William Gilpin sold Colorado as the "amphitheatre of the world," where settlement would enable the United States "to stir the sleep of a hundred centuries—to teach old nations a new civilization, . . . to unite the world in one social family."[83] Not for the last time, high-minded American rhetoric masked an exploiter's selfish designs.

TWO OTHER GROUPS, APART from Hispanics, suffered as a result of the severance of the northern territories from Mexico: black slaves in

Texas, whose prospects of emancipation vanished when the province became an independent republic; and those indios everywhere who had come to a formal accommodation or at least a modus vivendi with Spain or Mexico. Between secession from Mexico and absorption in the United States, Texas quintupled its numbers of slaves to about 40,000. The 1860 census showed that they numbered 182,000 out of a total population of somewhat over 600,000. (By then, Mexicans, both those who survived from before independence and those who had arrived later, numbered 12,000.)[84] Neither intermarriage nor any length of service could secure liberty under the laws of Texas—on the contrary, everyone tainted with black blood was condemned to perpetual bondage. The only escape was across the Mexican border. Four years before the census, slave conspirators in Colorado and Matagorda counties planned flight to Mexico and liberty. Whites depended on them and despised them in equal measure. The slaves' value was assessed at over $106 million in Texas—more than the combined value of all cultivated land. There were two factories in the state, making hats and other garments, both manned by slaves. Even after the Civil War, the effects of emancipation were limited. In symbolic rejection of black freedom, the constitution of Texas omitted the federal amendment freeing slaves. Blacks could still not testify against a white person in court. They had no right to vote: the franchise had to be forced on Texas by federal bayonets and was eroded and nullified by local ordinances and practices over which the federal courts were powerless to act even had they so wished. Blacks passed from slavery to peonage, with no means of acquiring land except as dependent sharecroppers in a new form of plantation economy.

For indios, the arrival of the United States on their borders or in their midst was always an unmitigated disaster. Under Mexican rule, they suffered depletion from disease, subordination in missions, reduction to debt peonage, and informal enslavement and maltreatment, but at least they had equal rights under the law, the possibility of redress, and immunity from chattelage. Texan and Californian independence and adhesion to the United States left them at the mercy of white predators. In California, where the indigenous population perhaps amounted to 150,000 when the United States took over, the Indian "Protection" Act of 1850 in effect transferred the initiative over native people's fate from their own hands to those of any Anglo settler with an interest in dispossessing or enslaving them. The act banned indios from testifying against whites. Article 2 authorized any white rival for indio land to apply to have part of it sequestered for his or her own use. Article 3 gave whites the right to enslave indio minors with their parents' consent. Article 14 gave any white person the right to acquire compulsory labor service from a convicted indio on payment of the fine due. Article 20 authorized any white citizen to denounce an indio for vagrancy or immorality, making the latter liable to hire "within twenty-four hours to the highest bidder . . . for any term not exceeding four months."[85] In 1851 Governor Peter H. Burnett told the Senate: "that a war of extermination will continue to be waged between the two races until the Indian race becomes extinct, must be expected; while we cannot anticipate this result with but painful regret, the inevitable destiny of the race is beyond the power and wisdom of man to avert."[86] David Phillips, who traveled the railroads in search of a good climate for his ailing son in 1876, denounced the rapacity of the owners and the moral indifference of the shareholders, but could spare no sentiment on Natives' behalf: "The Indians," he wrote, "are simply doomed, by their laziness and vices, to early extinction. . . . Why, then, make such an outcry about ejecting a lot of worthless Indians?"[87] By the end of the nineteenth century only about 25,000 Native Americans survived in the state.

In Texas there were about 80,000 indios, according to the best available estimates, at independence. Mexican laws reserved for them about a third of the territory of the province.[88] Most Anglos, however, had no use for them and continued the policies of extermination that had already depleted the native peoples of the United States.[89] The second president, Mirabeau Bonaparte Lamar, overturned Houston's policy of peaceful accommodation and declared war "without mitigation or compassion, until they shall be made to feel that flight from our borders without hope of return, is preferable to the scourges of war."[90]

Events unfolded according to these principles. In Texas, in 1839, the lands formerly allotted to the Cherokees were expropriated and the promised payment indefinitely deferred. Most other native peoples were too numerous, too well established, and too well organized for war to be easily defeated. The strategy of Texan and US governments therefore swung erratically over the next century between actively hounding the Natives on the one hand and on the other encouraging them indirectly towards extinction. No other future was imaginable according to popular late nineteenth-century social Darwinism, which antedated Darwin—as Burnett's and Phillips's prophecies of indio extinction show—but drew scientific support from perverse misreading of the theory of evolution. Inferior races were doomed to succumb in competition with their betters: to exterminate them was to waste time and effort on a project attainable merely by neglect. The predictions of social Darwinism seemed to be fulfilled: disease and hunger enfeebled and depleted the indios, while the sheer weight of settler numbers overwhelmed them. Under the presidency of Mirabeau Lamar, the indio frontier made little progress, though, at the tremendous cost of $2.5 million, which almost bankrupted the state, the central part of the state became more secure for white settlement, and Austin—the designated capital of the republic where no one wanted to settle for fear of hostiles—became a viable settlement. But west of the ninety-eighth meridian the plains remained Indian country, dominated by Apache and Comanche and guarded by lonely forts where the tough, insecure conditions of life induced neuroses and fretfulness.

On this frontier buffalo hunters were the vanguard of conquest. A treaty of 1867 guaranteed the immunity of the indios' herds, but the army commanders treated the hunters with benign inertia. In 1859 public subscription funded a scalp-bounty scheme that rewarded slayers of indios, or anyone with convincingly black hair, irrespective of the victims' deserts. General William T. Sherman, the deviser of the scorched-earth policy that had helped wreck the Confederacy, advocated the hunters' policy of "destroying the Indians' commissary. . . . Let them kill, skin, and sell until the buffaloes are exterminated."[91] In the long run, the destruction of the buffalo herds proved fatal to the peoples that depended on them. Of perhaps 60 million head in the plains in the early nineteenth century, fewer than a thousand remained when the last independent Cheyenne, Comanche, and Kiowa surrendered in 1875. By the same date, in Texas, Natives had dwindled accordingly. Out of a total population nearing 2 million, perhaps a couple of thousand indios survived.[92]

Reservations were no havens. In 1858 John Robert Baylor, a disgraced former Indian agent, carried to new extremes his campaign for the expulsion of all Native Americans from Texas, leading parties of killers onto the reservation on the Brazos River. The Texas Rangers refused the court's order to arrest the culprits, and Baylor threatened to massacre the entire population of the reservation. The authorities' solution, as so often, was to force the indios off the reservation and expel them to Oklahoma, while the local agent who had tried and failed to protect them likened their journey across the Red River to "the Bible, where the children of Israel crossed the Red Sea."[93] Treaties of surrender allocated 3 million acres to the vanquished of 1875, but once the indios were disarmed, most of their land was opened to settlers and distributed in grants.

In California, where the ecology that sustained Native Americans was less vulnerable than in Texas, more active measures of genocide were necessary. With some indios, the Spanish empire had, as we have seen, a long history of collaboration, rooted in the stranger-effect and in the mutual rivalries of indigenous peoples. Even on the eve or in the throes of secession or seizure of what became the southwestern United States from Mexico, the habit of working with some native peoples against others remained part of Hispanic politics. In Southern California in 1846, for instance, Coahuillas combined with Californios against the Luiseño Indians in a violent territorial dispute. There was more to the alliance, however, than the routine prosecution of ancient hatreds: the Luiseños befriended settlers and invaders from the United States, rather as some indigenous communities had welcomed the Spaniards in the previous century in the hope of securing help against native rivals. The collaboration of Californios and Coahuillas was part of a bigger story of resistance against the gringos,[94] who avenged indio depredations a hundredfold. The Hayfork massacre on the Trinity River in 1852 followed the death of one white man. The avengers slaughtered 150 Indians from the murderers' community. The three survivors, a woman and two children, were enslaved.[95] In California in 1852 an Indian agent, O. M. Wozencraft, tried to arrest whites who murdered at least thirty Indians on a reservation, but the district attorney refused to prosecute, and the leader of the gang was elected county judge.[96] In 1862 William F. Dole, California's Commissioner for Indian Affairs, observed that "there is no place where the Indian can experience that feeling of security which is the effect of just and wholesome laws, or where he can plant with any assurance that he shall reap the fruits of his labor."[97]

The secularization of the missions exacerbated the problem of how to accommodate indios in a burgeoning colonial society. The detritus of the missions challenged the social order. Some friars never had much confidence in their congregations' ability to live constructive lives beyond the reach of clerical tutors. When indios "get their heads full of liberty," wrote a friar of Santa Barbara to Governor Pío Pico just before the Mexican War, "there is no human power that can repress their scandalous conduct, which consists of drunkenness and the stealing of women and cattle."[98] The secularizations were ruinous. In 1842 Sir George Simpson, the future governor of Hudson's Bay territory in Canada, who was traveling the world apparently with no better purpose than to accumulate records of distances traversed, saw indios at General M. G. Vallejo's ranch near Sonoma, "about 300 in number, who were the most miserable of the race that I ever saw, excepting always the slaves of the savages of the northwest coast. . . . They are badly clothed, badly lodged, and badly fed, . . . they vegetate rather than live. . . . This picture which is a correct likeness not only of General Vallejo's Indians, but of all the civilized aborigines of California, is the only remaining monument of the zeal of the Church and the munificence of the State."[99]

Simpson, when responsible for buying hides, beef, and corn for Hudson's Bay, had been a realistic admirer of the missions, not because they were humane but because they were productive, and he deplored the decline of population and productivity that followed seculariza-tion. His opinion was confirmed by disinterested accounts. George C. Yount, a Napa Valley pioneer, concurred in lamenting the effects he observed in the year before the Gold Rush:

> It is not eight years since the above named valley swarmed with not less than eight thousand human beings, of whom there are now left as many hundreds. They have been hunted down by the murderous white man. . . . Diseases of the filthiest and most fatal kind have been contracted and disseminated from the same source, the same intruders have usurped the land, scat-tered and exterminated their game and fish, corrupted their habits, as well as infected the persons of their females, which has rendered them feeble, torpid and indolent. Hence they murder their offspring at birth, to rid themselves of the care and toil of nursing and raising them to life. If they do not mur-der them the little innocents come into life diseased and are born only to suffer and to die.[100]

Mass was celebrated for the last time in the San Fernando Mission in 1874.[101] Obstinately, some indios survived, after a saga summarized in 1875 by C. A. Wetmore, special commissioner for the former Mis-sion Indians, "forced by superior power to trade their patrimony and their liberty for civilized bubbles blown by the breath of political insincerity; trading by compulsion from bad to worse until they have, as the Mission Indians of California, simply the right to beg. They beg bread of their white neighbors on whose lands they are trespassers; on the roads where they are vagrants; and in the jails which are their only asylums. They have begged in vain for legal rights. Their right to peti-tion Congress has been ignored."[102]

For many indios, enslavement in effect or in law was the only future allowed. James Clyman, the mountain man and pioneer, visited J. A. Sutter's fort in 1846, where, he observed, "the Captain keeps 600 or 800 Indians in a complete state of Slavery" and fed them from troughs "like so many pigs." According to a critic of 1850, a method of getting labor is "to raise a posse and drive in as many of the untamed natives as are requisite, and to compel them to assist in working the land. A pittance of food, boiled wheat or something of the kind, is fed to them in troughs, and this is the only compensation which is allowed for their services."[103] In 1861 G. M. Hanson, superintendent of Indian affairs in Northern California, reported how a slaver justified his activities as "an act of charity . . . to hunt up the children and then provide homes for them, because their parents had been killed, and the children would have perished with hunger. My counsel inquired how he knew their parents had been killed. 'Because, he said, I killed some of them myself.'" In 1865 a newspaper reporter in Mendocino County described indios as "held here as slaves were held in the South; those owning them use them as they please, beat them with clubs, and shoot them down like dogs." He cited the case of James Shores, bound over for $1,000 for shooting an indio "because he would not stand to be whipped . . . but I have my doubts of finding a jury that will convict a man for killing an Indian up here."[104]

Unassimilated Apache were a different problem. Those whom the Spanish authorities failed to lure into farming and docility were viscerally intractable to offers of Christianization and "civilization." On both sides of the US-Mexican border, the authorities tried to control them by savage reprisals or eliminate them by genocide. Paying bounties for Apache scalps was a common but ineffective method, which uncoiled cycles of violence. James Kirker accumulated $100,000 worth in a career that began in 1838.[105] Mexican authorities revoked and restored his contracts as practical needs succeeded moral niceties. Kirker collected scalps indifferently, as long as the hair was black. When the Mexicans lost patience with him, they put a price on his own scalp—$9,000 in 1845, $10,000 in 1846.

In 1849 James S. Calhoun, President Zachary Taylor's personal emissary in New Mexico, revived the old Spanish policy of reducing Apaches to dependence on the government. Some tribes responded in a way that was increasingly typical of resistance to white imperialism all over the world—setting aside internecine hatreds to form alliances against the intruders. Mangas Coloradas, a Chiricahua chief, was the architect of the widest Apache alliance, which never got so far as to threaten white predominance but did create a short-lived Apache state in most of southwest New Mexico and eastern Arizona in the late 1850s and early 1860s. The Civil War, which gave Mangas Coloradas a chance of consolidating his achievement, evoked desperate measures on the part of the indios' enemies. In 1863 Californian militiamen seized the chief under a flag of truce, tortured, and shot him. The debate among the white men was between massacring the indios and enslaving them. The Union chief James H. Carleton and John Robert Baylor, who was by then the self-appointed Confederate governor of Arizona, advocated the former course, and Henry H. Sibley, Baylor's successor, the latter.

Peace between the states brought a reversion to the solution of confining the Apache in reservations. It also generated surplus manpower—desperate, demobilized soldiers and impoverished, emancipated slaves—to enforce the policy. In 1866 the US Army created the all-black 9th and 10th cavalry units, under such white officers as were willing to serve, to drive indios into reservations. With short rations and defective equipment, they also had to try to police an indefensible, porous border. In February 1871, when the Aravaipa Apaches settled at their own request at Fort Grant, Arizona, on the San Pedro River, the pattern of reservation life was established: braves used the secure base to launch raids. Settlers from Tucson with Mexican and Papago allies in tow clubbed over a hundred peaceful Aravaipas to death in retaliation. Reservations neither contained indios nor satiated the bloodlust of those who hated them. The problem of the mutual hostility of Apache tribes endured. If they had to accept confinement, they wanted reservations of their own, and many outbreaks of violent resistance occurred when government agents tried to compel hereditary foes to share quarters. Paradoxically, cross-tribal alliances sometimes ensued between groups the authorities would have been wiser to "divide and rule."

In some thinkers' minds, there was an alternative to extermination, confinement, and enslavement. Considered from one point of view, indios were for the United States just another minority to be assimilated, Americanized, and attuned to the majority culture like the European migrants who increasingly thronged the country, or like the many minorities whom emerging nation-states in Europe subjected to campaigns of indoctrination in national identity and social conformity to turn them into culturally indistinguishable fellow citizens. Richard Henry Pratt, who founded the Carlisle Indian Industrial School in 1879, tried the method with the Apache. He was a humane ex-soldier who served as one of the white officers in a black cavalry regiment, and a believer "in immersing the Indians in our civilization and when we get them under holding them there until they are thoroughly soaked."[106] His program of integration, however, was as destructive of Native American culture as the extermination policies he opposed. In 1886 Pratt began to recruit the children of Chiricahua prisoners for his school, which he ran on military lines. On arrival, the photographer lined them up in their first experience of regimentation. The children in their variously Europeanized dress, with sullen faces and unkempt hair, were living proof of the way white people's ways permeated their lives without quenching their people's tradition of independence. Pratt put the students in uniform, cut their hair, and made them do daily drill. On the whole, the experiment was a failure, as white people appropriated the students for their own purposes and the students stubbornly resisted transformation. Most were obliged to spend their vacations as servants in white households. Most of them had no economic opportunities on graduation and returned to their reservations, making their "education" seem pointless.[107]

By 1880, according to General John Pope, the self-proclaimed exterminator of Native Americans, policies of reservation and assimilation had failed. The Apache, he said, were "a miserable, brutal race, cruel, deceitful and wholly irreclaimable—although for years they have been fed by the government and 'civilized' by their agent they are in no respect different from what they were when the process began."[108] But his own policy of relentless war to the death had been equally unsatisfactory from the point of view of settlers who continued to fear indio guerrilla campaigns. Like the British Army against the Maori, soldiers turned in exaggerated claims of battles won and casualties inflicted, in part, perhaps, out of mendacious self-interest and in part out of genuine bafflement at the Apaches' ability to survive. Exasperated civilian petitioners in Silver City, New Mexico, in June 1880 denounced the army for describing victories "which have never been achieved," and making "reports which are untruthful throughout."[109]

In the same year, Victorio, an undomesticable Chiricahua chief, who had created an alliance among mutually long-alienated tribes and had repeatedly eluded or defeated the US and Mexican armies and militias, launched his last campaign. The Santa Fe *Weekly New Mexican* begged "in the name of peace, in the name of an unprotected people; in the name of the surviving families of those who have paid the forfeit of their lives for attempting to develop the resources of this rich territory; in the name of the thousands who now desire to make New Mexico their homes but are deterred by these fearful tidings, we ask that a sufficient force be sent here to prevent the threatened outbreak, and keep those bloodthirsty demons within their proper bounds."[110]

A combined Mexican and Ranger force killed Victorio in an engagement in October, in mountains south of the Rio Grande. In the final fight between indios and white men in Texas, Rangers trapped the last survivors of his band in January 1881, in the Diablo Mountains, by a pool of water that ended full of blood. The Rangers' captain remarked on "the beauty of the scenery . . . marred . . . by . . . the ghostly forms of the Indians lying around."[111]

Native resistance was now too heavily outnumbered and outgunned to prevail. The ecology that sustained traditional ways of life vanished as the ranchers, farmers, railroads, and cities occupied the indios' former niches. It was the same all over the Americas. In Mexico machine guns dispelled Yaqui resistance. General Roca blasted his way through the Argentine pampa and Patagonia. In Chile the Mapuche, who had resisted every conquistador for nearly half a millennium, succumbed. The last Sioux Ghost Dancers were massacred in 1890. In Southern California in 1902, by ruling of the US Supreme Court, the last Cupeño indios left Warner's Ranch, where they had withstood successive efforts to destroy them. In a last-ditch attempt to get the government to uphold their rights, the Cupeño captain, Cecilio Black-tooth, remarked to the Warner's Ranch Indian Advisory Commission:

You see that graveyard over there? There are our fathers and grandfathers. You see that Eagle Nest Mountain and the Rabbit-Hole Mountain? When God made them he gave us this place. We have always been here. We would rather die here. Our fathers did. We cannot leave them. If Harvey Downs says he owns this place, that is wrong. . . . If you do not buy this place, we will go into the mountains like quail and die there, the old people and the women and children. Let the government be glad and proud. It can kill us. We do not fight. We do what it says. If we cannot live here, we want to go into those mountains and die.[112]

Three years later, in Texas, Geronimo, the legendary Apache guerrilla who had surrendered in 1886, visited the Carlisle School. "You are here to learn the ways of white men," he told the students. "Do it well."[113]

THE EXPROPRIATION OF RESIDENTS of Hispanic ancestry was almost as thorough and ruthless as that of those other natives, whom gringos classed as Indians. As the indio world receded, the Hispanic past ebbed away. Mexican migration northward into formerly Mexican territory never stopped, but the lines of gringo migration crossed it and overlaid it like the thick lines in a plaid. By 1870 over 95 percent of Colorado's foreign-born were from Europe and Canada.[114] In 1876 the Southern Pacific Railway arrived on the western shore of the United States. The fare from Missouri to Southern California dropped from $125 to $100.[115] In 1887 the Santa Fe railway reached Los Angeles. That year 120,000 passengers arrived.[116]

The boom in transpacific trade, meanwhile, brought a new workforce of Chinese coolies to the west coast. There were perhaps 25,000 Chinese in California in the 1850s. The Central Pacific Railroad employed 10,000 of them. From 1868, by agreement with China, 16,000 arrived annually. Many went to factories in San Francisco, where "Little China" had nearly 50,000 residents by 1875. Violence and immigration controls followed. When the British writer Rudyard Kipling visited California in 1889, he could see "how deep down in the earth the pigtail [which all Chinese men had to wear under the Qing dynasty] has taken root."[117]

The demographics of Los Angeles illustrate the hispanos' relative decline, which, in the 1880s, amounted to collapse. The Mexican population was extremely unstable. Only about a quarter of families who lived in Los Angeles before 1848 were still there in the 1850s—about half as many as was typical in the rapidly sprouting western cities of the era.[118] Immigration kept topping up the numbers, but few Mexican migrants stayed long. A tenth left during the 1870s. Between 1866 and 1872, while the Mexican population of the city held steady, the overall numbers more than doubled, to 17,400.[119] In 1880 most rural hamlets of Los Angeles County were still 25 percent Spanish-speaking.[120] More than a fifth of the population still had Spanish surnames. But by 1887 Spanish-speakers, at 12,000 in total, were less than 10 percent of the inhabitants. So denaturalized had they become that the *Los Angeles Times* accused Reginaldo del Valle, leader of the Spanish-speaking community, of un-Americanism not for sympathy with Mexico but for supporting "free trade and other English ideas."[121] The last Hispanic participants in the city's government withdrew, to be replaced by gringos.

Mariano Vallejo, heir of one of the great estates that survived, albeit fragmented, from before the gringo conquest, acknowledged that California prospered under US rule "but," he added, "to the moral detriment of the inhabitants . . . demoralized by daily contact with so many immoral persons . . . and a large part of the blame and responsibility may be rightfully attributed to the national and state government." His brother, Salvador, was more philosophical: "[I]t is useless," he pointed out, "for mankind to protest against the decree of a wise Providence, whose deep mysteries we mortals are not allowed to fathom or interpret."[122]

Despite the horrors and atrocities that accompanied the US take-over from the Gulf of Mexico to the Pacific, despite the expropria-tion of Mexicans, the extermination of indios, the exploitation of slaves, and the repression of dissidence, most settlers from the United States, Europe, and China were normal, decent people who were more concerned to make a good life for themselves than to deprive others of it. Some of them took seriously their self-conferred *mission civilisatrice* on a savage frontier. They sustained, in 1860, seventy-one newspapers with a total circulation of about 100,000.[123] They built on a foundation of determined schooling that dated from Spanish days: probably about a quarter of the settlers of New Mexico before absorption by the United States could read and write and—dependent on their own efforts to create culture—set up many local schools.[124] The gringos added scores more—nominally, in Texas in 1860, forty academies, thirty-seven colleges, twenty-seven institutes, seven universities, and one medical college[125]—though these rarely did more than impart the rudiments of general education and basic professional training. When Texans got around to founding a state university, the legislature decreed that it should be "of the first class" and, eventually, it was.

Even some mining towns, with surprising rapidity, became exem-plary places of civic tranquillity in the 1860s, when, as a judge said in Gregory Gulch (where gold was first discovered in Colorado), "biz in the Police Court is dull."[126] The Hollywood image of gunslingers, cardsharps, and brawls and bawdy fueled by red-eye was accurate, typ-ically, for the early days of mining communities: Charles C. Post, a rich Ohio farmer who passed through Denver disapprovingly in 1859, "saw more gamblers and gambling than ever I saw before, and went to bed wondering what the Anglo-American race were approaching, and concluded that a universal triumph was its destiny."[127] His irony was strangely accurate. Cardsharping and saloon brawling continued but yielded, as foci of life, to the improving activities of a burgeoning bourgeoisie who held ice-cream socials and patronized sermons and visiting lectures. The embourgeoisement of Leadville was spectacular. In 1888 gambling was outlawed and *Harper's Weekly* found the place "as steady going as Salem, or Plymouth Rock," while old hands lamented its transformation into an "infernal Sunday-school town."[128]

With the indios confined and the hispanos repressed, it became possible for nostalgia to rewrite the story of "the Spanish border-lands" with no sense of danger from a past that the tide of history had washed safely from the shore. Helen Hunt Jackson transformed California's image in her bestselling novel, *Ramona*, of 1884 and *Glimpses of California and the Missions* (1883). Her aim was to change her countrymen's prejudices about indios, whom she depicted as victims of their own nobility, which made them deceivable by white men's lies and passive in the face of cruelty. She projected soft-focus, rosily lit images of the old Californio aristocracy, while depicting gringo invaders in stark relief as hard-bitten, rapacious, and insensitive. She idealized the Franciscan missions as havens of mutual understanding between Europeans and indios. In her work, the usual pattern of perceptions was reversed: California inherited civilization from the Spanish past, which barbarian invaders from Anglo-America destroyed. The misfortunes of Jackson's heroine, Ramona, who inherited her lustrous hair from a Native American mother, her bright blue eyes from her Scottish father, and her noble bearing from her adoptive Californio family, wrung the hearts of hundreds of thousands of sentimental readers as Anglo persecutors hounded her, despoiled her, and murdered her husband.

Theodore Roosevelt feared that the novel's impact would undermine Anglo supremacy. Rather, it bolstered it, by converting the realities of frontier conflict into comforting myths. Anglo-America appropriated a sanitized version of the Hispanic past, inventing fiestas and building pastiche Hispanic architecture. Architects from New York and Boston flocked to Florida and the Southwest to cash in on nostalgia by building romantic hotels in a supposedly Spanish style, like the Castañeda Hotel of 1894 in Las Vegas, New Mexico, with its baroque pediments, or the grandiosely turreted Ponce de León Hotel in San Agustín of 1885, or the vaguely Mauresque Alcázar in the same city—both commissioned by the railroad entrepreneur Henry Flagler to give tourists a spurious sense of continuity with Spanish tradition. The Mission Inn in Riverside, California, completed in 1902, even has a chapel and cloister to evoke the ghosts of friars who were never there. Charles Fletcher Lummis, a journalist who challenged the practice of removing indio children from their families for indoctrination in white men's values, founded the Landmarks Club in Los Angeles to restore old mission buildings in 1895 on the grounds that "[w]e shall . . . have the contempt of all thoughtful people if we suffer our noble missions to fall."[129] Railroads that did so much to ensure the triumph of Anglo-America adopted Spanish revivalism for the architecture of their depots, starting with the rippling roofscape of the San Capistrano station of 1894.

In Santa Barbara even the Unitarian Church was built in the Hispanic Revival style. The city was the site of a Spanish mission and garrison from the 1780s, so Hispanic affectations were not out of place. The continuity of the Spanish heritage was guaranteed by the marriage in 1836 of the daughter of the civic patricians, the de la Guerra family, with Alfred Robinson, a Yankee trader who defended the missions and opposed the Mexican War, just before California joined the United States. Robinson, who converted to Catholicism for the occasion, married in a tight Bostonian morning coat with a high, stiff collar, looking to a fellow countryman "as if he had been pinioned and skewered with only his feet and hands left free."[130] He sent his children to Boston for their early schooling. But thanks to his encouraging example, immigrants from the United States were happy to vote de la Guerra family members into office as mayors, judges, and senators, even after California joined the Union. To this day descendants are civic guests at the annual "Old Spanish Days" fiesta when the city celebrates its Spanish roots. The fiesta started in the 1920s, at the height of enthusiasm for the Spanish past, when Johnston McCulley's Zorro fantasies were selling books and movie tickets. In 1923, Charles Lummis urged the Hispanic revival on. "Stand fast, Santa Barbara!" he cried. "Save the centuried romance of old California in this, its last and most romantic stronghold." He founded his case on sense, sentiment, and the interests of "business." He argued that Spanish romance was of "greater economic benefit than oil, oranges, or even the climate."[131]

FOR A REALISTIC CHRONICLE of the making of the Anglo Southwest, the autobiography of Agnes Morley Cleaveland is unsurpassed. She recalled what it was like to be a settler in the wilderness during New Mexico's long, tough integration into the United States. Her father was a construction engineer on the Santa Fe railroad, which pierced Mexican North America like a fatal lance. Speeding the colonists who wrenched the land from native and Mexican hands, the railways ultimately turned the Southwest into a patchy, imperfect simulacrum of Anglo-America.

Ray Morley's job both symbolized and shaped the frontier, as he helped rivet the emerging gringo "nation" from east to west. Building the railway was a crazy, chaotic business. The route first projected for a coast-to-coast line across the southern United States showed how little East Coasters knew of the West: the line, if built as intended, would have run into impossible mountains and through impossible deserts. It would have had to make a detour through Mexican territory to reach its goal. Indeed, the Santa Fe line never reached Santa Fe: the topography of the Rockies forced it through the relatively minor outpost at Lamy, where a branch line took passengers and freight to the capital. Legal squabbles and cutthroat competition delayed the start of work and kept interrupting construction. Even so, when the lines began to be laid from Topeka, a little west of Kansas City, in 1868, surveying—conducted frantically, scramblingly in torturous terrain among terrifying Apache war bands—barely kept ahead of the tracks. Rival companies literally fought one another for control of the narrow gorges that pinched and squeezed the railway as it struggled westwards. Ray Morley worked for each company in turn, swapping contracts like a modern football pro. For the Santa Fe line he led a daring expedition to seize Raton Pass in 1878, keeping rivals out until his rails were laid. "Morley," said the chairman of the company, "builds railroads with one hand, fights Indians with the other, and lives on the bark of trees while doing it."[132]

Agnes Morley was only a little girl then, and she recorded the violence of frontier life with childish romanticism. Her tales of cowboy high jinks and gunslinger chivalry were worthy of an old-time Hollywood western. When her father gave up railroad construction, he became the editor of the local paper in Cimarron County, denouncing the land sharks and rustlers who persecuted poor ranchers. His big foe was Clay Allison, a legendary and in many ways typical gunfighter, whose journey to the margins of the law began with training in arms as a Confederate soldier. Gunfighting was a refuge from the restlessness of demobilization following the defeat of the Confederacy in the Civil War. Clay killed a Union man who tried to seize his ranch in Tennessee and fled first to Texas, then to New Mexico, where he led lynch mobs, terrorized towns, defied law officers, and reveled with impunity in a notorious series of death-dealing duels. In the Morleys' hometown, he allegedly assassinated the crusading local pastor, who wanted to "clean up" local lawlessness. When Morley's paper protested, Allison dumped the printing press in the river. Young Agnes, however, remembered him for his courtliness. When her mother confronted the gunman, wringing her hands at the loss of her husband's livelihood, Allison apologized and paid to replace the press, saying, "I don't fight women."[133] The combination of savagery and chivalry seemed routine to Agnes—or "it may be," she admitted, "that evilly-disposed men were less likely to go unhanged."[134] A "good" woman, she reported, was always safe—which suggests that a besmirched reputation might justify rape or other ill usage. Agnes, at least, had only once to defend her virtue at gunpoint. To the end of her days, throughout a life of impeccable matronly respectability, she remained wistful for the exciting scofflaw environment of her childhood and youth, when high spirits justified fisticuffs and even "gun-fighting and horse-stealing carried with them something of sportsmanship." "Shooting up"—the practice, hallowed in cowboy movies, of firing multiple, random, celebratory shots in the air accompanied by bloodcurdling whoops on the way in and out of town—was an intimidatory tactic disguised as a jovial rite. Agnes loved it and resented the law's efforts to curb it. Her family regularly hid relatively mild outlaws—fugitives from gun controls or other encroachments of the state; she was inspired to protect them because she felt the complicity of free spirits faced with officious threats to an unregulated way of life she and her neighbors were proud to lead. Later, when posses came frequently to her ranch to search for her desperado protégés, she pined for the days when law enforcement was "too far away to be useful."[135]

Agnes could evaluate the civilization—such as it was—of the frontier with some objectivity, since she never fully belonged to it. After her father's death from an accidental gunshot wound, her mother moved to an ever-failing highland ranch 8,300 feet up in Datil Canyon, where Agnes shared space with Apache rustlers and irritable she-grizzlies. Though the family's fortunes steadily deteriorated, there was enough money to school Agnes "back east" in a refined ladies' academy in Philadelphia. The experience was mildly alienating. When she exchanged letters with home, her high-tone received English got ever further removed from the ungrammatical patois of her brother and friends, who never distinguished accusative from nominative pronouns and mangled singular verbs with plural subjects. She cultivated the image of a virago in what (in the title of her memoirs) she called "no place for a lady." Her motive, perhaps, was to rehabilitate herself in her neighbors' eyes after the presumable dilution of her frontier spirit in the enervating east. Inevitably, back in Datil she was cast as the local schoolteacher, teaching children whose parents only "wanted them to read, write and figger," not to acquire her own fancy Philadelphia ways. In what sounds like a comic anticipation of the heroine's account of her family in *Annie Get Your Gun*, a recalcitrant student assured Agnes that "my grandpaw he couldn't spell 'cat' and he lived to be most a hundred." "Doin' what comes naturally" seems apt beyond the boundary of modernized life. "Modern medicine," for instance, was either unavailable or impractical in the land of Agnes's youth, where a Mexican *curandera* could cure gangrene with a poultice of onion and tobacco leaves.[136]

Agnes Cleaveland was the chronicler of the Americanization—or, more properly, what we might call the *estadounidificación*—of New Mexico, and her evidence, because it is neutral, is decisive in demonstrating that the United States was not a "civilizing influence." On the contrary, it brought more lowlifes, scapegraces, and refugees from civilization to the colony than ever before. Agnes reported two aspects of Americanization especially vividly: religion and language. She described two kinds of religion—one collective, one individual, both ecstatic and visionary, both recognizably rooted in the world of pre-Yankee piety of Miguel Quintana. On the one hand was the world of the *penitentes*—the confraternities of lay flagellants, overwhelmingly of Native American ancestry, whom the Spanish friars' example of furious self-mortification inspired to celebrate Holy Week with orgies of scourging. When she watched one of their processions, "My own mount, a cream-colored pony, was soon flecked with blood that spurted from self-lashed human backs as the yucca plant cat o' nine tails tore through raw flesh." The mob, outraged at her curiosity, which seemed to mock their devotion, made her feel threatened. The next night, she hid in the thick-walled adobe church, blanketed with Navajo rugs. Men crammed the sacred space on one side, women on the other. There were almost as many dogs as children. The doors opened to admit the flagellants, injecting a rare breath of fresh air in the fetid atmosphere. "Their once white trousers, brown and stiff with dried blood, their hair matted with it, they staggered as they came, carrying their yucca whips over their shoulders. The door behind them closed, shutting out all air, sanity, and hope." The secrecy and seclusion were part of the ritual because these excesses of asceticism were heterodox. The Church allowed them but remained aloof. No priest took part. A lay elder of the brotherhood, Juan de Dios, led the service. His "voice, hysterical now," Agnes reported,

was lifted in a final prayer for the souls of all the dead, and the last candle went out. The congregation held its breath for one second longer. The blackness and silence were as one. Then came the explosion with all the force of the rending of the heavens after the Crucifixion. . . . It came as a child's shrill terrified scream, swallowed up in an instant chaos of noise that cannot be described. Women's shrieks, the hoarse moaning of men, the howling of dogs. . . . Chains rattled, empty bottles were blown into producing a sound peculiarly weird, empty barrels were beaten, and riding high above it, the thin nerve-tingling wail of the penitente pito or flute, and the harsh clatter of their wooden rattles. But it was the now-and-then distinguishable scream of a child . . . that gave the final touch of horror to the bedlam.[137]

The service lasted an hour.

If the devotion of the *penitentes* represented the religious culture of New Mexico at one extreme, Francis Schlatter, who "came to town" in 1895, occupied the other pole. He was a charismatic delusive who believed, or claimed to believe, that God had ordained him to a healing ministry. He performed few miracles but many prodigies of fasting and traveling through deserts and wintry mountains. He was no mere charlatan. He took no money for healings but felt obliged to flee the "disappointment" provoked by his low tally of miracles. He took shelter with the Morleys, assuring them that "the Father has told me that Datil is the place He has selected for the New Jerusalem." He recovered his healing power, he said, by gymnastic exercise—swinging heavy clubs—but never retrieved the esteem of his former devotees.[138] His following seems to have been strongest among Protestant immigrants who lacked spiritual leadership from their own churches— such as Agnes Morley's susceptible mother. For Protestantism was still relatively new to New Mexico. In the 1870s, in anticipation of the arrival of the railroad, an irrationally persistent Methodist minister, Thomas Harwood, built a series of rather speculative schools and churches across the northern part of the state for worshippers and scholars who had yet to materialize. Before then, there were only a few communities in major settlements. Jean-Baptiste Lamy, whom Uncle Sam imposed in 1850 as head of the Catholic diocese in an attempt to make New Mexico less Spanish, probably did more than the Protestants to change the religious culture of the territory. He was the spiritual scourge of the self-scourgers, whom he tried unsuccessfully to suppress. He built churches that looked French, recalling his native land, rather than Spanish or Mexican. He tore down adobe and replaced it with stone. He tried to break the cosy, corrupt links—especially clerical concubinage—and intense, introspective local cults that impeded priests from demanding puritan morals and universal styles of worship from their congregations. He was a hero of Yankee Catholicism—the kind that Pope Leo XIII later denounced as sinfully "Americanist" for seeking to craft a kind of Catholicism peculiar to the USA, with patriotism replacing piety. Willa Cather based the hero of perhaps her greatest novel, *Death Comes for the Archbishop*, on Lamy. Her "Jean Latour" dressed appropriately "like an American trader." He strove to be "American in word and thought and—yes—in heart, too" and saw his task as helping the army to turn "Mexicans into good Americans."[139] The real bishop was equally zealous but less successful than his fictional counterpart in purging Native American and Hispanic traditions. Meanwhile, settler Protestantism never echoed the bloody, lachrymose excesses of Native Catholicism, but Schlatter's apostolate showed how in its own way it could be just as ostentatiously bizarre and just as deeply shot through with emotionalism and magic.

The balance of religious cultures never shifted decisively in favor of Protestantism. In Agnes Morley's observations, the shift from Spanish to English as a majority language was also slow. In 1888, when one of her neighbors was arraigned for murder after a violent dispute with a tenant, the only man in the courtroom who could not speak Spanish was the Washington-appointed judge. Nine of the jurors spoke only Spanish, which was the main language of communication between natives and settlers. Most anglophone settlers spoke a kind of macaronic among themselves. "Oye, amigo," said a typical citizen in an utterance Agnes transcribed, "how far down este camino before I hit the trail that goes otro lado Arroyo Seco?"

"Tres millas," came the reply, "and you had better quidado because there's been mucha agua coming down Arroyo Seco."

"I doubt," wrote Agnes, "if we said 'tomorrow' once in a hundred times. 'Mañana' is such a satisfying word."[140]

The abiding character of New Mexico as a Catholic, hispanophone land delayed statehood. Congress turned down fifteen applications before the status was finally confirmed in 1912. Historians have manufactured excuses of varying validity: some elites profited from territory status; southern congressmen conspired to exclude New Mexico because of the territory's liberal attitude to black civil rights. The decisive reasons for New Mexico's long exclusion, however, are clear: xenophobia verging on racism and a narrow-minded understanding of what it means to belong to the United States. Relentless demographic change made the difference. During Agnes Morley's lifetime, immigration anglicized the population. There were a little over 90,000 settlers in 1870, nearly 200,000 by 1900. The natives were "swamped"—to use the term now echoed by WASPs apprehensive of Hispanic immigration. Meanwhile, the courts wrenched property bit by bit from Mexican landholders, who lost 80 percent of their holdings between the end of the Mexican War and the coming of statehood. Indigenous tribespeople proved more robust in surviving in New Mexico than in almost any other present state of the union, but until the 1930s their numbers and lands diminished too, ground down by war, massacres, expulsions, forced migrations, deliberate starvation, forcible acculturation, and disease. New Mexico became a state when the balance between Anglos and others tipped. Now the trends that prevailed since the United States seized the region have gone into reverse. Nearly half the people of the state are native speakers of Spanish—outnumbering census contestants who class themselves as English-speaking whites. The state song is bilingual. The numbers of people of indigenous descent have recovered spectacularly.

About 10 percent of the population class themselves as Native Americans and nearly 5 percent speak Navajo at home. The Catholic communion is the largest in the state, comprising over a quarter of the population, but Protestants of all kinds hugely outnumber Catholics. As is common throughout Latin America, radical Protestantism has corroded the Catholic tradition among poor, educationally deprived minorities. The identities hispanophones and navajophones nurture are distinctive but not dissenting. Spanish-speaking groups share, overwhelmingly, two objectives in their public relations output: the first is the relaxation of anti-immigrant hostility in social attitudes, policing practices, and laws. The second is the proclamation of US allegiance, particularized in insistence that the use of Spanish is not an un-American activity. The Navajo nation's official publicity hardly ever refers to the long history of US oppression but highlights the contributions Navajos have made to the country's wars. The proudest and most prominent section currently on the nation's Web site celebrates the Navajo-speaking radio operators who baffled Japanese code breakers during the Second World War and kept key US operations secret.

So New Mexico has a relatively short part in the conventional story of the making of the United States from east to west. The older, longer-lasting story of a country made from south to north, or in gridwork and patches with contributions from all over the hemisphere and the world, has resumed there. It is a model of US pluralism, in which no community's culture is fixed, but peculiar traditions can be upheld without compromising overarching political unity. With well-intentioned effort and expenditure it could be the first genuinely bilingual state, where native English-speakers speak Spanish and native Spanish-speakers speak English, and the macaronic Agnes Morley recorded comes naturally to everyone.

CHAPTER SIX

THE REVENGE OF MORONI

The Triumph of Anglo-America, c. 1830–1898

Every night previous to the one just passed they had encamped in the great forests; but now they looked upon a vast expanse of level plain which, to the north and east, stretched trackless and unbroken by mountain or ravine to an infinitude—the boundless prairies soon to be mellowed and turned to a golden brown by the shafts of a burning sun already just below the edge of an horizon aglow with opaline tints. The Girl had ever been a lover of nature . . . but never until now had she realized the marvellous beauty and glory of the great plains. And yet, though her eyes shone with the wonder of it all, there was an unmistakably sad and reminiscent note in the voice that presently murmured: "Another day." After a while, and as if under the spell of some unseen power, she slowly turned and faced the west where she gazed long and earnestly at the panorama of the snow-capped peaks, rising range after range, all tipped with dazzling light.

—David Belasco, *The Girl of the Golden West* (1911)

I have never looked for utopia on a map. Of course, I believe in human advancement. I believe in medicine, in astrophysics, in washing machines. But my compass takes its cardinal point from tragedy. If I respond to the metaphor of spring, I nevertheless learned, years ago, from my Mexican father, from my Irish nuns, to count on winter. The point of Eden for me, for us, is not approach but expulsion.

~ *Richard Rodriguez*, *Days of Obligation:*
An Argument with My Mexican Father (1992)

R ELIGION STRETCHED OUT HANDS OPEN FOR PRAYER AND for gain westward to the end of American earth. In 1790 or thereabouts, according to a story recorded some forty years later, a shaman of the Spokan people, who lived beyond the Rockies, along the Spokane River, alerted his followers to the arrival "from the rising sun" of "a different kind of man" and "a book that will teach you everything."[1]

Such tales are nearly always false. Prophecies usually happen retrospectively, in search of validation by real occurrences. People construct them in an attempt to make strange and sometimes traumatic events intelligible: the comfort of pretending that someone foresaw them helps dull the cutting edge of unwelcome innovation. For native peoples whom intruders' empires subverted, the reassurance that their old shamans were right about something—even if only about their own destruction—legitimated lost or endangered traditions. For conquerors it is always flattering to be subjects of prophecy: it suggests divine preordination.

The Aztecs and Incas too are commonly said to have foretold their own undoing, though the evidence for the assertion crumbles at a touch and the stories are evidently early colonial lies—part of the web of myth that wrapped unpalatable truths in uncertainty and turned mayhem into mystery. Therefore, the Spokan prophet probably never pronounced. He may have inferred the newcomers' approach from the deadly smallpox that preceded them. He may have heard rumors about French and Spanish missions in the Missouri valley and the

Great Plains. He is unlikely, however, to have thought well of the intruders. Can he really have regarded their Bible—with its justifications of expropriation and massacre of the incumbents of the lands God's chosen ones conquered—as omnisciently authoritative and benign?

Still, the fact that the story circulated in the 1830s is evidence of what was going on at the time. In 1831 Nez Percé and Flathead pilgrims arrived in Saint Louis. They were wandering in search of spiritual experience; but US Easterners, variously eager for new congregations to convert and new lands to seize, misinterpreted their arrival as a sign of western tribes' hunger for gospels of love and lucre.

Prophecy is a common American vice, and the white people, of course, had prophets of their own. The common—albeit not constant feature—of settler religions was enthusiasm. Millenarianism was enthusiasm's extreme form.[2] Persecution in Europe drove millenarians to America, where toleration nourished Anabaptism, end-time fundamentalism, and sects invented by chiliasm-crazed prophets. The religion of Puritans, so staid in some ways, tended to get febrile when adherents thought about the end of the world. The founders of Massachusetts envisaged a refuge for those God intended "to save out of a general destruction." John Cotton, the Boston divine who collaborated in the expulsion of Baptism from Massachusetts, predicted the world would come to an end in 1655. Increase Mather felt he could hear God's "murdering pieces go off" as he watched the comet of 1680. The Shakers called themselves "the United Society of Believers in Christ's Second Coming."[3]

From the mid-eighteenth century, "Great Awakenings" reignited millennial fervor in British North America. A reaction against rationalism made popular idols of fervent preachers who sought "not to store heads but to stir hearts," as Jonathan Edwards—perhaps the most famous of the awakeners—explained to his congregations. "Outcries, faintings, convulsions and such like" replaced liturgy.[4] The Shakers experienced an "era of manifestations," during which Ann Lee claimed to have experienced the Second Coming in 1770. In 1803 self-professed prophet Georg Rapp led his followers from persecution in Germany to "the land of Israel" in Pennsylvania. There, after trying Indiana too, they settled down to await the return of Christ, which, Rapp foresaw, would happen in 1829. Meanwhile, in rural New York, William Miller, the founder of Adventism, was predicting that the world would end in 1844.

To be a prophet, it probably helps to be odd. Perhaps the oddest of the white prophets was Joseph Smith, who began, according to his own later account, to experience divine revelations in 1820, at the age of fifteen, and frequent angelic visitations from 1823. In 1830 he founded the movement that came to be known as the Church of Jesus Christ of Latter-day Saints. Like Hispanics and most other minorities, Mormons are, I think, undercelebrated in US history. From the perspective of a Hispanic history of the country, they were the vanguard of the anglicization of the West—the pioneers who breached the "Great American Desert" and made the lands beyond the plains into the frontier of Anglo-America. This chapter unfolds the story they began—of the decisive episode in the Hispanic history of the United States—the westward colonization that shifted the balance of the future and inaugurated a long spell of gringo dominance "from sea to shining sea." Most protagonists of the action in this chapter are, therefore, Anglos. But, like the makers of Anglo-America who were the focus of Chapter Three, the extenders of Anglo-America into the West are inescapably part of the Hispanic story.

As A HERESIARCH JOSEPH Smith was spectacularly successful, but he failed at whatever else he tried. His first vocation was as a professional treasure hunter, which led to impoverishment and allegations of chicanery. His stab at banking ended in bankruptcy and suspected fraud. He founded cities that had to be abandoned. His military career as the self-styled General Joseph Smith ended in defeat, his campaign for the US presidency in ignominy, and his self-projection as a political caudillo in accusations of treason, followed by his own death at the hands of a lynch mob. From wherever he established his followers they were expelled; yet there were scores of thousands of them in his lifetime and the Church he founded numbers many millions of adherents today.

If his life makes this outcome seem unlikely, his doctrines only deepen the problem. He said that an angel had revealed to him inscribed tablets of gold, which he could show to no one else; apart from a few of his close confederates, no one else has ever claimed to see them. He did not know the languages in which they were written, but he translated them by divine inspiration, finding luminous transcriptions, visible only to himself, inside his hat. The least surprising of the revelations was that Native Americans were descendants of a lost tribe of Israel, for that had been suggested many times before, for no good reason. More startling disclosures were that Jesus Christ had visited America; that the New Jerusalem would be built in America, preferably in Missouri; and that the territory of the United States, which had been the scene of destructive ancient wars between early Christians and apostates or infidels, would be the destination of Christ's Second Coming. Smith expressed all these claims and prophecies in language closely modeled on the Authorized Version of the Bible of the Church of England. His visions grew in extravagance as time went on. By the time of his death in 1844 he was imagining himself as king of a "theodemocracy."

It is hard to understand how so many people can have believed and even found genuine blessings in what an unsympathetic critic would be inclined to dismiss as a farrago of obvious nonsense. Some of Smith's appeal no doubt was the result of his personal charisma, which we can calibrate in terms of his apparent sex appeal. He dispensed himself and a few select disciples from the constraints of monogamy and accumulated at least twenty-five well-attested "marriages." His successor as leader of the Saints, or of the largest faction of them, Brigham Young, evinced similar charisma: reputedly, Young had fifty-six wives, all living under one roof in a long terrace where each woman had her own front door. Charisma could not, however, launch on its own such a vast movement as Mormonism, or recruit faithful beyond the range of the leaders' travels, or explain the success of missionaries who recruited thousands of converts as far afield as Canada or among the poor of Dickensian England. Most Mormons' inspiration seems rather to have come from Smith's writings.

The appeal of the *Book of Mormon*, in which most of Smith's output appeared in 1830, with his name on the title page as author rather than translator, was, I suspect, rather like that of *The Lord of the Rings* and its many cognate fantasies today. Whatever one thinks of the truth or sanctity of Smith's work, any reader must admire the genius with which he created and sustained a vast world of characters with innumerable stories of war and betrayal, love and hatred, fear and friendship, and remarkably few inconsistencies. Into his text he interwove—without elegance but not without crude skill—many justifications for rituals of his own devising and many sideswipes at existing churches. Once a reader commits emotionally to a literary world, it becomes for him or her a form of reality—as do radio and television soap operas for a public that grieves when characters die or sends money or gifts when one of the dramatis personae is in trouble. Many readers of the *Book of Mormon* responded to Smith's scripture with a similar degree of self-surrender, much as audiences responded to the writings of other unlikely heresiarchs, such as Luther and Muhammad. I am immune to the book's fascination. Its stilted language, uniform rhythm, hyperbolic rhetoric, and repetitive tedium leave me unmoved. But for one who is once moved, the power of a text develops a momentum of its own.

Of Smith's projects and promises, the building of New Jerusalem in America ignited most imaginations. Of his assurances to his followers, the divine guarantee of the holiness of America was the most durable, even among the many disappointments to which the founder's ambitions fell victim. "This," says the *Book of Mormon* concerning America, "is a choice land"—choice above all other lands, says a neighboring text, "and whatsoever nation shall possess it shall be free from bondage . . . captivity, and from all other nations . . . if they will serve the God of the land, who is Jesus Christ."[5] Brigham Young upheld the tradition. The American hemisphere, he said, "is the land of Zion, the land that the Lord gave to Jacob . . . and his posterity . . . wherein Jesus will make his appearance the second time."[6] The promise of ease in Zion came with the backing of a suitable threat: "and now, we can behold the decrees of God concerning this land, that it is a land of promise; and whatsoever nation shall possess it shall serve God, or they shall be swept off when the fullness of his wrath shall come upon them. And the fullness of his wrath cometh upon them when they are ripened in iniquity."[7]

The image of a land of promise enlivened by menace—which is what America was for migrants from hard times in Europe—elides easily into that of the Promised Land. Though Smith and Young had difficulty with audiences schooled in rationalism, skepticism, and the exercise of critical intelligence, their message was intelligible in the context of the day, especially to the people of modest education they primarily addressed. There was a long tradition of American utopianism: the very name of Utopia derived from Thomas More's satirical fiction of a voyager discovering a model republic across the ocean from Europe. Columbus and Cortés, when their secular ambitions faded, imagined a new apostolic age taking shape in the lands they discovered. The early Franciscan evangelists in New Spain rushed through their program of baptisms in anticipation of the imminent end of the world. Millenarianism animated Native resistance in parts of colonial Spanish America.[8] In the early days of Mormonism it was still possible to imagine a new start for the world in virgin American soils.

Secular utopians joined religious enthusiasts in seeking their own kinds of Zion. While Mormons touted the New Jerusalem, followers of Robert Owen, Étienne Cabet, and Charles Fourier constructed backwoods utopias on socialist principles—cities of Icarus that dared and failed. Fourier planned a settlement called Harmony, where even sexual orgies would be organized on egalitarian principles. In Texas in 1849 Cabet founded a town he called Icaria, where abolishing property and forbidding rivalry would prevent envy, crime, anger, and lust. Clothes, according to Cabet, ought to be made of elastic to make the principle of equality "suit people of different sizes." Although Owen was a militant atheist, he bought the site of his own doomed community in Indiana in 1826 from Georg Rapp, whose followers had already failed there, inadvertently symbolizing the continuities between secular and religious utopianism.

In 1831 Joseph Smith picked the site of the New Jerusalem: the town of Independence in Jackson County, Missouri, recently founded at the westernmost limits of US settlement, just short of the confluence of the Kansas and Missouri rivers. The influx of 1,200 of Smith's followers in the fledgling community alarmed the residents, who responded first with threats, then with violence, forcing the newcomers to flee. In 1833 Smith raised his own militia to conquer the promised land by force, but the locals prevailed. After expulsion from Missouri the Mormons tried Illinois, only to experience the same fate with even greater violence. In 1844 Smith used his militia, now thousands strong and clad in comic-opera uniforms with plumes, to stage a local coup, declaring martial law in the New Jerusalem. But the militia proved unable to withstand bombardment by state troops.

Evidently, the New Jerusalem would only thrive where there were no enemies to destroy or deride it, deep in the interior of the continent, beyond the jurisdiction of the United States. That, after Joseph Smith's death, was the view of the successor who attracted the allegiance of the vast majority of Smith's followers, Brigham Young. Among the justifications for the policy he imposed was that the Mormons would follow the course of the angel who had been the founder's chief celestial confidant. The angel Moroni was, according to some readings of Smith's work and some recollections of what the prophet had said, an avatar of a heroic Christian warrior, who had written much of the *Book of Mormon* in the form in which Smith supposedly received it and who had taken part in the last campaigns of the followers of Christ in ancient America. Surviving the debacle, he wandered inland until he died in single combat against a series of challengers from among the Native Americans, or "Lamanites" in Mormon jargon: having vanquished the first three, he succumbed to the fourth in exhaustion. The colonization of the interior would be the revenge of Moroni. A vision led Young to Utah, but practical considerations favored his choice: it was a long way from other settlers, in land superficially too unattractive to draw competitors; no one except Native Americans would want to fight for it; and it was beyond the frontiers of the United States in what was technically Mexican territory.

The migration Young led to Utah was a key episode in the making of modern America. I have been astonished at the amount of intolerance and even hatred Mormons still encounter at the hands of their fellow citizens in the United States. Although as a former resident of Massachusetts, I had no wish to see ex-governor Mitt Romney's presidential campaign succeed in 2008, I was aghast at the way his enemies used his religion against him. In the 2012 election the issue hardly cropped up, but detractors' voices, recalled from the previous campaign, seemed to echo in the silence, denying that Mormons can be Christians—whereas really, in their own strange way, they set out sincerely to follow Christ—and treating Mormonism as if it were an un-American activity, whereas really there is no religion more American than Mormonism, and none so fixated on the sacrality of America. The United States should honor the Mormons for making a vital breakthrough in the history of their country.

Until Brigham Young drew or drove scores of thousands of settlers into the far west, the interior was, in most Americans' perceptions, an obstacle to cross on the way to Oregon or California. It seemed uncultivable, fit only for nomadism and buffalo. The Mormons turned it into farmland and transformed the environment so thoroughly in the areas they settled that Young realized they would have to feed the Natives whose prospects of survival they had undermined. He had no romantic illusions about the Native Americans. On the contrary, he shared Mormon prejudices against the Lamanites. "There is a curse on the aborigines of our country," he said, "who roam the plains and are so wild that you cannot tame them. . . . God cursed them with this dark and benighted and loathsome condition."[9] Yet he ordered his followers to treat Natives with kindness, partly in the practical interests of peace, partly in deference to the Lamanites' status as fallen children of Israel, and partly in payment for the land taken from them. Principally, Young acknowledged, the duty of feeding them arose from the fact that the disappearance of their pastures and their herds left no other option.

Young personally deserves much of the credit or blame for effecting this transformation. His vision was always fixed on the far western interior of the hemisphere. Though he allowed migrants to go by ship via California, he always disdained proposals for an easier Zion on the Pacific coast. "We have been gathered to the valleys of these mountains," he said, "for the express purpose of purifying ourselves, that we may become polished stones in the temple of God."[10]

Typically, the pioneers traveled in wagon trains, which Young and his coadjutors organized with impressive care. The leaders' advice was to take two or three yoke of oxen and at least a couple of milk cows, and load each wagon with munitions, iron for smelting on the way, pulleys and ropes for traversing mountains, fishing gear for the journey, and tools, not only for farming on arrival but also for planting crops beside the route for subsequent wagoners to eat. A *batterie de cuisine* was recommended, with at least seven hundredweight of flour to cook with it. The Kimble family was among those who overestimated the amount they could carry. In 1847, as they approached the Rocky Mountains, they wrapped their piano in buffalo hides and buried it, sending a team of oxen to recover it and drag it to the Salt Lake Valley the following spring.[11]

In the 1850s, as the costs of the great migration mounted and the Church's money gave out, Young saved on the cost of livestock by designing carts for Mormons to pull, like huge wheelbarrows, across prairie, desert, and mountains, by unaided human muscle-power. The handcart pilgrims included some of the poorest migrants, especially those recruited in England, whose funds were depleted by the expenses of the transatlantic voyage. They journeyed with exhilaration described by a migrant from Liverpool: "People made fun of us as we walked, pulling our handcarts, but the weather was fine and the roads were excellent and although I was sick and we were very tired at night, still we thought it was a glorious way to go to Zion."[12]

For any who started too late in the season or encountered unexpected delays or unseasonable weather, the journey would probably be fatal. Hundreds perished from cold and starvation. Yet religious exaltation can be amazingly robust. By the end of the 1860s there were at least 60,000 Mormons settled on farms in Utah and neighboring territories.

Mormons' relationship with the United States was equivocal. Smith claimed to be able to exempt his followers from federal laws. His militias challenged fellow citizens in war. Brigham Young thought Zion transcended any modern polity and carefully located his colonies beyond US borders. When the federal government sent troops to remove Young from the governorship of Utah Territory, his followers responded to his call to resist in arms: "an armed mercenary mob, which has been sent against us at the instigation of anonymous letter writers . . . ; of corrupt officials who have brought false accusations against us, to screen themselves in their own infamy; and of hireling priests and howling editors, who prostitute the truth for filthy lucre's sake."[13]

But the Church raised a battalion of volunteers to fight against Mexico in the Mexican War, resisted the temptation to defy the federal government during the Civil War, and over time made many compromises over doctrine and choice of secular leadership in order to join and remain in the Union. Without the Mormons, the incorporation of the far western interior would surely have been much delayed. The fact that they helped shape the United States in a crucial way is as tenaciously ignored in conventional minds as the country's even longer Hispanic past.

OF COURSE, THE MORMONS could never have begun the colonization of the western interior if other explorers had not preceded them and established routes. The illusions of early colonists in New Mex-

ico and Virginia, who hoped that North America would be narrow
and easily traversable, took a long time to dispel. Practical transcontinental routes to the Pacific were elusive. Mountains seemed
everywhere to be in the way. Maps evolved by trial and error, tenta-
tive about the routes explorers probed and vague about what lay
between them.

In the 1770s extended Spanish navigation along the Californian
coast combined with the discovery of wonderful harbors at San
Francisco and Monterrey and the opening of coastal missions to
whet appetites for routes that would connect Northern California
with what Spaniards called the interior provinces. In 1776 Spanish
friars cut a stairway into sheer rock to cross the Sierra Nevada in a
failed attempt to open a direct route. The range of their journeys
exceeded local knowledge; so instead of on indios, they relied on
oracles to guide them, "having implored the intercession of our
most holy patrons in order that God might direct us in the way that
might be most conducive to his service."[14] Fray Silvestre Vélez de
Escalante chronicled the explorations that took them as far north as
Lake Utah and back across the Colorado at what has since been
known as the Crossing of the Fathers. The friars, who found time to
preach whenever they met unevangelized indios, refused to carry
arms (except for hunting) or trade goods and responded with naive
indignation when they discovered that some of their secular companions broke their promises to comply with these risky policies.[15]
Misunderstanding what the locals told them, they thought Lake
Utah was part of Salt Lake: in consequence, maps of the depths of
the Great Basin were long filled with a distortedly large inland sea.

One of the most enterprising missionaries, Fray Francisco
Garcés, made the attempt to trace a route across the mountains in
the reverse direction; but although he was famous for his winning
ways with Indians—conversing patiently in their fashion and eating
and praising their food, which fellow Spaniards generally condemned as unpalatable—Hopi hostility eventually forced him to
turn back near Oraibi. Spanish communications across the mountains therefore remained unsatisfactory; the Sierra Nevada contin-

ued to divide the Spanish dominions, and missions north of San
Gabriel remained dependent on seaborne links. For a moment it
seemed to the Spaniards that "the door will be opened to a new
empire" in the hinterland of California,[16] and missions were established accordingly on the Yuma River; but Indians wiped them out
in 1781 and the effort was not renewed.

America's spine of mountains had been revealed. Their extent
was baffling. But how impenetrable were they? Where were there
passes accessible to trade? Was there a lake-and-river route to the
Pacific that might bypass or cleave the mountains? Attempts to
answer those questions were renewed in 1804, when the Louisiana
Purchase changed the game. Thomas Jefferson speculated that a
single day's portage might carry an expedition from the uppermost
Missouri to the Columbia River and a swift descent to the sea. He
entrusted the effort to Meriwether Lewis, who had won the president's confidence as a member of his staff. Lewis in turn recruited
William Clark to be his co-commander. The two leaders were perfectly matched by temperament and perfectly linked by friendship.
"I assure you," wrote Lewis to Clark, inviting him to join the expedition, "that no man lives with whom I would prefer to undertake
the difficulties of such a trip than yourself." Lewis was urbane and
reliable, Clark rash and unreflective.[17]

Their primary objective was "to explore the Missouri River, and
such principal stream of it, as by its course and communication with
the waters of the Pacific Ocean offer the most direct and practicable
water communication across the continent, for the purposes of
commerce." Political objectives were paramount. The Spanish government knew what the United States wanted: a route under its
own control—a "way by which the Americans may some day extend
their population and their influence up to the coasts of the South
Seas." Lewis swaggered through Native American lands, claiming
suzerainty, demanding redress for banditry, confirming chiefs, and
at least once—among the Mandan—nominating one chief to be
paramount. These political interventions were marked by bestowals
of gifts. They did not mean much to the recipients, except occasions

of largesse. Native Americans were always being mistaken for willing, self-inscribed subjects of "great white fathers."[18]

The case of the Mandan, however, was special, because it was
representative of the displacement of Spanish power and pretension
from the North American center: the Mississippi and Missouri
drainage areas. Under the influence of John Evans (see above, p. 72),
the Mandan were the last indios to hoist the Spanish flag. Even
nominal transfer of their allegiance has, in retrospect at least, symbolic significance. The Great White focus of allegiance had slipped
from Madrid to Washington.

Lewis and Clark wintered among the Mandan, acquiring the
services of a precious guide. Sacajawea was the sixteen-year-old
wife of a French trader. Her people, the Shoshone, lived athwart the
passes that Lewis and Clark needed to cross to get to the far side of
the Rockies. After a long spell of captivity among the Mandan and
marriage to a French trader, she had the advantage of speaking a
number of languages that qualified her to be the expedition's principal interpreter. She was reputed, moreover, to be of chiefly birth
among her own people. The disadvantage was that she was in an
advanced stage of pregnancy, but she proved invaluable to the expedition and neither she nor her baby ever held the party up. As so
often in the modern history of exploration, everyone involved,
except a few great white chiefs and heroes, stays on the margins of
the story, even when occupying a central place in events. Sacajawea's
contribution is barely discernible in the records of the expedition,
but it was obviously crucial.

As they set off up the Missouri on April 7, 1805, Lewis com-
mended his "little fleet" as "not quite so respectable as those of
Columbus or Captain Cook." He celebrated the moment of departure as "as among the most happy in my life," although he felt
dwarfed in his "little vessels" at the realization that "we were now
about to penetrate a country at least two thousand miles in width,
on which the foot of civilized man had never trodden; the good or
evil it had in store for us was for experiment yet to determine."[19]

The party followed the Missouri until they could straddle it and

they reached the highest ridge of the mountains near the source of
the Lehmi River, roughly where modern Idaho and Montana join. A
short way downstream they came to salmon spawning grounds: proof
that the river they were on flowed on, ultimately, to the Pacific. They
were on a tributary of the Columbia River system. Many mountains
lay ahead and the rivers were unnavigable, even in canoes, with heavy
baggage. In October they descended the Snake River. Beyond the
Celilo Falls they found signs of the approach of their goal. Indians
with European trade goods appeared—assurance that the ocean was
not far away. They wintered near the mouth of the Columbia, where
the constant roar of the ocean kept Lewis awake on the coast of that
ill-named sea: "and I have not seen one pacific day since my arrival in
the vicinity, and its waters are foaming and perpetually break with
the immense waves on the sands and rocky coasts, tempestuous and
horrible." The return journey was arduous and dispiriting. They had
to barter for horses and hunt for food or scrounge both from the
Indians. They mismanaged their trade goods and ran out of truck on
the homeward voyage. Despite many excursions in search of a com-
mercially exploitable route through the mountains, they could not
find one. Though they cut a dashing swathe through difficult country,
the expedition was a heroic failure.[20]

THE EXPEDITIONS THAT FOLLOWED demonstrated the difficulties. Much of the West seemed unworthy of exploration: it led
nowhere and was effectively uninhabitable. When the French
vacated Louisiana, Spanish military scouts reconnoitered routes of
communication to link the Mississippi and Rio Grande, eventually
establishing a direct trail from Santa Fe to Saint Louis. But these
remained tenuous links between military outposts, not causeways of
commerce or highways for settlement. Even after wide-ranging
explorations of the rivers and plains of the West by the military, the
prairie seemed a desert. Stephen Long, who commanded the operations between 1816 and 1824, and crossed the prairie along the
line of the Platte River, denounced it as "almost wholly unfit for

cultivation, and of course uninhabitable by a people depending upon agriculture for their subsistence."[21] The technology that transformed the plains—the steel plows to bite the soil, the machined nails that built the towns, the railways that carried wood in and wheat out—had not yet arrived. The prairie, like the mountains, was an obstruction, not an opportunity, on the way west.

At first, therefore, settlement had to bypass or cross the prairie. The rich Pacific coastal territories in Oregon and California were the target of the great pioneer drive to the west. Cheap land was the lure. In the 1820s Jed Smith linked the Spanish trails into a continuous route across the Sierra. He was a trader with an oddly pantheistic religious vocation, who claimed to explore "that I may be able to help those who stand in need."[22] Between the lines, his copious journals disclose another motive: he could not bear his own ignorance of the country that surrounded him or accept reports he had not verified. His maps of the central Rockies and the Great Basin fed into the later, more self-consciously scientific cartography produced by federal expeditions and railway surveyors from the 1840s.

On the way to Oregon, meanwhile, propagandists advertised "a level open trail . . . better for carriages than any turnpike in the United States." Shrewd utopians such as the American Society for Encouraging the Settlement of the Oregon Territory bought up land to sell to settlers with the promise of a "city of Perfection" in the west. Misleading maps were available suggesting that there was an easy river passage from Great Salt Lake along nonexistent waterways. In 1813 the *Missouri Gazette* declared that "a journey across the continent might be performed with a wagon, there being no obstruction in the whole route that any person would dare to call a mountain." In the year of this overoptimistic pronouncement, a party of fur traders stumbled on a pass through the Rockies that would became the vital link for the Oregon Trail. South Pass, a fairly flat plain about twenty miles wide around the Wind River range in Wyoming, remained unpublicized until 1824, when Jed Smith saw it on a deerskin map made by Crow Indians.[23]

Ox teams carried Steinway pianos and seven-foot mirrors to

rough-necked mining boomtowns. The first trading wagons crossed South Pass as early as 1824. Fur traders traveled from Independence across the mountains and into Oregon in 1832, but without iron axles the wagons were too fragile for unbroken trails of this kind. In an arid climate where, in the words of a missionary's wife in 1836, "the Heavens over us were of brass and the earth of iron under our feet,"[24] dried-out spokes sprang out of place and iron rims slipped from shrunken wheels. Wagons had to be manhandled up steep climbs and then lowered down cliff faces with ropes—a feat that might take eighty men to one wagon. Ravines had to be filled with rubble.

The first settler wagons to make it across set out in 1840. The party of missionaries who pioneered the venture hired a trapper, Robert "Doc" Newell, to lead them and their two wagons from Green River on the eastern edge of the Rockies over the mountains to Fort Vancouver on the Willamette River. The party left Green River on September 27 and traveled as far as they could on their wagons, clearing a road as they went. When they could go no further, they shifted their goods to packhorses and stripped the wagons to their chassis. Eventually they broke one up to provide spares for the other. When they reached Fort Walla Walla in what is now Washington State, Newell built a barge and hauled the remaining wagon along the Columbia River to the mouth of the Willamette. Newell was jubilant, if wrong, when he wrote on April 19, 1841, "that I, Robert Newell, was the first who brought wagons across the Rocky Mountains."[25]

MEANWHILE, IN THE WAGON trains' rear the great grasslands that stretched from the Mississippi towards the Rockies remained largely immune from and resistant to white colonization. Forts and trading posts speckled the region; Native Americans roamed it. But there were few farmers, almost entirely confined to east Kansas and the fringes of the Missouri in Nebraska—some 8,000 in Kansas in the mid-1850s and fewer than 5,000 in Nebraska. Settlers mistrusted the prairie; promoters saw it as unprofitable; and the government was reluctant to do anything about it—poised inertly between Republicans, who wanted to divide the land among independent smallholders, and Democrats, who wanted to preserve the balance of power in Congress between south and north, slavers and emancipators. Pro-slavery gangs from Mississippi and Missouri harassed early cultivators in Kansas and burned their little town of Lawrence in 1855, while John Brown—whose body "mouldering in the grave" inspired Civil War federalists—helped lead the resistance. The early phases of the era of railway building, though it prepared the soil for settlement by supplying an infrastructure, displacing the Native Americans, and exterminating the buffalo, actually postponed the advent of farming by encouraging the exploitation of the grasslands for beef production to feed the workers. The era of the culture of lawless towns and trails, cowboys and outlaws, gunslinging and ghost towns was part of the result.

The extension of grazing was the first stage in the region's transformation. This was the common experience of previously underexploited grasslands in the period. (Much of southeast Australia and New Zealand became sheep-rearing country, though at first more for wool than for meat; Argentina became a major exporter of beef and mutton.) The North American prairie, however, exceeded other areas in productivity, partly because railway construction concentrated large, though temporary, labor forces in parts of the region. When the railways were built, the big concentrations of population in the Mississippi River valley and along the seaboards of North America became easily accessible to the products of the prairie. Grains soon became more important than meat, as wheat and maize replaced the native prairie grasses.

Most US histories invoke the homesteader ethos to explain the transformation of the prairie into a populous and productive region. The heroism of the brawny farmers striding through waving wheat fields in paintings of the Wisconsin school looks ridiculous to uninformed visitors to the university collection in Madison, but it is profoundly appropriate. Without homesteaders it is hard to see how the plains could have been wrested from the Native Americans: the land suitable for adaptation as slave-staffed plantations was limited, remote, and dispersed. And the stories of the people who eventually farmed the prairie have impressively heroic elements. Most of the tales emphasize their hardships. The early fiction of the settlement of the plains includes harrowing stories like O. E. Rolvaag's *Giants in the Earth*, in which the harshness and isolation of a Dakota farm, the locusts and hunger and capricious climate, break a Norwegian homesteader of the 1870s and drive his wife mad.[26] The first poet of plains life, Hamlin Garland, writing in 1892, recalled the sting of the salt sweat in his eyes as he toiled behind "the snarling plow." The most famous of all autobiographical novels of plains life, Laura Ingalls Wilder's *Little House on the Prairie*, which purports to recall the writer's early childhood in Indian Territory, Kansas, in 1869–70, is mawkishly sentimental but includes recollections of real hardships, including the "fever 'n' ague"—the mysterious illness that afflicted farmers—and the insecurity of a homesteading life, culminating in official eviction for having an imperfect title to the land. The secession of slaver states from the Union made it possible for Congress to open up the prairie as a mise-en-scène for emigrants from Scandinavia and Germany to play the role of yeomen. In 1862 the Homesteader Act granted free title on a claim of up to 160 acres for anyone who improved a plot in the plains. Promoters raised the strain:

> *Come along, come along, make no delay,*
> *Come from every nation, come from every way,*
> *Our lands they are broad enough, have no alarm*
> *For Uncle Sam is rich enough to give us all a farm.*[27]

Homesteading is part of one of Americans' favorite myths about themselves: that they are all rugged individualists who succeed, if they do, by self-help, whereas really US society is viscerally civic-minded and everyone normal should belong to a community—in the workplace, the alumni association, the neighborhood, the city, the church, the innumerable membership organizations that range from charities to criminal gangs. Yet the "free soil" slogan that animated the homesteaders and the heroic tales of perseverance in adversity resonate with the notion of the United States as "the land of the free and the home of the brave." The prairie home symbolizes the private-enterprise ideology of the Republican Party, which even most Democrats seem to share, because it was the result of the free alienation of public property to individual owners.

IN THE END, HOWEVER, the crucial story of the domestication of the Midwest was not one of individual heroism. The problems of adapting the plains were environmental as well as human. The solutions that enabled farmers to colonize the region were technological rather than matters of individual prowess or pioneer spirit. The prairie produced little in the way of plants naturally edible to humans. The soil, unaffected by the last Ice Age, was tough and invulnerable to preindustrial tools. The habitat lacked ecological diversity. Neighboring regions never housed enough population to generate potentially transforming demand. For most of the past, the abundance of game—giant quadrupeds in paleolithic times, great herds of bison when the giants became extinct—inhibited the introduction of agriculture. The inhabitants exploited grassland vicariously, hunting the creatures that ate the grasses. Although the way of life satisfied those who practiced it, the waste of energy is obvious. For maximum efficiency, the best strategy is to grow plants for human food rather than wait for the ruminants to convert grass into meat.

Even as late as 1827, when James Fenimore Cooper wrote *The Prairie*, it seemed a place without a future, "a vast country, incapable of sustaining a dense population."[28] Yet at the very moment that Cooper described it, the prairie was beginning to experience a slow invasion of white squatters, which would eventually contribute to a new look for the plains as a land of rich farms and cities. Today the Great Plains are the "breadbasket of the world." They also have a recent history of ranching, still practiced with prodigious success on the high plains to the west and south of the region. It seems incredible that a land now so thoroughly adapted to human needs should for so long have been the domain of nature, where farming was confined to a few poor and tiny patches and where sparse populations trailed the great American bison.

Only invaders from the Old World could effect this magic. The first stage was colonization by European weeds and grasses that made the pampa and prairie able to support sheep, cattle, and horses instead of just bison and guanaco. Purslane and Englishman's foot created what Alfred Crosby called "empires of the dandelion." Weeds made the revolution work. They "healed raw wounds invaders tore in the earth," bound soil together, saved it from desiccation, refilled vacant eco-niches, and fed imported livestock. The conscious transpositions followed: horses and cattle first—domesticable quadrupeds of a kind unknown in the New World since the Pleistocene.

Livestock came at first from the south. To Spanish cattlemen the great plains were the last frontiers of an enterprise that began in the Middle Ages, when ranching was adopted as a way of exploiting the empty, conquered lands of Extremadura and parts of Andalusia after the Muslim population had fled or been expelled. Although cattle were raised in parts of Anglo-America in colonial times, the herds that grazed the great grasslands, and most of the practices, traditions, and early personnel that accompanied them, belonged mainly to the Hispanic history of the United States—part of the northward colonization of the country from New Spain, arriving with Oñate, multiplying with the missions. The displacement of ranching by farming contributed especially to Hollywood and Broadway many stories of conflicts. The clash of incumbent ranchers with planters from the east was part of the narrative of the triumph of Anglo-America.

Yet wheat, the crop that transformed the plains, came at first from the south too. Mesoamerican wheat strains that Spanish settlers brought to their "interior provinces" adapted poorly to the plains. But in the 1840s entrepreneurs obtained suitable seed from Europe and China, while US experimenters developed hybrids that could flourish in a capricious climate on unglaciated soil while resisting local pests. A Mexican model of production—exploitation of wheatlands for export and for feeding a few urban centers with transitional or marginal ranching, perpetuated on unfarmed land— arrived in the North American plains. It did not take long for prodigious quantities to sprout from the soil of the Midwest. In 1840 Indiana and the states to the west of it produced less than 10 million bushels. The census of 1852 revealed an increase to 25 million.[29] By then, the output of the eastern states was in decline. When Anthony Trollope visited Buffalo in 1861, he was amazed at the quantities of grain—60 million bushels a year—passing through the city's depots. In Minneapolis he felt "grieved by the loose manner in which wheat was treated" with "bags of it upset and left upon the ground. The labor of collecting it was more than it was worth."[30] By 1900, 500 million acres of farmland had been added to the cultivated area of the United States.

The domestication of the prairie made the United States a truly continent-wide country. Space, that most underexploited of American resources, was being put to good use. For the transformation to be complete, four conditions had to be fulfilled. First, Anglo-America had to survive its own crisis of identity and perhaps of survival— the Civil War. Next, the indigenous peoples of the plains had to be expelled, exterminated, or severely confined. Then, industrialization had to supply the means of turning the sod and tilling the soil with limited manpower; and an industrial infrastructure of comprehensive railroads had to transport produce to markets. Finally, a demographic explosion was necessary to create the surplus population to settle the land and open enough mouths and markets to consume its output.

To TAKE THE CIVIL War first—the episode of their nineteenth century that people educated in the United States know best and study most—a useful way to add perspective is to see it in the context not just of US history but of the pasts of the hemisphere and the world too. Most nineteenth-century American republics were fissile—those of Hispanic America remarkably so—and were battlegrounds of rival political ideologies of centralization and evolution at intervals, almost throughout the nineteenth century. Brazil was the most conspicuous exception, managing to survive civil wars in the 1830s chiefly because the regions were incapable of collaborating in revolt and because the emperor supplied a powerful symbol of legitimacy for the new country. Meanwhile, states carved from former Spanish viceroyalties crumbled.

In the United States the major crisis of potential fragmentation was delayed, partly because centralists and devolutionists established a working, albeit precarious, compromise after independence, and partly because the settled part of the country was unified by relatively good maritime communications. The vast hinterland was like an escape valve for unconfinable movements and secessionist communities. The effective growth of the country toward the middle of the century exacerbated the tension between its culturally distinct moieties, South and North. The addition of the former Spanish and Mexican territories and the Mormon republic contributed by multiplying cultural differences and raised awkward questions about how much power the central government should have as territories matured into states and how US identity should be defined inside the new configurations: in particular, should it be a slaving identity? A lot was at stake—vast fortunes, entire ways of life—as the slave states ran the risk of losing their power in Congress.

In global perspective, the war, when it came, was one of many conflicts that broke out as central governments acquired advanced weapons, fast communications, and nationally mobilized and organized armies and police forces. They could now impose their will on traditional, particularist, and devolved sources of authority. All over the nineteenth-century world, local elites, tribal chiefs, territorial aristocracies, urban patriciates, churches or other religious hierarchies, and provincial satraps had to compromise with or fight centralizing governments. In ways that help one understand what happened, the US experience of civil war resembled roughly contemporary events in Italy, Germany, and Japan, where wars unified countries that were either fragmented or in danger of fragmentation.

Germany and Italy had long been disunited—"geographical expressions" divided among many different and often hostile states. Japan had a long history as a unitary state, but power over remote provinces had slipped out of the central government's control. The United States was still a new state, but its constitution had never really settled a crucial issue: whether the separate states had permanently and irrevocably renounced their sovereignty in favor of the federal government. When some of the slave-holding states exercised what they claimed was their right to secede from the Union, the federal government contested it by force.

In all four places war pitted industrializing or industrialized regions against agrarian neighbors. In Japan, the regions of Choshu and Satsuma in the south supplied most of the manpower and equipment on the victorious side. These were areas where the local rulers had invested most in modernizing their armed forces and producing munitions on a massive scale. In Italy, the armies that conquered the rest of the peninsula came mainly from the kingdom of Piedmont in the northwest, where most Italian industry was concentrated. In Germany and the United States, the stories of the wars were similar: broadly speaking, industrializing regions overcame unindustrialized ones, though in Germany the divisions were less clear-cut than in the American case.

The effects of consolidation, moreover, were similar in all four cases. Germany emerged instantly as a major power. Italy, Japan, and the United States were slower to emerge as potential superpowers after their wars of unification, but by the end of the century they were all beginning, at least, to display the same characteristics: rapid industrialization, military efficiency, and colonial expansion. In all four countries the leaders appealed, with varying degrees of sincerity, to conservative values to justify the revolutions that had imposed centralization and unity on sometimes reluctant communities. In Japan the term "Restoration" was coined to describe the revolution, on the spurious grounds that by abolishing the shogunate in 1868 the new regime "restored" the emperor to his rightful place at the head of the empire. In Italy the victors quoted medieval poets in praise of political unity and claimed to have contained radical elements in the nationalist movement. In Germany the conquerors called their new state an "empire"—evoking memories of medieval German empires—while adopting truly radical measures, including an aggressively secularist campaign against the social influence of the Catholic Church and the introduction of the world's first state-run social-insurance scheme. In the United States, the victorious North invoked the country's founding fathers and claimed to defend the Constitution, while undertaking profoundly radical policies, including the emancipation of all slaves, and "Reconstruction," which was really an attempt to enforce policies of racial equality on the defeated South that many of the northern states themselves did not practice.

Had southern secession succeeded, it might not have made much difference to the broad trajectory of US history, since during Reconstruction and for a long time after it the South was in any case an American backwater, making little contribution to and taking little share in the prosperity and expansion of the country. The fate of Hispanic North America might hardly have changed. Hispanic natives would still have been persecuted in the areas previously wrested from Mexico. Hispanic migrants would have continued to target the same regions of settlement in the American West. The way we perceive Anglo-America, however, would surely be deeply different. We would have an alternative Anglo-America to contemplate: a confederacy culturally rooted in a mainly British past, with institutions ultimately modeled on those of England and predominantly Protestant in religion, but with an economy and society more closely resembling some of those of Latin America and the Caribbean than that of the United States. The confederacy would demonstrate that it was possible for a WASP-led country to house an agrarian society of vast social and economic inequalities, dominated by a landowning elite definable in terms of race and color, producing primary goods for other countries' industries: a white-dominated, English-speaking country, in other words, classifiable with Latin American stereotypes of social and economic deficiency.

Even so, as we have seen, the South, while still powerful, did inhibit the settlement of the plains. Secession and defeat therefore removed an obstacle. The next big obstacle, the native inhabitants, were surprisingly resilient. Myth depicts the plains as an arena of "manifest destiny," where Native Americans were victimized by a white "evil empire." They are better described as a zone of imperial competition where the white men's empire contended with that of the native imperialists, the Comanche and Sioux, who by dint of organization and ethos focused on war almost succeeded in subjugating the other peoples of the prairie.

Contact with the Spanish monarchy transformed the peoples beyond the frontier more thoroughly, perhaps, than Rome transformed the Germans or China the Jurchen or Manchus before the great invasions. Horses transformed the economy and way of life. Loot transformed society and the distribution of power. War chiefs and leaders of mounted bands contested the power of shamans and hereditary chiefs. In the eighteenth century horse-borne hunting turned the Great Plains into an arena for competition between ever-growing numbers of migrant peoples—many driven, as much as drawn, from east of the Mississippi by the pressure of white empire building. Those with agrarian traditions edged toward or into nomadism. All tended to become herders of horses as well as hunters of buffalo, which forced them into volatile contiguity on shared trails and pastures. The plains began to resemble the "cauldron of peoples" in the Eurasian grasslands.

As we saw in Chapter Two, the Sioux became to the plains what the Mongols were to the steppes. They were converts to nomadism, a potentially imperial or hegemonic people who became the terror of a sedentary world still intact on the Upper Missouri. Meanwhile, huge kills of buffalo generated a trading surplus, which in turn introduced corn to the hunters' diets, whiskey to their rites, and guns to their armories. As the horses multiplied, the plains became a source of supply for the white colonies arrayed beyond the edges of the region. Trade probably aggravated exposure to killer diseases of European origin.

The Sioux took the initiative against white encroachment during the Civil War, but their attempt to reverse white colonization in Minnesota failed despite the army's commitment elsewhere. They resumed fighting in 1875, in response to white gold miners' invasion of their heartlands in the Black Hills of Dakota, and won one of the world's most famous victories by indigenous resisters of white imperialism at the Little Bighorn the following year. But the real war was being fought off the battlefields—the ecological war, in which the buffalo hunters crippled native resistance by exterminating the bison. The army did not have to defeat the natives—it was enough merely to protect the hunters. In the three years prior to the Battle of the Little Bighorn, 9 million buffalo perished. By 1900, the total Native American population of the United States was recorded as 237,196—a decline of probably 50 percent during the nineteenth century. The plains bore most of the loss, from a peak of perhaps 250,000 Native American inhabitants to little more than 100,000.

As the traditional ecology vanished, agriculture could take over the vacated niches, but without an industrial revolution the West might have remained the exclusive domain of inspired pioneers. The extermination of the buffalo was in part an effect of industrialization, procured by repeating rifles. Advertisements for the harvesting machines that the McCormick Company of Chicago produced in the midcentury illustrated vividly the difference industrialization made. Two horses and one man were all that were needed, the poster seemed to say, for vast fields that stretched toward distant mountains. The company produced 1,500 reapers a year in the 1850s and nearly 15,000 in the 1870s. "Balloon" framing, made from precision-milled sticks with cheap nails, housed settlers and spread cities in a region bereft of most construction materials.[31] Elevators, introduced in 1850, made it possible to store grain without vast amounts of labor. Giant flour mills pressed grains into marketable wares. From the outset, the farmers of the Midwest specialized in large-scale cash crops. They exported their own produce and imported what they ate.

Industrialized food products sustained both ends of the exchange. Montana settlers, according to one of them, Mamie Alderson, formerly of Virginia, in 1883, "lived out of cans."[32] Rusting trash heaps outside homesteads signified settlers' dependence on the industrial revolution.

THE ENTERPRISE OF THE prairies needed an industrial infrastructure to underpin it. Railways transported the grain across what would otherwise be uneconomic distances. In return, they brought more settlers, more building materials, more industrial tools, more population for the cities, and more manpower for the industries of the Midwest and beyond. The iron horse was a successor in a tradition already established by the horse of flesh and blood. The rail-borne invasion of the plains by industrial America was only the last and most destructive episode in a series of transformations. The railroads' role in riveting the United States together was vital.

The surveyors' exemplar was John Charles Frémont, who preceded them in the 1840s, investigating the routes to the West for wagoners on behalf of Congress. Though Frémont himself was among America's early railway builders, the railways barely pricked the interior of the continent when he first surveyed the West. A wagon route to Oregon existed, but there was not even a viable road for wagons to California when the 1849 gold rush sent scores of thousands of settlers hurtling across the plains and the Rockies to get there. Military expeditions against the Navajo sought a route as a sideline to their main missions over the following few years, but without success.

Merchants, meanwhile, chaffed at the frustrations of exploiting the gold-happy markets that gleamed on the Pacific coast. For American commerce, access to the Pacific and the "East India" and China trades had long been both vital and laborious. It generally took at least a hundred days to sail around the Horn. A transcontinental railway would cut prices and stimulate demand for oriental products all over the country, as well as ease the means of importing cheap Indian and Chinese labor.

Political deadlock between promoters of rival routes hamstrung decision making. The possibilities were numerous. The route originally proposed by Asa Whitney in 1844 would have linked the shores of Lake Michigan to the Pacific at the mouth of the Columbia River. Other promoters canvassed for routes from Chicago via South Pass, or Saint Louis via the Cochetopa Pass, or Memphis or Fulton along the thirty-fifth parallel, from Vicksburg along the Gila River, and from Springfield (Illinois) via Albuquerque—to mention only the most widely supported options. Every departure point and terminus had its boosters. In 1848–49 a preemptive attempt by Frémont to find a route that would favor his financial backers in Saint Louis exacerbated the problem. He tackled the task with deceptive optimism. Ten of his men died in the snow. Frémont had to turn back, still asserting that "neither the snow of winter nor the mountain ranges were obstacles."[33] No other private ventures in the following years accomplished much more or satisfied their rivals. As so often in the history of capitalism, competitors stifled one another. Federal action was the only way forward.

In 1853 Congress decreed that the government would fund a series of expeditions, complete with botanical and zoological specialists and official artists, to find railway routes across the continent. Science would determine objectively a decision that sectional interests disputed. Route finding went hand in hand with scientific inquiry, as the surveyors had to check the elevation and gradient of every pass and report on the climate, resources, and native peoples along the proposed routes. The model appeared in the instructions surveyor I. I. Stevens wrote for himself when he was dispatched to explore Whitney's suggestions. He was to examine geography and meteorology and, "in short, to collect every species of information bearing upon the question of railroad practicability."[34]

Congress's approach to the rival routes was selective: the route along the thirty-second parallel was exempted from the attentions of the surveyors, presumably because it was thought to be viable and because it was supported by strong sectional interests in the South, which, at the time, the federal government needed to appease.

Fixation with the thirty-second parallel probably arose from an error in the calculation of latitude made by Mormon frontiersmen in Guadalupe Pass in 1845.[35] Yet really the thirty-second parallel was effectively impassable. Even today the railway has to dip south into Mexican territory to cross the USA at about that latitude.

The thirty-fifth parallel offered much better prospects, and a survey conducted in 1853 proved that fact, cleaving a pretty straight route from Fort Smith on the Arkansas River to Los Angeles; in reputed desert the party found plenty of fertile valleys suitable for settlement along a route they deemed "eminently advantageous." But the officer responsible, Lieutenant Amiel Whipple, grossly overestimated the construction costs with deterrent, depressant effects. The official artist described the end of the expedition's tolerable discomforts, as the party approached Los Angeles, with unmistakable relish:

> [T]he wilderness had reduced most of the garments indicative of civilization to such a state of decay that they either hung in rags or had their deficiencies supplied by patches of leather blackened by the smoke of many a camp fire. The same useful material wrapped around the feet supplied the place of boots, a distinction of which few could boast even in the most attenuated form, and our round felt hats had assumed every conceivable fantastic shape, and seemed to adhere to the tangled hair, which in many cases hung down on the shoulders. But, though conscious that our costume and personal appearance might have admitted of some improvement, we were not without a certain feeling of pride in the evidence of our long and toilsome journey, afforded by the aspect of our brown and long-bearded company, and their meagre, tired cattle.[36]

The "cattle" consisted entirely of mules: the sheep and cows had all been killed off for food—even the oxen that dragged the vehicles.

Yet the biggest problem for a route along the thirty-fifth parallel was not topographical but political. Negotiations over the Mexican-US border after the Mexican War had confirmed Mexican possession of a stretch of desert, the Mesilla Valley, which was the best place for the proposed railway to go for fifty miles west of El Paso. To squeeze this last grant of land from Mexico, the Pierce administration had to bid for far more than the United States really needed. In 1853, resisting US demands for a huge cession of territory including Baja California and most of Sonora and Coahuila, Mexico sold the vital strip and some surrounding land amounting to a little under 30,000 square miles, for $10 million. For the next thirty years, however, political squabbles—Arizona against Texas, the Confederacy against the Union—and financial exigencies kept the railway out, and at best the newly acquired region served cattlemen as grazing.

For the rest, the railroad surveyors' reports were so voluminous, so opaque, so mutually contradictory, and so hard to compare that the fact was long obscured. In fact all the proposals were impractical, and the route of the Union Pacific Railroad, when it was finally built, was different from all of them.[37] While America waited for railroads, army engineers and sometimes private firms opened more wagon roads across the continent—dirt tracks enhanced by engineers who flattened awkward gradients, spanned gorges, and smoothed bumpy rides. These roads were monuments not so much to the patience of the topographers as the impatience of the public. In May 1856, 75,000 Californians petitioned Congress for a wagon road from the frontier of Missouri.[38]

Eventually the railways became realities. The first railroad from sea to shining sea—or, strictly speaking, from New York to Sacramento, where a steamer passage completed the trip to San Francisco—opened in 1869. The effect on ranching was transformative. Herders in preindustrial and early industrializing societies drove their stock to points of slaughter: the cowboys who fed the rail gangs in the American west from the mid-nineteenth century provided the most strenuous, spectacular, and long-range instance in history. Even as they did so, they were contributing to the demise of their own age-old way of life. When the networks were complete, the railways carried the live cattle. When refrigeration came in, from the 1870s onwards, butchered carcasses could be delivered in edible condition over any distance covered by rail.

The revolution in transport also affected supplies of less perishable items, which could be carried unrefrigerated. Wheat was the most important because of the dual development of railroads and wheatlands in the North American prairie in the second half of the nineteenth century. When I was a visiting professor at the University of Minnesota, my balcony in downtown Minneapolis looked out over derelict evidence of this once-mighty combination. The empty factories of Pillsbury and General Mills, decorated with fading proclamations of the glories of their flour, were being converted into hotels and apartments. Alongside, the Milwaukee Road railway station, saved from demolition, was undergoing rebirth as an upscale shopping mall. The old trade has shifted from downtown but is still vigorous in relocated, modernized mills, silos, and weigh stations. The rails, where they remain unrusted, carry hardly any passengers but are still the arteries of commerce in grain.

MEANWHILE, STEAM POWER WAS affecting maritime routes, cheapening and facilitating migration to the United States, bringing the increased population that created demand for the food of the Midwest. The effects accumulated slowly. For a long time operators of regular packet lines eschewed steam as unreliable. The first transatlantic steamer kept up steam for only eighty hours of the crossing: she was scrapped and sold as a sailing ship.[39] Gradually, however, technical improvements to propulsion and fuel consumption confirmed the steamers' future. Steam-powered vessels did not need new routes. Nor, on the whole, did they make use of them: most early steamships spent the greater part of any journey under sail and used their engines only for supplementary power or as a device to escape calms. Even ships that dispensed with sailing rig altogether still found the assistance of winds and currents useful. In some respects, however, steam vessels could buck the wind. The effect was most noticeable in the North Atlantic, where the busiest westward routes, between northern European and North American ports, were extremely laborious for sailing ships because of the detours imposed by the prevailing westerlies. The first transatlantic steam-packet service opened in 1838. By the late 1840s, a ten- or twelve-day crossing was normal.

Steamers could strike more directly across the ocean, taking the risk of sticking close to the limits of favorable conditions. They had to sail in all weathers, for regularity was as important as speed to the commercial appeal of the service. Paintings (there is a great collection in the Peabody Essex Museum in Salem, Massachusetts) bring the discomforts home. Vessels plunge and buck through stormy seas. Sometimes, in the propaganda spirit of the artists' commissions, they outperform sail. Sometimes the painters include symbolic hints of better times—a shaft of sunlight, a glimpse of blue skies. Sometimes they stick to the bland ease of summer. The best and most dramatic pictures share the "staggering, heaving, wrestling, leaping, diving, jumping, throbbing, rolling and rocking" Charles Dickens described on his Atlantic crossing of 1842. His vision of the ship braving the headwinds "with every pulse and artery of her huge body swollen and bursting" is recognizable in some of the canvases. Most transatlantic migrants headed for the United States, which gained more than 128,000 migrants in the 1820s and over 500,000 in the 1830s. Numbers trebled in the next decade. Until then, most migrants came from Germany, Britain, and Ireland. A further leap in the 1880s brought the total to over 5.25 million from all over Europe and especially from Scandinavia, Italy, central Europe, and the Russian empire. This was the manpower that fueled continental expansion and industrialization. In 1884 the Statue of Liberty arrived in New York City from France in 214 crates to welcome the wretched of teeming shores. The cost of erecting it ($100,000, around $5 million in today's money) almost prevented it from being unpacked. From 1890 to 1920, migration brought a net gain of 18.2 million people to the United States—

more than in the entire previous history of the country. In combination with industrialization, this turned the United States into a major world power.

European immigration obscured but, as we shall see in the next chapter, did not eclipse the continuing contribution of northward migration from Mexico into the United States. It did, however, reinforce a trend adverse to the maintenance of a substantial level of Hispanics in the population at large. Foreigners from Europe, many of whom had no allegiance to Anglo-American values and scant knowledge of English, guaranteed the triumph of Anglo-America.

In the late nineteenth century the railroads linked up with steam-powered sea routes. Intersecting rail and shipping lines were the scaffolding of the world, along which trade and travelers could clamber to every part of it. British steam tonnage at sea exceeded that under sail from 1883: ocean routes would never be fully independent of weather, but their dependence on the elements was easing. Minnesota's railroad king, James Hill, whose sole munificence built the marble cathedral of Saint Paul, had his own fleet of steamships. They joined the terminals of the fastest railroad across the Rockies with those of the Trans-Siberian Railway, which reached the Pacific in 1903. The completion of these links was of more than symbolic significance. Land transport could now take bulk cargoes across continents as easily as over seas. The great food-producing and -consuming belt of the northern hemisphere, from Vancouver to Vladivostok, was linked by steam transport. Trade could defy geography.

The results included a new form of worldwide specialization, as food no longer had to be produced near the point of consumption. In industrializing areas, agriculture declined. British agriculture virtually collapsed in the last generation of the nineteenth century. All over western Europe, wheat production was abandoned in the face of cheap long-range imports. The rock-ribbed farmland of New England began its long, slow reversion to forest as food production shifted west.

Colonization of the Midwest and the western interior, with the ecological invasions that preceded and accompanied the settlers, was surely the most complete and surprising transformation of a natural environment by human agency in the history of the world. When one considers the vastness and intractability of the prairie, its hostile soil, and its ornery climate; when one remembers the origins of wheat in wild grasses hardly reducible by human jaws and barely digestible by human stomachs; when one considers for how long this near-desert was incapable of sustaining more than its own sparse, indigenous population: when all this is taken into account, the achievement that has made the American Midwest what it is today seems hardly credible. It transformed the human profile of the region as well as its look and landscape. Anglo-America—with the Irish, German, Slav, Italian, and Scandinavian footsloggers and railway travelers who carried the mainstream culture in their baggage or acquired it on their way, displaced Hispanic America and Native America alike, and diluted Black America.

IN 1893 THE US Census officially declared the land frontier closed. The country was now settled from coast to coast. Anglo-America had triumphed inasmuch as the ruling institutions had been formed in the old British colonies and transmitted westwards with the federal army and the colonists. The Midwest and the western interior were culturally consistent—albeit not uniform—with the seaboards. Frederick Jackson Turner, perhaps the most influential of all historians of the United States, discerned one source of difference. Frontiers, he observed, are socially and institutionally creative because they attract vanguards and open gaps between march and metropolis—generational gaps, because the young go to the frontier to escape gerontocracy; social gaps, because frontiers draw outcasts and entrepreneurs; wealth gaps, because the frontier is a land of opportunity; and political gaps, because frontiers leave central governments and aristocracies behind. According to Turner's reading of the US past, these effects modified the old world of the eastern seaboard in turn, keeping the republic young, roping it to frontiersmen's love of freedom.

However that may be, the United States—perhaps because men steeped in reverence for both the classics and Christianity founded it—was the effective laboratory of democracy for the nineteenth-century world. Democracy as we usually understand it today—with political parties and a representative legislature elected on a wide suffrage—was in effect an American invention. In the 1840s Tocqueville made European aristocracies understand it and contemplate it without fear. His successor in the 1880s was James Bryce, an Oxford professor who became ambassador to the United States. His book, *The American Commonwealth*, helped to convince many states to adopt democratic or democratizing constitutions in the late nineteenth century. In some ways, US democracy never went as far as some of its imitators: the American executive is not formally subordinate to Congress, for instance, as is the çase in most European and Latin American democracies. Nonetheless, all major US officeholders under the president have to submit to confirmation by the Senate and all, including the president, report to Congress, which has—and sometimes indulges in—a right to impeach them. Despite major imperfections—slaves, Native Americans, and women were excluded from political rights—democracy developed early in the history of the new republic. Some of the states were more generous than others in enlarging the franchise, but by the early 1840s, almost all adult, white, and free males could vote in all the states of the United States.

IN SOME WAYS, THE arrest or self-limitation of expansion guaranteed the triumph of Anglo-America within the United States. The prospects that the United States would annex more of Mexico, or even the whole of it—retuning itself as part of the Hispanic world— were real at intervals until well into the twentieth century. At the end of the Mexican War, Congress heard over and over again the case for continuing to occupy all conquered territory. Some US citizens defied the order to withdraw from Yucatán. Others raised conquistador expeditions of their own. Annexation fever increased with the election in 1852 of President Franklin Pierce, who wanted to take over Britain's Central American colonies, buy Cuba from Spain, and, as we have seen, bid to acquire most of northwestern Mexico. A daily paper in Upper California expressed the mood: "That Mexico must be Americanized is clear to every thinking man."[40] The clarity struck slavers most forcibly: territory seized from Mexico could be converted to slavery, adding to the constituency against emancipation in the United States or—should abolitionists prevail—turned into a refuge for slave owners and a land of perpetual plantations.

In 1853 the Gadsden Purchase transferred the city of Tucson and nearly 30,000 square miles of Mexican territory to the United States in order to accommodate a railroad link to San Diego. Thereafter, US governments contained their appetite for Mexican territory and—officially, at least—did not risk trying to digest millions of hispanos at a gulp. Like so much US activity, the role of empire building devolved to private enterprise. In the 1850s, on at least seven separate occasions, adventurers led unsuccessful attempts from the United States to detach Baja California, Tamaulipas, and Sonora from Mexico. Joseph C. Morehead (so he called himself, though the Texan family of that name disclaimed all connection) turned from a career of extortion and banditry in California to launch an invasion in 1851. His men fled when they encountered resistance. More persistent were the efforts, begun at about the same time and sustained on and off for five years, of José-María Jesús Carbajal, who had converted to Protestantism and Anglophilia during long residence in the United States as a refugee from Mexican efforts to prosecute his violations of trading laws. Protesting innocence of his schemes, the US authorities did nothing to stop him, except to exonerate him of wrongdoing in a farcical trial in 1854.[41] Had Carbajal's efforts or those of his many counterparts and emulators succeeded, there were plenty of imperialists in the US political establishment who advocated replicating the fate of Texas and annexing any more parts of Mexico that split from the republic.

Carbajal aspired to carve out a state to rule himself. William Walker, a pugnacious New Orleans journalist, took over an existing one. After failed efforts to incite rebellion in Baja California and Sonora, he took advantage of a civil war in Nicaragua to invade with an army of mercenaries and seize the capital in 1856. He proclaimed himself president, reinstituted slavery, declared English the national language, and incited his fellow countrymen to migrate to join him. His rule lasted a few months before the combined outrage of his new subjects and their neighbors in the other Central American republics ousted him. The allure survived. In 1880 Ernest Dalrymple, an otherwise obscure Pennsylvanian who called himself "General Dalrymple," planned the conquests of Mexico and Central America, claiming to have raised money in Germany for the attempt: "Behold a vision of enchantment, a continent lulled by the waves of two oceans . . . undying glory crowns the knight whose daring arm unveils the dazzling future."[42]

US cupidity aroused pan-Hispanic sentiments that had been largely dormant since the collapse of the Spanish empire. José Martí, the hero of the Cuban independence movement, who was working at the time as a journalist in New York, denounced US warmongers who "see Mexico as their own property and stir race hatred" against "our fatherland, which is one, starting at the Rio Grande and stretching to the hills and marshes of Patagonia."[43] The US establishment seemed to arrive at a consensus against further territorial expansion at Mexico's expense on the grounds that most of what was profitable in the neighbor country was already in the hands of Yankee investors,[44] but ambitious individuals and syndicates could not yet be restrained. Another outburst of what US journalists called "filibustering" targeted Baja California in 1888–90. Invaders from the United States who called themselves socialists and proclaimed political subversion of the Mexican state as their objective tried again in 1911, in an attempt to exploit the Mexican Revolution.

At intervals over the next six or seven years, while conditions in Mexico became unstable, arguments for taking over the country repeatedly resurfaced in the United States. In 1913 the caricaturist José Posada depicted gringo imperialists as a modern version of the horsemen of the apocalypse, along with fraudsters, corrupt politicos, syphilitic prostitutes, and "bad Mexicans who help the foreigners." Border incidents culminated in the occupation of Veracruz by US troops in 1914. A major security operation followed, deep into Mexican territory, by a US force of 10,000 men in 1916–17. The object was to capture or kill Pancho Villa, the charismatic revolutionary and warlord of Chihuahua, whose career wavered between service to banditry and democracy. Villa provoked US wrath by his habit of ignoring the border in search of munitions and money with which to keep his army supplied. Like other US incursions into Mexico during the remainder of World War I, the expedition ended ignominiously. The commander, General John Pershing, confessed to his brother-in-law that "having dashed into Mexico with the intention of eating the Mexicans raw, . . . we are now sneaking back home under cover like a whipped cur."[45] The consequences included Villa's elevation to heroic status in Mexican legend. He remains a model and reference for gringo baiters, who still call, "Long live Pancho Villa!" to taunt hostile US authorities.[46]

ALTHOUGH MEXICO ESCAPED FURTHER losses of territory (until a small boundary adjustment by agreement in 1970), the United States began to overspill the continent almost as soon as the country had occupied the land within its own latitudes, seizing Hawaii in 1898, American Samoa and Wake Island in 1899 (with various other small Pacific islands added at intervals until the 1940s), Puerto Rico, Guantánamo, the Philippines, Guam and the Northern Marianas from 1899 to 1902, and the Panama Canal Zone in 1903. The last big acquisition of territory, the formerly Danish Virgin Islands, was made by purchase in 1917. Most of the new subjects the United States gained in these last convulsions of imperialism were from Spain. Except, however, for Puerto Rico, they added little to the Spanish heritage of the United States. Guantánamo, though never decolonized, is a small military base, effectively isolated from the rest of Cuba. The Canal Zone, under US occupation from 1903 to 1979, was largely populated by temporary US émigrés. The Philippines was a region where Spanish culture was shallow, except among the elite, as missionaries had always used indigenous languages as media of evangelization. Few Filipinos who moved to the US mainland during the occupation of their homeland spoke Spanish or shared a sense of belonging with Hispanics from the Americas.

Except in religion and in the architecture of public buildings, Guam and the Northern Marianas were only superficially affected by Spain. Their Spanish history began in earnest in 1668, when Chief Quipuha, in a classic instance of the stranger-effect, welcomed Spanish missionaries to Guam, gave them land for a church, accepted baptism, and allowed Spain to use the island as a base for the galleon trade between China and New Spain. As so often in the history of Spanish empire building, good relations broke down. The Jesuits who manned the Spanish mission tried but failed to do without Spanish troops and to exclude lay Spaniards, whose provocations contributed to worsening relations. Vested interests in the islands united against the missionaries: defenders of pagan shrines, practitioners of polygamy, formerly powerful priestesses whose position would be untenable under Jesuit tutelage. The incumbent beneficiary of the stranger-effect, a Chinese migrant who exercised a great deal of informal local influence, helped organize violent resistance. The martyrdom of the Jesuits' leader in 1672 sanctified the war from the conquistadores' point of view and inaugurated a generation of brutal repression. Thanks, however, to the Jesuits' cultural sensibilities, and those of the Augustinian and secular priests who succeeded them in the eighteenth century, the islands were evangelized in the native language. The indigenous elite never took on Spanish airs or speech, as they did in the Philippines. When the US Navy arrived at the end of the Spanish-American War, a native clergy was on hand to replace the Spaniards, and a native aristocracy entirely eager to see off their former colonial masters.[47] Today the people of Guam and the Northern Marianas can hardly be counted as part of the Hispanic minority in the United States.

The war that freed them from Spanish rule only increased WASP contempt for Spain. According to the US press, it started because of Spanish perfidy and ended quickly because of Spanish cowardice and incompetence. The truth, of course, was more complex. For many years before the outbreak of the Spanish-American War, successive US governments had coveted Cuba with its precious sugar production, and tried to negotiate the island's purchase from Spain. According to Leonard Wood, who commanded US forces in the Philippines, the island was "easily worth any two of the Southern States" of the United States. With Cuba, he thought, "we shall soon practically control the sugar trade of the world."[48] By the mid-1890s, the US government, far from sponsoring Cuban independence, began to contemplate intervention to crush Cuban resistance. The launch of the war in 1898 was a preemptive strike designed to prevent the Cubans from winning independence on their own and to transfer the island to US control.

In January of that year, the US warship *Maine* arrived in Havana, ostensibly as a gesture of friendship to Spain but really in order to intimidate islanders and Spaniards alike. The following month, in a nineteenth-century equivalent of a Wikileak, the US press inflamed public opinion by publishing a private letter in which a Spanish minister lampooned the US president as a "feeble rabble-rouser." A few days later an explosion rent and sank the *Maine*, still in Havana harbor, with the loss of 266 lives. Official Spanish and US inquiries both found that the cause was an onboard accident, but US media insisted on blaming "a Spanish act of treachery." The US consul in Havana recommended that the administration exploit the pretext to annex Cuba, and that "the Cuban people would not be a factor." President William McKinley still hoped to acquire the island cheaply by purchase, but agreed that "we must . . . occupy and . . . own" it. Despite the warnings of Cuban insurgents that they would resist US imperialism as tenaciously as Spain's, the United States launched an invasion in April and prepared expeditions against all Spain's Caribbean and Pacific possessions, including the Philippines, Guam, the Mariana Islands, and Puerto Rico.[49]

The outcome was inevitable, as soon as the US Navy blew Spain's outdated and neglected Caribbean and Pacific fleets out of the water. Despite impressive resistance on land, Spain could not realistically hope to go on defending her possessions without any means of reinforcing or supplying her troops. Spanish resistance proved remarkably effective until the government in Madrid, realizing its futility, called it off. In the land campaigns, a combination of Spanish tenacity and yellow fever worsted the invaders, although to no avail in the long term.

In peace negotiations from which Cubans and Filipinos were shut out, Spain effectively capitulated, handing all the disputed territories over to the United States. Imperialists extemporized various justifications for holding on to their conquests, but underlying all the rhetoric were racist assumptions voiced by one of the US generals in Cuba, Samuel Baldwin Young; he declared the Cubans "no more capable of government than the savages of Africa" and advised that "the relationship of the white men to the tropical people must be one of dominance."⁵⁰

In Guam and the Marianas the population succumbed bloodlessly. In the Philippines and Puerto Rico, thanks to the ruthless tactics of Leonard Wood and his fellow commanders, the invaders contained native insurgency. In Cuba, however, the insurgents were well organized and had links to liberal and democratic opinion in the United States. In 1902, rather than continue to hold Cuba by force, the administration decided to install a nominally independent government, while retaining effective control of the new state's foreign policy and trade. "We mean business," declared the US investor in Cuba George B. Hopkins, "and not a thing in Cuba should be allowed to get away from the Americans."⁵¹ The island remained in effect dependent on the United States for more than half a century.

One of the redoubtable Spanish commanders in the interior of Puerto Rico was the remarkable Julio Cervera Baviera, one of the great polymaths of the age. His career included surveying Spanish North Africa, introducing Freemasonry to Morocco, collaborating with Marconi in the invention of wireless telegraphy, and taking the lead in developing voice transmission by radio. The outcome of his efforts, and those of his fellow soldiers, was disillusioning. He blamed Spain's defeat on the colonists' indifference or hostility and regarded their allegiance as saleable. Within twenty-four hours, he said, of Spain's capitulation, "the people of Puerto Rico went from being fervently Spanish to enthusiastically American. . . . They humiliated themselves, giving in to the invader as the slave bows to the powerful lord"[52]—with consequences we shall see in Chapter Eight. For the time being, the war seemed to set the seal on the triumph of Anglo-America and demonstrate its superiority over Hispanic America.

HISTORICALLY WELL-EDUCATED PEOPLE IN the United States—admittedly, a very small minority—can remember the Alamo with respect for the victors and the *Maine* with sympathy for the vanquished. It is now almost obligatory for US presidential candidates to make some effort to say something in Spanish. Nothing confirms the triumph of Anglo-America more than the fact that some Anglos can contemplate the Hispanic past without a sense of menace. If their transition to indifference to or appreciation of their Hispanic neighbors is imperfect or selective, it is because the growing size of the Hispanic minority has revived some people's cultural fear and racial hatred. The Hispanic revanche was already going on under cover of the events narrated in this chapter. As we shall see in the next, a newly rehispanized United States was incubating under the shell. While millions of migrants from Europe were coming to America, Mexicans were undertaking their own return to Aztlán.

PART THREE

PARADISE REGAINED?

*The Second
Hispanic Colonization,
c. 1898~2012*

CHAPTER SEVEN

THE RETURN TO AZTLÁN

Americanization and Resistance in the Age of Mexican Countercolonization, c. 1898–1986

———

But is this new conquest of the Americas, by the Americas and for the Americas? This mutual transcontinental, translinguistic, trans-racial osmosis? If so, it is a far cry from the conquistadores to these frightened hybrids, from those who knocked down the door of a new world, to those who knock at the door of a richer world. . . . It is a far, heartrending cry from those Spaniards to these Ameri-caniards.

~Felipe Alfau, Chromos (1936?)

This is what we live here for: proud of this America of ours, to serve her and honor her.

*~José Martí, speech to the
Sociedad Literaria Hispanoamericana* (1885)

IN 1886 THE STATUE OF LIBERTY ROSE OVER NEW YORK HARBOR, welcoming—according to the inscription at her feet—the "wretched refuse" of the poor and oppressed. The giant cast a dark shadow.

The idea for a landmark of liberty on the threshold of the United States began not in America but in France, for purposes of French politics, among Frenchmen who wished to liberalize the regime of Napoleon III, to express solidarity with republican traditions, and to curtail imperialistic adventures. Four hundred thousand dollars were raised among French subscribers. F. A. Bartholdi and Gustave Eiffel bent all their engineering genius to the problems of design and construction. Nearly twenty years elapsed before an American envoy accepted the completed work. Twenty-four crates shipped it across the ocean in kit form. Enthusiasm was much less at Liberty's destination than in her country of origin. The delicately articulated structure—the central iron pylon, the complex, flexible truss-work innards, the cladding of hammered copper—seemed destined to remain crated for lack of funds to pay for a pedestal, until Joseph Pulitzer's newspaper campaign shamed the American public into scraping up the $100,000 needed to put the statue in its place.

From her perch on Bedloe's Island, Liberty presided over a new era in American immigration. Apart from black slaves, the United States banned or deterred no migrants until 1875, when Congress enacted the first restrictions on allegedly potentially subversive arrivals from China. In 1882 the Chinese Exclusion Act followed—the first in a series of measures designed to keep Chinese out altogether. From 1885, a new law forbade the importation of contract labor. Restrictions similar in effect limited and then virtually outlawed Japanese immigrants in the early years of the twentieth century. Meanwhile, in 1891, Congress set up a board of inspection to process applicants for immigration and reject communicators of "loathsome disease" or of "moral turpitude."

Just as Liberty's statue went up, the inscription on her pedestal seemed to go out of date, as selective immigration heaped travail and indignity on the wretched and oppressed whom she claimed to welcome. From 1892, the year the hemisphere celebrated the four hundredth anniversary of Columbus's first Atlantic crossing, the authorities filtered immigrants according to suitability. Undesirables—mostly carriers of suspected diseases, but also political suspects, such as anarchists, or moral rejects, such as prostitutes and polygamists—were combed out like lice from a pelt. Ever-narrower quotas were enforced. The Statue of Liberty had arrived just in time to witness the erosion of liberality in America's immigration laws under the impact of a migrant movement hugely bigger in numbers than had been experienced before and vastly more extensive in range of provenance.

It is not surprising that rising immigration and tighter controls should go hand in hand. When newcomers' numbers mount and trigger anxieties, communities worry about the adulteration of their culture, the pollution of their womenfolk, pressure on jobs, and the "swamping" and "squeezing" effects of mass immigration. The late nineteenth-century migrants came, driven in part by misery at home and drawn in part by opportunity in America. For the United States was as hungry for labor as immigrants were for work. Two circumstances account for the shortage of manpower. First, industrialization multiplied work and opened up new economic possibilities, though its effects on labor were not uniformly benign: it substituted machine power for muscle, imposed mind-numbing routines, and magnified the workforce by making possible the mobilization of females in factories, with equivocal effects on women's freedom and happiness. Moreover, in a related phenomenon, as we saw in the last chapter, industrial methods hugely expanded the amount of land available for exploitation in the United States.

The combination of bonanzas in land and demand meant that the United States could gobble up large numbers of immigrants. Even as the hoops got tighter, more people squeezed uncomfortably through them. Newcomers came from ethnicities new to American experience or previously underrepresented, from areas deep in eastern Europe, beyond the western seaboard states that had formerly predominated.

From 1899, when Jews were first separately enumerated, until 1924, 17 percent of new arrivals were Italians, 14 percent Jews, and 17 percent Slavs. Well over 10 percent were Mexicans.

Mexico could provide because of its own phenomenal demographic buoyancy. At the time of the Mexican War, the country contained about 7 million people. The numbers more than doubled by 1915. By then, popular revulsion against the importation of Chinese and Japanese labor and the multiplication of hoops in the way of European migrants made Mexicans more than ever the prime targets for the recruiters of cheap hands north of the border. The rehispanicization of the United States began toward the end of the nineteenth century, and although, as we shall see in the next chapter, plenty of other Spanish-speaking people played a part, Mexicans were its prime vectors. They still are. According to 2011 figures, self-identified Mexicans in the United States form nearly two-thirds of the total Hispanic population, and well over 60 percent of the foreign-born Hispanic community. They account for nearly a quarter of all foreign immigrants.[1]

In a sense, the transgressors of the border, when the late nineteenth-century upturn in migrants' numbers occurred, were the first wave of what was to be a major global phenomenon of the twentieth century. I call it "countercolonization": the reversal of the direction of global migration, which—instead of flowing outward from center to periphery or from the metropolitan "mother countries" to colonized lands—began increasingly to originate among the subject peoples or former victims of colonialism. They set out to reclaim lost territory, or colonize regions previously reserved for the imperial master races, or head for the center and set up home in imperial heartlands. Maghribis in France, Caribbeans and subcontinentals in Britain, Surinamese in the Netherlands, Latin Americans in Spain, Somalis in Italy, and people from central Asia and the Caucasus in Russia all exemplify the trend. So do Mexicans in the United States.

Theirs is genuinely a phenomenon of countercolonization. David Villaseñor, a Tucson shoe smith from Guadalajara, said in 1927 that Mexico would someday recover the territory the United States had seized.[2] Antonio Orendain, a leading farm-labor organizer, was hiding from the police when he first entered the United States without documents in 1950; a companion reproached him: "You're a coward! Don't you know this is our land? This is Mexican territory that Santa Anna sold."[3] When a migrant arrives wetbacked from the Rio Grande or tumbled from the back of a truck that bounces across the desert night, "he sometimes asks," according to the revered Mexican intellectual Carlos Fuentes, "hasn't this always been our land? Am I not coming back to it? Is it not in some way ours? He can taste it, hear its language, sing its songs, and pray to its saints."[4]

As MEXICAN BORDER CROSSINGS multiplied in the 1890s, so did the resentments and hatreds of the migrants' hosts. An incident in the remote copper-mining communities of Clifton and Morenci in Arizona in October 1904 exposed the depths of the oppression of Mexicans.

The Sisters of Charity ran a foundling hospital in New York City, where they cared for abandoned children—typically the offspring of poor Catholic and therefore, in New York at the time, commonly Irish single mothers. When their charges were about four years old, the sisters sought foster families for them. The work was not only charitable: it was evangelistic. The sisters were responding to the depredations of Protestant adoption agents, who rounded up Catholic children on the streets in what were sometimes genuine rescues and sometimes acts of naked abduction, and placed them with zealots who brought them up in alienation from their traditional faith. The sisters' policy was to find suitable Catholic households to take over the care of the growing foundlings. The search led ever farther west, as the frontier and the Foundling Hospital both filled up. In 1904 Arizona was beyond the range of the sisters' previous efforts, but in Clifton and Morenci the priest in charge—a temporarily installed new arrival from France, where the diocese recruited many of its priests—reported great willingness to help on his congregations' part. The destination was too far away for the sisters to make in advance the usual preliminary enquiries about the proposed families' suitability, but they decided to take children to the territory and perform checks on the spot.

When they got there, they found a mephitic environment. Sun burned. Dust blew. Sulfurous clouds from the merciless mines polluted the atmosphere. The acid in the air attacked the lungs with a sting like "boiling lime."[5] Stench from unpiped privies and uncleared donkey droppings hung among the fumes. Hostile topography twisted the little towns into tortured shapes and scattered precipitous homes over wearisome slopes. The savage, spendthrift mining ethos lined the streets with saloons, gaming houses, and brothels. Nightly entertainments included bar brawls and bandit ballads. Memories of a menacing, violent strike of the previous year divided the population and exacerbated the cultural chasm that separated workers from bosses: the miners were mostly of Mexican ancestry. They spoke Spanish for preference. The Anglo management and middle class beheld them with emotions ranging from defensiveness to fear, from contempt to hatred. The place seemed godless. Church attendance, Protestant and Catholic alike, was minimal. Miners' wives were the most pious element in the population.

The sisters had no means of knowing or understanding the nature of local feelings. To them, the miners' wives were Spanish. "Mexican" was not a category that meant much to New Yorkers. The women's deferential manners seemed decorous, whereas really they were the effects of underdog status and repressive and humiliating treatment at the hands of the Anglo elite. Their attire—shawls and sandals and unstructured skirts—contrasted, but not unfavorably, with the tawdry finery the soi-disant "white ladies" affected. They were all covered with dust. None had the education or taste or command of language that the nuns might have associated with superior social status. The sisters were wary of placing children with "Indian" families, and reflected the prejudices of their time in favor of relatively light pigmentation. Though they had never faced a comparable situation before, they seem to have been dimly aware that their children needed to fit the families to whom they were assigned. They turned away some would-be foster parents on the basis of what seems to have been almost instinctive prejudice. On the whole, however, the applicant households were recognizable to the sisters as "respectable." They were often competent in English and eloquent in Spanish. The higher-paid miners earned adequate wages, saved earnestly, expressed Catholic sentiments, and housed, fed, and treated their wives and children well. The women were house-proud, devout, and hungry for motherhood.

The placing of white children in what the Anglo elite regarded as racially inferior families provoked an extraordinary outbreak of hate-filled mass hysteria. "White ladies" demanded that they should have the exclusive privilege of mothering the "little ones" from the east. By preferring families of Mexican origins or traditions, the priest and nuns seemed simultaneously to insult white superiority and imperil the children's welfare. Women mobilized their menfolk into a mob that threatened and effectively imprisoned the nuns. They sent posses to Mexican homes to round up the children at gunpoint and redistribute them among the supposedly more deserving whites. The "great orphan abduction" became a cause célèbre, which transmitted harrowing tales of intimidated nuns and tearful Mexican foster-mothers all the way to the Supreme Court of the United States. When the case came to court, the representatives of the Foundling Hospital, while suing for the children to be returned to the nuns, never questioned the opposition's case that the Mexican families were unsuitable and unreliable fosterers. Some of the sisters complied with their adversaries' racism, admitting that some Mexicans were "dark skinned ragged people, . . . a destitute and uninviting lot . . . like a horde of savages."[6]

Some anti-Catholic feeling intruded. Objectors accused the nuns and priests of the kinds of venality and cruelty with which Know-Nothing tradition typically besmirched Catholics. The Church, according to local deponents, sold children to the Mexicans for "silver coins" in a crude allusion to the Judas story, "as they would deal with so many packets of merchandise."[7] The foundlings' caretakers suffered accusations, which the evidence clearly contradicted, of neglecting and maltreating their charges, selling them to Indians, abandoning them to die en route, and—in calculatingly delicate language—exposing or subjecting them to sexual abuse and enslaving them for prostitution. Anti-Catholicism was clearly not, however, the objectors' main inspiration. Some of them even claimed to be Catholics themselves, though they had never gone to Mass or identified themselves as such to their parish priest (who thought everybody locally except for the Mexicans was "either a Protestant or a Freemason.")[8] In some cases they even offered unconvincing promises to bring the children up as Catholics if confided with their care. One of them, a miner's wife whose husband earned little more than the best-paid Mexicans, explained that she could not go to church because "white people or Americans" could not consort with Mexicans. She was willing, however, for the priest to call on her in her own home.[9]

The objectors' main grounds for denouncing the Mexicans and demanding to foster the children themselves were broadly cultural or crudely racial. The Mexicans sickened the infants with tortillas and beans, or allowed them to drink morally imperiling beer (though saloonkeepers were among the abductors who kidnapped and kept some of the orphans). They were illiterate—though the objective evidence is that those who have left records could read and write with fluency. The owner and superintendent of the mines—who seized children from the nuns for purposes of their own—derided the Mexicans' poverty, though it was they who fixed the wages at exploitatively low levels, and denounced their dirtiness, though it was they who refused the workers' demands for washing facilities at the mines. "They have no intellect," insisted the superintendent, and "drink up everything they can."[10] The charges were groundless. The Mexican fosterers had generally good records of solvency, and objective witnesses endorsed the cleanliness of their homes and persons. Deponents testifying in court in the aftermath of the great abduction always insisted that they "knew" Mexicans, but the rules of society in Clifton and Morenci prevented them from doing so: they always admitted that they never went into Mexican houses, did not know most of their Mexican neighbors by name, and "weren't supposed to associate with Mexicans at all."[11] Fraternization was unthinkable.

It was hard for a Mexican to be "white," except in the sisters' perception or that of the parish priest, who listed the number of his

THE RETURN TO AZTLÁN ～ 253

nonwhite parishioners as zero in the census.[12] In local usage, "white" was an economic category, constituting entitlement to a higher rate of wages than Mexicans were usually allowed. Typically, anyone perceived as a foreigner, "dago," or "bohunk" was, at best, of imperfect whiteness. Birth or naturalization in the United States could not dispel the taint. In Texas in 1921, as a congressman put it, 250,000 Mexicans were born in the state, "but they are 'Mexicans' just as all blacks are Negroes, though they may have five generations of American ancestors." Southerners with backgrounds in racist cultures predominated in the "white" population of the mining districts and transferred from blacks to Mexicans their accustomed language and prejudices. The mothers the Sisters of Charity favored as foster-parents were, according to Laura Abraham, who wanted a child for herself, members of "a class of people even lower than the negro of the south and almost as dark."[13] Vigilantism targeted Mexicans, along with Chinese, in the Southwest as much as blacks in Mississippi or Alabama. Countervigilantism occurred, but was rarely effective. "You can hang a Mexican, and you can hang a Jew, and you can hang a nigger, but you can't hang an American citizen!" according to a Tucson newspaper in 1873.

Frontier justice ruled.

The rioters called themselves "the citizens" and "the people." The notion that citizenry and the people might include people of Hispanic background did not arise in a land where no juries empanelled people with Spanish-sounding names and where Mexican testimony was banned from courts. Hispanics indeed tended increasingly to opt out of a political community in which they were victimized and deprived of rights. Their share of the population of registered voters fell in Arizona from over 44 percent in 1894 to less than half that figure at the time of the orphan abduction. By 1922 the numbers had collapsed to 8 percent.

The spirit of redneck democracy, according to which the will of the mob is always right, animated the hysteria. The mob that besieged the nuns in 1904 screamed "the dirtiest names possible"[14] at them along with threats of lynching and burning, and dragged tar, feathers, rope, and coal oil to the scene to spike their attempts at intimidation. The sheriff and deputies submitted to the mood and lent the mob an air of legality. In Clifton the abductors could not prevail on the local judge to legitimize their claims to have adopted the children they kidnapped; but neither would he order the return of the orphans to their legal wards, the representatives of the Foundling Hospital of New York. The idea that laws made in Washington or Albany should command respect in Arizona was an affront to local feeling and to the particularism that shivers America into legal and political fragments, as if the motto of the land was "Ex uno plures." Despite—or perhaps because of—a nationwide Catholic campaign against the abductors and an amicus curiae brief by a US attorney on the nuns' behalf at the request of the president of the United States, the district court ruled that against "half-breed Mexican Indians . . . impecunious, illiterate, . . . vicious" good "Americans . . . assisted in the rescue of these little children from the evil into which they had fallen."[15] Over the next few years, the Ku Klux Klan lit crosses in Clifton, the Catholic priest's house was bombed in the course of a clear attempt to murder him, and dynamiters twice attacked his church.[16]

THE HISTORY OF ANTI-CATHOLIC prejudice in the United States is inseparable from that of the problems of immigrants from Latin America. Self-appointed guardians of American values often assume that Protestantism is a defining feature of the heritage of the United States, that civil liberties grew out of freedom of faith, and that despotism and popery are natural allies. Contempt for the Irish and hostility to Spain were among the values inherited from the old country by some Americans of English descent. Religious fissures divided the German-American minority in the late nineteenth and early twentieth centuries, reflecting, in part and for a time, the metropolitan *Kulturkampf*—the government-sponsored campaign against the freedom and social influence of the church in Germany in Bismarck's Reich. Anti-Catholicism united with ex-immigrants' natural resentment of their successors in a political movement, officially called the

American Party but better known by its ironic soubriquet: the Know-Nothing Party. Samuel Morse, the inventor of cable telegraphy, who suspected that the United States was the target of a Jesuit plot, summoned Catholic immigrants to his fellow citizens' minds in "a loathsome picture of degradation, moral and physical," of "a secret enemy" who had "stolen in among us . . . that he may . . . do his nefarious work."[17] In the 1890s the American Protective Association, which stood for the exclusion of all Catholics from US citizenship, backed candidates pledged to remove Catholics from government jobs.[18] The influence of anti-Catholic organizations peaked in the 1924 elections, when the Ku Klux Klan, "the largest and most cohesive, most efficiently organized political force in the state," according to the Denver Post,[19] secured the election of one of its members as Colorado governor. Clarence Morley promised to ban Catholic immigrants and prohibit sacramental use of wine. But Democrats and liberal Republicans blocked the measures.[20]

Condemned by their own Catholicism, Mexicans suffered from their hosts' racism. Those able to distinguish Mexicans from blacks commonly labeled them "Indians" or "half-breeds" or "renegades" when groping for pejorative classifications. According to the folk orthodoxy of the time, which many supposedly scientific authorities endorsed, racial impurity caused degeneracy. In California in 1870, Pablo de la Guerra, who had held many public offices, became "no longer eligible to vote, hold office, testify in court against a white person, or hold land" because he did not look white enough. He could afford lawyers who were able to establish that he was white enough to be a US citizen, but his case confirmed the state's right to exclude "non-white Mexicans" from citizenship.[21] In 1884 Reginaldo del Valle, a crucial but until recently largely unacknowledged contributor to the foundation of the school that became the University of California, Los Angeles, lost an election for Congress to an opponent whose campaigning line was, "No decent man has ever been born of a Mexican woman."[22]

By that time, as we have seen, Darwinism, or bastard social-Darwinian versions of it, had reinforced nineteenth-century assumptions about the ranking of races. The basis for the hostile assumptions was that many Mexicans were "of mixed Indian and renegade American blood."[23] Louis Agassiz, the distinguished Harvard professor who died in 1873, thought that racial interbreeding was an evolutionary stigma that condemned half-breeds, like mules, to infertility and extinction.[24] He was wrong, but his ideas persisted in uncritical minds. Mexicans were Indians, in which case they were "brown" or "red" and racially inferior to anyone who was white, or they were mixed-race products of white or black and Native American interbreeding, in which case they were "degenerate." Degeneracy, filth, ignorance, indolence, and an insistence on Mexicans' supposedly "mongrel" origins, tainted by admixture with or resemblance to blacks and Indians, recur monotonously in late nineteenth-century justifications of gringo supremacy.[25] Real prejudices, which occluded the genuine reasons for social problems in the Southwest, were among the results. An Arizona social workers' magazine in 1907 addressed the statistically glaring problem of why Mexican-American felons thronged courts and jails. The article suggested one good reason: migrant populations always included a relatively high number of fugitives from justice. It admitted a further, even more compelling fact: hostile expectations prejudiced US policemen and courts against Mexicans.

In 1920 Texas congressman John C. Box argued against a relaxation of immigration controls on the grounds that in the war of Texan independence Americans confronted Mexicans and "found they could not live with them on genial terms. . . . In a contest which arose then the Mexican showed both his inferiority and savage nature," further exemplified in the self-destructive violence of the Mexican Revolution. The influence of trickle-down Darwinism is unmistakable.[26] It affected otherwise clear-thinking, well-disposed individuals. Walter Prescott Webb, who died in 1963 and was a major figure in the intellectual establishment in the United States in the 1920s and 1930s, was an admirable Texan and a pioneering historian. He was a prophet of environmental history and an early ecologist who foresaw how the abuse of irrigation would gradually make the prairie he loved unfarmable. His genuine originality of mind, however, was not strong enough to subvert racist prejudices. Webb thought that Mexicans'"cruel streak . . . may be a heritage from the Spanish of the Inquisition; it may, and doubtless should, be attributed partly to the Indian blood." He said that Mexican-American blood was "ditch water."[27] He undiscriminatingly admired the Texas Rangers, to whom he devoted much of his lifetime of scholarship, and characterized a typical Ranger as "a very quiet, deliberate, gentle person who could gaze calmly into the eye of a murderer, divine his thoughts, and anticipate his action, a man who could ride straight up to death." Webb praised Captain Bill McDonald, the Ranger who led a shootout in which Mexican-American residents of Rio Grande City were massacred in 1906. The courts exonerated the Rangers' act of "self-defense," in which they suffered no casualties.[28]

The racism that afflicted Hispanic migrants in the United States has to be understood against the background of US imperialism. The 1890s were, perhaps, the high-water mark of US empire building. Officially, in that decade, the "republican empire" filled the continent, as the shining sea gleamed in close-up. Almost immediately, with the closing of the frontier, American imperialism spilled into the oceans. In the Pacific, the Hawaiian kings had fended off European predators for years and sustained a clever diplomatic balance to keep potential conquerors at bay. But the numbers of foreign immigrants to Hawaii increased, and the economic power of traders from the United States became dominant. The game Hawaii's native rulers played therefore got harder, until white settlers overthrew the monarchy in 1893 with American military and diplomatic support. Annexation to the United States followed in 1898.

Meanwhile, the United States also annexed American Samoa in the South Pacific and, as we saw in the last chapter, seized the Philippines, Guam, and Puerto Rico after defeating Spain in 1898. The acquisition of Puerto Rico closed a circle: US territory now included a colony more than a hundred years older than any Anglo settlement. As we have seen, Spain's former colony of Cuba, which was nominally independent after 1901, became a virtual US protectorate, and Washington took permanent possession of a naval base there at Guantánamo Bay. The United States also acquired the Canal Zone from Panama in 1904 after enabling Panama to secede from Colombia—the sort of project the filibusters had long cherished and the government now copied. The whole American hemisphere became a US sphere of influence and "Uncle Sam's backyard."

Like most European empires, that of the United States relied on racism for its ideological justification—the right of rule of the superior over the inferior, the *mission civilisatrice* of a higher over a lower order of beings. The Spanish monarchy, founded and mostly lost before scientific racism began, was largely spared explicitly racist self-legitimation. Rather, medieval and Renaissance models animated the empire: of Rome, with its universal citizenship; of natural law, with the concept of the "community of mortals"; of sovereignty as "supreme lordship," according to which all vassals had access to equal justice under the crown; and of the Church, embracing all humans as of common descent and shared prospects of salvation or damnation. Indigenous elites could command respect, retain power, marry Spaniards, and acquire the ornaments of honor. So could free blacks, especially if they could plausibly claim distinguished ancestors in their societies of origin. Even so, other rankings kept Spaniards at the top of the hierarchy of prestige and ordinary indios and blacks at the bottom. Priests' paternalism rated them as infantile; cultural prejudices characterized them as barbarous or underdeveloped.

The US empire, by contrast, grew up in and beyond its home continent, like those of Britain, France, and Germany in Africa and the Pacific, in an age of unashamed racism, when soi-disant scientific anthropology stacked the peoples of the world in order of pigmentation, dodgy calculations of cranial size and shape, and supposed resemblances to apes. The categories that confined nonwhites to inferior status were tighter than formerly; the effects, though exacerbated, were essentially the same. White leadership was presumed to be a favor to races of feebler capacity. In 1900 Senator Albert Beveridge of Indiana used language already well established among European imperialists, when he told Congress that "God . . . has made us the

master organizers of the world . . . that we may administer government among savage and senile peoples."[29] The previous year William
Rheem Lighton, whose novels romanticized the American West and
idolized its heroes, had published an eponymous story about "the
mestizo, the Greaser, half-blood offspring," whose "Spanish appearance is not his dominant characteristic. His skin has been sunbrowned
for centuries; his nose and cheeks are broad; his lips are thick; his
brows are heavy."[30] Lighton transposed onto the greaser the physiog-
nomy of the missing link. The features he enumerated were those
Petrus Camper and Arthur de Gobineau—the leading figures in the
development of racist anthropology in the eighteenth and nineteenth
centuries, respectively—alleged against blacks as evidence of closeness
to apes and distance from white people. The name "greaser" stuck to
people of Hispanic background with the tenacity of a fatty stain.

DISCRIMINATION AGAINST HISPANICS WAS systematic and official. From the 1890s, in Texas and California schools were segregated
on grounds justified by naked racism. Forcible Americanization—a
sort of "culturecide" paralleled by Russification in the Russian empire
and Magyarization in parts of the Austro-Hungarian empire at the
time—banned Spanish from schools and bombarded deracinated
Catholics with Protestant propaganda. Even New Mexico, as we shall
see (below, p. 316), where the use of Spanish enjoyed nominal constitutional protection, endured campaigns to proscribe the language in
schools in the early twentieth century.

The evidence that police and the courts continued to pick on Hispanics is statistical, impartial, and overwhelming. But only individual
stories capture the real-life experience that the statistics shroud. In
1913 a Mexican consul in Galveston reported that "court cases involv-
ing Mexicans are always decided against the Mexican."[31] In 1923,
after a series of cases in Texas that exonerated the murderers of Mexicans, a Mexican official drew an amply justified conclusion: Mexicans
felt, he said in a letter to the US secretary of state, "that no offense
committed by an American citizen against a Mexican citizen will ever

be punished, regardless of evidence or of the severity of the crime."[32]
In 1929 a social worker at an immigrant-assistance center in San
Antonio approached a peaky-looking old woman who was waiting in
line to seek advice on transport to Chicago, where she was heading to
join her son. Would the *señora* like to take some fresh air without losing her place in line? "No, no, no, *niñita*," the old one replied, "I would
rather die than see another gringo with a pistol around his waist. He
might stop and question me again."[33] The huge expansion of the Texas
Rangers during the scare years of the Mexican Revolution incorporated hoodlums and white supremacist paramilitaries in the ranks of
law enforcers. Inevitably, the outlook even of the most honorable and
magnanimous officials reflected the prejudices at large in the culture
of the day.

Lynchings continued well into the twentieth century, though they
became rare compared with the previous century's tally, and merged
into the background of routine civil violence against immigrants,
which the police and courts never addressed with appropriate solem-
nity or effort and in which, indeed, they often colluded or even partic-
ipated. Twenty-four lynchings occurred in Texas, heartland of the
practice, between 1889 and the 1920s, though Hispanics were underrepresented among the victims by comparison with blacks, who dangled fatally ninety-four times in the same period.[34] In April 1915,
rumors from the World War I battlefront alarmed US public opinion:
German persuasion would lure Mexico into the war. Germany would
finance Mexican insurrection or invasion. The rumors were false, but a
kind of *Grande Peur* convulsed the borderlands. Among a series of
lynchings in that year, the most horrifying occurred when deputies in
Greaterville, Arizona, tried to extort confessions by hanging from the
neck three Hispanic brothers whom they suspected—apparently
falsely—of homicide. Two of the brothers died. The deputies were
released under the governor's pardon.[35]

The immigrants' predicament and the igneous, volcanic intensity
of hostility between migrants and hosts were probably at their most
perilous during the second and third decades of the twentieth century.
The Mexican Revolution rattled US security. The World War and the

lurches of the global economy made immigration policy swivel and twist like a lynching victim. One manifestation of danger was the frequency of violent labor conflicts in areas of production where Mexican manpower was important—in ranching, fruit harvesting, and, above all, mining. In August 1913 nearly 3,000 people turned up for 1,000 jobs at a ranch in Wheatland, California. Police opened fire when a riot ensued. In the same year Rockefeller mining moguls in Ludlow, Colorado, provoked a strike by evicting miners from the "tied" housing that was part of the workers' compensation package. The National Guard moved in with machine guns and bombs. In the summer of 1914 the press in Mexico and the United States agreed in applying the "race war" tag to bloody demarcation disputes among Arizona miners.

Some Mexicans literally fought the system. Cross-border terrorism or banditry exacerbated Anglo fears. In 1915 a Mexican-American malcontent, Basilio Ramos, was arrested with an inflammatory document in his pocket. This Plan of San Diego called for a "Liberating Army of Races and Peoples," of Mexican Americans, African Americans, and Japanese to pry Texas, New Mexico, Arizona, California, and Colorado from gringo grasp. In an obvious attempt to ape and reverse the events of the 1830s and 1840s, the document envisaged an independent republic, which might seek reunion with Mexico. The plan was authentic, but elaborations in the press added distortions that turned it into a Mexican equivalent of the *Protocols of the Elders of Zion*, invoking threats to massacre all adult Anglos. The following year, a cross-border raid by Pancho Villa, the legendary revolutionary leader in Chihuahua, provoked the US "intervention"—or, more accurately, invasion, described in the last chapter—and an attempt to occupy the Mexican side of the border.

Discrimination kept Hispanics mired in poverty and excluded from the social and economic opportunities of the "American Dream." In five elementary schools in Denver in 1925–26, 80 percent of the pupils were Spanish-speakers; only seven of them made it into junior high and only two into full high school. In Pueblo, in the same year, 12 percent of school-age children spoke Spanish as their first language, but only 3 percent of the high-school population did so.[36] At around that time the number of immigrant Mexican farmworkers along the South Platte and Arkansas rivers was growing spectacularly—but not the number of Mexican children in schools. As a local school superintendent explained, "the respectable people of Weld County do not want their children to sit along of dirty, filthy, diseased, infested Mexicans." A resident confirmed, "We wish the Mexicans were not there." Segregation extended to restaurants, cinemas, and housing zones. Comparisons with the sufferings blacks endured are instructive. In 1940 the average income of blacks in Colorado was 62 percent below that of whites; the income of Spanish-speakers was less than half that of Anglos and other whites. Thirty-four percent of blacks owned their own homes. The corresponding figure for Hispanics was 11 percent. For every 1,000 live births, 65 black babies died, compared with 205 Mexican babies. The way US society restrained and frustrated Hispanics seemed ineradicable. Blacks and Hispanics were tied in underprivilege almost continuously until the 1960s. After World War II, there were twice as many Mexicans as blacks in substandard housing in Denver, and their per capita income was, on average, half that of their black neighbors. In 1967, 72 percent of Chicanos lived in what city officials designated as "poverty areas," compared with 37 percent of blacks.[37]

MORE SIGNIFICANT FOR THE long-term history of the United States than all the migrants' sufferings and all the peculiarities of border life was the diffusion of Hispanics, especially of Mexicans, in the wider territory of the United States. The acceleration of the influx into northern Colorado began in 1900, when the Colorado Fuel and Iron Company brought in Mexican labor. The sugar-beet industry drew seasonal immigrants who constituted 60 percent of the workforce by 1927. There were fewer than 15,000 Hispanics in the state in 1910 and more than 40,000 by 1930 census.[38] Many of the economic opportunities for migrants spread beyond lands that had ever effectively belonged to Mexico. Migrants penetrated every state of the union and every significant city in the first four decades of the twentieth century, but Chicago can serve as an exemplary case: it has been a magnet for Hispanics, especially for Mexicans, and unlike other big concentrations of Hispanic population such as Miami and New York, it had no historic links with the migrants until they began to settle there in enormous numbers, from the second decade of the twentieth century onwards. In 1910, 1,224 Mexicans lived in Chicago. Ten years later there were almost 20,000. They constituted 40 percent of railroad maintenance crews in the city.[39] The boom echoed across the Midwest. The number of Mexicans in Ohio, Indiana, Michigan, Wisconsin, and Illinois increased eightfold in the same period.

The Mexican Revolution stimulated the flow. For Ernesto Garlaza, whose family fled from the revolution as soon as it began, and settled in Sacramento, "the barrio was a colony of refugees." It was "like a sponge that was beginning to leak along the edges, squeezed between the levee, railroad tracks, and the river front. But it wasn't squeezed dry, because it kept filling with newcomers who found families who took in boarders: basements, alleys, shanties, run-down rooming houses and flip joints where they could live."[40]

US conditions, however, rather than Mexican ones, determined the rhythms of the human traffic. In 1918 Herbert Hoover demanded the abolition of border restrictions: "We need every bit of this labor we can get and we need it badly . . . for years to come."[41] He was wrong. After the labor hunger of the late nineteenth and early twentieth centuries, the depression that followed World War I provoked mass repatriations—including many of dubious legality and notorious inhumanity, as migrants were shipped out of cities and left to starve or expelled by mobs under the threat or smart of violence. Some public-health officials' attitudes were revealing: Mexicans' health was seen in two ways—either as a threat in the form of pathogens or filth, or as an obstacle to efficient exploitation. In promoting Mexican health in 1920, Los Angeles County Health Department member Dr. Charles Bennett sought to "conserve the energy of [Mexican] laborers for efficient work."[42]

From 1921, federal and state legislatures passed frantic legislative curbs on immigrants because, according to President Coolidge, "America must be kept American." This abuse of the name of Americans to exclude Americans from outside the United States was and remains typical gringo usage. At first the restrictions overlooked Mexicans, neither explicitly banning them nor granting them the guaranteed quotas available to intending European immigrants, but regulations that imposed high cash fees for processing documents drove many migrants into secretive, undocumented ways of life. Congress authorized border patrols in 1924. US policy, rather than the wishes of immigrants, decreed migrants' movements. It still does. When the United States wants cheap labor, Mexicans respond. When the employment market north of the border is glutted, the barbed wire gets taut, the border patrols fix bayonets, the vigilantes get busy, and the walls go up.

The pace of immigration in the years leading up to the Great Depression was bound to arouse fear and provoke reaction. The Mexican-born population in the United States was probably less than 5 million in 1900, perhaps three times that number in 1929. Nowhere experienced a more spectacular rise than Los Angeles, with 5,000 Mexican residents, by official counts, in 1910 and 30,000 in 1920, when the total population was approaching 1.5 million. The numbers of Mexicans grew to 97,000 in 1930 and 219,000 in 1940, of whom 65,000 were Mexican-born.[43] Anglo supremacy withered as the city turned into the "Oildorado" satirized in Upton Sinclair's novel *Oil*, where derricks—some of them phony, installed to drive up real estate prices—appeared "right alongside Eli's new church, and another by that holier of holies, the First National Bank." The new elite, however, was not Mexican. It included Irish Americans, like Edward Doheny, an oil prospector who built St. Vincent de Paul Church—still a major city landmark under its obese, multicolored dome—and whose house had a deer park, a conservatory for a hundred types of orchid, a dome of Tiffany glass, and a dining room, supported on Sienese marble columns, for a hundred guests. The film industry diffused power to another newcomer set of largely Jewish film producers.

Between 1925 and 1929 more than 283,000 Mexicans entered the United States. In 1930 there were some 1,500,000 resident Mexican

immigrants and their children, not counting native hispanos. All but
150,000 were concentrated in California, Texas, New Mexico, Colorado, and Arizona. *El Lavaplatos*, an anonymous *corrido* (a narrative
ballad for bardic performance) of the late twenties or early thirties
narrates the singer's story, which, though fictional, was highly representative of its era. Longing for Hollywood, he fled revolution, becoming in the United States first a railroad builder, then a harvester of
tomatoes and beets. Life was like a penance of the kind Mexicans
practice on the ascent to the shrine of Our Lady of Guadalupe, climbing on bleeding knees:

> *I got indulgences for free.*
> *Struggling on bended knee*
> *For four miles or five*
> *Kept me alive.*

> *[Y allí me gané indulgencias*
> *Caminando de rodillas.*
> *Como cuatro o cinco millas*
> *Me dieron de penitencia.]*

He became a cement worker, straining at the "torture" of manhan-
dling the mixer for fifty cents an hour. He escaped into dishwashing,
then into a circus—"clowning and shabby showmanship"—before
going home poorer than before, regretful of the whole experiment:

> *How I repent, repent there*
> *The day I went there!*

> *[¡Qué arrepentido*
> *Qué arrepentido*
> *Estoy de haber venido!]*

Deportations resumed with the Depression. Over half a million
Mexicans were forced out of Los Angeles County in the 1930s during

a "deportation era," when "streets were closed off, trolley cars stopped and searched, and anyone who 'looked Mexican' was liable to be forcibly deported." Four hundred people were rounded up as they emerged from Sunday Mass one day in 1931 at La Placita. Many US citizens were deported in consequence, because they had no proof of residency to hand.[44] No one knows for certain how many Mexicans were forced home because so many operations were ad hoc, illegal, sub rosa, or the work of vigilantes. If one includes people coerced into repatriation by harassment or the withdrawal of food rations or unemployment relief, two million or so is the figure that represents specialists' best guesswork for the number of people returned to Mexico between 1929 and 1939.[45] Over half, perhaps as many as three-quarters, were US citizens or had the right of US citizenship.

The hardships of recession, the fate of compatriots, and the necessity of mutual help increased the sense of solidarity among Mexicans who clung on in the United States. The thirties saw a revival of Mexican-American welfare organizations, cultural sodalities, mutual funds, trade unions, labor radicalism, and political activism. The Mexican-American Movement, founded in 1934, showed how Mexican-American identity was coagulating, like bloodclots on the surfaces of migrants' wounds. The Congreso de Pueblos de Habla Española, founded in Los Angeles in 1938, was almost entirely a Mexican-American organization, but its inclusive name demonstrated the potential for an alliance or fusion between various Hispanic groups.

No AMOUNT OF ACTIVISM, however, could arrest the deportations. The Second World War, in consequence, provoked a labor crisis as severe as that of the First. In May 1942 Mexico joined the war against Germany and Japan, making allies of the neighbor states along the Rio Grande—mutually congratulatory democracies fighting against authoritarianism and totalitarianism. The US government took the opportunity to negotiate a deal for hiring Mexican workers. The first laborers—*braceros*, as the workers were known by the Spanish term— arrived in September with high hopes that soon collapsed.

Braceros were tied to specified, low-paid, explicitly temporary, backbreaking jobs: railroad construction or maintenance and manual harvesting. Like serfs in medieval Europe or the indios attached to Spanish encomiendas in the early sixteenth century, they could not dispose of their own labor, negotiate their own terms, or switch bosses. If they did, they were liable to deportation. The agreement guaranteed prevailing wage rates, but the US authorities never undertook measures to enforce the clause.[46] An account of the enlistment process for the scheme in the National Stadium of Mexico City evokes eerie reminiscences of slave-market scenes: "A young, athletic American, of a playful and jolly nature, took my right arm and yanked me with his lion-like paw. Were it not for my physical strength . . . I would have landed on all fours and this man would have manipulated me like a puppet. He then began to feel my biceps and he checked my hands, giving signs of satisfaction."[47]

Documentation made little difference in everyday life, as Ascensión Higueras found, when the failure of her family retail business forced her into the fields along with Mexican fruit pickers in 1947. She was a US citizen, and guarded her birth certificate jealously, but felt as exposed to abuse and exploitation as her undocumented fellow workers. She later joined the religious Society of Helpers and became an activist with the Farm Workers' Union.[48] The maltreatment of braceros ignited unrest, protests, attempts at organizing bracero labor, and occasional riots. The mutual hostility of Anglos and immigrants spiraled, to the point where the Mexican authorities suspended the program in Texas in 1943 owing to "the number of cases of extreme, intolerable racial discrimination."[49]

From the braceros' point of view, however, the program had its attractions: if you were willing to tolerate the abuse and exploitation, you could live cheaply in a labor camp and save money to send home. When Manuel Padilla, a truculent worker who had not been able to hold down a job in Mexico, decided to become a bracero in 1944, he had to wait in line with thousands of applicants, who would spend up to two months outside the office that issued required documents, because "the people had great need; they were hungry." When the line grew disorderly, the police or troops intervened with hoses or even, on one occasion, by firing into the crowd. Eventually, restive at the sense of being at the bosses' mercy, and tortured by abuse—one boss would not let him pause in his work to go to the lavatory, another made him pick oranges with blunt scissors—he deserted the program and worked illicitly, with slightly higher wages and even less security.⁵⁰ When Mexico suspended the program in Texas, Mexicans continued to go to work there, sacrificing in favor of undocumented status the feeble security the program provided. Viviana Salguero crossed the frontier on foot, with a baby at her breast, walking by night, hiding from the patrols, swapping hunger for starvation.⁵¹ In the late fifties and early sixties, Ofelia Santos kept her family alive in Oaxaca on her husband's earnings as a bracero. When the program folded, she had to take to selling food and candy in the street, until a new US labor program gave her husband work as a bricklayer in 1986.⁵²

By the end of the war, the system allowed for 75,000 Mexicans on the railroads and 50,000 in the fields at any one time. The labor shortage eased, but bosses lobbied to keep the system going because they liked the cheap labor. Thanks to a faltering, stuttering series of renewals and short-term, ad hoc exemptions, the program, or something very like it, staggered on, formally until 1964 and with modifications until 1967, admitting over 4.5 million workers shunted back and forth across the border to meet employers' quotas.⁵³ Phil Ochs, the swaggering, self-destructive counterculture hero of the sixties, was not Mexican, but he watched the workers come and go, first from his childhood home in El Paso and later from the privileged altitude of Beverly Hills. He saw men effectively enslaved by poverty—herded in camps, compelled to forfeit basic rights such as freedom to sell one's labor and go where one likes. If anyone found the pace "killing," he sang, others would be willing. Tom Lehrer, the most effective satirical songwriter of the era, credited the immigrant-unfriendly senator from California, George Murphy, with a suggestive defense of the system: US citizens should not have to pick fruit because "no one but a Mexican would stoop so low" and "[e]ven in Egypt the pharaohs/Had to import Hebrew *braceros*." Murphy was just the kind of politician to inspire Lehrer's contempt—a clownish colleague of sorts, who made a living, outside politics, from a vaudeville song-and-dance act.

Licensed migration was never sufficient to match demand. Undocumented workers are always attractive to unscrupulous or hard-pressed employers because they earn little and come tax-free. Workers who served the system suffered in at least one respect more than their undocumented counterparts, who eluded taxation: most of them never received back the overpayments deducted from their wages, although their entitlement to reimbursement was guaranteed by treaties between the United States and Mexico. Most of the court cases generated by the confiscation of migrants' money have still not been resolved.

In some ways, the inertia of the bracero system alleviated Mexicans' misery. The 1940 census no longer made Mexicans a separate racial category but counted them as "white."[54] The first breakthrough in antisegregation customs and laws in the United States came not in the context of black civil rights struggles in the Deep South, but in the case of *Mendez v. Westminster School District of Orange County*, 1946–47, which ended by outlawing the exclusion of Mexicans from "white" schools and provoked repeal of segregation legislation in California.[55]

OFFICIAL PROGRESS LEFT ROUTINE perceptions unaffected. In 1942 a report of the Los Angeles County sheriff's department said of Mexican crime that "it is difficult for the Anglo-Saxon to understand the psychology of the Indian or even the Latin," and—extraordinary as this may seem—actually traced Mexican violence back to Aztec human sacrifice.[56] The department's Captain Duran Ayres, investigating twenty-two Hispanic suspects for murder, alleged that the violence of Mexican criminal gangs had a biological basis, breeding "total disregard for human life," traceable not only back to the Aztecs but even to the remote "Asiatic origins" of native peoples.[57] "The Mexican element," he declared, "desire to kill, or at least to let blood. . . . This inborn characteristic . . . has come down through the ages."[58] The defendants Ayres's department had arraigned were not even guilty.

Carey McWilliams, who chaired the committee that secured their exoneration on appeal, described the trial. The accused were not allowed to sit with or communicate with their attorneys. They were denied haircuts or clean clothing, while the prosecutor "pointed to the clothes and style of haircut of the defendants as evidence of guilt."[59]

What the press called "the Sleepy Lagoon murder case" was the worst of a long, comparable series of injustices Mexicans endured at the hands of police and prosecutors while the bracero program was under negotiation or in its early stages of operation. The sequence culminated in June 1943 in the so-called Zoot Suit riots, named after the fashionable dancing clothes that aficionados of Latin dance affected, with tight pants cuffs, high waists, and roomy shoulders. After a street fight on the night of June 3 between sailors and allegedly local boys in a Mexican barrio of Los Angeles, the police organized what they frankly called a "vengeance squad," while the press reported escalating violent incidents between sailors and "zooters." Police followed hell-bent sailors around "'to mop up' by arresting the injured victims of the mob."[60] By June 7 the mob was thousands strong. According to Carey McWilliams, the violence was undiscriminating, encompassing blacks and anyone who looked Mexican, irrespective of attire: "From affidavits which I helped prepare at the time, I should say that not more than half of the victims were actually wearing zoot-suits. A Negro defense worker, wearing a defense-plant identification badge on his workclothes, was taken from a streetcar and one of his eyes was gouged out with a knife. Huge half-page photographs, showing Mexican boys stripped of their clothes, cowering on the pavements, often bleeding profusely, surrounded by jeering mobs . . . appeared in all the Los Angeles newspapers."[61]

Even those inclined to exonerate Mexicans from an aeons-old damnosa hereditas reproduced racial stereotypes. The Los Angeles journalist Al Waxman, reporting the riots truthfully and fearlessly, opined that "Mexicans as a race are easy-going, peace-loving people," fixated on "fiesta, siesta, mañana, religion."[62] Copycat riots followed in San Diego, Philadelphia, Chicago, Detroit, Harlem, and in small towns as far apart as Texas and Indiana. A "residue of hatred and resentment remained."[63] Relations between the United States and Latin American allies in the United Nations were temporarily envenomed, but the bracero program was too important to be imperiled.[64]

NO NARRATIVE CAN CAPTURE the experience of migrating. To understand what the adventure and adversity feel like, we have to turn to migrants' testimonies in memoirs, autobiographies, works of fiction and art, such as the votive paintings that barely literate migrants dedicate to the saints and Virgins who save them from the dangers of their journeys, sustain them through the traumas of alienation, and feed them amid the alien corn.[65] The most abundant sources from Hispanic migrants to the United States in the twentieth century are the oral histories that sociologists and historians have collected. Transcriptions sometimes have romantic touches—evocative terms reproduced in Spanish, occasionally stilted rhythms and interjections characteristic of people mentally translating from a language not their own. The fidelity of translations is not always verifiable. Yet interviewers' work is precious, because it captures thoughts and feelings, otherwise undocumented, of ordinary people trapped in the cultural and psychological no-man's-lands that borders create, even when successfully crossed.

The experience starts with the journey to the border. For migrants with papers, it can be a routine bus ride. For others, it is either painful or fearful or both. You can travel on your own initiative, like Viviana Salguero, with only your life to lose, spending days in the desert with no more food and water than you can carry; or you can trust yourself to the coyotes—the people traffickers who charge thousands of dollars to smuggle you in fetid trucks or guide you in footsore gangs. The coyotes speak openly of buying and selling people.[66] Some are frauds who take migrants' money and abandon them. On Antonio Orendain's odyssey in 1950, he set off to walk all night, seeking the red light of the station at Encanto, California, jumping fences, eluding dogs, surviving gunfire, getting lost and finding his own tracks. When he reached Escondido, he slept under dried avocado leaves, shaking "like a rattlesnake" from the cold and reduced to such misery and penury that he hoped the border patrol would seize him. "At least," he thought, "I'll get a ride to Mexico." Fellow illegals rescued him and found him work. Eventually he became a US citizen and a leading labor organizer.[67] Teresa Villanueva got across by wading through mud while the arrest of other illegals distracted the guards.[68]

After the journey to the border, the crossing. Stories of crossings are always hurtful to read, animated by danger, lashed with sacrifice. "Cruzar es morir un poco," as the songstress Juana Váldes Patiño put it in 1978—"to cross the border is to die a little."[69] Sometimes it is to die, period. Immigrants used to have to submit to a bath in gasoline and DDT to "fumigate" them for the typhus and lice they were assumed to carry. In 1916 several Mexicans burned to death in the process when the gasoline ignited. Vigilante predators now patrol the border, looking for opportunities to practice extortion or indulge sadism. Sometimes they kill. In June 1993 an official border-patrol agent, Michael A. Elmer, shot Dario Miranda twice in the back and concealed his body; the court acquitted the killer on grounds of self-defense. In May 2000, near Bracketville, Texas, Samuel Blackwood killed an illegal immigrant, who had begged him for water, by shooting him in the back; his sentence for homicide was 180 days in jail.[70] As the numbers of migrants increase, so do reports of unexplained disappearances on "caminos sin regreso"—one-way journeys.

When not fatal, the experience of crossing the border has long been intrusive and degrading: in the old days, male guards watched female migrants strip for the bath. Even without the menace of the gas baths, the business of the border was fearsome and traumatic. The experiences of Lupe Macías, who made a typical crossing from Durango to Lynwood, California, in the 1970s show what it meant to get through the perils of the border. She was on her way to look after the children in a five-room house full of fifteen *compadres*: "The line was very slow. After a while, I could see where they were checking everyone. Oh, no! There was a very fat woman—like this—with her *pistolas. ¡Ay! ¡Madre mia!* And she was sending back so many people. I went asking the benediction of the little saints. . . . Well, . . . the fat woman was talking to the man next to her and would you believe, she didn't ask me anything. She just glanced at my card and went back to talking with the other *migra* and off I went. *¡Ay!* little *Dios*, I passed, I passed!"[71]

The incident captures many commonplace anxieties of the border: fear of the officials' apparently arbitrary decisions; terror at their bristling, menacing weapons; revulsion from their unfamiliar, unsympathetically shaped bodies; bafflement at their unintelligible speech; the sense of exclusion that arises when officials ignore their public and talk only to each other. Lupe's best recourse was supernatural: hoping the saints would see her through her ordeal. Her best strategy was self-effacement—just keeping in line. Her best outcome was to be overlooked. The migrants who succeed in entering the United States commonly do so only by performing acts of wretched submission. Lupe had documentation, but that did little to allay her fear in the face of a capricious system. Manuel Padilla had no papers and was aghast, when he reached the frontier in 1950, to see "many people with their heads completely shaved" after being caught three times without documents. He was caught many times—once, he claimed, five times in a single day. He got a beating but eluded head shaving by giving false names.[72]

If they get across the border, immigrants face longer, more tenacious trauma. Migration breaks families up, partly because of the usual pattern: the breadwinner travels abroad to face danger and loneliness, while dependents have to stay behind, looking after immovably elderly relatives or children who are locked into their schooling. In general, the farther from the border migrants traveled, the lonelier and more isolated their lives. The demographics of migrant communities make the problems quantifiable: in 1930, according to census returns, there were almost as many Mexican men as women in San Diego, San Antonio, and Los Angeles. In Chicago there were more than twice as many men as women, in Detroit three times as many.[73] Immigration laws and authorities make it hard for normal family life to resume, even when sundering obligations relax or disappear. US law, which shifts the burden of proof of good intentions on spouses seeking to

remain united, severs families, and implicitly licenses bigamy, desertion, and sham weddings.[74] "Let them give us a gringo girl to marry,"
sang the subtly bitter poet Luis Armenta Malpica in a corrido dedicated to celebrating the resilience of undocumented migrants, "and,
once we've got the green card, to divorce."[75] Cuauhtémoc Menéndez,
a construction worker, traveled alone in 1973 "like a tramp, in the
trains." He returned home for good when he was out of work and
poverty broke up his relationship with a woman he met in America:
that was another unfamiliar feature of the culture—the dependence of
love on money, the apparently widespread addiction to divorce. "Sure
you feel bad," he concluded, "to eat only beans in Mexico . . . but you're
not so lonely, you're in your own country with your family."[76]

Even in families who stay together on the road across the border, conflicts of culture alienate generations. Newcomers feel shame
at peasant origins, especially when they raise urbanized, Americanized children. They blame themselves for inflicting on children and
spouses the permanent discomfort of suspension between cultures.
Above all, the alienating effect of intrusive language, as English slices
into Spanish-speaking families' lives, widens generation gaps. Lumber
boss Miguel Rodríguez, for instance, reflected, in conversation with
the sociologist Marilyn Davis, "We always thought that there was
another world on the other side of the border that we wanted our
children to know. Many people here think that this is the whole world.
There are children who speak only English and can't communicate
with their grandparents, and then there are children who speak only
Spanish and won't have opportunities here." [77]

Disillusionment and alienation are common experiences in a chal-
lengingly new environment. The first shock the United States delivered to Celestino Fernández, when he arrived at the age of eight, was
that the food tasted different, even if it was nominally Mexican food.
In Mexico his mother cooked it on an open fire, which imparted a
different flavor from the bottled gas they used in the family's early
days beyond the border. Lard imparted its special flavor, unattainable
with the commercial vegetable oil that replaced it in the United States.
The milk Celestino was used to came warm from the cow, and you

could taste the differences in it according to the season and the cows' diet. Nuns who taught him in Mexico gave him a superior grounding and discipline, but in his junior year in advanced track, prejudice held him back.[78] He always got a grade C from his instructor, try as he might; so he swapped work at the end of term with an Anglo friend whose grade, equally invariably, was A. Their respective marks were unchanged. He eventually made good, getting a PhD in sociology from Stanford in 1976, and becoming a vice president at the University of Arizona. Another educated Mexican American, Roberto Carrasco, who has a PhD in Latin American literature, voices a common sense of disappointment, contrasting memories of a Mexico "rich in culture" with a sense of US philistinism, "personified by Donald Duck, by superficiality, and a philosophy of screwing anyone who lets himself be screwed."[79] The judgment is itself superficial, but it is representative.

Migrants' stories are full of the poignancy of modest aspirations, sometimes heartbreakingly postponed. In 1980 Julia García de Morales joined her husband in Los Angeles, which, she found, was "not the same as Guadalajara." She worked at a humble job, making collars for dogs and cats and packing pets' Christmas stockings with treats and novelties. "I can't explain my work to my friends in San Juan," she said, partly, perhaps, because the thought of so much luxury lavished on cats and dogs would seem incomprehensible to victims of human poverty, but also in part because the job seemed shameful. If one encountered in a novel an image of a woman who could barely afford to celebrate Christmas stuffing goodies into commercial stockings for cats and dogs, one would read it as a symbol of warped values and exploitative economics. For Julia, however, it was an opportunity she celebrated gratefully, because it gave her a chance to realize the project of which she dreamed: not the "American Dream" of me-centered material prosperity, but a Mexican dream of votive offerings to God and the saints. She wanted to go back to Mexico to paint the pews in her hometown church. "I promised," she added in her interview with sociologist Marilyn Davis, "that I would buy new robes for *el padre*. Then I want to buy little strings of lights for each pillar in the church. They have some here that are very pretty and they blink on and off. This is what we're thinking: to bring new robes for *el padre*, and then lights for the pillars, and a crown of lights for in between the first pillars, just in front of the altar. I would also like to find a smaller crown of lights for outside above the arch of the doorway. That's what I've been thinking."[80]

Juana María Cadena Torres, who worked as a housemaid in Texas from 1985, suffered border anxieties repeatedly as her sister went back and forth, smuggling enchiladas and picadillo across the border, with chorizos wrapped around her like a belt. Three ambitions kept Juana María in the United States. She wanted to make a pilgrimage to Rome. Next, she would go to Spain to see the Mexican soccer idol Hugo Sánchez Márquez play for Real Madrid. At last, she would go back home to see Mexico's national soccer team in live action. Her frustrations seem as romantic, in their way, as those of Novalis, yearning hopelessly for the Blue Bloom, or Keats's lover, trapped in unfulfillment on the surface of the Grecian urn. But there is no literary artifice in the migrants' accounts.

OF COURSE, THOUGH MIGRANTS suffer, they travel in pursuit of advantages and commonly get them. In the early twentieth century, the frontier lured labor with wages that rose roughly in proportion to the latitude attained. In 1900 a laborer's wage was typically 23 cents a day in a city in the Mexican interior, or 12 cents a day on a farm. In the United States the same work could command up to $2.00. Miners received up to 37 cents in Guerrero for work that earned $2.00 in Sonora, and up to $3.00 in Arizona.[81] Enriching experiences—some merely material, some genuinely life-enhancing—are among migrants' strongest themes, and many of the witnesses Marilyn Davis recorded seemed happy to rate their positive experience of the United States above the hardships and sufferings they endured to get there or stay there. One of the first emigrants to the United States from the tiny village of La Barranca de los Laureles in Jalisco was Santiago González, who made the crossing in 1914, when the US still welcomed Mexican labor and the main obstacle was poverty, not bureaucracy. He had to walk 300 kilometers to find work, but when he returned home he wore a "pure cashmere suit" and "washed the patio with good tequila" at his godchild's christening. "Well," according to Davis's informant, "many of the men" from the village followed his example. Don Ezekiel Pérez underwent typical privations: he was beaten, swindled, harassed by the migra, deported five times, frozen by the Montana climate, bombarded by unwelcome evangelical propaganda, imprisoned, and subjected to the suffering of separation from his children. But when he went back to La Barranca he had enough money for "several parcels of land and . . . horses, cows and pigs." He could educate his children, who espoused bourgeois professions. Two became teachers, one a lawyer, one a doctor. Juan Montoya, an accomplished guitarist from Guanajuato, walked for nine days northward from the Rio Grande in 1985, subsisting on the fire-roasted flesh of an armadillo he killed with a slingshot. He harvested tobacco in North Carolina for $3.35 an hour after inadequately explained deductions "for taxes." On his way home, the Miami police arbitrarily seized his car and took $500 from him in exchange for a receipt for $250. "They told us we didn't have any rights because we were here illegally," he reported. He still got home with $250—enough to start a ceramics business.[82] Even for ruthlessly exploited workers, the wage differential on the US side of the border has usually been worth having.[83] In 1946, according to migrants' recollections, a lumber mill on the US side of the border paid 25 cents an hour, when you could get only 6 centavos for the same work in Guadalajara. In the 1980s Ventura Gómez earned three times as much picking cotton, pound for pound, in the United States as she could in Mexico, even though she was wickedly exploited at well below the legal minimum wage.

For some migrants, the rewards of US life are more than material. Miguel Rodríguez, who arrived in Chicago in 1979 and rose to manage his lumberyard, said, "Here you can have anything you want if you're willing to work for it. That's not true in Mexico." His wife, Elena, praised the United States for equality of rights for rich and poor, and for the fact that people did not ask for her papers in places of schooling and employment. She was lucky, however: the sort of tolerance she encountered is capricious and precariously dependent on local and short-term conditions.[84]

THE THREAT OF A new "deportation era" like that of the 1930s always looms. In the US, migrants live in fear of deportation, especially, but not solely, if their documents are imperfect. José Gabaldón, who started working life as a bootblack and ended it as a janitor, spent much of his life from the late 1950s, when he was fourteen years old, crossing and recrossing the border without documents, prey for the border police, who confiscated his money; but as he could make $20 to $30 a week selling newspapers—up to three times what he earned in Mexico—he counted himself lucky.[85]

In 1953 a combination of zealous policing, inflated reporting, lax defining, and a genuine increase in undocumented migration led to 865,000 border arrests. The following year, government officials spoke loosely of a million "illegal" immigrants annually—apparently taking their cue from President Eisenhower, who had a tendency to round up figures and who had long been anxious about immigration rates. The perceived problem was especially acute in Texas, where, to elude the Mexican government's ban on the bracero program, employers had recruited undocumented labor unrestrainedly. Eisenhower ordered a crackdown and put General Joseph "Jumpin' Joe" Swing of the 101st Airborne Division in charge of it. The general ran Operation Wetback like a military campaign. Beginning in Texas, Colorado, and Arizona in June 1954, his men expelled an average of 1,727 Mexicans every day in the first few weeks of the operation, although most migrants were within the law as it then stood. The Immigration Service claimed a total of 1.3 million expulsees, including those intimidated into flight.

The police who conducted the swoop confiscated identity documents, earnings, and possessions of all kinds without compensation. They rarely took family ties into account when selecting individuals for deportation. Visitors and tourists suffered along with migrant workers.[86] Raymond Ramirez (in a typically self-abnegatory act of assimilation, he anglicized his Christian name and suppressed the accent that crowns his Spanish surname) only just escaped the sweep. He had arrived in the United States with his family in 1925–26, when the US was hungry for labor and unfastidious about who crossed the border. At first the family slept on the floor with one mattress. Raymond and his seven brothers fought in World War II. "I think if I hadn't volunteered in the service, I'd probably have been sent back to Mexico," he reflected in conversation with Marilyn Davis. "Once they send you back to Mexico it's very, very hard." Later, one of his sons was wounded in Vietnam.[87] The roundup that Ramirez eluded was a victimization operation still recalled with pride and admiration by anti-immigration campaigners. Recent trends suggest their hope of reviving conspicuous exercises in mass deportation is not forlorn. In 2010, officials deported 392,000 alleged "illegals." By July 2012, without encouragement from the White House, the administration of President Obama had overseen 1.4 million deportations—a rate one and a half times faster than that of the previous president.[88]

The label of "illegal" is a maddeningly unjust stigma, coined—it seems to me—to create an atmosphere of prejudice against honest people whose undocumented state is often the fault of the system. Many, perhaps most, "illegals" honestly want to regularize their status and are without documents only because they have been denied them. Most contribute to the US economy with their labor and their taxes. Many are in the United States because of official connivance to meet labor needs. Ostensibly, the Simpson-Mazzoli Act of 1986 (the "Immigration Reform and Control Act") responded to a bipartisan commission headed by the famous liberal churchman Notre Dame's Father Theodore Hesburgh, which wanted relief for suffering immigrants. But the legislation was deliberately framed to keep agriculture supplied. While demanding new standards of employers' compliance with required documentation, the act exempted some agricultural workers from documentation and granted amnesty, under penalty of a fine, to about 3 million undocumented US residents. In the wake of the act, the Immigration and Naturalization Service turned a blind eye perhaps to as many as 600,000 imperfectly documented workers.[89] Simpson and Mazzoli made no provision, however, for families of amnestied illegals. In 1989 an amendment designed to bring them relief got stymied in Congress. Since then, every US administration has aired or promised some sort of scheme for the relief of illegals; but no help has materialized for them, and, as we shall see (below, p. 326) their plight has worsened as states take measures against them— denying, in various cases, access to health care, schooling, and social-welfare programs.

EVEN IN THE OBSCURE world of the undocumented, one conclusion seems to glare sharply out of the twilight: there are many similar minorities in the United States, who are both wanted and unwanted, hated and needed in almost equal measure, trapped between the rival ideologies of Americanization and pluralism, trying to integrate and self-identify at one and the same time. The aims are mutually contradictory and success in one usually implies failure in the other. Italian Americans have forfeited their language, deserted their neighborhoods, and bowdlerized their food: spaghetti and meatballs is as American as apple pie. But they maintain a sentimental relationship with Italy and have created a band for themselves in the spectrum of what it means to be American. German Americans, Polish Americans, and almost every other community of hyphenated Americans who brandish a partly European identity have traveled a similar trajectory and occupy a similar place. Irish Americans, from my perch at the University of Notre Dame, seem to me to be exceptionally successful, having overturned the prejudices that oppressed them in the nineteenth century, partly by beating WASPs at American football. Black Americans or African Americans seem increasingly at ease in what most of them recognize as their only homeland; but tensions abide between the African or more generally black and American components of their identity, and between movements that look outside America—to Islam, to an idealized Ethiopia, to African nationalism—and the black American mainstream that flows, contained, between sea and shining sea.

In a sense, the black journey towards an American identity began

in Latin America. Early in the twentieth century, Afro-Cuban scholars in newly independent Cuba began to treat black languages, literature, art, and religion on terms of equality with white culture. In 1906,
Fernando Ortíz was interviewing black inmates in a Cuban jail. He
had, as far as is known, no black ancestry himself. He was working on
a thesis on the connections between race and crime. What impressed
him, however, was the way the black inmates retained elements of
culture—music, language, food, religion—that originated in Africa.
Ortíz became an advocate of the African input to Cuba's heritage and
an enthusiast for the work of black artists. Partly thanks to his success,
white advocates and imitators of black speech, music, prose, and
imagery became numerous. It was relatively easy for black Cubans to
feel thoroughly Cuban, especially since most people in the country
had at least some black family connections. The poetry of Nicolás
Guillén (1902–1989), one of the twentieth century's greatest poets,
expresses this attitude. In the late 1920s he became a leading expo-
nent of the assimilation of black influences in literature, especially in
his masterful use of the rhythms of black music and the street talk of
black Cubans.

Coincidentally, white musicians discovered jazz, and white primi-
tivist artists began to esteem and imitate African "tribal" art. The effect
in the United States was to shake up existing black self-perceptions.
During the nineteenth century, black Americans had felt Africa call
to them. But the notion of returning "home" to Africa was out of favor
by 1900. The senior black spokesman of the time, Booker T. Washington, opposed it. W. E. B. Du Bois, his successor, the most influential
black intellectual in the United States until his death in 1963, was
more radical than Washington. Du Bois was not content for black
people simply to accept their lot and rely on education and economic
improvement to raise them toward equality. He demanded social
reforms. His major book, *The Souls of Black Folk,* was full of references
to Africa. Du Bois was convinced that a common history connected
black people throughout the world, but that history was now in the
past. Black Americans had to be "both a Negro and an American." The
Jamaican immigrant Marcus Garvey was among the black leaders

who dissented. In 1916, he launched the slogan, "Africa for the black peoples of the world."

The idea that black culture embodied values superior to those of white culture was the next phase. The idea became a movement, spreading wherever black people lived—and, on its way, transforming the self-consciousness of those who were still under colonial rule or suffering under social inequalities. In French West Africa in the 1930s, Aimé Césaire and Léon Damas became brilliant spokesmen for the black self-pride they called *négritude*. As a result, as African independence movements gained strength, so did civil rights movements wherever black people were still denied equality under the law. In the late twentieth century, when those battles had been more or less won, the struggle continued against racial prejudice and remaining forms of social discrimination against black people in predominantly white countries. The black consciousness movement in the United States was a case in point, encouraging the rediscovery of African roots and even of African allegiances. "Philosophically and culturally," said the Black Muslim leader who called himself Malcolm X in 1964, Afro-Americans "need to 'return' to Africa."[90] Rastafarianism, a movement that identified Ethiopia as the spiritual homeland of black Americans, became popular in the same period—to the puzzlement of the Ethiopians themselves. The parallels with Hispanic movements are strong: there are communities of allegiance to places outside the United States—to "México lindo" among Mexicans, or to Cuban nostalgia among Cubans, or other national homelands—or to spatially unlocated extra-American concepts such as the Church or *el idioma*, which in any case, despite the Univisión slogan, "Unidos por un solo idioma," is a ragbag of *hablas*. Like blacks or African Americans, Hispanics or hispanos or Latinos do not know what to call themselves, or even whether they all want to call themselves by a common name. Of course, black and Hispanic identity often overlaps in a single individual. Tato Laviera, the distinguished puertorriqueño poet of New York, is one of the most eloquent spokesmen for Hispanic blackness, especially in a poem he placed in the mouth of a fictional Cuban exile, Pedro Morejón, who explains blackness to the poet "in front of an abandoned building." The US dollar symbol, British fair play, Catholic colors—all come from Africa. And

> Hear me, brother, but don't repeat it
> If the Klansmen catch me I'll be defeated.
> Squashed by a German, swastika-smacked,
> Head severed, but here's a fact
> Two white folks can't make one black.[91]

> [Óyeme, consorte, pero no repito esto,
> porque si me coge el ku klux klan
> me caen encima con un alemán
> me esparrachan con un swastika
> y me cortan la cabeza, pero es verdad:
> dos blancos no pueden hacer un prieto.]

The dilemma closest to that of Hispanics in the United States is perhaps that of people who call themselves Native Americans, despite the disparity in numbers, partly because both have a relationship with the land—strong, at least, among Hispanics in the Mexican case—that predates colonization by the United States, and partly because of their overlapping ancestry. Native Americans' responses to the white man have never been consistent, and official US policy has wavered between integration, separation, and genocide as solutions to the "Indian problem." With the effective suppression of indigenous resistance in the late nineteenth century, however, most participants on both sides—if one can speak of two sides, the "red" and the "white"—settled on integration as the best option. In 1872, when the end of Native resistance was only barely foreseeable, and some of the Natives' greatest victories against the whites were still to come, the US secretary of the interior foretold the future he expected for the Indians, extolling "our duty to coerce them, if necessary, into the adoption and practice of our habits and customs."[92]

The integrationist spirit was most perfectly exemplified in the career of Richard Henry Pratt, whom we met in Chapter Five (see above, p. 184). As a cavalry officer in charge of Indian prisoners in the early 1870s, he found that he could turn them into friends by putting them in uniform, cutting their hair, and subjecting them to white routines of military discipline. "In Indian civilization," he declared, "I am a Baptist, because I believe in immersing the Indians in our civilization and when we get them under holding them there until they are thoroughly soaked."[93] From 1879, as we have seen, as superintendent of what became the Carlisle Industrial School in Pennsylvania, he applied the methods to Indian children orphaned or seized in the course of Indian wars or, increasingly, surrendered by their families in order to be Americanized. In most respects the experiment was a failure. Few graduates of the school got the opportunity to play an unobstructed part in mainstream American life. Most returned to their reservations. Some took jobs with Buffalo Bill's Wild West show, aping the savagery Pratt had sought to fillet out of them. But Pratt inspired similar, variously, patchily successful programs in hundreds of other schools. There could be no more impressive endorsement of the integrationist agenda. Though the federal government revised and sometimes reversed it at intervals—notably in the 1930s and 1960s—distinctive indigenous cultures have withered in practice, almost to the point of extinction. Revivals of "tribal ways" seem contrived nowadays—often little more than costume reconstructions or sentimental pantomime. "Indian rights" today usually means the right to exploit gambling casinos, golf courses, and shopping malls.

The next big question for Hispanics in the United States, therefore, is whether they will assimilate as other minorities have in varying degrees, or whether a distinctive relationship with the rest of the country is available to them. That is also the question for the final part of this book.

CHAPTER EIGHT

THE REPUBLIC OF HESPERUS

The Remaking of the Hispanic United States,
c. 1914–2012

———

America has traditionally chosen to describe itself as an east-west country. I grew up on the east-west map of America, facing east. I no longer find myself so easily on that map.

~ *Richard Rodriguez,*
Brown: The Last Discovery of America (2002)

ONE OF THE PARAMEDICS LOOKED AT A SMASHED BODY THAT stuck to the hot cement on a street near the DC zoo. "He looks Hispanic," he said.

A female passerby, "clutching her purse to her chest," spoke next. "Maybe he's from Central America. . . . A lot of them live in this neighborhood. . . . You know, they come here fleeing the wars in their countries . . ."

"If he's not from El Salvador, he must be from Guatemala," agreed one of the paramedics. "Although now they're coming from all over: Bolivia, Peru, Colombia. We used to be the ones who invaded their countries; now they invade ours. Soon Washington will look like Latin America."[1]

The scene, which occurred in a novel published just before the beginning of the present century, by Mario Bencastro, a *salvadoreño* resident of the United States, sums up what happened in the Hispanic story of the United States in the late twentieth century. The numbers of immigrants shot up. Their provenance diversified. Expectations grew—hopes for some, fears for others—that they would transform the culture of the country. The word "invasion" was double-edged, likening the Hispanic inflow to an unwelcome takeover yet conveying a sense of justice, complementing the invasions the United States had launched many times into Mexico, Central America, and Caribbean states. Other people's perceptions of the newcomers remained racialized: formulated in terms of how they looked, or how DC or the whole United States might come to look as the immigrants' numbers increased. The female character's words captured the power and accuracy of the image of lands of Hispanic origin as violent and conflictive. Also apparent in Bencastro's dialogue is the way people in the host country condensed all the arrivals, from many different places, in a single category, as Hispanic—an identity many of them barely felt, if at all, and some resisted.

Official forms at every stage of life invited or required one to opt for an ethnic descriptor. You could not choose to be *salvadoreño* or Cuban or Mexican or Nicaraguan. But the term "Hispanic" beckoned everyone who did not feel at home in other, even more generalized categories. I have always checked the "Hispanic" box when filling in forms, not chiefly because the epithet matches my own sense of identity, but rather out of sympathy and solidarity with others who do the same. Marilyn Espitia, a sociologist working in Texas, recently described her own experience of the identity options available:

> During my elementary school years, my teachers annually took
> a head count of all the "Spanish" children in my class. Although
> the purpose of this exercise was unclear to me at the time, I
> knew to raise my hand to be included for the tally even though

my parents were from Colombia and I was born in the United States. Intuitively, I knew that the count consisted of all the Spanish-speaking children regardless of their birthplace. Later, in middle school, I noticed on my standardized test forms that I was no longer classified as Spanish, but, mysteriously, I had somehow become "Hispanic." This new category apparently still included all the Spanish-speaking children regardless of their birthplace, but now, in addition, actual language capabilities in Spanish seemed not to be required. In high school, when I began using the label Hispanic as a self-referent, my college-educated brother quickly informed me that the politically correct term was now "Latino," even though it appeared to represent the same people previously referred to under the old umbrella term, Hispanic. It wasn't until my undergraduate years, when I began to meet other Colombian-origin Latinos, that my specific background came to the forefront for others and myself. Since then, it has remained in the forefront, even in California and Texas, where I have at different times been presumed to be Puerto Rican (because of my New York City origins) or Chicana. With Colombian pop-star crossover sensation Shakira currently recognizable in the U.S. mainstream, I finally see a glimmer of acknowledgment in others when I tell them I am Colombian American.[2]

Potentially, identity is like a layer cake. You can slice it where you like, and all the levels will appear. I find it relatively easy to combine my mixed native and adopted identities, and commit to all those I have been told I have. I can feel simultaneously Galician (the identity of all my paternal ancestors from time immemorial), Spanish (the nationality to which they belonged or came to belong), European (the transcendent identity co-workers in the European Union strive to achieve), and English (my mother's nationality and the descriptor of the land of my upbringing). I also have an enormous emotional investment in the interests and welfare of the United States, where I work. Apart from giving me a remarkably dispassionate outlook during certain international and interregional soccer matches, the complexity of my identity has no obviously incapacitating effect. Can my fellow Hispanics in the United States be equally comfortable with their identities of origin, without missing out on feeling Hispanic or making a wholehearted commitment to belonging to the United States?

A sense of identity is never self-ascribed. You get it from the community that surrounds you. But where does the community get it from? Usually, it is imposed or projected from the outside, or arises from collective comparisons we and our fellows make with outsiders. Migrations often make people aware of fellow feeling they never previously knew they had. I recall a brilliant paper by a friend of mine, the Dutch historian Leonard Blussé, on Chinese migrant workers in eighteenth-century Borneo. Most of them never thought of themselves as Chinese until their Dutch employers referred to them as such. They came from various provinces and ethnic groups, spoke dissonant languages and, to one another, looked ill-assorted and strange. But they acquired from their hosts the habit of seeing themselves collectively. They transmitted it home in their letters.

In a similar way, migrants from the fragmented statelets of pre-Risorgimento Italy all became self-consciously Italian in America, whereas previously they would have designated themselves by descriptors relating to their home regions, as *romagnol*, or *toscano*, or *siciliano*, or *pugliese*, or whatever. The process works in reverse, too: no natives of the Americas called themselves indios or Indians or Native Americans, or thought they had any level of shared identity with natives of other local or tribal or linguistic communities than their own, until outsiders arrived to provide a point of comparison and a collective perception. A big question for Hispanics in the United States is: will they adopt and maintain a common identity and work for a shared future? Will they submerge the identities they bring with them in self-ascription to a "Hispanic" category (or some near-equivalent, such as that of "Latinos," which is currently favored by generators and receivers of academic jargon)? Will the United States become the republic of Hesperus?

In ancient Greek myth, Hesperus was a divine personification of the Evening Star, whose daughters, the Hesperides, tended a fabulous land known by their name, toward the setting sun. One tradition represented Hesperus as a brother of Atlas, who bore the world on his shoulders. As a result of his brother's collaboration with Hercules, in a version of the myth popular in medieval and Renaissance Spain, Hesperus succeeded the hero as ruler of the Iberian peninsula at an uncertain date, which a consensus of sixteenth- and seventeenth-century authorities fixed as 1658 BC. Convoluted reasoning led Gonzalo Fernández de Oviedo, the myth peddler who, as we saw in Chapter One, identified Florida as the location of the Fountain of Youth, to represent Hesperus as the ruler of a prefigured Spanish empire. His fabulous realm spanned both sides of the ancient Atlantic, and included the Indies—the name for the Americas current in Oviedo's day. "From true and authentic sources," Oviedo wrote in 1535,

> we understand that the land of the Hesperides lies forty days' sail to the west of the isles of . . . Cape Verde. And just as in Spain and Italy . . . and Mauritania . . . there are places named after Hesperus, twelfth king of Spain, so the islands that are called the Hesperides . . . must undoubtedly be these Indies and must have been part of the dominions of Spain in the time of Hesperus. . . . And . . . it follows that 3,193 years ago to this day, Spain and her king, Hesperus, ruled these islands of the Indies of the Hesperides. And therefore, in conformity with this most ancient title, . . . God restored this dominion to Spain after so many centuries. And it appears that divine justice has restored this dominion to Spain, as it was formerly hers, so that it may remain hers forever.[3]

Oviedo's motive for this crazy claim was rational. He wanted to pretend that his sovereign's title to the Americas derived not from a contract with Christopher Columbus, or a grant from the pope, or any revocable human agency: it was God-given. The justice of Spain's conquests in the New World did not depend—the claim implied—on the assent of the inhabitants or treaties with other powers, but was rooted in a basic principle of just war theory: a state's right to recover its own former territory, albeit after a supposed lapse of thousands of years. Of course, Oviedo was wrong at every stage of his argument. There never was a King Hesperus. He never ruled Spain. The Hesperides never existed. They did not correspond to the New World or any part of it. Even if the rest of the argument had rested on truth, it would not mean that God approved of anything that had happened. Nor was there any reason to suppose that Spain's power would last forever—as indeed it did not, although so far, most of the western hemisphere has remained in a Hispanic tradition in terms of its predominant language and religion. And Oviedo's prophecy might yet come true, in a sense, if the area of predominantly Hispanic culture expands to include the United States. In the continental Americas, that would leave only Brazil, the Guyanas, Belize, and Canada outside the reconstituted realm of Hesperus.

FOR MOST OF THE twentieth century, rehispanicization proceeded too slowly to make such a future imaginable, even though, from the 1890s until the 1960s, immigration restrictions in the United States worked broadly to Hispanics' advantage. The regulations and the prejudices of officials favored new arrivals from Europe—still the place of origin of three-quarters of immigrants into the United States as late as 1960. Asians and Africans were almost totally debarred. But temporary work, with the possibility of extending its privileges, was accessible to Latin Americans, and at times relatively openly so—albeit, as we have seen, at the cost of much hardship—to Mexicans. Cultural swing and game-changing legislation in the 1960s opened a new era.

It was the era of belief in multicultural solutions to the problems of plural societies. Rainbows filled skies. The White Australia policy dissolved. The civil rights movement transformed the United States. An almost unnoticed side effect was the modification of national quotas for immigrants in 1965, and the introduction of a system that, according to President Lyndon Johnson, "rewards each man on the basis of his merit."[4] The sponsors of the new law were Democrats Emanuel

Celler of New York and Philip Hart of Michigan, backed by Ted Kennedy. They intended only to obliterate the scandal of racial quotas, not to change the demographic profile of the country. The outcome, however, was to reverse the proportions of immigrants from Europe and the rest of the world. By 2000, Europeans accounted for only 15 percent of immigrants. The numbers, once negligible, arriving from Asia and—in the long term—Africa soared. Would-be migrants from within the Americas faced at first serious competition from visa seekers in those previously underrepresented areas; but in the longer term the new regime sluiced a brain drain for well-qualified candidates from countries that had previously supplied few migrants.

The results benefited those coming from everywhere except Mexico. The United States admitted nearly a million of them in the course of the 1960s—more than there had been in the country at the start of the decade. And decade by decade the arriving numbers increased. Overall, from 1971 until the end of the century, immigrant status was granted to 7.3 million arrivals from Asia, a little over 5 million from Mexico, and nearly 6 million from the rest of the Americas including the Caribbean but not counting Puerto Rico, whose people were US citizens. Immigrants accounted for nearly 60 percent of Hispanics in the United States in the 1970s and 1980s, but the proportions diminished as their children and grandchildren multiplied. US-born Hispanics accounted for 55 percent of the total in 1990, 57 percent in 2000, over 60 percent in 2012.[5]

The effect was to shift the balance of the US population in favor of Hispanics and, among Hispanics, away from the previous absolute preponderance of Mexicans. Mexican numbers, however, received an unrecorded boost, perhaps doubling the totals, from the relatively large cohorts of undocumented workers who crossed the border. An increase in the number of undocumented migrants was an unforeseen consequence of the new legislation, since workers with poor qualifications were now condemned to a low place on the waiting list for visas.

In the shadow of the civil rights movement, Hispanic self-perception and self-presentation also began to change in the 1960s. The first activist was a disturbingly quixotic figure in the tradition of American prophets. Reies López Tijerina was an outsider by self-exclusion. His career of elective conflict with the social mainstream began when he started a religious community of his own in Arizona, with a barely intelligible doctrine that mixed elements of evangelicalism and Islam. The revulsion and persecution he drew from his Anglo neighbors and the representatives of law and order aggravated his already acute sense of injustice. During long years in the late fifties and early sixties as a fugitive from suspiciously unconvincing charges, including an alleged attempt to spring his brother from jail, he launched a campaign to draw attention to the long-ago illegal seizure of Hispanics' land in New Mexico and Colorado in the aftermath of the Mexican War. He had alighted on a cause with two advantages: a sound basis in historical fact, and a large number of interested parties among the descendants of dispossessed landowners. In 1962 he launched a movement, popularly known as La Alianza, and a radio station. The protests, marches, cavalcades, and demonstrations he organized over the next few years provoked the authorities but attracted attention from other campaigners for minority rights. His attempt to make a citizens' arrest on a New Mexico district attorney who had banned one of his demonstrations ended with López Tijerina's imprisonment, the status of a martyr, and the embrace of Dr. Martin Luther King. Prison seems to have induced a spell of paranoia, and the level of his activism was much diminished on his release, but his case electrified Hispanic sympathies and helped inspire other, generally more effective movements.[6]

More impactful in Texas, perhaps, was the campaign waged by Democratic Party managers to mobilize Hispanic voters with a *¡Viva Kennedy!* campaign in the presidential election of 1960. Kennedy carried the state by the fingernail margin of 46,000 votes. The power of Hispanic voters suddenly became apparent. Crystal City, Texas, the self-proclaimed "spinach capital of the world," with a population of fewer than 10,000 people, became the focus for an unprecedented form of Mexican-American activism. People of Mexican origin or ancestry formed a big majority in the town, but Anglo gerrymandering had previously kept them out of municipal office. In 1963 a group of them organized the vote and swept the board. The winners were radicals with trade-union links, and conservative opponents turned them out at the following elections, but Hispanics were never again excluded from the council or the electorate. The Crystal City experience inspired wider activism, and the town remained a tinderbox for Mexican-American politics.[7]

By then, the Vietnam War had begun to get nasty—vicious, unstoppable, corrupted with atrocities—alienating many young people in every constituency in the United States. It seemed tyrannous to serve a state committed to a war that was simultaneously stupid, unjust, and illegal. For Hispanic opponents of the war, the Democratic Party became an unworthy object of trust. Some Mexican-American activists, meanwhile, adopted the name "Chicanos" as a badge of identity that implied dissent, somewhat in the spirit of civil rights leaders, who would rather be "blacks" than known by some euphemism or morally neutral term.

César Chávez was the Chicanos' unlikely hero. He was born in 1927 on the smallholding his grandfather farmed in Yuma, Arizona. From early childhood he accumulated instances of injustice at Anglo hands. Swindled out of their farm and modest grocery store, his family espoused poverty as migrant farmworkers in California. "Maybe," Chávez later mused, "that is where the rebellion started."[8] At school, Anglo teachers and classmates victimized César for speaking Spanish. He was a third-generation US citizen but sat in segregated seating at the movies. Restaurants turned his family away. In the navy, anti-bohunk prejudice confined him to menial tasks. In 1952, when he was twenty-five years old, he met a life-transforming patron, the radical activist Fred Ross, who trained Chávez and many other young idealists to organize labor, mobilize voters, use the media, and challenge exploitative bosses and corrupt officials. Chávez was short, shy, quiet, and ill-educated, but he electrified audiences and attracted followers perhaps because of his convincing sincerity and unremitting pursuit of justice. He communicated simply, factually, clearly, with reticence unadorned by rhetoric. When he set out to organize a farmworkers' union in 1962, the prevailing opinion was that his task was impossible:

every previous attempt had broken down between the bosses' power and the workers' fear. He built a following slowly, unspectacularly, without provoking agribusiness into repression until his organization achieved a critical mass. In 1965 he launched an apparently hopeless, overambitious campaign of attrition against grape producers for the right of collective bargaining: he enlisted interunion cooperation, founded a radio station to disseminate propaganda, launched mass marches, and won the applause of churches, the sympathy of most of the public, and the endorsement of politicians. After five years, the growers recognized the union.

The success of the farmworkers' organization Chávez founded was short-lived. He had garnered over 100,000 members by 1978, when his fame compelled the prosecuting authorities to release him after his arrest for defying antipicketing legislation in his native Arizona. But it is the tragedy of trade unions that they thrive on workers' poverty and degradation and wane when they improve their members' lives. The conservative turn of the 1980s represented a check for the labor movement throughout the developed world. The new glut after the 1986 Immigration Act cheapened labor. Chávez's union dwindled and his power waned. Even the term "Chicano" gradually fell out of favor. But Chávez had genuinely ignited communal self-awareness among Mexican Americans and inspired emulation in other Hispanics.

Among the evidence of a new mood of Hispanic self-assertion in the sixties were the high-school students' walk-outs that started in Los Angeles in 1968 and spread across the Southwest, demanding the inclusion of Hispanic history and culture in the syllabus and parity for Hispanics in student representation. Many universities responded to the demand for reformed curricula. In 1969 the Plan de Santa Bárbara emerged from a gathering of *chicanista* activists at the University of California, Santa Barbara. Essentially, it was a program for creating Chicano Studies courses in universities, but its rhetoric was more far-reaching. The plan proclaimed a "Chicano renaissance" and condemned "the socio-economic functions assigned to our community by Anglo-American society—as suppliers of cheap labor and dumping ground for the small-time capitalist entrepreneur," alleging that this was why "the barrio and *colonia* remained exploited, impoverished, and marginal."[9] The program was potentially vexatious and despotic, demanding common assent from Chicano educators irrespective of whether their views had been heard. But it proved extremely powerful in addressing, not only for Chicanos, one of the cruelest problems that afflict Hispanics in the United States: the low status and prestige that accrues from underrepresentation in higher education and, in partial consequence, top jobs.

Meanwhile, a further breakthrough in political organization occurred with the launch of what the founder, Rodolfo "Corky" Gonzales, called the Justice Crusade. He was an ex-professional boxer—an exemplar of the unappealing options available for Hispanics who sought a profession with a means of social ascent. He was genuinely indifferent to materialism, and borrowed a line from Spanish intellectuals of the early twentieth century who claimed that their country's economic failure, compared with the hard-nosed capitalism of some competitor nations, was evidence of spiritual superiority. In a poem written as if by the bandit-hero Joaquín Murrieta (see above, p. 166), "My parents lost the economic struggle," Gonzales admitted, "but triumphed in the battle for cultural survival." He denounced "gringo society" as suffering from "American social neurosis, sterilization of the soul, and a full belly." He called himself heir of both Cuauhtemoc and Cortés, celebrating a syncretic identity, simultaneously Spanish and indio. He hardly vacillated in taking to its logical conclusion the case for the restitution of land that López Tijerina had made. "This land," he said, referring explicitly to his home state of Colorado and implicitly to the whole hemisphere, "is ours."[10] In March 1969 he organized the first national get-together of Chicano activists in a "Youth Liberation Conference" in Denver. It produced a luridly over-written joint statement, called the Plan Espiritual de Aztlán: "in the spirit of a new people that is conscious not only of its proud historical heritage but also of the brutal 'gringo' invasion of our territories, we, the Chicano inhabitants and civilizers of the northern land of Aztlán from whence came our forefathers, reclaiming the land of their birth and consecrating the determination of our people of the sun, declare that the call of our blood is our power, our responsibility, and our inevitable destiny."[11]

Remarkably, the Chicano movement pinned its credentials to the same myth that Gaspar Pérez de Villagrá had invoked, as we saw in Chapter Two, to justify the Spanish invasion of New Mexico nearly four hundred years before. The language of blood, race, nationalism, and *mission civilisatrice* that animated the document was already old-fashioned in its day and doomed to become politically incorrect or at best obsolete. But at the time it excited real commitment among thousands of enthusiasts to the program the plan outlined: seizing control of the ruling institutions of "our barrios, *campos*, pueblos, lands, our economy, our culture, and our political life." The formation of a Chicano political party, La Raza Unida, in May 1969 was among the results, with a flurry of local election gains to its credit in its brief spell of fluorescence in the early 1970s. Though the party did not last, it was influential in establishing networks of cooperation among Chicanos who remained in political life in the mainstream parties.

Although the Plan de Aztlán recognized "no capricious frontiers in this bronze continent," and Rodolfo Gonzales used "*mejicano, español*, Latino, hispano, Chicano, or whatever I call myself" as if there were no difference, the Chicano movement derived both its great strength and its greatest weakness from addressing and embracing Mexican Americans in an increasingly plural United States. The best hope for Hispanics to advance together lay in collaboration across traditional categories. None of the changes of the 1960s would have happened if Hispanics' numbers had not grown. Demographic buoyancy gave them clout in the marketplace and power in competitive recruitment environments in the worlds of trade unionism and higher education.

AFTER CHICANOS, THE SECOND biggest group of Hispanics defined by where they and their ancestors came from consisted of Puerto Ricans. Strictly speaking, Puerto Ricans are not immigrants, as all Puerto Ricans are born on US soil, and Congress extended US citizenship to inhabitants of Puerto Rico in 1917, just in time to make them liable for service in World War I. But they joined a country where most people considered them, if they thought about them at all, as members of "an alien and inferior race."[12] The island's first US military governor reported that "the so-called white race have a decided color—a reddish brown not unlike the color of those persons in the US who have more or less Indian blood." Whitelaw Reid, a US delegate at the Paris conference at the end of World War I, feared the "degeneration" threatened by Puerto Rico's "mixed population, a little more than half colonial Spanish, the rest negro and half-breed, illiterate, alien in language, alien in ideas of right, interests and government." Puerto Ricans commonly encounter some of these prejudices to this day.[13]

The courts repeatedly restricted islanders' rights, openly acknowledging that the citizenship of Puerto Ricans was second-class, and excluded, for instance, the right to vote in federal elections and the right to be a candidate for the presidency. Among the most terrifying effects of racial prejudice was the repeated and systematic selection of Puerto Rican patients and prisoners to be human guinea pigs in medical experiments. Pedro Albizu Campos, the independence-movement leader who exposed the scandal in connection with cancer research in 1932, was probably himself the victim of experimental radiation exposure when he was in prison on faked charges more than thirty years later.

In 1922 the Supreme Court ruled that Puerto Ricans did not enjoy all the rights of citizens under the Constitution unless they were on the soil of a state of the union. This restriction continued to apply even after 1940, when legislation formally defined Puerto Rico as US soil—but not, of course, the soil of a state. In 2005, the *Puerto Rico Herald* pointed out that it was still the case that "in effect, a plane ticket can give to a Puerto Rican civil rights that the Congress has so far refused to grant to those who remain on the island."[14]

In 1921, in the first flush of the concession of nominal US citizenship, there were fewer than 12,000 Puerto Ricans in the whole of the continental United States. By the 1930s, there were over 50,000 in

New York City alone. Toward the end of the decade, a probably pseudonymous poet, claiming to be Colombian, described them in a long praise poem about New York, in which the city seemed magnificent, towering, glittering, but the lives of people in it were oppressed, burdened, and degraded. Puerto Rican women, "dark against the glimmer of the neon advertising, search Manhattan for the light of their star [ofuscadas por el llamativo anuncio luminoso, buscan por Manhattan la luz de su estrella]."[15] They sewed shirts for Jews, washed dishes in Broadway diners, made elevators work, shifted weights on the docks, painted lampshades in gloomy factories, kept going on marijuana. For Alfredo Ortiz Vargas, as the poet called himself, though perhaps not for the women, their lives were a national humiliation, a political sacrifice:

> *And in their little defeats*
> *The condescending shadow*
> *Of a foreign flag*
> *Engulfs them forever.*[16]

> *[Y la sombra indulgente*
> *de la extraña bandera,*
> *en sus pobres derrotas*
> *para siempre se hundieron.]*

The great leap in numbers came in the 1940s, when the Second World War and its aftermath boosted demand for labor. From nearly 70,000 at the start of the decade, Puerto Ricans on the mainland multiplied to over 300,000, concentrated overwhelmingly in New York City.[17] They enjoyed one advantage over fellow Hispanics from other places: citizenship made them hard to deport or expel or brand as "illegal." But they came below blacks and other Hispanics in every measure of prosperity, including average income, welfare dependence, school dropout rates, and standards of nutrition. As the poet Pedro Pietri recalled in *Puerto Rican Obituary* in 1973, "They worked ten days a week and were only paid for five."[18] They acquired the aura of

danger that surrounds every minority that becomes suddenly conspicuous as a result of increasing numbers. After World War II, when
MaCarthyite hysteria gripped the United States, the fact that politically radical Puerto Rican labor dominated many industries in New
York invited persecution. Meanwhile, the island economy, previously
monopolized by sugar, began to diversify; new opportunities should
have reduced the amount of surplus labor, but population growth out-
stripped them and emigration increased. As Puerto Rico became the
home of an urban society, internal migration pulled up peasants' roots
and dissolved traditional constraints on migration.

Even for whole communities that transferred more or less en
masse from Puerto Rico to Spanish Harlem or the South Bronx, New
York was a poor fit. Pedro Juan Soto, "the classic delineation of a
divided psyche,"[19] felt mocked for bad English in New York and bad
Spanish in Puerto Rico. "Well what can you do?" he asked. "You shut
your mouth and live in a no-man's land." This was perhaps a disingen-
uous claim, as he was a well-educated intellectual who became a university professor. Salvador Agrón had a rockier road to intellectual
respectability via the violent street gangs that dominated other New
Yorkers' image of their Puerto Rican fellow citizens in the 1950s. In
his midteens he joined the Mau Maus, whose name, called after the
Kenyan resistance movement against British colonialism, conveys a
sense of the political airs the gangs sometimes gave themselves. In
1959 he stabbed to death two bystanders who were not even participants in gang war, evincing shocking insouciance at his trial but
obtaining a reprieve because of his obvious immaturity. Prison made
him. He learned to read and write, took a degree, discovered a talent
for poetry, and reinvented himself as a political activist and freedom
fighter. In 1998 he achieved a kind of posthumous apotheosis, glori-
fied as the hero of a Broadway musical flop by the folksy rocker Paul
Simon and Derek Walcott, a distinguished black English poet. It was
not, after all, far to Broadway from El Barrio.

Piri Thomas could recall gangland with candor. Before publishing
his autobiography in 1967 and becoming a famous writer, he escaped
the trammels of the gangs and the drugs to devote himself to the reha-

bilitation of fellow addicts and the redemption of fellow gangsters. He was "a skinny, dark-face, curly-haired, intense Puerto-REE-can,"[20] half Puerto Rican, half Cuban, and mainly black, divided between shame at his crinkly hair and the greater shame he felt when he had it restyled and greased down to ape white looks. His mother remembered Puerto Rico through a romantic veil as "muy pobre, but happy," a lush, soft, sinuous, scented land full of flowers. The concrete-hard, right-angled reality that surrounded Piri in El Barrio stank and hurt. In turn, he romanticized gang warfare when he fictionalized it later, larding it with camaraderie, sharing, humor, and pathos in his story of "The Blue Wings and the Puerto Rican Knights," whose sidewalk braggadocio escalated into a shooting war. Pedro Pistolas, the crazy man of the gang, fell to a shotgun blast. "The steel pellets tore away most of Pedro's childlike face," but the author succumbed to slushy yet emotionally convincing sentiment. "Nobody would ever again turn his dreams into nightmares," Thomas wrote of the victim.[21] Sometimes, whole gangs self-reformed. The Young Lords, a Chicago street gang, mutated into a national political party militating among continental Puerto Ricans on behalf of the island's independence movement.

Despite discrimination and restricted opportunities, Puerto Ricans were bound to benefit from the booming US economy of the 1950s. In 1957, Leonard Bernstein's brilliant musical *West Side Story*, with Stephen Sondheim's ingenious lyrics, romanticized gang life and, when it transferred to the cinema in 1961, transformed perceptions of Puerto Ricans. In some ways, it captured the realities of the Puerto Rican dilemma, caught between attraction to promised prosperity and indignation at actual injustice. "Life is all right in America," sings a member of the girls' chorus, referring, in the loose usage that seems irremediable, to the United States. "If you're all white in America," reply the boys. The girls sing of credit, Cadillacs, and washing machines, the boys of money-grubbing, capitalism, and crime. The antiphony represents the dilemma. Like Corky Gonzales, the male characters sense the moral superiority of poverty.

Most things in the United States, however, rise and fall with the bottom line, and the rhythms of Puerto Rican migration followed those of the economy. Whenever there was a downturn or slump—in 1963, for instance, or the 1970s—Puerto Ricans' thoughts turned homeward. As Anita in *West Side Story* said to her admirer when he was thinking of going back to San Juan, "I know a boat you can get on." According to the *New York Times* in 1978, Puerto Ricans were the first community in the United States collectively to give up on the American Dream,[22] but tension between materialism and spirituality has become a common topos of Hispanic rhetoric about the United States. Corky Gonzales voiced it. Sondheim caught its tone. The sociologists Nathan Glazer and Daniel Patrick Moynihan took a snapshot of Puerto Ricans in their classic 1963 study of migrants in New York City.[23] Their picture was of a community condemned to poverty by bad health, poor education, low skill levels, a neglectful Church, feeble communal institutions, and "multi-problem families, afflicted simultaneously by a variety of miseries—a child who is a drug-addict, another who is delinquent, a father who is psychologically or physically unable to work, or perhaps is not there." The authors raised the possibility—only to doubt or dismiss it—that Puerto Ricans might ascend to the general population's levels of prosperity and security "by the same path that Italians took" forty years before. Increased political activism drew Glazer's and Moynihan's attention. For most of the 1970s, poor economic conditions held back all of the city's poor, among whom Puerto Ricans were disproportionately represented. Gang warfare returned in the early seventies, disciplined by bloodily enforced bans on addictive drugs, equipped with assault weapons instead of the zip guns, shotguns, and knives of the era Bernstein had romanticized.

In the last generation of the twentieth century and early in the twenty-first, however, the Puerto Rican profile in the continental United States changed. It became increasingly bourgeois, not only because of the enfeeblement of US manufacturing. Among new migrants there were so many teachers, nurses, and social workers that Puerto Rico itself suffered a shortage of workers in those occupations. Puerto Ricans spread beyond New York, Chicago, and their other traditional pockets of concentration. In Florida their numbers quadrupled from 1998 to 2000.[24] Since then the rate has slowed, but the total number has grown by about 18 percent to over 850,000. It has become easier for Puerto Ricans to dissolve or attenuate their difference as they have dispersed, and as their island has succumbed increasingly—more even than the rest of the world—to mainstream US cultural influences. Coca-Cola-diluted rum.

For the Puerto Rican historian Fernando Picó this was a matter for self-congratulation. "We have given up celebrating Candlemas with bonfires," he wrote, "[n]or do we eat funche (cornmeal) with the feast of St Peter and St Paul. . . . We no longer sow tobacco on the feast day of St Rose of Lima . . . nor do we sing bomba at Michaelmas. . . . Halloween has replaced the solemnities of the Feast of All Souls. . . . But along the way we have incorporated St Valentine, . . . graduation days."[25] I suspect Picó exaggerates the attenuation of traditional culture. The famous salsa duo Richie Ray and Bobby Cruz popularized Christmas bomba, a form of music derived from African rhythms, in New York in the 1980s, adding laments for Puerto Ricans' sufferings to the lyrics. Some Puerto Rican leaders—notably Herman Badillo, the first to serve in the US Congress, from 1970 to 1977—have demanded bigger sacrifices of culture, including the abandonment of Spanish, in the interests of absorption in the United States. But whatever the effects on Puerto Ricans' assimilability in the US mainstream, the innovations in migrant history of the last few decades have stimulated contact, collaboration, and fellow feeling with other Hispanics on the mainland.

CUBANS—THE NEXT BIGGEST HISPANIC group by country of origin—have been in some ways the hardest Hispanics to induce into a sense of shared destiny because of the distinctive trajectory of Cuba's history, compared with that of other Hispanic-American republics. Among the first Cubans in the United States, revolutionaries predominated. They came as refugees from the independence struggles of the second half of the nineteenth century—perhaps about 100,000 of them in all, mainly to work in the cigar industry exiles set up, with its center in Tampa. The subsequent trickle of migrants became a flood from 1959, when Fidel Castro's revolution subverted the dominance of the rich and the bourgeois in Cuba. The more people the revolution victimized, the more migrants fled—nearly a quarter of a million by 1962, over a third of whom did white-collar jobs.[26] This fact immediately set Cubans apart from most other Hispanic communities, who were, for the most part, economic exiles with modest education. In September 1965, largely in order to be rid of troublesome opponents, Castro decreed that exiles could collect members of their families and take them to the United States without enduring sanctions. Nearly 300,000 people left the country while the window remained open, until April 1966.

In the second half of the decade, the Cuban profile and that of other Hispanic immigrants converged as the legislation of 1965 took effect. In the 1970s and 1980s, moreover, economic refugees predominated from Cuba, where government intransigence towards the market reforms that revitalized other economies prolonged the global economic crisis of the seventies. In April 1980 Castro again relaxed the regulations, after police volleys killed alarming numbers of dissidents who were seeking shelter in the Peruvian embassy in Havana. Something like 125,000 people, released as subversives from the obligations of Cuban citizenship, fled in boats across the strait to the United States. Reinaldo Arenas was one of them. "Before boarding the boats," he recalled, "we were sorted into categories and sent to empty warehouses: one for the insane, one for murderers and hard-core criminals, another for prostitutes and homosexuals, and one for the young men who were undercover agents of State Security to be infiltrated in the United States."[27]

During most of the remainder of the century, "boat people" undertook risks to life comparable to or greater than those of wetbacks who swam across the Rio Grande. In 1994 the coast guard arrested 38,000 would-be Cuban migrants at sea. After a spell of internment, they all found homes in the United States.

Shared experience with Mexicans and other migrants showed in the way Cuban literature of exile reflected the frustration and exclusion of life in the US. Elías Miguel Muñoz, in his 1991 novel, *The Greatest Performance*, even expressed greater enthusiasm for the old colonial masters in Spain than for the new ones who oppressed him in Garden Shore, California, where his protagonist's Cuban family sought "the promised land.... But to me it became the vivid representation of hell." He wanted Spain, where "there were good-looking people who spoke pure Spanish and there was gorgeous music and crowded plazas" instead of "only cars, freeways and solitary houses" in empty streets.[28]

On the other hand, Cubans seem in some ways to have been less invested in—more alienated from—their homeland than counterparts in other migrant communities. They accounted, for instance, for 12 percent of US naturalizations during the seventies, at a time when Mexicans supplied only 6 percent of newly naturalized citizens.[29] In part this reflects the discriminatory nature of US legislation in favor of Cubans and in revulsion from Castro: since 1966, even nominally illegal Cuban immigrants have enjoyed the right to be fast-tracked to permanent resident status. Conflicting Cuban sentiments about the United States reflected divisions at home in a postrevolutionary society where the contending sides were never reconciled. The cause célèbre was that of five-year-old Elián González, whom fishermen rescued from the sea on Thanksgiving Day, 1999. They found him clinging to the inner tube of a tire off Fort Lauderdale, the survivor of the wreckage of an aluminum boat full of poor migrants fleeing from Cuba. Most of the occupants drowned, including Elián's mother and the lover with whom she was fleeing not only, or perhaps primarily, from Cuba, but also from her husband.

The case was an unpleasant reminder that not all exiles were political refugees or seekers of economic opportunity in the land of the free. The political divisions among Cubans, however, clouded the moral issues. Elián boarded in Miami's Little Havana with relatives who contested court proceedings to return the boy to his father, and threatened, with support from the Cuban mayor of Miami's Dade County, where 700,000 Cuban voters lived, to defy the law if the courts found against them. One of Miami's most influential Cuban journalists, Belkis Cuza Malé, declared, "Elián represents the salvation of a people, the slandered and unseen exile, the homeland in chains, and in the purest sense, our condition as human beings who find ourselves in another land."[30] Cuza Malé might, perhaps, be excused for this apparently disproportionate language: she had fled to the United States with her own little boy after she and her husband were imprisoned for criticizing Castro. Oddly, the case overturned the usual parameters of US politics. Normally, Republicans would want to chastise illegal immigrants and uphold parents' rights. But Florida's Republican legislators, Senator Connie Mack and Representative Bill McCollum, introduced a bill to thwart Elián's father's rights by making the boy a US citizen. Federal agents forestalled the attempt by forcibly removing Elián from his fosterers in April 2000 and handing him to his father, who took him back to Cuba a few months later, when legal proceedings reached the point of exhaustion.[31] Over the following ten years, Cubans arrived in the United States to make permanent homes there at the average rate of over 10,000 a year. Thereafter the numbers leapt as the Cuban regime relaxed its own restrictions, reaching nearly 40,000 a year. The privileges Cubans enjoy—accelerated access to Green Cards, Republican patronage, sufferance of "illegals"—helps, perhaps, to keep them distinct in the perceptions of other Hispanics.

THE FOURTH BIG COMMUNITY of Hispanics in the continental United States, after those of Mexicans, Puerto Ricans, and Cubans, is Dominican. The scale of Dominican immigration reflects the Dominican Republic's status as a quasi-colonial territory of the US empire for much of its history. In 1904 the US government took over management of the Dominican national debt, which had never been under control owing to the costs of the war for independence. US forces occupied and ran the country continuously from 1916 to 1924. The Trujillo dictatorship from 1930 to 1961 represented a reversion to nominal national sovereignty but relied increasingly on US support as the Cold War, from the late 1940s, and the Cuban revolution of 1959 made right-wing regimes seem endearing to Washington. The dictator's death removed the emigration controls that Trujillo had regarded as essential to prevent a drain of talent to the United States. To some extent his fears were well grounded in history, as the relatively few emigrants who went to the United States in the late nineteenth and early twentieth centuries were overwhelmingly well-to-do professionals who were fast-tracked through Ellis Island. In reality, however, the pattern of emigration after Trujillo's downfall hardly matched his expectations. Economic hardship, especially after the austerity plan of 1982 aimed to control the perennial budgetary deficit, became the main reason for people to leave. Unemployment stood officially at 30 percent in 1988. The Dominican Republic became a major exporter of people who, in contrast to the early emigrants, had modest educational attainments and accepted low rates of pay. Entrepreneurialism, however, was characteristic of the community. In 1991 an estimated 70 percent of New York City bodegas, or small Hispanic groceries, were in Dominican hands. This was a spectacular reversal of the historic balance, which, of course, was heavily weighted in favor of Puerto Rican owners. New York was by then the second most populous city in the Dominican world. Generation by generation, moreover, Dominicans registered distinctive patterns of social ascent. Their second generations have produced, typically, twice as many professionals as their parents.[32]

Some of those professionals—certainly the best known—are baseball players. Baseball is the imperial game of the United States, spread by empire as surely as cricket was spread by the Raj. It appeared in some places ahead of US power. Spanish authorities banned it in Cuba in the 1880s because the take at the gate went to finance freedom fighters. It appeared in Japan in the 1920s. In Venezuela the game has seeped into popularity beyond the reach of US imperialism. But wherever it is played on a large scale outside the US, Yankees either introduced it or reinforced it. Today baseball is more popular and exerts more influence in Cuba and the Dominican Republic than in the United States, mobilizing relatively more fans, colonizing more column inches. "They took their baseball seriously in the Dominican Republic," reported Juan Marichal, the famously fast-armed pitcher for the Giants. "They still do."[33] The Dominican baseball commentator Pedro Julio Santana told the historian Rob Ruck that US colonialists "have not given us anything else that in my opinion is of any value except baseball. And here baseball is king." To be a baseball star is the commonest boyhood ambition in the Dominican Republic.[34]

If Puerto Ricans were equivocal about their home island, and Cubans tended to recall it with hostility, Dominicans were outstandingly adept in forging transnational links that kept their US neighborhoods in close touch with those of what still seemed like home. The sociologist Peggy Levitt has described the links that bind Miraflores, near the southwest coast of the island, with the Jamaica Plain district of Boston, Massachusetts, which, despite its name, has little in common with the Caribbean except for the 25 percent or so of the population who now come from the Dominican Republic, Cuba, or Puerto Rico. By 1994, 65 percent of homes in Miraflores had relatives in Boston, especially in Jamaica Plain, where people from that one hometown monopolized several streets. Forty percent of the households in Miraflores relied on remittances from Boston for at least 75 percent of their income. The ebb and flow of influence was constant. In Miraflores, T-shirts with names of Boston businesses abounded, "even though they often do not know what these words or logos mean." Anyone visiting Miraflores would quickly become familiar with Cremora, juice made from Tang, SpaghettiOs, and Frosted Flakes, and with park benches inscribed with the names of migrants who made good in Boston. Conversely, Dominicans in Boston brought aspects of a Dominican look and lifestyle with them, decorating their fridges with magnets that had fruit motifs, adorning their shelves with plastic animals, and hanging ornamental curtains around their doorframes.[35] On the other hand, a stay-at-home relative of migrants from the Dominican Republic told Levitt how materialism corrupted emigrants from his hometown of Miraflores. "Life in the U.S.," he admitted, "teaches them many good things but they also learn some bad things. . . . People come back more individualistic, more materialistic. They think that 'things' are everything rather than service, respect, or duty. They are more committed to themselves than they are to the community."[36] Not everyone wants to go "home." *In the Heights* by Lin-Manuel Miranda was a musical that went from a student production at Wesleyan University in 1999 to Broadway in 2005, full of characters hobbled by poverty, conflicted by race, and rejected by the Anglo world. The plot hovered between options of returning to the Dominican Republic and staying to try to make it in New York. The doyenne of the barrio, Abuela Claudia, died planning to use her lottery winnings to take the whole community home, but the youngsters decided their home was in the United States. They knew no other. The generations edge away from the old homeland to the new.

Nonetheless, Dominicans and Hispanic immigrants generally are exceptionally zealous in staying in touch with home. Most migrants from other parts of the world do not make frequent journeys home or send anything like as much money to the families they leave behind. In valuing their roots, too, Dominicans are typical of fellow Hispanics. A recent opinion survey organized by Harvard's Kennedy School put at 83 percent the proportion of Hispanics who rate the preservation of their cultures of origin as important. Nearly 70 percent of those who marry choose partners from their country of birth.[37]

THE DIVERSIFICATION OF HISPANIC immigration has brought increasing numbers from other communities. Central Americans, mainly *salvadoreños*, numbered little more than 330,000 in 1980. They had quadrupled by the end of the century and supported their families back home with $3.5 billion in annual remittances.[38] South America supplied the United States with well over half a million immigrants in the 1990s. Recently the variety of Central and South American countries that filed amicus briefs in court proceedings against fastidious state immigration laws in the United States shows the range of communities interested in the welfare of their emigrants. In 2011 Bolivia, Colombia, El Salvador, Guatemala, Nicaragua, Peru, and even Paraguay, which of all Latin American countries has fewest of its citizens in the United States, filed separate, nearly identical motions to join Mexico's against Arizona's restrictions.

Not only is the provenance of Hispanics in the United States becoming more diverse, but migrants are spread ever more widely across the country.[39] The patches are far more extensive today than ever before as a result of the freedom of migration within the United States. The name of Chicago's Pilsen neighborhood betrays its past, but now the old monuments with inscriptions in Czech or Slovak are interspersed on streets teeming with mariachi bands and lined with Mexican restaurants. There are over 10,000 restaurants in Chicago, every one of which has at least one Mexican worker in the kitchen.[40] Hartford, Connecticut, was once the capital of Yankeedom. Now, in a city of more than 110,000 people, there are over 47,000 Hispanics. Most are Puerto Ricans—the city has had two mayors of Puerto Rican background in a row—but there are also 25,000 Peruvian families in Connecticut.[41] In two counties in eastern Washington State, Hispanics now form a majority of the population. In nearby Yakima County, 45 percent of the population is Hispanic according to the census. In these places the phenomenon has been sudden, as numbers of immigrants have hurtled upward in response to job opportunities, and, in contrast to the situation in Hartford, political representation has not caught up in the ten counties where they are the highest percentage of the population. Of 1,891 local elected offices in those counties—from city councils to cemetery-district boards—only 78 were held by Latinos as of December 2009, and Yakima has no Hispanic representatives on the City Council.[42]

The number of US states from which substantial remittances now reach Latin American countries demonstrates vividly the widening distribution of the Hispanic population. "Twenty years ago," according to Sergio Bendixen, a Miami pollster who surveyed some 2,500 immigrants in 2006, "the money was coming from four or five states; now it's coming from every corner of the country." Bendixen's investigation, commissioned by the Inter-American Development Bank, found that 1.2 percent of the residents of Pennsylvania were born in Latin America, as were 0.7 percent of those of Ohio and 2 percent of the population of Indiana. Transfers from Indiana approached $400 million. Those from Pennsylvania exceeded $500 million. Ohio produced well over $200 million in remittances. "These were states," the report observed, "with virtually no Latino immigrants five years ago."[43] He left West Virginia and Montana out of his inquiry on the grounds that they contained too few Hispanics to make the exercise worthwhile. Two years later, however, those states were yielding, respectively, over $10 million and some $5 million.

After a spectacular rise—by more than half as much again from 2004 to 2006—the total remit stabilized at around $45 billion as a result of the failing economy in 2008, and declined as recovery faltered. But the trend toward an ever more widely dispersed Hispanic population across the United States has continued. Indeed, economic difficulties, forcing workers to look ever farther afield for work, has probably stimulated the trend. Mexicans moved in substantial numbers, for instance, from familiar Illinois to previously little-known Pennsylvania in 2006. "Somebody who is already here hears about a new plant opening and goes there," Jeffrey S. Passel, a demographer at the Pew Hispanic Institute, told the *New York Times*. "After a while, the word gets back to Mexico, and the migrant stream is no longer from California to a meatpacking plant in Iowa. It's Mexico to a plant in Iowa."[44] The reconstruction of New Orleans after Hurricane Katrina provides an example of how immigrant populations coalesce around jobs. In New Orleans, by 2006, Hispanic workers accounted for half the reconstruction force, with 54 percent of them working in the United States illegally. Remittances to Latin America from Louisiana topped $200 million in 2006, a 240 percent increase since 2004.

———

THE MULTIPLICATION OF MIGRANTS' destinations has converted Hispanics into a national minority, rather as the Great Migration out of the rural South made blacks significant nationally. I suspect— though evidence is lacking—that, by spreading Hispanics more thinly among non-Hispanic communities, it has also stimulated the development of pan-Hispanic feeling. At the same time, diffusion probably increases pressure on Hispanics to assimilate—that is, forgo their own culture in order to be more like their non-Hispanic neighbors.

Which trend will predominate? If Hispanics are to function as a cohesive minority and collaborate with one another in the conservation of culture, the key areas of resistance to erosion will be those they traditionally share or are currently acquiring. Latino music, for instance, is a new kind of pan-Hispanic culture, where formerly there was Mexican or Cuban or Puerto Rican music, or that of other national and local traditions. But music is unlikely to sustain a common sense of identity, precisely because its appeal is so wide. It is Latino, not Hispanic, and owes major debts to Brazil and non-Hispanic parts of the Caribbean. It has rapidly transcended any particular constituency and is now part of the global popular culture that carries a US brand in the world at large.

In the long term there is little chance that Hispanics will reunite enduringly around common political interests, because those interests are limited. Cubans tend to have a stake in the anti-Castrista Republican agenda many of them share. Mexicans, whose economic success rate in the United States is relatively low, have a strong interest in the labor and tax policies of the Democrats. Many Hispanic communities are divided between values-driven politics, which inclines them towards the Republicans' rhetoric of the family, and interest-driven commitments to the more radical social policies of the Democrats. Allegiances are volatile and unpredictable. In the 2012 presidential election immigration policy was like a noose, drawing Hispanics tightly together because the Republican Party—with a presidential candidate widely suspected of liberal sympathies—had to work to get out the xenophobic voters who form part of the party's core. The Republicans espoused self-destructive nativist rhetoric. They are not likely to make the same mistake again (see above, p. xix).

For the future of the Hispanic United States, the most promising common cultural traditions Hispanics share are religious and linguistic. Problems beset both. Take religion first. The Catholic tradition might be expected to form a focus of identity for Hispanics, and the Church to provide both a forum of exchange and a forge of power. César Chávez appreciated that "it is not just our right to appeal to the Church to use its power effectively for the poor, it is our duty to do so. . . . We ask for its presence with us, beside us, as Christ among us."[45] Visiting New York in 1996, John Paul II told his congregation that he "also loves the sons and daughters of the Church who speak Spanish. Many of you have been born here or have lived here for a long time. Others are more recent arrivals. But you all bear the mark of your cultural heritage, deeply rooted in the Catholic tradition. Keep alive that faith and culture."[46] In some ways the Church does function as a guardian of Hispanic identity and tradition. Generically Hispanic styles of worship cram congregations from all parts of Hispanic America into the same spaces for Mass.[47] Gringo Catholics have adapted to some of the traditions Hispanic Catholics have brought with them, wearing white for first communion, displaying Our Lady of Guadalupe in the sanctuary. Anthony Stevens-Arroyo, one of the foremost specialists in the devotions of Hispanic migrants in the United States, insists on the importance of common features of their religious culture:

> The expression of religious belief covers every niche in Latino society, from the churchgoers singing in processions on Good Friday or gathering families for Sunday school to the Latino pugilists who bless themselves with the sign of the cross before a boxing match and the gang members who have religious images tattooed on their arms and chests. . . . Our homes have crosses over the bed and altars with candles and holy pictures or estampillas are found in ceremonial niches, especially in the poorest homes. Latinos revere the unadorned elements of nature by placing earth, rocks, and plants within these sacred spaces. Concern for sexuality and success often find expression in rituals derived from African religions or from beliefs in reincarnation and spiritism.[48]

The power of the Church to influence Hispanic life, however, is slight, partly because of the very diversity of forms of popular religion that differentiate communities of worship from different places of origin. The Church, moreover, has been extremely bad at retaining the allegiance of Latin Americans, whether in their home countries or the United States. Secular culture has enfeebled that allegiance. Protestant evangelization often usurps it. Only 65 percent of US Hispanics called themselves Catholic in 1990, less than 60 percent by 2001,[49] though according to 2012 statistics the percentage has recovered a couple of points meanwhile.[50] In any case, the US Church has always been rife with the heresy Pope Leo XIII called Americanism—assigning priority to the projection of a distinctive image of Catholicism for the United States to accommodate WASP prejudices and forestall know-nothing hatred. The hierarchy has long been divided over the extent to which the Church should encourage Hispanic religious autonomy. The most glaring conflict occurred at Christmas Mass in Los Angeles in 1969. Chicano activists, who had celebrated Mass in Spanish on the steps outside the stark, machinelike, concrete volumes of St. Basil's Church in the densely Catholic Wilshire district of Los Angeles, were locked out of the English-language Mass that followed at the high altar. Those who got in were forced out, while riot police emerged from the cardinal's palace "wearing helmets, bearing shields, and swinging billy clubs." Cardinal McIntyre blamed the demonstrators as resembling "the rabble as they stood at the foot of the cross, shouting, 'Crucify him!'" A week later, the visiting Puerto Rican archbishop Antulio Parrilla Bonilla celebrated Mass in Spanish with victims in the open air within sight of the cathedral.[51] Even in Spanish-speaking communities in the nineteenth century, the hierarchy had a penchant for appointing French priests. The native Spanish-speaking priesthood is proportionately underrepresented to this day.

THE SPANISH LANGUAGE LOOKS, at first sight, like a more probable unifying force than the Church. Command of Spanish can be prestigious, even sexy. One of Eusebio Chacón's fictional protagonists is a Don Juan who abuses his knowledge of the literature of Spain to ensnare the admiration of a victim of his seduction. When I stayed in a club in Chicago, waiters gathered around my table for the pleasure of hearing my Castilian way of talking. It is common for me—because

I speak the English of England—to have difficulty getting my speech across to interlocutors in the United States. When I switch to Spanish, however, Spanish-speakers understand me wherever they come from. This, I suppose, is a sign that Spanish-speakers genuinely do form a community, disposed to make the effort to understand forms of the language that are unfamiliar. The former slogan of the television station Univisión—"Unidos por un sólo idioma," united by a single language—looks convincing from a distance, especially to those who do not speak Spanish, and perceive only the solidity and size of the world's hispanophone community.

When you look up close, you see how that community, like "global English," is riven by differences of dialect and problems of mutual intelligibility. Univisión's commercial needs, in any case, have proved stronger than its crusading vocation, and the station is unwatchable for anyone intelligent or educated. The *telenovelas* that provide pabulum for its viewers do encourage people to see into one another's home countries, but the similarities the series disclose are so crass, banal, tawdry, and morally dodgy that it could only inspire revulsion in someone of normal sensibilities.

Those who expect Spanish to survive in the United States and even to establish itself as the second language of a bilingual nation have to confront the fact that no linguistic minority has retained its own language throughout a process of integration in the country. Ortiz Vargas noticed in Puerto Rico in the 1930s how women who lived almost entirely isolated in their own linguistic communities responded to the tug of the anglophone world:

> *They corrupted their speech*
> *With the bizarre jargon*
> *Of a tongue that was foreign*
> *And that no one could teach.*

> *[Corrompieron su lengua*
> *con la mezcla bizarra*
> *de la lengua extranjera*
> *que jamás aprendieron.]*

Persuaded by the establishment's prejudices, Spanish-speakers, uneducated in the literature of their own language, think that they must privilege English in order to acquire prestige or trigger success. A famous, anonymous satire, *Jíbaro en Nueva York*, recorded in the 1960s, recounts a subway meeting with an old friend from the highlands of Puerto Rico, who answered Spanish questions in broken English. His friend persevered but:

> *He still didn't want*
> *To admit he was* hispano.
> *I asked, "How's your* hermano?*"*
> *He said, "Oye esto, brother,*
> *I love my father and mother,*
> *Just like a real* americano.*"*[52]

> *[Aún por eso no quería*
> *declararse que era hispano.*
> *Le pregunté por su hermano*
> *Y me dijo, "Oye esto, brother,*
> *I love my father and mother*
> *igual que un americano."]*

Piri Thomas, whose dialogues in his stories about Puerto Rican life in New York have the macaronic quality of the fiction of Junot Díaz (see above, p. xxviii), has a poignant dialogue between two lovesick teenagers: Juanita has just arrived from Puerto Rico and wants to transform herself into "Jenny" but has difficulty understanding the rapid English of George, the immigrants' son from the apartment downstairs. He realizes her Spanish is "without fault, unlike many Puerto Ricans born in the States who mixed their English and Spanish together" but cannot speak it well himself. "In a way," he tells the women who live upstairs, "you are teaching me about my heritage. Not enough of us kids born here know what Puerto Rico is about."[53] Some of the interviewees whose transcripts the sociologist Oscar Martínez published in 1994 had the same attitudes. Juan Hinojosa was a student whose parents, both native Spanish-speakers, spoke only English to him because his mother "determined that her children would lead middle-class lives." His fellow student, Daniel Fisher, rejected his mother's attempts to teach him her native Spanish "because I wanted to Americanize" but came to regret his self-alienation from his roots. Greg Rocha, whose parents spoke to him only in English to spare him the discrimination they felt they had suffered, thought he was "returning home" when he visited Mexico, but his inability to communicate left him feeling "a stranger in a foreign country."[54] In one of his popular Mambo Mouth videos, the entertainer John Leguizamo portrays an incarcerated Mexican in the United States, who tries to talk Spanish to a cop of Dominican origin outside his cell. The cop declines to reply. The prisoner calls him a "coconut—white inside, brown outside." Realizing that his problem is that speaking Spanish is derogating, he tries to talk his way out of jail by pretending to be successively Swedish, Irish, Israeli, and Japanese.

Yet the strength of emotional commitment to Spanish may triumph over the inconstancy of linguistic renegades. To understand how deeply Spanish-speakers can feel about the survival of their language, one has to appreciate the depth of persecution they and their ancestors suffered for the sake of Spanish. In 1914, for instance, shortly after the admission of New Mexico as a state of the Union, some school boards banned instruction in Spanish. The ruling was contrary to the amiable modus vivendi, which, as we saw in Chapter Five (above, p. 191), Agnes Cleaveland described in the previous generation, as well as to the state constitution, which guaranteed Spanish-speakers' rights to the use of their language. In November 1914 a versifier in the *Revista de Taos* appealed to legislators to enforce protection. His case anticipated every device of argument and rhetoric since deployed to justify Spanish in the United States: cultural sentimentalism, human rights, the facts of history, the international usefulness of a Spanish-speaking community, and the richness of the literary legacy open to users of the tongue.

> *Know that my native tongue,*
> *That I sucked at my mother's breast,*

Spoken in Spain and long
Famous, is now wrung
From the land, proscribed, oppressed.

[Sabed que el idioma natal
Que en los pechos he mamado
El idioma celebrado
Que se habla en la España actual
Es proscrito y desterrado.]

Spanish, the author pointed out, was the language of Cervantes, Lope, Calderón, Isabel la Católica, more than twenty nations, and "the original settlers of this land."[55] In 1934 a similar outrage occurred in Puerto Rico, where the US military government tried to impose English as the sole medium of instruction in schools. The poet Tomás Gares responded by asking whether his fellow Puerto Ricans would surrender their language along with "our all, like slaves, . . . our sacred freedom, tradition, customs, . . . and our human dignity."

The language that my grandparents used,
That as children we learned for bedside oration,
Must endure forever in this, my nation,
Never corrupted, never confused.[56]

[Mas . . . el idioma aquel de mis abuelos
Aprendido de niños al rezar . . .
Ese idioma en mi Patria será eterno
Nunca, nunca le habremos de cambiar.]

The children persecuted for using Spanish in New Mexico and Puerto Rico were not immigrants in anglophone territory: they were native users of Spanish in parts of the United States where it was the long-standing official language. Immigrants suffered in their own way. Stories of being bullied or beaten for speaking Spanish in school have become a topos of Hispanic autobiography. Gloria Anzaldúa's memoir of her Texan childhood, published in 1987, is the locus classicus. Speaking Spanish at recess merited "three licks on the knuckles with a sharp ruler. . . . If you want to be American," her teacher told her, "speak American. If you don't like it, go back to Mexico where you belong."[57] César Chávez told a similar story about himself. So did Richard Rodriguez, a conservative opponent of affirmative action, who in his *Hunger of Memory*, published in 1981, focuses on an episode in his childhood when his teachers asked his parents—ostensibly for the sake of their child's social and economic advancement—not to speak Spanish at home.

In an attempt to frustrate Spanish, most states of the Union have legislated for the exclusive official use of English. It is not clear what this means, or whether it would override a defendant's right, for instance, to hear accusations and proffer defense in a language he or she dominates to perfection. People hostile to the use of Spanish have treated such laws as invitations to abuse. In one instance in Colorado, an elementary-school bus driver stopped children from speaking Spanish on their way to school. In 2004 in Scottsdale, Arizona, a teacher who slapped students for speaking Spanish in class claimed to be implementing English immersion policies. In Kansas City in 2005 school authorities suspended a student for speaking Spanish in a hallway, explaining, "This is not the first time we have [asked] Zach and others to not speak Spanish at school."[58]

Bilingual education has not worked because it has not been properly tried. Under present protocols, the effect is to mire economically deprived children in monoglot stagnation. Because they tend to be the poorest and most educationally deprived of Hispanics in the United States, fewer than 50 percent of Mexican immigrants speak fluent English. "They start below other Hispanics," a leading authority tells us, "and never catch up."[59] Their children start school with little exposure to English. They are either condemned to enduring a disadvantage in competition with anglophone peers, or to nominally bilingual education—a term unimaginatively interpreted in the United States to mean teaching Anglos in English and Hispanics in Spanish. In a genuinely bilingual system, both language communities would benefit from instruction in each other's language, and school time divided equally between Spanish and English would be supplemented by sub-titled television and e-entertainment that would encourage people to perfect their command of their second language.

The Netherlands and some Nordic countries have made English their own second language without even having native English-speaking communities. For the United States, the fact that a large number of native Spanish-speakers is at hand to help anglophones learn Spanish is a precious resource, which ought to be celebrated and encouraged. A bilingual United States would benefit not only from the cultural enrichment and life enhancement that command of more than one language brings to everyone who knows the pleasure and privilege of it, but would also better equip the country for the ineluc-table political and economic future, immersed in hemispheric circles of trade and cooperation. It would also be popular. Opinion sound-ings show that just about every Hispanic parent in the country wants English to be a medium of instruction in schools, and that 87 percent of non-Hispanic whites and 88 percent of African-American parents want their children to know Spanish.[60] To make real bilingualism hap-pen, people who speak only one language have to overcome their fear of the other. In the United States the task is hard because the country happened to absorb vast numbers of immigrants during a brief period when linguistic nationalism dominated the world. The false assump-tion that national unity depends on the enforcement of linguistic con-formity is an unfortunate legacy. Most other countries have gotten over it. The fact—which I declare on my faith as a historian—is that, typically, enduring and successful states have had more than one lan-guage and have been better and more robust in consequence.

FEAR OF HISPANICS GOES beyond fear of the need to learn a second language. For some well-educated but imperfectly rational people, it arises from cultural defensiveness: investment in the notion (which is false) that culture has essential, inalienable characteristics; the belief (which, as we shall see in the next chapter, is invalid) that the culture of the United States is characterized, in this essential sense, by a white, Anglo-Saxon Protestant heritage; and the claim (which is questionable) that whatever is valuable in this culture is threatened by the presence of large numbers of people of different heritage. These are important fears (and we shall return to them in the next, final chapter); but I do not think many US citizens share them, except in connection with language. The fears that really impede Hispanics and inspire attempts to subordinate or exclude them are racial, demographic, and economic. Racism is always excited when an easily identifiable minority expands rapidly. To understand the force of racism when exerted against Hispanics, it is worth acknowledging that they are relatively philoprogenitive. During the generation of accelerated immigration from the mid-1960s, when white denizens of the United States were already anxious about being swamped by newcomers of unprecedentedly varied provenance and appearance, Hispanics' fertility boosted the numbers of their unfamiliar neighbors, while the whites' own fertility declined alarmingly. The proportion of births to non-Hispanic white mothers in that period fell from two-thirds to around one-third. Births to Hispanics rose to be more than half the total. These are just the sorts of circumstances one should expect to ignite racism. Associated fears arose from prejudices about Hispanics' social and economic condition: that they would impoverish the economy, degrade society, increase crime, spread disease, and multiply antisocial behavior. In 1971, when David Hayes-Bautista, an outstanding public health specialist at UCLA, published a prospect of the effects of the coming boom in Hispanics' numbers, he faced a barrage of adverse reaction from members of the public who, he observed, "imagined that Latinos were largely gang members, welfare mothers, high school dropouts, and drug users."[61]

These opinions were durable. In 1994 California governor Pete Wilson's focus groups "denounced immigrants for ruining the state," taking jobs, crowding hospitals, gobbling tax dollars, and increasing crime rates. A great fear obsessed the state: undocumented migrants were so numerous that they would exhaust the state's resources. An advertisement for one state senator's reelection campaign claimed that "two thousand each night" slunk across the border. Petitioners alleged that the nightly total was 5,000. If true, this would produce an undocumented population of nearly 22 million, at a time when the total population of the state was only 27.8 million. In reality, there were almost certainly fewer than half a million undocumented people in California, probably closer to 250,000. Despite the absurd basis of the fears, Wilson proposed an initiative that set the pattern for a lot of recent anti-immigrant legislation. He wanted teachers and social workers to be made to deny services to "anyone who appeared to be illegal." Voters endorsed the policy in a referendum.[62]

One effect was to animate Hispanic political activism. Another was to exacerbate intercommunal tensions. In a legal battle that continued for five years, Hispanic community organizations got the federal court to rule the proposal unconstitutional. They also achieved unprecedented success in uniting and mobilizing Hispanic voters. In 1990 there were only seven Hispanics in the state legislature. A decade later there were twenty-seven.[63] Anglos fought back with traditional gerrymandering. Abuse of the redistricting system kept numbers of ethnic voters low in each district and created only one new Hispanic-majority district where the demographic logic mandated two. In September 2001 the *Los Angeles Times* reported that the plans for redrawing district boundaries "largely thwart the desires of Latinos and Asian Americans to win additional seats in Congress." The following month the Mexican American Legal Defense and Educational Fund filed a lawsuit against the scheme, but the court found that "the protection of an incumbent" was "a well-established, legitimate districting criterion" and pointed out, correctly, that non-Hispanics often voted for Hispanic candidates.[64]

Meanwhile, across the country, deportations multiplied. A case that drew public attention in 1998 was that of John Collado, a successful, middle-aged family man from the Dominican Republic with three children and a restaurant of his own in New York. When he was a young immigrant, nineteen years old, he was arrested for fornicating with his consenting but underage girlfriend, which was not an offense punishable by deportation at the time. Nearly twenty-five years later, immigration authorities arrested him, imprisoned him, and informed him that, as his offense had been reclassified, he would be deported. The courts freed him, but only after an ordeal of sixteen months, during which his life was subverted and his livelihood imperiled.[65] Of 179,000 people deported the following year, more than 92 percent were Hispanic.[66]

The fears that provoked these episodes, and continue to influence US politics, were and are illusory. The values that US voters hold dear are not on the whole peculiarly US values. Some are common, decent human values. Others are shared by the modern, democratic, capitalist world. Hispanics are commonly guardians and enthusiastic practitioners of the same values. Hayes-Bautista's 1971 study showed that despite "poor education and low incomes, most Latino populations . . . exhibit middle-class behaviors and extraordinary health outcomes. They do not fit a 'minority' model." They had the lowest death rates of comparable sections of the population, except in New Mexico and Colorado, and maintained good health records in spite of the poverty that restricted their access to insurance. Hispanic mothers gave birth to drug-exposed infants at only one-third the rate of non-Hispanic whites and one-tenth the African-American rate. A Mexican American Legal Defense and Education Fund advertisement in 1997 realistically showed Latinos teaching, returning from war, buying homes, and graduating, but the public rejected it because the image did not match the stereotype.[67] In June 1999, Robert Lopez, a reporter who had been a schoolboy in a notorious Belmont, California, high school, found that of his Mexican and *salvadoreño* classmates, 77 percent went to college, 28 percent earned degrees (the same proportion as non-Hispanic whites statewide). Eighty percent had white-collar jobs and 34 percent were homeowners.[68] Hayes-Bautista concluded that "from 1940 to 2000, Latinos have behaved more like members of the 'American' middle class than middle-class 'Americans' themselves have: Latinos exhibit the most vigorous workforce participation; the lowest public welfare usage; the strongest family structures; the fewest heart attacks; lower cancer rates and fewer strokes; the healthiest babies; and a five-year-longer life expectancy, compared to non-Hispanic whites and African Americans."

Fears are irrational and you cannot dispel them simply by demonstrating their false basis. They were containable while the economy was doing well. The eighties were boom time. In the nineties, the government paid off debt and ran up surpluses. Then, in 2001, George W. Bush took office as president and embarked on a risky strategy of simultaneously cutting taxes and increasing expenditure. Profligacy became uncontrollable when, with what at the time seemed stunning irresponsibility, the United States launched two concurrent wars, first in Afghanistan, then in Iraq. The wars proved budget-busting, or at least helped to bust the budget. As the United States plunged into deficit, the world's economy slowed. In 2008 it became apparent that US institutions—both public and private—had overinvested in property in the expectation of infinitely rising real estate prices. The property market collapsed. Leading banks defaulted. The government committed to hundreds of billions of dollars in bailouts for tottering businesses—money that, owing to the profligacy of the previous few years and the trillions wasted on the wars, it did not have. Europe, where some governments had been as prodigal as Mr. Bush, opted for austerity. The world flailed into recession.

One of the effects was to exacerbate unemployment in the United States and reinflame resentment of immigrants. Tom Tancredo, who sought the Republican nomination for the presidency in 2008 and got over 650,000 votes when he ran for the governorship of Colorado, was the most consistent spokesman for reawakened fears. He blamed terrorism in the United States on "twenty million aliens who have come to take our jobs." Calls for fencing the border—mandated by Congress in 2006 but only halfheartedly implemented or in some places abandoned as impractical, antienvironmental, morally repugnant, and economically destructive—became a thermometer for the heat of the passions involved. In 2010 Sarah Palin, the presidential hopeful who had been the Republicans' vice-presidential candidate in the last election, came out in favor of fencing the entire Mexican border, reinforcing it with ten or fifteen thousand National Guardsmen.[69] Presidential hopefuls for 2012 Michele Bachmann and Herman Cain were reported as saying that they wanted, respectively, a barrier "across every foot" of the frontier and an electrified wall that could kill people trying to enter illegally.[70] In the 2012 general election, the Republicans' official manifesto called for the completion of a fence along the entire border.

As usual in any persecution, the poorest and weakest were the first to suffer. There are all too many unintended jokes in the US Congress. But in September 2010, a real comedian spoke up before a subcommittee on immigration. The satirist Stephen Colbert appeared in the character he plays on television—a right-wing chat-show host who lampoons extremism by taking conservative positions to their logical conclusion. But there was a solemn side to his contribution. When committee members asked him serious questions, he suspended his comic role and replied seriously. His views were pertinent, because he was one of only a handful of committed respondents to a nationwide challenge from the United Farm Workers of America to "take our jobs"—to try their hands at the backbreaking, ill-paid work immigrants do in US orchards and fields. Rednecks and xenophobes charge Latino—chiefly Mexican—laborers with "taking our jobs." So the union dared the grumblers to take some of those jobs back. The result demonstrated what anyone with any knowledge of the subject already knew: that immigrants accept work so hard and so unremunerative that citizens reject it. Far from taking citizens' jobs, they keep vital sectors of the economy going.

A student at my university reported the conditions he observed in Immokalee, Florida. Journeymen had to line up every day before dawn in the hope of getting picked for a work gang. If they were lucky enough to attract a taskmaster's attention, they struggled for ten hours in 100 degrees Fahrenheit, under a cruel sun and the weight of a thirty-two-pound bucket of tomatoes. To earn an amount equal to the minimum daily pay nominally allowed under the laws of the state, a worker would have to pick two and a quarter tons. Large numbers of workers have never negotiated the bureaucratic obstacles one must overcome to have the support of the legal and judicial system. So

exploiters, intimidators, and blackmailers can victimize them unrestrainedly. Immigrants typically pay exorbitant sums for any transac-
tion that demands documentation—deals on accommodation or loans
or the costs of the money transfers on which their families back home
depend.[71] Employers can coerce them to the point of slavery. Applica-
tion of antislavery legislation has freed more than a thousand workers
in Florida in the last dozen years.

Racism is one of the characteristics of the white empires of the
nineteenth and twentieth centuries. The subjection, subordination,
exploitation, and degradation of Americans of Spanish-speaking and
Native American ancestry were steps along a single road that began
with conquest. The way US employers have always undervalued Hispanic Americans' labor is a means of calibrating the oppression. Discriminatory differential wages succeeded virtual or actual peonage and
coerced labor in the nineteenth and early twentieth centuries. Anglos
justified the discrimination on the grounds that inferiors did not need
as much money as white people. When Congress outlawed racism,
beginning with the series of civil rights acts from 1964, employers
perpetuated the system by confining their victims to low categories of
work and keeping skilled and managerial jobs for the master class.

The main target of revived fear has been the migrants we commonly refer to as "illegals." The term is hateful, because most people in
the category are law-abiding. "Illegals" are often in the United States
because of official connivance to meet labor needs. Under a statute of
1986 (see above, p. 279), which was deliberately framed to keep agriculture supplied, the Immigration and Naturalization Service turned
a blind eye perhaps to as many as 600,000 imperfectly documented
workers.[72] The act made no provision for families of amnestied illegals
to join them, and an amendment proposed in 1989 to remedy that
definition failed because of delays in Congress. Many undocumented
immigrants have an idealistic or romanticized notion of the United
States as a country where the rule of law can be respected. In most
cases the only laws they might consciously have evaded are, to them,
oppressive, denying them a livelihood or the right to family life.

I write with feeling because I think of the woman who used to clean my apartment when I lived in Somerville, in suburban Boston, Massachusetts. I do not know her immigration status, but an allusion she once made to the cost of her journey to the United States from her homeland in Central America made me think that she had been in the hands of extortionists. She was a profoundly good woman: selfless, generous, sentimental, unswerving, impressively hardworking, and devoted, often to the point of tears, to the children she had left at home, whom she was working to educate. She was always cheerful, but below the surface of her smiles she endured suffering only dispelled on the day she could show me the photos of her boy and girl in their graduation outfits. The United States, it seemed to me, was better for having such people in it. I could not understand how anyone would want to pass legislation to victimize someone so deserving.

In 2010–11, however, such legislation cascaded onto the statute books or stacked up in court corridors. It started in Arizona in April 2010,[73] when Governor Jan Brewer signed a bill that, according to President Barack Obama, would "undermine basic notions of fairness that we cherish as Americans, as well as the trust between police and our communities that is so crucial to keeping us safe." The law, which the Supreme Court upheld, makes it a crime for an immigrant to be unable to show proof of status if challenged by the police. It also mandates police to demand to see the documents of anyone "where reasonable suspicion exists that a person is an unauthorized alien," and jail people on suspicion of being in the country illegally. Typically, victims will stay in jail until their immigration status can be confirmed. To immigrants, this looks like a move to encourage the sort of harassment and discrimination against Hispanics, regardless of their citizenship status, typical of such infamous precedents as Operation Wetback and the periodic, vindictive roundups of potential deportees that seem to happen whenever the US economy is in serious trouble. Arizona's legislature has also endorsed a plan to fence off the state's entire southern border, at an estimated cost of $3 million a mile, to be raised with private donations.

Alabama followed Arizona's lead in June 2011, making it a crime to be an illegal immigrant in the state of Alabama, on pain of up to a year's imprisonment. The law's sponsor, Republican representative Micky Hammon, was frank about the nature of his bill, which, he said, "attacks every aspect of an illegal alien's life" and "is designed to make it difficult for them to live here so they will deport themselves." The 2012 Republican presidential candidate, Mitt Romney, endorsed the measure. In Georgia, a similar law the following month enjoyed the patronage of former gubernatorial candidate Nathan Deal, who advocated punishing the children of undocumented immigrants by withholding health care and barring them from college education. Unless the courts overrule it, his law will replicate the contents of those of Arizona and Alabama, while also imposing on employers the obligation of checking the status of every employee against federal records. Deal's proposal for meeting the employment shortfall in agriculture, as migrants fled Georgia, was to fill the 11,000 openings with some of the state's 100,000 ex-convicts, about 25 percent of whom are unemployed.[74] Early in 2011 South Carolina enacted a similar law, which, to supplement the measures introduced in other states, established a special police force dedicated to the pursuit and punishment of imperfectly documented immigrants.

Meanwhile, vigilantes had been patrolling the border and undertaking persecutions of their own. From 2005, an organization that called itself Minutemen intimidated immigrants with videos that appeared to show killings of alleged illegals. Arnold Schwarzenegger, governor of California, praised the vigilantes' "terrific" work and said they were welcome to patrol the California border. Suspicions abounded that the Minutemen really did undertake violence and commit murders in the course of victimizing immigrants. In February 2011 a long-standing Minutemen operative, Shawna Forde, who had a long criminal record, including offenses of burglary and prostitution, was convicted of the murder of a nine-year-old girl and her Mexican-American father in their home in Arivaca, Arizona. According to allegations made in court, her aim was to steal funds to support vigilante operations. In an interview she explained that she was resisting "getting third-world values in a first-rate country."[75]

By then, however, a reaction seemed to be setting in. Arizona legislators dropped a series of even more draconian measures that were on their way to the statute books: these would have evicted undocumented immigrants from their homes, banned them from schools and colleges, and made it a crime for them to drive. Realization had set in that the persecution of a critical part of the labor force would cripple the state. "It's time for us to call time out," explained a state senator.[76] Utah demonstrated that it was possible to formulate a law that addressed public concerns about undocumented immigrants without cruelty and without inflicting much economic damage on the state. The Utah Compact, which the Chamber of Commerce drafted, called for "a focus on families and empathy in immigration policy, and using police to fight crime rather than enforce immigration laws." The legislature responded, limiting police investigations of immigrants' status to cases of serious suspected crime and creating a fast track, via an amnesty and a means-adjusted fine, to official work permits for undocumented immigrants of blemishless record.[77]

It looks, therefore, as if the Hispanic minority is going to continue to grow, and that even the undocumented immigrants will be allowed to augment it. A CNN report of May 24, 2011, summed up the statistics. The Hispanic population exceeds 50 million, a 43 percent increase from a decade previously. Hispanics account for more than half of the nation's overall growth of 27.3 million. A quarter of US Americans under eighteen years old are Hispanic. Between censuses, the Hispanic population more than doubled in nine states, including Alabama, Kentucky, and Maryland. In New Mexico, the Hispanic population (46 percent) exceeds the white population (40 percent). In some city concentrations the numbers are even more impressive, because nearly half the nation's Hispanics live in just ten metropolitan areas: 5.7 million of them—11 percent of the national total and 45 percent of the city—are in Los Angeles alone. In Miami, 66 percent of the population are Hispanics, who are also a substantial majority in San Antonio. In Riverside, they constitute the biggest community, at 47 percent of the total urban population. They account for about a third of the populations of Houston and Phoenix and exceed 20 percent in New York, Dallas, San Francisco, and Chicago.[78] Hispanics have become the country's biggest official ethnic minority. In the 1970s they were little more than half as numerous as blacks. In the 1990s they approached parity. By 2010 they numbered 47.8 million, more than blacks and Asians together.

In one of his Mambo Mouth videos, John Leguizamo plays with amusing mock-menace on Anglo fears of a Hispanic takeover of the United States. "We were here first," he points out, summarizing, in effect, the first couple of chapters of this book. He reminds Anglos how they need Hispanics to keep their country clean and make guacamole. "We'll push you so far up," he threatens, "you'll be in Canada. We won't deport you, we'll let you clean our toilets." The audience laughs good-naturedly, showing that they take this seriously, if at all, only as an ironic inversion of the way Hispanics have been treated. Nobody expects Hispanic revanche. The chances of fellow feeling embracing a large proportion of the Hispanic people of the United States are good, but if this happens, it will be on the basis of a common religion—and we have seen how limited is the potential of religion to bring Hispanics together or galvanize them in action—or of the Spanish language, which still does not command universal allegiance and which may not endure. Rehispanicization is most likely to be a relatively painless process. For reasons we must now address, it may even benefit the United States in future in previously unanticipated ways.

CHAPTER NINE

RETROSPECT AND PROSPECT

Why the United States Is—and Has to Be—a Latin American Country

———

Parochialism must not mislead us into assuming that the fair-skinned folk of our hemisphere are congenitally or irremediably wicked, just because they do not speak our language, or think of home as we do, or have political scandals of the same sort as ours, or value leaders with querulous tempers and dark complexions, or look charitably—from their precariously superior eminence—on neighbors who, with fewer historical advantages, are laboriously climbing the steps every republic must ascend. Nor should we hide the obvious facts of a problem that can be solved, in the interests of a long and peaceful future, by means of study, good judgment, and the quiet, strong impetus of the single soul that the whole hemisphere shares.

—José Martí, "Nuestra América" (1891)

WHEN A FRIEND DIES, THINGS LEFT UNSAID BECOME IMPORTANT. I got to know Samuel Huntington, the famously provocative political scientist, in the last few years of his life, when I worked in Boston,

Massachusetts. We disagreed about almost everything academic, but he was a delightful man, infinitely courteous, with the quality of character that academics need more, perhaps, than any other, if they are to be happy in their profession: he would not take professional disagreements personally.

When we met, I had written a duly appreciative but broadly adverse review of his best-known book, *The Clash of Civilizations and the Remaking of World Order*. In that work, published in 1996, he predicted that the era of global ideological conflicts, which was coming to an end with the collapse of most of the communist "bloc," would yield to a period in which civilizations—generally but not consistently characterized in terms of their religious traditions—would be the foci of contention. The concept was amazingly influential. Fanatics rushed to realize it, moderates to forestall it. Both focused on it. Huntington's categories disposed people to think that opposition between communism and capitalism would yield to conflict between Islam and the West. The prophecy seemed to come true, perhaps because it had the power of self-fulfillment.

I rejected the Huntington thesis partly because of my reading of history, which, I think, shows that collaboration is normal between civilizations and religious communities: even those with histories scarred by conflict, like Islam and Christendom, have spent longer in fruitful dialogue than at war. Partly, too, my own experience of belonging to more than one culture has convinced me that loyalties to civilizations are too weak and overlapping on their own to inspire violence. Talking it over with Sam, I found that he was by no means the rigid, reactionary authoritarian his foes depicted, though he found it hard to believe—hard, perhaps, to understand—the experience of a cultural mongrel like me, who could belong to more than one tradition without sacrifice of love or loyalty. We never got around to thrashing out our differences over his next controversial book, *Who Are We? The Challenges to America's National Identity*, which appeared three years before the author's death. Pressure of work kept me from reading it for a while. By the time I got around to it, it was too late.

Huntington's book had a minatory tone of *la patrie en danger* from immigrants. His quarrel was not with immigrants, whose value he acknowledged and appreciated. But he did reject pluralism. For him, the only good immigrant was an assimilated one. He interpreted the commonplace characterization of the United States as "a nation of immigrants" in a distinctive way, insisting that newcomers joined a country that already had a definitive culture made not by immigrants but by settlers in its formative period, which he dated to the seventeenth and eighteenth centuries. I would have liked to talk with him about that. Culture is not—it seems to me—like a house whose character is fixed when the building is completed. It is a much more flexible kind of edifice, which is never finished but changes continually, at different paces and rhythms at different times, like the home of Jerome Kern's "Folks Who Live on the Hill." There is no moment at which we can say that the process is arrested. The character of the house depends on the décor and on the changing composition of the residents, as well as the external building. Late additions to the structure, moreover, can develop it and improve it. People who came to the United States after 1776, or 1784, or 1865, or whatever date one cares to assign, contributed to the developing culture, just as those who preceded them did.

In three important ways, Huntington distinguished nineteenth- and early twentieth-century immigrants from their successors in the 1960s and after. First, he claimed that the earlier migrants had to make a total commitment to their new country because of the effort they endured, the ties they severed, and the difficulty of keeping in touch with their former homes. Recent immigrants, by contrast, could travel with relative ease, retain ties with home, and even uphold dual nationality. (These points, I think, are good ones, although there is room to debate whether they constitute a problem rather than an opportunity.) Second, according to Huntington, the new wave of immigrants was special because Hispanics predominated.

Never before had a single linguistic minority been so numerous in the United States. Here again, Huntington was right about the facts, at least for the period before the 1986 legislation opened up immigration from Asia and Africa (see above, p. 279), but the fears he felt as a result were misplaced.

His first fear was for the place of the English language in US culture. As the last chapter made clear, I am not sanguine about the survival of Spanish as the country's second language, but if the United States really were to become bilingual, I think it would be very much to the country's enrichment and advantage. Still, Huntington believed that Hispanics menaced more than the linguistic status quo. He thought they had a culture of *mañanismo*, putting work off till tomorrow, and were relatively unschooled in participatory civic, institutional, and political life. On these points, I think he was simply wrong— misled in part by a traditional caricature of Latin laziness and anarchism, and in part by his own experience of Latin America. He had advised the Brazilian government on democratization in the 1970s, urging a gradual approach—not without the selective use of repressive measures—and was inclined to attribute the ultimate success of democracy in that country to his own prudent counsel.

When Sam was dying, one sentence in his book resonated vexingly in my mind and I would have loved to pick over it with him: "Would the U.S.," he asked rhetorically, "be the country it has been and largely remains today if it had been settled in the 17th and 18th centuries not by British Protestants but by French, Spanish or Portuguese Catholics?"

The question, like all counterfactual questions, is tiresome because it is hard enough to know what did happen in the past without worrying about what might have happened if what did happen had not happened. In practice we use counterfactuals all the time in order to identify real or plausible relationships of cause and effect. I have done so repeatedly myself in the course of this book. But counterfactuals only make sense in contrast with genuine facts.

The factual basis of Huntington's question is false. A lot of what is now the United States was settled by French and Spanish Catholics in the seventeenth and eighteenth centuries. Not all the British settlers were Protestants. Quite a lot of the country was settled, involuntarily, by Africans, who numerically matched or exceeded Protestants of British origin in many regions. Until 1804, most of what is now US territory belonged to the empires of romance-speaking, Catholic powers. All states where more than 20 percent of the population is

Hispanic today were acquired from Spain between 1810, when the United States annexed the so-called Republic of West Florida (see above, p. 126), and 1848, when the Treaty of Hidalgo-Guadalupe ended the Mexican War. The Adams-Onís Treaty of 1819, in which Spain, beleaguered by widespread rebellions, ceded the rest of Florida in exchange for US renunciation of claims to Texas, was the main intermediate event in the sequence.

In any case, Huntington's question makes no allowance for the variety of the United States. This is a mistake more commonly made by outsiders, especially Europeans, who tend to assume that the US is culturally homogeneous. But those of us who live there and look around the place can see that there is at least as much difference between, say, Minnesota and Alabama as between New Mexico and, say, Sonora. In order to understand the United States, it may make better sense to compare parts of it with parts of other countries than to limit comparisons between unwieldably huge units whose borders are, in any case, often arbitrary—the results of historical compromises rather than of real cultural or environmental boundaries. It may be more instructive, for instance, to compare California with Baja California, or the Great Plains with the pampa, than to compare the whole of the US with the whole of Mexico or the whole of Argentina.

Belief in the exceptional character of the United States underpins Huntington's question, whereas it is at least worth asking whether it is helpful to emphasize US exceptionalism. All countries are exceptional in the sense of having features that distinguish them from all others. All are exempt from some generalizations. But is the United States more exceptional than anywhere else? Is it, as a whole, more different, say, from Argentina than, say, Chile is from Belize, or Canada from Paraguay?

THE ASSUMPTIONS OF HUNTINGTON'S question are culturalist: that is, the questioner assumes that cultural influences were uniquely responsible for shaping the history of the country. But culture and environment penetrate and affect each other and should never be considered in isolation. A glance at a map is sufficient to suggest that the implication of Huntington's question—that the United States is different from Latin America—can be understood at least as much as an effect of environment as of culture (though of course both have their place in any explanation that aims to be complete). The main reason why parts of the United States are extremely unlike most of Latin America is that the hemisphere is top-heavy, skewed towards the north, so that the United States and Canada have no fully tropical zones, and the rest of the Americas have no boreal ones. The United States has a vast amount of land that belongs, ecologically speaking, in the category of temperate forest, of which there is relatively little elsewhere in the Americas.

The biggest single difference, if one compares what we loosely call Latin America collectively with the United States and Canada, is that from the Rio Grande to the Paraguay, European colonists encountered large, densely settled incumbent populations with whom they could collaborate in building colonial societies, whereas in what became the United States and Canada, Native American peoples—or "First Nations" in Canadian parlance—were too thinly distributed to be useful as a pool of labor. Their economic traditions were, for colonists' purposes, unexploitable. Therefore the United States became a land of white people and black slaves, where the Native Americans were exterminated or expelled or confined to tiny patches. Meanwhile, all the countries of Latin America except Chile and Argentina (whose histories resemble that of the United States in many respects) retained huge indigenous populations and elements of precolonial economies and culture.

Where there are duplications of environment, however, between parts of the United States and parts of Latin America, one finds that the economies and cultures are similar too. Ranching is an outstanding example. Highland farming, too, is similar, with similar crops, in Idaho and in Peru. The same strains of wheat grow equally well in parts of Mexico as in parts of Washington State. Arid desert is much the same, in effect, wherever you find it. Québec is Catholic and romance-speaking, but politics and economics there resemble those of environmentally similar parts of the United States—in, say, parts of Minnesota or Michigan or upstate New York. Chile has been as receptive as Chicago to Chicago economics. So there seems to be nothing in culture—nothing, at least, in language or religion or historical experience—that narrows particular political or economic outcomes, whereas environmental conditions genuinely do limit what people can achieve.

Huntington's belief that culture is autonomous, indifferent to environmental constraints, and autocatalytic—as a scientist might say, generating its own dynamic of change—arose from his schooling in the tradition of one of the founding fathers of sociology: the great German thinker of the late nineteenth and early twentieth centuries, Max Weber. In particular, Huntington owed to Weber his belief in the "Protestant work ethic," which, he thought, was part of US culture's legacy from Puritan settlers and helped to account for the country's economic success. He acknowledged that Catholics could adopt the Protestant work ethic without abandoning their own religion, but in order to do so, Huntington contended, they had to make a cultural compromise with a distinctively Protestant habit of life and thought. For him (as with a supposedly non-US language, such as Spanish), a supposedly non-US religion such as Catholicism was permissible as long as those distinguished by it were willing to assimilate to mainstream values. By implication, his fear was that because most Hispanic immigrants were Catholics, they would all be Catholics together, just as they would all speak Spanish together, and assimilation would be deferred or impeded.

THE PROTESTANT WORK ETHIC demands a solemn and sustained digression because, in spite of the fact that there never was any such thing, people believe in it with desperate, defiant tenacity. I am constantly surprised at the persistence of the notion among sociologists. An influential Harvard history professor has recently endorsed it at length in a popular television series. Even some of my Catholic students at Notre Dame were taught to believe in it in high school. I must begin, in fairness to readers, with two admissions. First, I am a Catholic. It is important to point this out, because a lot of people love to hate Catholics and I regard it as an obligation of Christian charity to give people a chance to hate me, if that is what turns them on. Some people, moreover, think that Catholicism disqualifies its adherents from contributing to rational debate on the grounds that we are mired in dogmatism. If I have any such readers, I can only assure them that I am completely open-minded and beg them to treat me with the same open-mindedness in return. My second confession is that I am lazy. So I am both lazy and Catholic. But there is no necessary connection between the two, just as there is no necessary connection between Protestantism and hard work.

I wish the Protestant work ethic really existed, because I hate work and, on good biblical authority as well as by personal inclination, I think it a curse. If it were really true that Protestants' values typically elevate work into a kind of morality, I would take it as evidence of the moral superiority of Catholicism. The logical outcome of an ethos that overvalues work is the praise of work that hung over the gates of Nazi death camps: *Arbeit Macht Frei.* The historical consequences popularly supposed to flow from the Protestant work ethic—capitalism, imperialism, industrialism—are, when taken to excess, evils of which I would love to be able to exonerate Catholics. But they are not particularly Protestant vices: they are human vices, in which, unfortunately, Catholics have been as deeply implicated as everyone else.

Luther and Calvin urged the virtue of work. But so did almost every sixteenth-century moralist. "Teach me, good Lord," prayed Saint Ignatius of Loyola, "to toil and not to seek for rest. . . . to labor and not to ask for any reward." Saint Thomas of Villanueva advocated setting up poor people in business as the best form of alms. "Laborare est orare," as every Benedictine monk knows, is a Catholic slogan, a thousand years older than the Reformation. It is true that in the first few centuries of Protestantism, Protestant states sometimes persecuted the work-shy, coerced "sturdy beggars" into pointless labor, and enslaved them in workhouses. But there is nothing ethical about that. You might call it a work fetish, not a work ethic. Catholics, while engaging in plenty of other persecutions of their own, did not share in the persecution of beggars, not because they favored idleness, but because they had good reasons for respecting mendicancy. When I was little, my mother made me give money to beggars and thank them for taking it. They were doing me a favor, she explained, by giving me a chance to perform a work of mercy.

Protestants, who deny the salvific effect of good works, have no incentive to give to beggars and can find no place for them in society. But the money Protestants save on almsgiving does not typically get reinvested in work. It gets squandered on leisure and luxury just as much as in Catholic societies. Think of those Dutch interiors, full of gilded paintings and million-guilder tulips, hiding the "embarrassment of riches" behind the facades of the Heerengracht; or the conspicuous consumption of such staunchly Protestant builders of Elizabethan country houses as Lord Burleigh and Francis Drake; or Barthélémy d'Herwarth, supposedly the exemplar of the seventeenth-century Calvinist ascetic-turned-entrepreneur. He demolished a duke's palace to build a bigger one for himself. In any case, ordinary, everyday experience tells us that people are idle or industrious according to circumstances, genes, opportunities, personality, or psychological traits, but rarely if ever because of their religion. Jules Siegfried, the French industrial magnate sometimes hailed as an icon of the Protestant work ethic, had "to work is to act" engraved on his cufflinks. But he retired at the age of forty-four.[1]

So why does anyone believe in the Protestant work ethic, except at the level of rhetoric honored in the breach? How can anyone have thought the theory up in defiance of the obvious facts in the first place?

Whenever we evaluate a theory, we have to ask the question Cicero asked about all crimes. *Cui bono?* Whose agenda does the theory serve? The first time the Protestant work ethic appeared in print was in 1905, nearly four hundred years after the Reformation. Weber, the phrasemaker, was responding, in part, to his own childhood. My mother gave money to beggars. His did not. She was a hardened Calvinist harridan who tyrannized little Max into work rates that ultimately turned him into a top examinee and a precocious professor. Max, moreover, was searching for an answer of his own—an evangelical, bourgeois answer—to Marxism, which for Weber was the great bogey, the dominant intellectual force of his era. It was Max versus Marx. Marx said economics precede religion. Weber said religion precedes economics. Marx denounced religion as an opiate for workers. On the contrary, Max claimed, religion stimulated work.

Weber's thinking also reflected a wider intellectual context. He published his theory of the Protestant work ethic in the same year that Einstein published the theory of relativity. Science was the fashion. Weber wanted to craft a science of society in which predictable consequences flowed from identifiable causes. Now, really, human cultures do not work like that. They are a chaotic mess and change at random. But Weber, who was very active in evangelical politics, wanted to make values, especially religiously inspired values, the cause of everything else—the motor of civilization, in the way that evolution is the motor of organic life. A theory so elastic that it can explain everything is not exact enough to explain anything. It would be wonderful if societies really did conform to religious values. The world would be so much better if Christians practiced universal love and Buddhists actively strove for enlightenment. But practically nobody does. Except as a justification for violence and hatred, religion is unhappily overrated as a source of influence in society. To understand Weber, one also has to realize that he was obsessed, in an entirely healthy and positive way, with Judaism. He could not be sure how—by migrations, perhaps, from medieval centers of protocapitalism, and by individual conversions—but he thought Protestants had inherited what he called "inner-worldly asceticism" or *innerweltliche Askese* from Jewish antecedents. Outward signs of this inner asceticism, he thought, included contempt for ostentation and respect for reinvestment. This was not a realistic way of looking at Judaism. Jews' modesty was the result not of any religious belief but of the need to camouflage themselves against predation and persecution.

Nor was Weber's a convincing picture of capitalism. Overwhelmingly, the big capitalists in early modern Europe, whom Weber misidentified as predominantly Calvinist, turn out on close inspection to have been a mixed and undogmatic bunch who predictably guarded their wealth the way the Vicar of Bray guarded his living—by switching religion according to whoever was in power. In any case, if we look beyond the history of the West, we find that the really big wielders of capital in the early modern period were not Protestants but Chinese or Muslims or Jains, or even Hindus in a period before commerce was thought to pollute caste. And Protestants who are serious about their beliefs have often tended to be anticapitalist, emphasizing the apostolic model of common life, material equality, and shared goods. "Buying and selling," said the Leveller leader Gerrard Winstanley, "is an art whereby people cheat other."[2] Weber looked at Protestant capitalists and inferred the existence of a work ethic. He might just as well have looked at Protestant anticapitalists and inferred a social ethic.

Protestantism, however, seemed to him to happen at just the right time to explain early modern commercial empire building. In the seventeenth century the Protestant Dutch expanded at Catholic Portuguese expense. The new powers included Protestant England and Sweden, while decline supposedly afflicted Catholic Venice, Poland, and Spain. But the correspondences were inexact, the data false. Muscovy rose without the benefit of Protestantism. Turkey declined without the curse of Catholicism. France rose in spite of it. The difficulties of Portugal and Venice had nothing to do with religion. If Weber was wrong about the past, what about the world of his own day? Protestant Prussia beat Catholic Austria and France. The Protestant United States had defeated Catholic Mexico and Spain. Protestant British held Catholic Ireland and repeatedly got the advantage of Catholic France and Orthodox Russia. These events nourished fantasies about Anglo-Saxon or Nordic racial superiority over degenerate Latins, Celts, and Slavs. They were also convenient fodder for upholders of the doctrine that Protestantism was progressive, while Catholicism and Orthodoxy mired their adherents in stagnation. Anti-Catholic crusades, like the German *Kulturkampf* or the Know-Nothing movement in the United States, were, in part, efforts to preserve national purity from the supposedly debilitating effects of Catholicism.

Again, however, facts that Weber overlooked undermined the theory. If Protestant Britain was "the first industrial nation," Catholic Belgium was the second. In the nineteenth century, the Protestant-ruled Kingdom of the Netherlands was industrial Belgium's rural back garden, supplying primary materials and food for its more advanced neighbor. Belgium's productivity in iron and steel outdid both Britain and Germany by 1870. Industry concentrated in other Catholic zones—the Spanish Basque country and Catalonia, the Italian Piedmont. And there was nothing necessarily Protestant about Britain's "gospel of work": it was essentially a secular ethos calculated to justify inhuman hours in factories. "A servant with this clause makes drudgery divine" was a useful line *The English Hymnal* appropriated from a seventeenth-century poet—conveniently so, when you want to force women into dark satanic mills and children down mines. Meanwhile, in a Catholic simulacrum of the work ethic, French factory masters consecrated their work to the glory of God; anyone lucky enough to have a Jesuit education will know how Catholic a habit that is.

LIKE THE WORK ETHIC, most of the other supposed advantages a Protestant legacy conferred on Anglo-America turn out on close examination to be chimerical. Individualism is a particularly frustrating example. It would be hard to imagine a world organized economically for "enlightened self-interest" or politically along lines of "one person, one vote" without individualism. American novels and movies of self-discovery, the cult of psychiatry in the modern US, the feel-good values, existential angst, and the self-obsessions of the "me generation" would all be unthinkable. As we have seen, however, the role of individualism in the making of the United States has been grossly exaggerated: the country is distinguished by strong communitarian values of neighborliness and civic-mindedness. Liberation from self-abnegation had to begin—or at least have one of its starting points—in religious minds, because godly institutions, in the Middle Ages, were the major obstacles to self-realization. The watchfulness of fellow congregants disciplined desire. The collective pursuit of sal-

vation diminished individuals' power. The authority of godly establishments overrode individual judgment. The fact that in Western
literature and art, evidence of introspection and egotism multiplied in
the sixteenth and seventeenth centuries surely has at least as much to
do with humanism and mysticism as with Protestantism. Mysticism
has been overlooked, but for worshippers with a hotline to God, institutional religion is unnecessary. Sufis, Catholic and Orthodox mystics,
and Protestant reformers were all, therefore, engaged, in one sense, in
the same project: firing the synapses that linked them to divine energy;
freeing themselves to make up their own minds; putting clerisy in its
place. In any case, it is not necessary to be Protestant to have a strong
sense of the self. The Catholic Descartes used it as the foundation of
his conviction of the reality of everything else. Nor do Protestants
typically put a higher value on themselves than other people do.

Claims that Protestantism is particularly conducive to science, or
industrialization, or democracy, are all based on the same sort of special pleading as the supposed link between Protestantism and work or
Protestantism and capitalism or Protestantism and individualism: all
such claims arise from the assumption that the Reformation was a
liberating force, liberating conscience from authority, reason from
repression, research from surveillance, critical opinion from immersion in the vast solvent of Christian unity, and self-awareness from the
smother-love of the Church. But the Reformation was merely one
strand in a movement across Christendom that affected Catholic and,
to a lesser extent, Orthodox traditions in similar ways at about the
same time.[3] In some ways, Protestantism introduced or perpetuated
inhibitions to progress. In most Protestant communions, the authority
of the Church was attenuated, perhaps, and diffused among rival
denominations, but not abolished. Protestants' elevation of the Bible
to be a unique and sufficient disclosure of divine revelation actually
demoted a source of guidance in which, for Catholics, human reason
always had a big part. Nor was the throne room of conscience an
exclusively Protestant sanctum. Conscience can play as big a part in a
Catholic's decision to defer to Rome as in a Protestant's to defy it. As
for science and intellectual innovation, in the aftermath of the Refor-

mation, the monetary theory of value, the concept of international law, the heliocentric theory of the universe, the study of comparative ethnology, and the modern theory of sovereignty as absolute legislative power were all formulated in Catholic milieus. The inquisition did not deter Fallopio from discoveries in anatomy. Copernicus was on the syllabus in Salamanca before the end of the sixteenth century. Jesuits taught Galileo's discoveries in China. The data bank for the delineation and measurement of the earth was in the Paris of that scourge of Protestants, Louis XIV. Where political freedoms are concerned, most scrutineers will be fair enough to judge the Catholic record not by the tabloid history of cloister and hearth or pit and pendulum, but by the genuine history of the theories of tyrannicide and of the right of resistance. For obvious reasons, they were particularly attractive to persecuted communities, irrespective of their particular faiths, and were at least as widely canvassed among Catholics as Protestants.

So the answer to Huntington's question is not that the United States would be unchanged without the Anglo-American legacy, but that the WASP heritage is not the whole of the story, and that it accounts for surprisingly little difference between the US and other American countries. The United States is already a Latin American country in patches—not only because of the influx of Latin American immigrants in recent times, but also because some places have never lost continuity with the Spanish past, or have consciously reestablished it. We have seen, for instance, how a sense of Spanish heritage endured in Santa Barbara through the period of Yankee dominance, and how it revived in other places. Throughout this book, instances have arisen that make the United States seem, in some places, and in some respects, like a typical Latin American country. We have seen the resemblances, arising from conscious imitation, between Spanish and English conquistadores. We have also seen how similar creole cultures grew up in both British and Spanish America, contributing to the emergence of independence movements with similar sources of inspiration in the Enlightenment. Some areas have even resembled

Latin America historically, even though they saw few Hispanics. The Deep South, as we have seen, was a land of plantations that were the domains of latifundistas, with a racially defined underclass and a dependent economy, producing primary products for other people's industries. Bonanza towns resembled one another from Potosí to Dawson City. Much of the Southwest was for a while, even after the expropriation of Spanish and Mexican rancheros, a cattle-rich land, with a way of life that originated in medieval Andalusia and Extremadura and continued in Mexico and the South American cone.

Nor has the United States been entirely exempt from two vices conspicuous in the minds of Samuel Huntington and other believers in the severance of the United States from Latin America: *caudillismo*— the replacement of political institutions by individual leaders, installed or backed by force—and a politicized military. The fact that English has to appropriate a Spanish word to express *caudillismo* is suggestive. According to Salvador de Madariaga's theory, every country's national character consists in the terms that cannot be translated into other languages.[4] Conversely, you can read what one nation thinks of another by looking at the terms it borrows. Three English words—coup, putsch, and pronunciamiento—express the same event: a military takeover of political institutions; all three are naturalized from foreign languages, because English-speakers think political violence is a peculiarity of foreign cultures. In reality, of course, *caudillos* emerge, military interventions happen, and coups take place in all kinds of settings. We have already met some conspicuous North American *caudillos*: Aaron Burr, Joseph Smith, Brigham Young, and even Sam Houston in his distinctive way, all tried to take power by armed force. A more recent case was that of Huey Long, the great demagogue of Louisiana, who abjured the word "please" and boasted of "dynamiting" opposition out of his path. In 1932, when challenged for occupying the governorship and a Senate seat simultaneously and unconstitutionally, he called out the National Guard to remove his successor and overawe the state legislature. Perhaps, had I cited this instance to Samuel Huntington, he would have objected that Louisiana is a state with a big French heritage and that Long was in cahoots with elements in the Catholic Church. But those very facts, surely, make clear the point that the United States cannot be understood in terms of a single, WASP heritage. I suppose Huntington would also have pointed out, fairly, that *caudillos* are relatively rare in US history and that most of them have been prepared, like Houston, to yield power to constitutionally based institutions, following the model of Cincinnatus resigning the dictatorship of Rome to return to his plow. This makes the difference between the United States and most other countries in the Americas a difference of degree: from Bolívar to Pinochet, Latin American dictators have sometimes shown the same willingness to retire.

It is true that the US Army, Navy, and Air Force have almost unimpeachable records of abstention from politics, and that—to an unusual, even perhaps unique degree—US governments have rarely used the regular army against their own people since the Civil War. But the National Guard has a long history of abuse in strike-busting operations and still frequently takes part in the repression of civil disobedience. There have been instances of the use of regular troops, too. The army had to intervene to stop the Ludlow Massacre of 1914, when state militia opened fire on striking miners in Colorado. In 1944, 5,000 troops took over Philadelphia's transport system as part of the government's efforts to force white workers to accept black colleagues. The most notable case was in 1957, when President Eisenhower sent an airborne division into Arkansas to enforce the desegregation of Little Rock High School. The president also federalized the Arkansas National Guard, whom the governor had ordered to bar the way of the nine black children who turned up for class. In a sense, the president's was a repressive—albeit a laudable, just, and necessary—act, since the local electorate repeatedly voted for segregation, installing segregationists in the legislature, the governor's mansion, and the school boards, and allowed or encouraged a vicious campaign of bullying against black children in formerly white schools. In any part of America south of the Rio Grande, the use of the army would have been denounced as evidence of the vices of a militarized society, a democratic deficiency, and the fatal inheritance of the Spanish past.

STILL—AND NOT ONLY IN the parts of North America where the environment has no parallel in Hispanic America—it must be acknowledged that the divergences between the United States and the countries farther south have been substantial since the coming of independence. The United States survived threatened dismemberment in the nineteenth century, whereas many other American states, especially Hispanic ones, did not. The United States has had a record of more or less continuous democratic development, constitutional propriety, and the rule of law such as few formerly Spanish republics can rival. Precocious industrialization, rapid economic development, a major role in global trade, and ascent to the status of a global superpower were grounds for treating the United States as *hors de pair* in its hemisphere, while Hispanic America seemed mired in economic stagnation and incapacitated by political chaos. The turnaround seems surprising and relatively sudden when one takes into account the wealth and stability of Hispanic America in the eighteenth century and the glowing accounts of its potential presented by scientific reporters such as Alessandro Malaspina, who masterminded a major official survey of the resources and governance of the Spanish monarchy in 1788–94, and Alexander von Humboldt, who conducted an independent scientific mission, under the protection of the Spanish monarchy, in 1801–3. Both disclosed a populous, rich, expanding empire—albeit in need of political reform and improved defense—with prodigious cities and institutions of arts and learning such as Anglo-America was only beginning to match.

Witnesses of the divergence that followed—which left the United States as a hemispheric hegemon and reduced Hispanic America to a global backwater—commonly blamed it on a fatal inheritance from Spain. This was understandable, since Spain too seemed convulsed by similar problems in the same period: military ineffectiveness; unstable politics, punctuated by civil wars; and a very selective record of industrialization. Two of the Hispanic republics' common difficulties were indeed the result of Spanish colonial policies. First, maritime protectionism helped to deny to the Spanish colonies the huge, locally run merchant marine that enriched New England in the eighteenth century and gave the independent United States a springboard for further wealth creation. Second, the militarization of Hispanic-American societies, which cursed them with politically committed military establishments, began with Spanish policies: commending colonies with their own defense and mobilizing large militias.[5] Of course, however, Spain was not really to blame for all Latin America's ills: former and continuing colonies of Portugal, Britain, France, and the Netherlands in the region shared in the basic problems of economic underdevelopment and dependency in the nineteenth and twentieth centuries.

As well as blaming Spain, scholars in the nineteenth century, and for much of the twentieth, invoked cosmic theories about race and climate to explain the superiority of the United States over Latin America. A useful summary appeared in 1912 in the work of Francisco García Calderón, a Peruvian diplomat who was struggling to explain to himself as well as to his readers the frustrating powerlessness of Latin America in the face of what he called Yankee imperialism. Tropical climates, according to a widespread but obviously false belief, encouraged laziness and drunkenness. Whereas racial segregation in the United States wisely, according to assumptions of the time, preserved racial purity, miscegenation in Latin America corrupted races and concentrated vices in their blood: *mañanismo*, fanaticism, arrogance, lawlessness, and *barroquismo*—Calderón's code word for a fatalistic attitude to life, characterized by indifference to reality and a taste for tragedy, illusion, and suffering supposedly typical of seventeenth-century Hispanic art. Catholicism, of course, made the effects worse by discouraging work and encouraging servility.[6]

I do not think any reflective or well-informed person would endorse this sort of analysis today. The *longue durée* is dying. Contingency has taken over. We know that historical events lurch unpredictably and we no longer scour the remote past for their origins or expect them to have universal causes. When I was young, historians believed in gradualism. Great events were like great trees: they grew from long roots. Few people seem to think this anymore. When we consider the fall of the Roman Empire, we no longer do as Gibbon did and go back to the time of the Antonines (when the empire was doing well), but refer to the crisis of barbarian intrusions in the late fourth and early fifth centuries. No serious historian of the English Civil War still sees it in the context of the Whig interpretation of English history, as a deferred outcome of an aeons-old quest to recover the freedom of the Germanic woods; today's scholars are more likely to claim that the revolutionary events of 1642 can best be understood as the outcome of stresses caused by the war with Scotland of 1638. When we study the French Revolution, we no longer do as Tocqueville did and start with Louis XIV, under whom the French monarchy was extremely robust, but concentrate on the financial crisis induced by the costs to France of participation in the American War of Independence. To explore why the First World War broke out, we no longer do as Albertini did, and scour the European diplomatic system of the nineteenth century (which was fairly good at keeping the peace), but chronicle the break-down of that system in the few years prior to the war—or even blame the defects of the railway timetables of August 1914. I do not know whether our current emphasis on the random twists and turns of history gets us closer to the truth, but it is clearly part of a habit of our times, paralleled in the sciences, where punctuations and sudden mutations disturb evolution and the flap of a butterfly's wings can summon up a storm.[7]

In any case, an understanding of the causes of the divergence between US and Latin American history is adequately provided by a study of the immediately relevant period—the period when the divergence really happened—in the early nineteenth century. In 1818, in a debate in the US Congress about whether to recognize Argentina as a separate state, Henry Clay summarized the crucial difference that made Spanish America's independence struggles dev-astating in a way that the United States had not experienced during its own revolutionary war. He identified Spain's rebels as "patriots struggling for the same objectives as ourselves: their freedom and independence" but observed how their uprisings had been "stained with excesses of ferocity unparalleled in our experience" and "execrable outrages, such as we did not have to endure, committed by the troops of the mother country. . . . If our slaves had risen," he added, "like those in Venezuela, who can doubt but that Gen Washington would have had recourse to a policy of retribution?"[8] Participants affirmed the peculiar destructiveness of Spanish America's severance from the monarchy. Simón Bolívar lamented how "our three centuries of culture, enlightenment, and industry have disappeared" and noted that although the theater in which he was most engaged, in New Granada, saw peculiarly intense and savage warfare, other areas had witnessed "horrible butchery. Opulent Mexico, Buenos Aires, and Peru and unhappy Quito are almost like vast cemeteries."[9] We have seen how even Texas, remote from the main scenes of fighting, suffered terrible devastation.

In consequence, the Hispanic-American republics began their independence crippled, with populations diminished, societies divided, economies subverted, and infrastructures destroyed. Nothing comparable happened in the British colonies, although of course there were atrocities, especially against Native Americans, who were considered to be outside the laws of civilized combat, and in the backcountry of the Carolinas, where the revolution took the form of a bitter civil war; and, of course, there were destructive episodes. Newport, Rhode Island, for instance, never recovered from the burning; but the war in general was conducted with surprising restraint on both sides. The British commander in chief forbade burning and misappropriation of property; General Clinton discharged the loyalist militia because he feared "their vengeful spirit will inspire excesses." The orders of both sides were full of the rhetoric of humanity and virtue, lifted from the philosophical textbooks of the European Enlightenment.[10]

The contrast with the Latin American wars had nothing to do with racial or cultural differences between Latins and Anglo-Saxons. Nor was it attributable, as Bolívar's sidekick Daniel O'Leary thought, to a spiritual transformation of "the essential being of a South American" (*el ser suramericano*) under the malign influence of Spanish rule.[11] To a small extent it was a consequence of the participation of French and

Spanish armies in the Revolutionary War, which helped to protect the population from the worst consequences of direct encounters with the enemies, and a straightforward result of the facts that in British America the wars were swifter and the concentrations of population less dense. Mainly, however, the wars of the northern and southern moieties of the hemisphere were different because of the time lag that occurred between them. The British colonies won their independence in a war of the age of Enlightenment, with small, professional armies that respected the laws of war as formulated by the most influential theorist of warfare in eighteenth-century Europe, Emmer de Vattel. "A man of exalted soul," de Vattel wrote, "no longer feels any emotions but those of compassion towards a conquered enemy who has submitted to his arms. . . . Let us never forget that our enemies are men. Though reduced to the disagreeable necessity of prosecuting our right by force of arms, let us not divest ourselves of that charity which connects us with all mankind."[12] Typically, though not of course uniformly, the officers who led in the campaigns of the Revolutionary War respected these principles.

Commanders in the early nineteenth century could not be relied on for the same commitment to salutary doctrines. In the meantime, the French Revolution had dissolved the Enlightenment in blood and sanctified crimes committed in liberty's name. The levée en masse and Napoleonic Wars had replaced professional armies with "the people in arms." Romanticism now hallowed passions. The change of mood was manifest in Bolívar's accounts of what he called his "delirium"—the extraordinary mystical visions in which he claimed to feel "ignited by a strange and superior flame."[13] One cannot imagine George Washington uttering such a sentiment any more than one can imagine him authorizing massacres of the kind Bolívar justified on the grounds that "Americans must patiently allow themselves to suffer extermination, or destroy an iniquitous race, which will work to annihilate us for as long as it draws breath."[14] The proof that warfare had grown generally more destructive and that savagery in conflict was not solely a Hispanic vice is in the report of a committee of Congress on the War of 1812, accusing the British, in terms unprecedented in the Revolutionary War, of massacres, wanton destruction and rapine, and lamenting "breasts violated by unrestrained lust."[15] Had the Revolutionary War been postponed until then, its character might more closely have resembled its Latin American counterparts.

If we accept that the wars of independence set the Hispanic republics back, the problem remains of why it took them so long to recover and why they never emerged as competitors with the United States for power and wealth in the hemisphere. One reason is implicit in the experience of the independence wars: their legacy included highly politicized armies such as the United States never had to cope with until the Civil War. We have already mentioned the advantage political unity gave the United States. The main reason, however, why the divergence became permanent is probably a simple matter of the balance of exploitable resources. In preindustrial and industrializing economies, no resource is more important than manpower; in a world without free trade, no source of demand is more important than domestic demand. What we now call Latin America contained about 5 million people in 1650, when what is now the United States had only about 50,000. Not surprisingly, therefore, the balance of wealth and power in colonial times favored Spanish America. By the mid-nineteenth century, the United States had nearly caught up, with about 23 million inhabitants, compared with some 50 million in the rest of the Americas, giving her an enormous advantage over the individual republics. By the time Latin American inferiority filled García Calderón with despair, the US had about 100 million people and Latin America only about 65 million.

Apart from people, the other fundamental resource for nineteenth-century states was land for producing food. We have seen how the transformation of the Great Plains from wasteland to wheatlands enriched the United States and equipped the country for greatness. The Spanish republics had less grassland to work this magic with, and the Argentine pampa, because of its remoteness from major centers of consumption and efficient long-range transport systems, remained consecrated mainly to ranching while the North American prairies went under the plow. Historians have alleged many reasons for the economic and military success of the United States. The size of the internal market and the availability of vast, uniquely exploitable lands exceed all others in importance.

IF I AM RIGHT so far, it is obvious that people in the United States need to rethink their history in order to face their future. The United States still has a big and growing internal market, thanks to immigrants, without whom, to judge from the long-standing pattern of birthrates, the population would almost certainly shrink. It is inconceivable, however, that the US alone, even with immigrant labor to boost productivity and swell domestic demand, can continue to compete with other, bigger or potentially bigger competitors in China, India, and the European Union without joining in a larger free trade area. Other American states are the only obvious partners. The United States has no underexploited resources left to rely on, apart, perhaps, from some ecologically precarious reserves of fossil fuels. The Great Plains are likely to become less productive as the aquifers that sustain dry farming vanish. For the twenty-first century, the equivalent resources—the vast areas of underexploited but exploitable terrain for the Americas—will be in Amazonia and the Chilean and Argentine Antarctic (and to some extent in boreal Canada, a country already reconciled to its own biculturalism, with its native patch of "Latin," Catholic, romance-speaking America in Québec). Coming generations of US citizens are going to need the rest of the Americas.

In these circumstances it will be helpful for people in the United States to acknowledge the hitherto unappreciated fact that theirs is already, in some respects, a Latin American country, with more features in common with most of the rest of the Americas than mainstream opinion has so far conceded. It should also be useful to adopt the perspective advocated in this book and see the United States as a country with a Hispanic past as well as a Hispanic future. Migrants from Hispanic America need not be feared as intruders: they can be welcomed as homecomers. Their language need not be treated as a threat, but relished as an enhancement and embraced as an opportunity. The

United States does not need to be an Anglo redoubt in order to remain itself. On the contrary, it is, by the inescapable virtue of history, a model of pluralism, with a strong Hispanic dimension. To be true to the country's past, American patriots can commit without fear to a similarly plural future. In the United States we must make pluralism work because, paradoxically perhaps, it is the one creed that can unite us.

This will not mean that particular constituencies among citizens and residents will cease to cherish the collective memories that matter to them—including those with emotional investments in a sense of the uniqueness of the United States and in the British heritage. The United States will always remain at least as different from all other countries as each is from the rest. The distinctive legacy of British settlers will always account for part of that difference. The common-law tradition will always distinguish the country, along with Canada, Guyana, and Belize, from other countries on the American continent, just as within the United States elements of civil law tradition mark out Louisiana and have lingering resonances from the Spanish past in the laws and, to some extent, in court proceedings in Arizona, California, Nevada, New Mexico, and Texas. Latino music will never drown out other sounds. Spanish, as we have seen, will not displace English, though it might achieve something like parity. The influence of Protestantism will always be detectable in the United States—not in the mythical effects foolishly ascribed to the work ethic or suchlike, but in Catholic churches. US Catholic worship has absorbed many Protestant influences, such as the use of the vernacular, the prominence of hymns, the adulation of the Bible, and peculiar liturgical practices in some places, such as holding hands during the Pater Noster—which is commonly said to have originated in meetings of Alcoholics Anonymous but is almost certainly an intrusion from charismatic Protestant congregations. The drift of Hispanics into Protestantism seems unarrestable, both in and out of the United States; so Protestants in the US need not fear for their traditions but might rather expect reinforcement from immigrants.

In any case, the real dilemma for the future of the religious culture of the United States is not between rival kinds of religion, but between religion and secularism. In a secularizing world, religious people of all faiths are natural allies in trying to preserve the traditional balance, which is one of the defining characteristics of the United States, between a secular polity and a religious people. Religion has flour-ished in the United States precisely because there is no "establishment of religion"; in consequence, all faiths have had equal freedom. There is room for honest debate about where exactly the perfect balance lies: whether, for instance, prayers in public places or references to God in traditional patriotic texts can fit into the space the Constitution fences off from the threat of established religion. But the fact that most His-panics profess religious beliefs does not increase the threat. Rationally religious people understand the value of preserving a secular state: they know that they will always have a place in pluralism and that the principle of a secular state guarantees religious pluralism.

So what's to fear? It is hard to resist the temptation of thinking that what the immigrants' enemies really resent is poverty. Expensive labor fears cheap labor. Struggling markets long for big spenders. Plutocrats fear the poor. Some political campaigners against immi-gration have explicitly repudiated the promise of Liberty to the "huddled masses yearning to breathe free," and do not want the United States to become home to any more homeless, tempest-tossed, wretched refuse.[16]

Political opportunists stoke fears when they can. It seems unlikely, however, that they will be able to focus resentment on Hispanics for much longer. The flurry of anti-immigrant legislation of 2010–11 seems to be over already. The present or recent alarm will vanish as the numbers of immigrants, and especially of undocumented immigrants, falls, as it is bound to do with the limited economic opportunities available in an ailing US economy. Between 2005 and 2010 about 1.4 million Mexicans moved to the United States—almost exactly the same number as left. By April 2012 the Pew Hispanic Research Cen-ter reported that net immigration from Mexico had fallen to zero "and perhaps less."[17] The fall, of course, is from a peak. While the decline of Hispanic immigration is bound to allay fears, Hispanics' existing strength in numbers will protect them from further persecution. Hispanic voters punished the Republican Party for alignment with anti-immigration policies in the 2012 presidential election and triggered a scurry for new Hispanic-friendly policies among the party leadership (see above, p. xviii).

At every stage in this book we have seen how myths inspired people to explore and settle what has become the United States. Spanish pioneers sought the cities of Cíbola and, reputedly, the Fountain of Youth. Some of them got their inspiration from tales of Queen Calafia and similar fantasies of chivalric and romantic literature. English intruders and Puritan conquistadores came in search of King Arthur, their Spanish counterparts in pursuit of King Hesperus. Avengers of Moroni were among the first domesticators of the interior wastelands. Zorro animated or perhaps, rather, embodied defenders of the Hispanic tradition. Countercolonists saw themselves as heading for Aztlán. Immigrants today are still pursuing the most pervasive myth of all—the American Dream of prosperity and independence in a land of opportunity unrestricted by barriers of class and creed (albeit not yet entirely by those of race). Will that dream prove as illusory as all the other potent myths that have helped to make the United States?

ACKNOWLEDGMENTS

I AM GRATEFUL TO MY COLLEAGUES IN THE UNIVERSITY OF Notre Dame for the kindness and indulgence they always show to me and to one another. The University's Institute of Latino Studies, which is full of outstanding scholars who know far more than I about almost every one of the many topics I touch on, has been an immeasurable help to me, providing opportunities for self-education at many gatherings and uniting a formidable collection of books and art for study. The munificence of the Fundación del Pino made it possible for me to work on the subject of this book, and I am especially grateful for many generous attentions from the director, Amadeo Petitbò Juan, and Almudena Díez Bartolomé, who is in charge of research projects. The family of the late Rafael del Pino, the great engineer and entrepreneur who set up the foundation, have been exemplary guardians of the founder's memory and intentions. The support of the president, María del Pino y Calvo-Sotelo, for all the foundation's work, including my small part in it, has been unflinching. I thank Professor Ilan Stavans for sending me a proof copy of selections from *The Norton Anthology of Latino Literature* (New York, 2011), which was of enormous help and value. Dakota Ferrantino kindly helped me check references: any still in error are among those he left to me. Steve Forman read the manuscript and made many wonderfully acuminous suggestions. Defects that remain are the result of my failure to apply his good advice. I am grateful for opportunities to try out some ideas and material at a colloquium at the Centre of Latin American Studies, University of Cambridge, and a conference in Tampa, organized by the University of South Florida, the Tampa Historical Society, and the Centro Cubano of Tampa.

Note to the paperback edition: I am grateful to Lawrence Downes and other readers who pointed out errors of transcription in the original edition.

Felipe Fernández-Armesto
Notre Dame, Indiana
March 2013

NOTES

Epigraph: E. Olivares Briones, *Pablo Neruda, Los Caminos de América: tras las huellas del poeta itinerante III*, 1940–50 (Santiago de Chile: LOM, 2004), 378.

NOTE ON USAGE

1 *When I Was Puerto Rican* (1993), quoted in I. Stavans, ed., *Becoming Americans: Four Centuries of Immigrant Writing* (New York: Library of America, 2009), 1701.

INTRODUCTION

Epigraph: R. Knox, *The Three Taps: A Detective Story Without a Moral* (London: Methuen Publishing, 1927).

1 A. Kopicki and W. Irving, "Assessing How Pivotal the Hispanic Vote Was to Obama's Victory," The Caucus: The Politics and Government Blog of *The Times*, November 20, 2012; http://thecaucus.blogs.nytimes.com/2012/11/20/assessing-how-pivotal-the-hispanic-vote-was-to-obamas-victory/.

2 http://www.newsday.com/news/nation/republicans-debate-how-to-woo-hispanic-vote-1.4199694.

3 H. H. Bancroft, *Essays and Miscellany* (San Francisco: The History Company, 1890), 234.

4 H. E. Bolton, *The Spanish Borderlands: A Chronicle of Old Florida and the Southwest* (New Haven: Yale University Press, 1921), 1.

5 H. E. Bolton and T. M. Maitland, *The Colonization of North America, 1492–1783* (New York: Macmillan Co., 1920).

6 R. M. Magnaghi, *Herbert E. Bolton and the Historiography of the Americas* (Westport, CT: Greenwood Press, 1998); L. Hanke, *Do the Americas Have a*

Common History: A Critique of the Bolton Theory (New York: Knopf, 1964); J. H. Elliott, *Do the Americas Have a Common History?*, presented on the occasion of the celebration of the 150th anniversary of the founding of the John Carter Brown Library, November 13, 1996 (Providence, RI, 1996); G. Pérez Firmat, *Do the Americas Have a Common Literature?* (Durham, NC: Duke University Press, 1990); F. Fernández-Armesto, *The Americas: A Hemispheric History* (New York: Random House, 2003).

7   P. Richardson, *American Prophet: The Life and Work of Carey McWilliams* (Ann Arbor: Michigan University Press, 2005).

8   C. McWilliams, *North from Mexico: The Spanish-speaking People of the United States* (New York: Greenwood, 1968), 35–47.

9   Earl Pomeroy, "Toward a Reorientation of Western History: Continuity and Environment," *Mississippi Valley Historical Review* 41 (1955): 579–97; M. P. Malone, "Earl Pomeroy and the Reorientation of Western History," in R. W. Etulain, ed., *Writing Western History: Essays on Major Western Historians* (Reno: University of Nevada Press, 2002), 311–33; P. N. Limerick, *The Legacy of Conquest: The Unbroken Past of the American West* (New York: Norton, 2006), 256.

10 O. Handlin, *The Uprooted: The Epic Story of the Great Migrations That Made the American People* (Boston: Little, Brown, 1951); J. Higham, *Strangers in the Land* (New Brunswick, NJ: Rutgers University Press, 1955).

CHAPTER ONE: THE FOUNTAIN OF YOUTH

Epigraph: G. Santayana, *Winds of Doctrine: Studies in Contemporary Opinion* (London: J. M. Dent & Sons Limited, 1915), 187.

1   V. Murga Sanz, *Juan Ponce de León* (Río Piedras: Universidad de Puerto Rico, 1971), 39.

2   S. Sondheim, "America," *West Side Story* (New York: Leonard Bernstein Music Publishing Company LLC, 1956, 1957, 1958, 1959).

3   G. Fernández de Oviedo, *Historia general y natural de las Indias*, bk. XVI, chap. 1.

4   Murga Sanz, op. cit., 35.

5   F. Fernández-Armesto, *Columbus* (London: Duckworth, 1996).

6   E. Fernández Méndez, *Las encomiendas y esclavitud de los indios en Puerto Rico, 1508–50* (San Juan, Universidad de Puerto Rico, 1976).

7   Murga Sanz, op. cit., 38

8   J. Krippner-Martínez, *Rereading the Conquest: Power, Politics, and the History of Early Colonial Michoacán* (University Park: Pennsylvania State University Press, 2001), 145.

9   M. Restall and F. Fernández-Armesto, *The Conquistadores: A Very Short Introduction* (Oxford: Oxford University Press, 2012).

10 Murga Sanz, op. cit., 66; Fernández de Oviedo, op. cit., XVI, 8.

11 Fernández de Oviedo, op. cit., XVI, 3.

12 Ibid., XVI, 4

13 Ibid., 7.

14   M. W. Helms, *Ulysses' Sail* (Princeton, NJ: Princeton University Press, 1988); Helms, *Craft and the Kingly Ideal* (Austin: University of Texas Press, 1993).

15   F. Fernández-Armesto, "The Stranger-Effect in Early Modern Asia," *Itinerario* 24 (2000): 80–103.

16   Fernández de Oviedo, op. cit., V, 3.

17   I. Caldwell and D. Henley, "The Stranger Who Would Be King," *Indonesia and the Malay World* 36 (2008), 163–75.

18   Fernández de Oviedo, op. cit., XVI, 2.

19   Murga Sanz, op. cit., 77.

20   Ibid., 86.

21   Ibid., 90.

22   Ibid., 160.

23   Ibid., 118.

24   Fernández de Oviedo, op. cit., XVI, 5.

25   Ibid., 11.

26   Murga Sanz, op. cit., 239.

27   D. P. Henige, *Numbers from Nowhere* (Norman: University of Oklahoma Press, 1998).

28   F. Picó, *History of Puerto Rico* (Princeton, NJ: Weiner, 2006), 102.

29   Picó, op. cit., 101.

30   D. J. Weber, *The Spanish Frontier in North America* (New Haven: Yale University Press, 1992), 52.

31   Ibid., 67.

32   Ibid., 70.

33   A. Taylor, *American Colonies: The Settling of North America* (Harmondsworth, UK: Penguin, 2002), 76.

34   Weber, op. cit., 77.

35   E. Ruidiaz y Caravia, *La Florida: su conquista y colonización por Pedro Menéndez de Avilés* (Madrid: Hijos de J. A. García, 1893), 104; W. Lowery, *The Spanish Settlements within the Present Limits of the United States: Florida, 1562–1574* (New York: G. P. Putnam's Sons, 1905), 213.

36   Lowery, op. cit., 343.

37   C. M. Scarry and E. J. Reitz, "Herbs, Fish, Scum and Vermin: Subsistence Strategies in Sixteenth-century Spanish Florida," in D. H. Thomas, ed., *Columbian Consequences*, vol. 2 (Washington, DC: Smithsonian, 1990), 343–54.

38   Lowery, op. cit., 216.

39   J. M. Francis, K. M. Kole, and D. H. Thomas, *Martyrdom in Spanish Florida: Don Juan and the Guale Uprising of 1597* (New York: American Museum of Natural History, 2011).

40   Lowery, op. cit., 354.

41   H. E. Bolton, ed., *Arredondo's Historical Proof of Spain's Title to Georgia: A Contribution to the History of One of the Spanish Borderlands* (Berkeley: University of California Press, 1925), 61.

42   J. J. TePaske, *The Governorship of Spanish Florida, 1700–63* (Durham, NC: Duke University Press, 1964), 197.

43 Weber, op. cit., 90.
44 Ibid., 112.
45 TePaske, op. cit., 81.
46 Ibid., 42–44, 79.
47 Ibid., 53–56.
48 Ibid., 73–76.
49 Weber, op. cit., 176.
50 Ibid., 179.
51 Weber, op. cit., 304.
52 Ibid., 300.
53 TePaske, op. cit., 210.
54 Ibid., 211.
55 Ibid., 221.
56 Ibid., 157.

CHAPTER TWO: THE CITIES OF CÍBOLA

Epigraph: C. Hallenbeck, ed., *The Journey of Fray Marcos de Niza* [1539], (Dallas: Southern Methodist University Press, 1987), lxx.

1 A. Reséndez, *A Land So Strange: The Epic Journey of Cabeza de Vaca* (New York: Basic, 2007).

2 R. Adorno, ed., *Alvar Núñez Cabeza de Vaca: His Account, His Life, and the Expedition of Pánfilo de Narvaez* (Lincoln: University of Nebraska Press, 1999), 249–51.

3 Reséndez, op. cit., 226.

4 W. Brandon, *Quivira: Europeans in the Region of the Santa Fe Trail, 1540–1820* (Athens: Ohio University Press, 1990), 27.

5 I. Stavans, ed., *Becoming Americans: Four Centuries of Immigrant Writing* (New York: Library of America, 2009), 41.

6 G. Parker Winship, ed. and trans., *The Journey of Coronado* (Golden, CO: Fulcrum, 1990), 31.

7 Ibid., 117.

8 Ibid., 129.

9 Ibid., 119.

10 Brandon, op. cit., 36.

11 R. and S. C. Flint, *Documents of the Coronado Expedition, 1539–42: They Were Not Familiar with His Majesty nor Did They Wish to Be His Subjects* (Albuquerque: University of New Mexico Press, 2005), 379.

12 D. J. Weber, *The Spanish Frontier in North America* (New Haven: Yale University Press, 1992), 81.

13 G. P. Hammond and A. Rey, eds., *Don Juan de Oñate: Colonizer of New Mexico, 1595–1628* (Albuquerque: University of New Mexico Press, 1953), 6.

14 Weber, op. cit., 314.

15 G. Pérez de Villagrá, *Historia de la Nueva México, 1610*, ed. M. Encinas, A. Rodríguez, and J. P. Sánchez (Albuquerque: University of New Mexico Press, 1992), 88–89.

16 P. Fussell, *The Great War and Modern Memory* (Oxford: Oxford University Press, 1975).

17 Villagrá, op. cit., 3.
18 Ibid., 186.
19 Ibid., 187.
20 Ibid., 183.
21 Ibid., 189–90.
22 Ibid., 150.
23 Ibid., 146–47.
24 Ibid., 114–22.
25 G. Espinosa, ed. and trans., *History of New Mexico by Gonzalo Pérez de Villagrá* (Los Angeles: The Quivira Society, 1933), 143–44.
26 Villagrá, op. cit., 102.
27 Ibid., 124–25.
28 Ibid., 292.
29 Ibid., 224–26.
30 Weber, op. cit., 82
31 Ibid., 81.
32 Ibid., 82.
33 G. P. Hodge, F. W. Hammond, and A. Rey, eds. and trans., *Fray Alonso de Benavides' Revised Memorial of 1634* (Albuquerque: University of New Mexico Press, 1945), 100.
34 J. E. Ivey, "The Greatest Misfortune of All: Famine in the Province of New Mexico, 1667–1672," *Journal of the Southwest* 36 (1994): 76, 100.
35 J. M. Espinosa, *Crusaders of the Rio Grande: The Story of Don Diego de Vargas and the Reconquest and Refounding of New Mexico* (Chicago: Institute of Jesuit History, 1942); J. A. Esquibel and J. B. Colligan, *The Spanish Recolonization of New Mexico: An Account of the Families Recruited in Mexico City in 1693* (Albuquerque: Historical Genealogical Society of New Mexico, 1999).
36 F. A. Lomelí and C. Colahan, eds. and trans., *Defying the Inquisition in New Mexico: Miguel de Quintana's Life and Writings* (Albuquerque: University of New Mexico Press, 2006), 23.
37 Ibid., 122.
38 Ibid., 126.
39 Ibid., 125.
40 Ibid., 31, 126, 173.
41 G. C. Anderson, "Wakantapi and Juan Sabeata," in R. W. Etulain, ed., *Western Lives: A Biographical History of the American West* (Albuquerque: University of New Mexico Press, 2004), 5–28.
42 Weber, op. cit., 187.
43 P. N. Limerick, *The Legacy of Conquest: The Unbroken Past of the American West* (New York: Norton, 2006), 229.
44 Weber, op. cit., 167.
45 C. W. Hackett, ed., *Historical Documents Relating to New Mexico, Nueva Vizcaya, and Approaches Thereto*, vol. 1 (Washington, DC: Carnegie Institution, 1937), 395.
46 T. Falkner, *A Description of Patagonia and the Adjoining Parts of South America* ([London]: Hereford, printed by C. Pugh, 1774), 121, 123.
47 R. B. Hasrick, *The Sioux: Life and Customs of a Warrior Society* (Norman: University of Oklahoma Press, 1964), 68.

48 P. Hämäläinen, *The Comanche Empire* (New Haven: Yale University Press, 2008).

49 N. Kanellos et al., eds., *Herencia: The Anthology of Hispanic Literature of the United States* (Oxford: Oxford University Press, 2002), 71.

50 Weber, op. cit., 27.

51 A. Taylor, *American Colonies: The Settling of North America* (Harmondsworth, UK: Penguin, 2002), 410–13; C. Abbott, S. J. Leonard, and D. McComb, eds., *Colorado: A History of the Centennial State* (Boulder: Colorado University Press, 1982), 27–29.

52 Weber, op. cit., 36–37.

53 Ibid., 224.

54 J. E. Officer, *Hispanic Arizona, 1535–1856* (Tucson: University of Arizona Press, 1987), 61–62; A. B. Thomas, *Forgotten Frontiers: A Study of the Spanish Indian Policy of Don Juan Bautista de Anza, Governor of New Mexico, 1777–87* (Norman: University of Oklahoma Press, 1969), 275–89.

55 Ibid., 209–11.

56 Ibid., 228.

57 Ibid., 229.

58 J. L. Kessell, *Spain in the Southwest: A Narrative History of Colonial New Mexico, Arizona, Texas, and California* (Norman: University of Oklahoma Press, 2002), 309.

59 K. McCarty, *Desert Documentary: The Spanish Years, 1767–1821* (Tucson: Arizona Historical Society, 1976), 82–92.

60 W. P. Webb, *The Great Plains* (Boston: Ginn, 1931), 87.

61 G. Williams, *Madoc: The Making of a Myth* (London: Methuen, 1979).

CHAPTER THREE: THE PURSUIT OF KING ARTHUR

Epigraphs: S. Daniel, "Musophilus," in *Poetical Essays* (1599); M. Twain, *A Connecticut Yankee in King Arthur's Court* (New York: Harper & Brothers Publishers, 1889), 1.

1 J. Truslow Adams, *Building the British Empire* (New York: Scribner's, 1938), 16.

2 A. J. Nouryeh, "Shakespeare and the Japanese Stage," in D. Kennedy, *Foreign Shakespeare: Contemporary Performance* (Cambridge: Cambridge University Press, 1993), 254–69.

3 The figure is selected at random: annual statistics are published from time to time in *Theater Heute*. The 1988–89 season was notable for the number of West German productions exported to what was then the Democratic Republic: see M. Hamburger, "Shakespeare auf den Bühnen der DDR in der Spielzeit 1988/89," *Shakespeare Jahrbuch* 126 (1990): 180–93.

4 W. Isaacson, *Benjamin Franklin: An American Life* (New York: Simon & Schuster, 2003), 459.

5 P. N. Limerick, *The Legacy of Conquest: The Unbroken Past of the American West* (New York: Norton, 1987).

6 N. Bunker, *Making Haste from Babylon: The Mayflower Pilgrims and Their World* (New York: Knopf, 2010).

7 P. J. French, *John Dee: The World of an Elizabethan Magus* (London: Routledge, 1984), 184.

8   F. Fernández-Armesto, "Inglaterra y el atlántico," in A. Bethencourt et al., *Inglaterra y Canariads a través de la historia* (Las Palmas, Spain: Casa de Colón, 1999), 14–15; C. Artese, "King Arthur in America: Making Space in History for The Faerie Queene and John Dee's Brytanici Imperii Limites," *Journal of Medieval and Early Modern Studies* 23 (2003): 125–41.

9   D. B. Quinn, *New American World: A Documentary History*, 5 vols. (New York: Ayer, 1979), 5: 238.

10 W. Strachey, *The Historie of Travaile into Virginia Britannia (1612)*, ed. R. H. Major (London: Hakluyt Society, 1849), 56–61.

11 Virginia Council [London], "Instructions, orders, and constitutions to Sir Thomas Gates, Knight, Governor of Virginia," in *The Records of the Virginia Company of London* (Washington: US Government Printing Office, 1906–1935).

12 J. Smith, "The True Travels, Adventures, and Observations of Captain John Smith in Europe, Asia, Africa," in P. L. Barbour, ed., *The Complete Works of Captain John Smith* (Chapel Hill: University of North Carolina Press, 1986), 1: 152.

13 F. Fernández-Armesto, *Columbus* (London: Duckworth, 1996), 207.

14 T. Studley, "The Proceedings of the English Colonie in Virginia," in Barbour, ed., op. cit., 2: 318.

15 Strachey, op. cit., 59–61.

16 K. O. Kuppermann, ed., *Captain John Smith* (Chapel Hill: University of North Carolina Press, 1988), 129.

17 Strachey, op. cit., 289–90.

18 L. G. Tyler, ed., *Narratives of Early Virginia, 1606–25* (New York: Scribner, 1907), 239–44.

19 J. Smith, *The Generall Historie of Virginia, New England and the Sumer Isles* (Glasgow: J. MacLehose, 1907), 306.

20 S. M. Kingsbury, ed., *Records of the Virginia Company of London*, 4 vols. (Washington, DC: US Government Printing Office, 1906–35), 3: 243.

21 H. E. Bolton, ed., *Arredondo's Historical Proof of Spain's Title to Georgia: A Contribution to the History of One of the Spanish Borderlands* (Berkeley: University of California Press, 1925), 100.

22 Ibid., 104–7.

23 Ibid., 107.

24 J. Winsor, *The Westward Movement: The Colonies and the Republic West of the Alleghenies, 1763–98* (Boston: Houghton Mifflin, 1897), 551.

25 B. Bailyn, *Voyagers to the West: Emigration from Britain to America on the Eve of the Revolution* (New York: Knopf, 1987), 8–20.

26 J. H. St. J. de Crèvecoeur, *More Letters from an American Farmer and Sketches of Eighteenth-century America: An Edition of the Essays Left Unpublished by Crèvecoeur*, ed. D. D. Moore (Athens: University of Georgia Press, 1995), 178.

27 Bailyn, op. cit., 23.

28 Ibid., 43.

29 Winsor, op. cit., 60.

30 Ibid., 101.

31 T. Burnard, *Creole Gentlemen: The Maryland Elite, 1691–1776* (New York: Routledge, 2002).

32 C. Kidd, *British Identities before Nationalism, 1600–1800* (Cambridge: Cambridge University Press, 1999), 274; J. Cañizares-Esguerra, *How to Write the History of the New World* (Stanford: Stanford University Press, 2001), 211, 230–34.

33 F. Anderson, *The Crucible of War: The Seven Years' War and the Fate of British North America* (New York: Random House, 2000).

34 T. Chávez, *Spain and the Independence of the United States: An Intrinsic Gift* (Albuquerque: University of New Mexico Press, 2002), 39.

35 Ibid., 88.

36 Ibid., 32.

37 Ibid., 61.

38 Winsor, op. cit., 42.

39 A. Smith, *An Inquiry into the Nature and Causes of the Wealth of Nations*, ed. E. M. Cannan, 2 vols. (Chicago: University of Chicago Press, 1976), 2: 138.

CHAPTER FOUR: THE REALM OF QUEEN CALAFIA

Epigraph: G. Rodríguez de Montalvo, *Las sergas de Esplandián* (Seville, 1510).

  1 G. Brotherston, *Image of the New World* (London: Thames & Hudson, 1979), 58–60.

  2 D. Monroy, *Thrown Among Strangers: The Making of Mexican Culture in Frontier California* (Berkeley: University of California Press, 1993), 21.

  3 Ibid., 24.

  4 H. E. Bolton, *The Spanish Borderlands: A Chronicle of Old Florida and the Southwest* (New Haven: Yale University Press, 1921), 103.

  5 Monroy, op. cit., 66.

  6 W. Shaler, "Journal of a Voyage between China and the North-west Coast of America, Made in 1804," *American Register* 3 (1808): 153.

  7 D. J. Weber, *The Spanish Frontier in North America* (New Haven: Yale University Press, 1992), 263.

  8 Monroy, op. cit., 107.

  9 Ibid., 61.

10 Ibid., 50.

11 R. F. Heizer, ed., *The Indians of Los Angeles County: Hugo Reid's Letters of 1852* (Los Angeles: Southwest Museum, 1968), 74–76, 101–2.

12 R. F. Heizer and A. F. Almquist, *The Other Californians: Prejudice and Discrimination under Spain, Mexico and the United States to 1920* (Berkeley: University of California Press, 1971), 40.

13 T. Blackburn, "The Chumash Revolt of 1824: A Native Account," *Journal of California Anthropology* 2 (1975): 225–27.

14 Heizer and Almquist, op. cit., 8–9.

15 Ibid., 48.

16 E. B. Webb, *Indian Life at the Old Missions* (1851; repr. Los Angeles: Lewis, 1952), 49.

17 Heizer and Almquist, op. cit., 87–89; R. H. Jackson and E. D. Castillo, *Indians, Franciscans, and Spanish Colonization: The Impact of the Mission System on California Indians* (Albuquerque: University of New Mexico Press, 1995);

J. Sandos, *Converting California: Indians and Franciscans in the Missions* (New Haven: Yale University Press, 2004); S. Hackel, *Children of Coyote, Missionaries of Saint Francis: Indian-Spanish Relations in Colonial California, 1769–1850* (Chapel Hill: University of North Carolina Press, 2005).

18 Monroy, op. cit., 25.
19 Ibid., 108.
20 J. E. Officer, *Hispanic Arizona, 1536–1856* (Tucson: University of Arizona Press, 1987), 41.
21 Weber, op. cit., 327.
22 Ibid., 308.
23 Monroy, op. cit., 61; Weber, op. cit., 329.
24 R. H. Dana, *Two Years before the Mast* (London: Dent, n.d.), 85, chap. 13.
25 J. Winsor, *The Westward Movement: The Colonies and the Republic West of the Alleghenies*, 1763–98 (Boston: Houghton Mifflin, 1897), 183.
26 Ibid., 389.
27 Ibid., 396.
28 M. L. Davis, ed., *Memoirs of Aaron Burr* (New York: Harper, 1837), 376.
29 Weber, op. cit., 281
30 Ibid., 280.
31 Ibid., 296.
32 J. L. Kessel, "Juan Bautista de Anza," in R. W. Etulain, *Western Lives: A Biographical History of the American West* (Albuquerque: University of New Mexico, 2004), 55.
33 Weber, op. cit., 296; Monroy, op. cit., 73.
34 Winsor, op. cit., 374.
35 Ibid., 557.
36 Weber, op. cit., 304.
37 Ibid., 300.
38 Ibid., 282.
39 Winsor, op. cit., 547.
40 J. P. Ronda, "Pike and Empire," in M. L. Harris and J. H. Buckley, eds., *Zebulon Pike, Thomas Jefferson, and the Opening of the American West* (Norman: University of Oklahoma Press, 2012), 61–80.
41 D. A. G. Waddell, "International Politics and Latin American Independence," in L. Bethell, ed., *Cambridge History of Latin America*, 6 vols. (Cambridge: Cambridge University Press), 3: 197–228.
42 O. B. Faulk, *The Last Years of Spanish Texas* (The Hague: Mouton, 1964), 47.
43 J. McNeill, *Mosquito Empires: Ecology and War in the Greater Caribbean* (New York: Cambridge University Press, 2010); R. Earle, *Spain and the Independence of Colombia, 1810–25* (Exeter, UK: Exeter University Press, 2000).
44 Weber, op. cit., 301.
45 Monroy, op. cit., 119.
46 Ibid., 120.
47 Ibid., 124–26.
48 Ibid., 125, 161.
49 Heizer and Almquist, op. cit., 114.
50 Monroy, op. cit., 79.

51 B. Leutenegger and M. B. Habig, "Report on the San Antonio Missions in 1792," *Southwestern Historical Quarterly* 77 (1974), 487–98.

52 Officer, op. cit., 112–14.

53 J. A. Sandos, "Levantamiento! The 1824 Chumash Uprising Reconsidered," *Southern California Quarterly* 67, (1985), 109–33.

54 Officer, op. cit., 7.

55 Ibid., 167.

56 N. L. Benson, "Texas as Viewed from Mexico," *Southwestern Historical Quarterly* 96 (1987): 219–91.

57 S. H. Lowrie, *Culture Conflict in Texas* (New York: Columbia University Press, 1932), 52.

58 H. H. Bancroft, *Essays and Miscellany* (San Francisco: The History Company, 1890), 73.

59 C. Abbott, S. J. Leonard, and D. McComb, eds., *Colorado: A History of the Centennial State* (Boulder: Colorado Associated University Press, 1982), 38–40.

60 C. E. Castañeda, ed., *The Mexican Side of the Texan Revolution* (Dallas: Turner, 1928), 310–11.

61 Ibid., 324–25.

62 Bancroft, op. cit., 133, 137; C.A. Hutchinson, "General José Antonio Mexía and His Texas Interests," *Southwestern Historical Quarterly* 82 (1978), 117–142.

63 Ibid., 165.

64 N. W. Stephenson, *Texas and the Mexican War* (New Haven: Yale University Press, 1921), 47; Lowrie, op. cit., 134–36.

65 Monroy, op. cit., 160.

66 Ibid., 200.

67 Dana, op. cit., 118, chap. 21.

68 Monroy, op. cit., 174–76.

69 Ibid., 163.

70 Dana, op. cit., 68, chap. 13.

71 Ibid., 82, chap. 13.

72 Ibid., 50, chap. 9.

73 Ibid., 59, chap. 11.

74 Ibid., 63, chap. 13.

75 Lowrie, op. cit., 39.

76 Ibid., 46.

77 Stephenson, op. cit., 5–22.

78 Lowrie, op. cit., 69, 128–29.

79 Castañeda, op. cit., 328.

80 N. Doran Maillard, *The History of the Republic of Texas* (London: Smith, Elder, 1842), xvi.

81 W. J. McConnell, *Social Cleavages in Texas: A Study of the Proposed Division of the State* (New York: Columbia University Press, 1925), 27.

82 C. E. Castañeda, ed., op. cit., 7, 17, 181.

83 Dana, op. cit., 14, chap. 21.

84 R. M. McElroy, *The Winning of the Far West* (New York: G. P. Putnam's Sons, 1914), 13.

85 Ibid., 15.

86 R. Roberts and J. S. Olson, *A Line in the Sand: The Alamo in Blood and Memory* (New York: Free Press, 2001), 144–47.

87 W. Kennedy, *Texas: The Rise, Progress and Prospects of the Republic of Texas*, 2 vols. (London: R. Hastings, 1841), 2: 228.

88 McElroy, op. cit., 26.

89 Ibid., 46.

90 Ibid., 131.

91 Weber, op. cit., 339.

92 H. S. Foote, *Texas and the Texans*, 2 vols. (Philadelphia: Thomas, Copperthwaite, 1841), 2: 83.

93 P. N. Limerick, *The Legacy of Conquest: The Unbroken Past of the American West* (New York: Norton, 1987), 241.

94 T. J. Farnham, *Life, Adventures, and Travels in California* (New York: Sheldon, Lamport, and Blakeman, 1855), 139–40.

95 Heizer and Almquist, op. cit., 4.

96 A. Robinson, *Life in California during a Residence of Several Years in That Territory* (New York: Wiley, 1846), 355–56.

97 J.-M. Rivera, *The Emergence of Mexican America: Recovering Mexican Peoplehood in U.S. Culture* (New York: New York University Press, 2006), 60.

98 R. H. Ferrell, ed., *Monterrey Is Ours: The Mexican War Letters of Lieutenant Dana, 1845–1847* (Lexington: University Press of Kentucky, 1990), 75.

CHAPTER FIVE: THE CURSE OF ZORRO

Epigraphs: Letter to Wm Heath, in N. Kanellos et al., eds., *Herencia: The Anthology of Hispanic Literature of the United States* (New York: Oxford University Press, 2002), 100; H. H. Bancroft, *Essays and Miscellany* (San Francisco: The History Company, 1890), 214; D. Belasco, *The Girl of the Golden West* (New York: Grosset & Dunlap, 1911), 25.

1 D. Montejano, *Anglos and Mexicans in the Making of Texas, 1836–1986* (Austin: University of Texas Press, 2003), 27.

2 H. H. Bancroft, *Popular Tribunals* (Los Angeles: The History Company, 1887), 167.

3 Montejano, op. cit., 27–28.

4 R. H. Ferrell, ed., *Monterrey Is Ours: The Mexican War Letters of Lieutenant Dana, 1845–1847* (Lexington: University Press of Kentucky, 1990), 74.

5 F. A. Rosales, *Testimonio: A Documentary History of the Mexican American Struggle for Civil Rights* (Houston: University of Houston Arte Público Press, 2000), 18.

6 Ibid., 29.

7 Ibid., 40.

8 L. Pitt, *The Decline of the Californios: A Social History of the Spanish-speaking Californians, 1846–90* (Berkeley: University of California Press, 1966), 43.

9 Ibid., 85–86.

10 D. Monroy, *Thrown among Strangers: The Making of Mexican Culture in Frontier California* (Berkeley: University of California Press, 1990), 114.

11 R. Glass Cleland, *The Cattle on a Thousand Hills* (Berkeley: University of California Press, 1975), 25–29.

12 Pitt, op. cit., 93.

13 D. J. Weber, *The Mexican Frontier 1821–46: The American Southwest under Mexico* (Albuquerque: University of New Mexico Press, 1982), 190.

14 Ibid., 197.

15 Pitt, op. cit., 94.

16 R. M. McElroy, *The Winning of the Far West* (New York: G. P. Putnam's Sons, 1914), 113.

17 P. N. Limerick, *The Legacy of Conquest: The Unbroken Past of the American West* (New York: Norton, 2006), 237.

18 Pitt, op. cit., 106, 275.

19 Montejano, op. cit., 52.

20 T. R. Fehrenbach, *Lone Star: A History of Texas and the Texans* (San Antonio: Da Capo, 2000), 511.

21 Bancroft, op. cit., 173–75.

22 Pitt, op. cit., 91.

23 Ibid., 93.

24 A. E. Bestor, *David Jacks of Monterrey* (Stanford, CA: Stanford University Press, 1945).

25 Pitt, op. cit., 97.

26 Ibid., 101.

27 Montejano, op. cit., 44.

28 Pitt, op. cit., 84.

29 Ibid., 96.

30 J. E. Officer, *Hispanic Arizona, 1536–1856* (Tucson: University of Arizona Press, 1987), 261.

31 Pitt, op. cit., 97.

32 McElroy, op. cit., 271.

33 T. B. King, *Report of the Honorable T. Butler King on California* (Washington, DC: Gideon, 1850), 8.

34 McElroy, op. cit., 322.

35 Officer, op. cit., 230.

36 Pitt, op. cit., 53.

37 McElroy, op. cit., 102.

38 King, op. cit., 68.

39 Pitt, op. cit., 58.

40 Officer, op. cit., 247.

41 Pitt, op. cit., 60–64.

42 Pitt, op. cit., 187.

43 Weber, op. cit., 186.

44 Pitt, op. cit., 145.

45 Weber, op. cit., 196.

46 Pitt, op. cit., 248.

47 Ibid., 286–93.

48 H. Lamar, *The Far Southwest 1846–1912: A Territorial History* (New York: Norton, 1970), 310; P. R. Way, "Overland via 'Jackass Mail' in 1858: The Diary of

Phocion R. Way, parts 1–4," ed. W. A. Duffen, *Arizona and the West* 2 (1960), 35–53.

49 Lamar, op. cit., 149; Limerick, op. cit., 237.

50 V. Sánchez, *Forgotten Cuchareños of the Lower Valley* (Charleston, SC: History Press, 2010), 95–96, 105.

51 *Maria von Blücher's Corpus Christi: Letters from the South Texas Frontier, 1849–79* (College Station: Texas A&M Press, 2002), 99–100.

52 R. J. Rosenbaum, *Mexicano Resistance in the Southwest* (Dallas: First Southern Methodist University Press, 1998), 53–124.

53 Ibid., 59.

54 Kanellos et al., op. cit., 117.

55 McElroy, op. cit., 212.

56 Limerick, op. cit., 256.

57 *Difficulties on the Southwest Frontier* (U.S. Congress Report, Washington, DC, 1860), 80–81.

58 J. Thompson, *Cortina: Defending the Mexican Name in Texas* (College Station: Texas A&M University Press, 2007), 53.

59 Ibid., 47.

60 Ibid., 56.

61 Ibid., 57.

62 Ibid., 49.

63 Ibid., 67.

64 *Maria von Blücher's Corpus Christi*, op. cit., 117.

65 Thompson, op. cit., 87.

66 Ibid., 215.

67 P. Cool, *Salt Warriors: Insurgency on the Rio Grande* (Austin: University of Texas Press, 2008).

68 R. J. Rosenbaum, "Las Gorras Blancas of San Miguel County," in R. Rosaldo et al., eds., *Chicano: The Evolution of a People* (Malabar, FL: Krieger, 1982), 128–33.

69 C. Abbott, S. J. Leonard, and D. McComb, eds., *Colorado: A History of the Centennial State* (Boulder: University Press of Colorado, 1982), 51.

70 Ibid., 40.

71 Ibid., 51–54.

72 Ibid., 64.

73 Ibid., 46.

74 Ibid., 80–87.

75 Ibid., 83.

76 Ibid., 73.

77 D. Brundage, *The Making of Western Labor Radicalism: Denver's Organized Workers, 1878–1905* (Champaign: University of Illinois Press, 1994), 10.

78 G. E. Hyde, *Life of George Bent Written from His Letters* (Norman: University of Oklahoma Press, 1968), 140.

79 Abbott, Leonard, and McComb, op. cit., 74–77.

80 Ibid., 102.

81 Ibid., 107.

82 Ibid., 90–94.

83 Ibid., 80.
84 Fehrenbach, op. cit., 287.
85 indiancanyon.org/ACTof1850.html; Montejano, op. cit., 185–86.
86 R. F. Heizer and A. F. Almquist, *The Other Californians: Prejudice and Discrimination under Spain, Mexico and the United States to 1920* (Berkeley: University of California Press, 1971), 26; Monroy, op. cit., 189.
87 D. L. Phillips, *Letters from California: Its mountains, valleys, plains, lakes, rivers, climate and productions. Also its railroads, cities, towns and people, as seen in 1876* (Springfield: Illinois State Journal Co., 1877).
88 N. Doran Maillard, *The History of the Republic of Texas* (London: Smith, Elder, 1842), 233–34.
89 G. C. Anderson, *The Conquest of Texas: Ethnic Cleansing in the Promised Land, 1820–1875* (Norman: University of Oklahoma Press, 2005).
90 W. P. Webb, *The Texas Rangers: A Century of Frontier Defense* (Austin: University of Texas Press, 1965), 31.
91 Fehrenbach, op. cit., 538.
92 F. Todd Smith, *From Dominance to Disappearance: The Indians of Texas and the Near Southwest* (Lincoln: University of Nebraska Press, 2008).
93 Fehrenbach, op. cit., 505.
94 Limerick, op. cit., 217.
95 Heizer and Almquist, op. cit., 28.
96 Ibid., 29.
97 Ibid., 90.
98 Ibid., 18.
99 Ibid., 19; G. Simpson, *An Overland Journey Round the World* (Philadelphia: Lea and Blanchard, 1847), 177–78.
100 C. L. Camp and G. C. Yount, "The Chronicles of George C. Yount: California Pioneer of 1826," *California Historical Society Quarterly* 2, no. 1 (April 1923): 3–66.
101 Montejano, op. cit., 186.
102 Heizer and Almquist, op. cit., 90.
103 Ibid., 19.
104 Ibid., 58.
105 J. A. Stout, *Apache Lightning: The Last Great Battles of the Ojo Calientes* (New York: Oxford University Press, 1974), 12.
106 L. F. Witmer, *The Indian Industrial School, Carlisle, Pennsylvania, 1879–1918* (Carlisle, PA: Cumberland County Historical Society, 2002), 19.
107 R. H. Pratt, *Battlefield and Classroom: Four Decades with the American Indian*, ed. R. Utley (New Haven: Yale University Press, 1964); J. Fear-Segal, *White Man's Club: Schools, Race, and the Struggle of Indian Acculturation* (Lincoln: University of Nebraska Press, 2007), 157–83.
108 Fehrenbach, op. cit., 118; R. M. Ellis, *General Pope and U.S. Indian Policy* (Albuquerque: University of New Mexico Press, 1970).
109 Stout, op. cit., 145.
110 Ibid.
111 J. B. Gillett, *Six Years with the Texas Rangers, 1875–81* (New York: Cosimo, 2007), 209.

112 C. F. Lummis, "Preliminary Report of the Warner's Ranch Indian Advisory Commission," United States Commission to Investigate the Conditions of the Mission Indians of Southern California (Los Angeles, 1902), 23, 26, 29, 31.

113 B. Landis, "Carlisle Indian Industrial School History," http://home.epix .net/~landis/histry.html.

114 Abbott, Leonard, and McComb, op. cit., 188.

115 Monroy, op. cit., 236.

116 Ibid., 249.

117 D. H. Stewart, ed., *Kipling's America: Travel Letters, 1889-95* (Greensboro, NC: ELT Press, 2003), 23.

118 Ibid., 273.

119 Ibid., 236.

120 Ibid., 262.

121 Ibid., 273.

122 Ibid., 279.

123 Fehrenbach, op. cit., 302.

124 Weber, op. cit., 168.

125 Fehrenbach, op. cit., 303.

126 Abbott, Leonard, and McComb, op. cit., 69.

127 L. R. Hafen, ed., *To the Pike's Peak Gold Fields, 1859* (Lincoln: University of Nebraska Press, 2004), 54.

128 Ibid., 109.

129 Monroy, op. cit., 264; C. F. Lummis, "In the Lion's Den," in *The Land of Sunshine* 4, no. 1 (December 1895): 44.

130 R. H. Dana, *Two Years before the Mast* (London: Dent, n.d.), 285, chap. 27.

131 R. L. Sagarena, "Building California's Past," *Journal of Urban History* 28 (2002): 429-44.

132 A. M. Cleaveland, *No Life for a Lady* (London: M. Joseph, 1942), 9.

133 Ibid., 12.

134 Ibid., 115.

135 Ibid., 162.

136 Ibid., 103-22.

137 Ibid., 96.

138 Ibid., 182.

139 W. Cather, *Death Comes for the Archbishop* (New York: Knopf, 1932), 37.

140 Cleaveland, op. cit., 218.

CHAPTER SIX: THE REVENGE OF MORONI

Epigraphs: D. Belasco, *The Girl of the Golden West* (New York: Grosset & Dunlap, 1911), 343; R. Rodriguez, *Days of Obligation: An Argument with My Mexican Father* (New York: Penguin, 1992), 29.

1 L. Spier, *The Prophet Dance of the Northwest and Its Derivatives* (Menasha, WI: Banta, 1935), 58.

2 F. Fernández-Armesto, *The Americas: A Hemispheric History* (New York: Random House, 2002), 60.

3 E. Weber, *Apocalypses* (Cambridge, MA: Harvard University Press, 1999), 170.
4 G. M. Marsden, *Jonathan Edwards: A Life* (New Haven: Yale University Press, 2003), 218.
5 Book of Ether 2:12.
6 J. A. Widtsoe, ed., *Discourses of Brigham Young* (Salt Lake City: Deseret, 1925), 183.
7 Ibid., 9.
8 F. Graziano, *The Millennial New World* (New York: Oxford University Press, 1999); J. L. Phelan, *The Millennial Kingdom of the Franciscans in the New World* (Berkeley: University of California Press, 1970); G. Baudot, *Utopie et histoire au Mexique: Les premiers chroniqueurs de la civilisation mexicaine* (Toulouse: Privat, 1977).
9 Widtsoe, op. cit., 186.
10 Ibid., 183–84.
11 W. Slaughter and M. Landon, *Trail of Hope: The Story of the Mormon Trail* (Salt Lake City: Shadow Mountain, 1997), 23–24.
12 L. R. and A. W. Hafen, *Handcarts to Zion: The Story of a Unique Western Migration, 1856–60* (Glendale, CA: Clark, 1960), 82.
13 http://law2.umkc.edu/faculty/projects/ftrials/mountainmeadows/martial law.html.
14 L. R. and A. W. Hafen, *Old Spanish Trail: Santa Fe to Los Angeles* (Glendale, CA: Clark, 1954), 68.
15 H. E. Bolton, ed., *Pageant in the Wilderness: The Story of the Escalante Expedition to the Interior Basin, 1776* (Salt Lake City: Utah Historical Society, 1950), 159.
16 B. Miera y Pacheco, in G. G. Cline, *Exploring the Great Basin* (Norman: University of Oklahoma Press, 1963), 53.
17 F. Fernández-Armesto, *Pathfinders: A Global History of Exploration* (New York: Norton, 2006), 323.
18 Ibid.
19 B. DeVoto, ed. *The Journals of Lewis and Clark* (Boston: Houghton Mifflin, 1953), 92.
20 Fernández-Armesto, op. cit., 324.
21 R. L. Nichols and P. L. Halley, *Stephen Long and American Frontier Exploration* (Newark: University of Delaware Press, 1980), 167.
22 Hafen, op. cit., 108.
23 Ibid., 327.
24 C. M. Drury, ed. *First white women over the Rockies; diaries, letters, and biographical sketches of the six women of the Oregon Mission who made the overland journey in 1836 and 1838*, 3 vols. (Glendale, CA: Clark, 1963-66), 1: 77.
25 Ibid.
26 W. Prescott Webb, *The Great Plains* (New York: Grosset & Dunlap, 1931), 470–82.
27 A. E. Sheldon, *History and Stories of Nebraska* (Chicago: University Publishing Co., 1914), 112.
28 J. F. Cooper, *The Prairie* (New York: Putnam, n.d.), 6.
29 *The National Era*, December 23, 1852.

30 A. Trollope, *North America* (New York: Harper, 1862), 149, 160, 167.

31 W. Cronon, *Nature's Metropolis: Chicago and the Great West* (New York: Norton, 1991).

32 P. N. Limerick, *The Legacy of Conquest: The Unbroken Past of the American West* (New York: Norton, 1987).

33 W. H. Goetzmann, *Exploration and Empire: The Explorer and the Scientist in the Winning of the American West* (New York: Knopf, 1966), 270.

34 Ibid., 279.

35 Ibid., 257.

36 B. Möllhausen, *Diary of a Journey from the Mississippi to the Coasts of the Pacific with a United States Government Expedition*, translated by Mrs. P. Sinnett, vol. 2 (London: Longman, Brown, Green, Longmans, & Roberts, 1858), 335.

37 W. H. Goetzmann, *Army Explorations in the American West, 1803–63* (New Haven: Yale University Press, 1959), 263–66.

38 Ibid., 343.

39 F. Fernández-Armesto, *Millennium: A History of the Last Thousand Years* (New York: Simon & Schuster, 1996), 406.

40 J. A. Stout, *Schemers and Dreamers: Filibustering in Mexico, 1848–1921* (Fort Worth: Texas Christian University Press, 2002), 206.

41 Ibid., 14–24.

42 Ibid., 72; J. A. Stout, *Apache Lightning: The Last Great Battles of the Ojo Calientes* (New York: Oxford University Press, 1974), 166; "Dalrymple's Delusions," *New York Times*, August 10, 1880.

43 J. Martí, *Obras completas*, 23 vols. (Havana: Centro de Estudios Martinos, 1963–2000), 12: 48–49.

44 Ibid., 205.

45 M. Boot, *The Savage Wars of Peace: Small Wars and the Rise of American Power* (New York: Perseus, 2002), 210.

46 O. J. Martínez, *Border People: Life and Society in the U.S.-Mexico Borderlands* (Tucson: University of Arizona Press, 1994), 156.

47 R. F. Rogers, *Destiny's Landfall: A History of Guam* (Honolulu: University of Hawaii Press, 1995).

48 J. McCallum, *Leonard Wood: Rough Rider, Surgeon, Architect of American Imperialism* (New York: New York University Press, 2006), 214–30.

49 P. Foner, *The Spanish-Cuban-American War and the Birth of American Imperialism, 1895–1902* (New York: Monthly Review Press, 1972), 208–64.

50 Ibid., 394–95.

51 Ibid., 472.

52 J. Cervera Baviera, *La defensa de San Juan* (San Juan de Puerto Rico: Capitanía General, 1898), 4.

CHAPTER SEVEN: THE RETURN TO AZTLÁN

Epigraphs: Quoted in I. Stavans, ed., *Becoming Americans: Four Centuries of Immigrant Writing* (New York: Library of America, 2009), 231; Speech to the Sociedad Literaria Hispanoamericana, in *Nuestra América*, ed. H. Achúgar (Caracas: Biblioteca Ayacucho, 2005), 30.

376 - NOTES TO PAGES 248-60

1 census.gov/population/hispanic/data/2011.html.

2 F. A. Rosales, *¡Pobre raza! Violence, Justice, and Mobilization among México Lindo Immigrants, 1900–36* (Austin: University of Texas Press, 1999), 23.

3 O. J. Martínez, *Border People: Life and Society in the U.S.–Mexico Borderlands* (Tucson: University of Arizona Press, 1994), 157.

4 C. Fuentes, *The Buried Mirror: Reflections on Spain in the New World* (Boston: Houghton Mifflin, 1992), 343.

5 L. Gordon, *The Great Arizona Orphan Abduction* (Cambridge, MA: Harvard University Press, 1999), 91.

6 Ibid., 288.

7 Ibid., 74.

8 Ibid., 188.

9 Ibid., 281.

10 Ibid., 150.

11 Ibid., 184.

12 Ibid., 103.

13 Ibid., 280.

14 Ibid., 114.

15 Ibid., 294.

16 Ibid., 305.

17 S. F .B. Morse, *Foreign Conspiracy against the United States* (New York: American and Foreign Christian Union, 1855), 99, 116, 162.

18 Ibid., 205.

19 colorado.gov/dpa/doit/archives/govs/ morley.html.

20 C. Abbott, S. J. Leonard, and D. McComb, eds., *Colorado: A History of the Centennial State* (Boulder: University Press of Colorado, 1982), 271.

21 L. Pubols, *The Father of All: The de la Guerra Family, Power, and Patriarchy in Mexican California* (Berkeley: University of California Press, 2010), 26.

22 D. E. Hayes-Bautista, *La Nueva California: Latinos in the Golden State* (Berkeley: University of California Press, 2004), 199.

23 Rosales, op. cit., 4.

24 N. Stepan, *Picturing Tropical Nature* (Ithaca, NY: Cornell University Press, 2001.

25 A. de Leon, *They Called Them Greasers: Anglo Attitudes to Mexicans in Texas, 1821–1900* (Austin: University of Texas Press, 1983); C. Douglas, *A Genealogy of Literary Multiculturalism* (Ithaca, NY: Cornell University Press, 2009), 156–72.

26 Rosales, op. cit., 193.

27 W. P. Webb, *The Texas Rangers: A Century of Frontier Defense* (Austin: University of Texas Press, 1965), 14.

28 Ibid., 151.

29 N. de Genova, ed., *Racial Transformations: Latinos and Asians Remaking the U.S.* (Durham, NC: Duke University Press, 2006), 6.

30 J.-M. Rivera, *The Emergence of Mexican America: Recovering Stories of Mexican Peoplehood in U.S. Culture* (New York: New York University Press, 2006), 51.

31 Ibid., 124.

32 Rosales, op. cit., 103.

33 Ibid., 75.

34 Ibid., 119.

35 Ibid., 86–87.

36 Abbott, Leonard, and McComb, op. cit., 295.

37 Ibid., 298–302.

38 Ibid., 296–98.

39 R. F. Acuña, *Occupied America: A History of Chicanos* (London: Longman, 2011), 188, 192.

40 E. Garlaza, *Barrio Boy* (1971), quoted in I. Stavans, ed., *Becoming Americans: Four Centuries of Immigrant Writing* (New York: Library of America, 2009), 194.

41 R. I. Mize and A. C. S. Swords, *Consuming Mexican Labor: From the Bracero Program to NAFTA* (North York: University of Toronto Press, 2011), xxxiv.

42 N. Molina, *Fit to Be Citizens? Public Health and Race in Los Angeles, 1879–1939* (Berkeley: University of California Press, 2006).

43 Acuña, op. cit., 46, 95.

44 Hayes-Bautista, op. cit., 17–18.

45 Acuña, op. cit., 208.

46 A. Schmidt Camacho, *Migrant Imaginaries: Latino Cultural Politics in the U.S.–Mexico Borderlands* (New York: New York University Press, 2008), 69.

47 E. Gonzales-Berry and M. Mendoza, *Mexicanos in Oregon: Their Stories, Their Lives* (Corvallis: Oregon State University Press, 2010), 32–33.

48 F. Moralez, "Latina Women of Spirit," *American Catholic Studies Newsletter* 39 (Spring 2012): 1–12.

49 C. McWilliams, *North from Mexico: The Spanish-speaking People of the United States* (New York: Greenwood, 1968), 270.

50 Martínez, op. cit., 152–54.

51 J. Lackie, *I Don't Cry But I Remember: A Mexican Immigrant's Story of Endurance* (Tucson: University of Arizona Press, 2012), 55–68.

52 L. Velasco Ortiz and O. F. Contreras, *Mexican Voices of the Border Region: Mexicans and Mexican Americans Speak about Living along the Wall* (Philadelphia: Temple University Press, 2011), 87–89.

53 D. G. Gutiérrez, *The Columbia History of Latinos in the United States since 1960* (New York: Columbia University Press, 2004), 45–46.

54 Hayes-Bautista, op. cit., 31.

55 Ibid., 93.

56 Genova, op. cit., 9.

57 Ibid., 77–79.

58 Hayes-Bautista, op. cit., 32–36; McWilliams, op. cit., 233–35.

59 McWilliams, op. cit., 230–31.

60 Ibid., 247.

61 Ibid, 250.

62 D. Montejano, *Anglos and Mexicans in the Making of Texas, 1836–1986* (Austin: University of Texas Press, 1987), 76, 82–83.

63 McWilliams, op. cit., 257.

64 R. Griswold del Castillo, "The Los Angeles Zoot-suit Riots Revisited: Mexican and Latin American Perspectives," *Mexican Studies-Estudios Mexicanos* 16 (2000): 367–91.

65 J. Durand and D. S. Massey, *Miracles on the Border: Retablos of Mexican Migrants to the United States* (Tucson: University of Arizona Press, 1995).

66 Velasco Ortiz and Contreras, op. cit., 134–44.

67 Martínez, op. cit., 157–59.

68 Ibid., 161.

69 M. P. Davis, *Mexican Voices, American Dreams: An Oral History of Mexican Immigration to the United States* (New York: Henry Holt, 1990), 113.

70 Schmidt Camacho, op. cit., 294–96.

71 Davis, op. cit., 115.

72 Martínez, op. cit., 148–55.

73 Rosales, op. cit., 57.

74 Davis, op. cit., 197.

75 C. Fernandez and J. E. Officer, "The Lighter Side of Mexican Immigration: Humor and Satire in the Mexican Corrido," *Journal of the Southwest* 32 (1989): 471–96.

76 Davis, op. cit., 258.

77 Ibid., 189.

78 Ibid., 262.

79 Martínez, op. cit., 88.

80 Davis, op. cit., 218, 228.

81 Gordon, op. cit., 51.

82 Davis, op. cit., 15–21, 174.

83 Ibid., 19.

84 Ibid., 213, 235–40.

85 Martínez, op. cit., 172–74.

86 J. Samora, *Los Mojados: The Wetback Story* (Notre Dame, IN: University of Notre Dame Press, 1971); J. R. Garcia, *Operation Wetback: The Mass Deportation of Mexican Undocumented Workers in 1954* (Westport, CT: Greenwood, 1980).

87 Davis, op. cit., 229.

88 washingtonpost.com/blogs/wonkblog/wp/2012/08/27/obama-is-deporting-more-immigrants-than-bush-republicans-dont-think-thats-enough/.

89 Hayes-Bautista, op. cit., 144.

90 malcolm-x.org/docs/let_laac.htm.

91 N. Kanellos et al., eds., *Herencia: The Anthology of Hispanic Literature of the United States* (New York: Oxford University Press, 2002), 247.

92 E .H. Spicer, *The American Indians: Dimensions of Ethnicity* (Cambridge, MA: Harvard University Press, 1980), 182.

93 R. H. Pratt, *Battlefield and Classroom: Four Decades with the American Indian, 1867–1904*, ed. R. M. Utley (Lincoln: University of Nebraska Press, 1964), 335.

CHAPTER EIGHT: THE REPUBLIC OF HESPERUS

Epigraph: R. Rodriguez, *Brown: The Last Discovery of America* (New York: Penguin, 2002), 2.

1 M. Bencastro, *Odyssey to the North* (Houston: Houston University Arte Público Press, 1999); N. Kanellos et al., eds., *Herencia: The Anthology of His-*

panic Literature of the United States (New York: Oxford University Press, 2002), 423.

2   D. G. Gutiérrez, ed., *The Columbia History of Latinos in the United States: 1960 to the Present* (New York: Columbia University Press, 2004), 257.

3   Fernández de Oviedo, *Historia general y natural de las Indias*, bk. II, chap. 3.

4   L. B. Johnson, *Public Papers of the Presidents of the United States* (Washington, DC: US Government Printing Office, 1966), 1037–40.

5   D. E. Hayes-Bautista, *La Nueva California: Latinos in the Golden State* (Berkeley: University of California Press, 2004), 8, 94; census.gov/compendia/statab/cats/population.html.

6   R. López Tijerina, *They Called Me King Tiger: My Struggle for the Land and Our Rights* (Houston: Arte Público, 2000).

7   D. G. Gutiérrez, "Introduction: Demography and the Shifting Boundaries of Community," in Gutiérrez, op. cit., 1–86, at p. 54.

8   R. J. Jensen and J. C. Hammerback, eds., *The Words of César Chávez* (College Station: Texas A&M University Press, 2002), xviii.

9   *El plan de Santa Bárbara: A Chicano Plan for Higher Education: Analyses and Positions by the Chicano Coordinating Council on Higher Education* (Oakland, CA: La Causa Publications, 1969), 9.

10   Kanellos et al., op. cit., 196–97.

11   http://www.sscnet.ucla.edu/ooW/chicano101-1/aztlan.html; L. Váldez and S. Steiner, eds., *An Anthology of Mexican American Literature* (New York: Knopf, 1972), 402–6.

12   L. Thomas, *Puerto Rican Citizen: History and Political Identity in Twentieth-Century New York City* (Chicago: University of Chicago Press, 2010), 6.

13   Ibid., 27–29.

14   *Puerto Rico Herald*, February 25, 2005.

15   A. Ortiz Vargas, *Las torres de Manhattan* (New York: Chapman & Grimes, 1939).

16   Kanellos et al., op. cit., 354–56.

17   F. Picó, *History of Puerto Rico: A Panorama of Its People* (Princeton, NJ: Markus Wiener, 2006), 274.

18   Kanellos et al., op. cit., 212.

19   R. Carr, *Puerto Rico: A Colonial Experiment* (New York: New York University Press, 1984), 302–3.

20   P. Thomas, *Down These Mean Streets* (New York: Vintage, 1997), x.

21   P. Thomas, *El Barrio* (New York: Knopf, 1978), 86–102.

22   Carr, op. cit., 335.

23   N. Glazer and D. P. Moynihan, *Beyond the Melting Pot: The Negroes, Puerto Ricans, Jews, Italians, and Irish of New York City* (Cambridge, MA: MIT Press, 1963), 116–22.

24   K. A. Santiago-Valles and G. M. Jiménez-Muñoz, "Social Polarization and Colonized Labor: Puerto Ricans in the United States, 1945–2000," in Gutiérrez, op. cit., 122.

25   Picó, op. cit., 313.

26   M. C. García, "Exiles, Immigrants, and Transnationals: The Cuban Communities of the United States," in Gutiérrez, op. cit., 153.

27 R. Arenas, *Antes que anochezca* (1992), quoted in I. Stavans, ed., *Becoming Americans: Four Centuries of Immigrant Writing* (New York: Library of America, 2009), 593.

28 Kanellos et al., op. cit., 500.

29 García, op. cit., 174.

30 C. Parikh, *The Ethics of Betrayal: The Politics of Otherness in Emergent US Literatures and Culture* (New York: Fordham University Press, 2009), 141.

31 Ibid., 174–85.

32 P. Levitt in Gutiérrez, op. cit., 230, 240.

33 J. Marichal, *A Pitcher's Story* (New York: Doubleday, 1967), 24.

34 R. Ruck, *The Tropic of Baseball: Baseball in the Dominican Republic* (Westport, CT: Bison Books, 1991); T. Miller, *Trading with the Enemy: A Yankee Travels Through Castro's Cuba* (New York: Athenaeum, 1992); A. Zimbalist, "Baseball and Society in the Caribbean," *New West Indian Guide–Nieue West-indische Gids* 68 (1994): 101–4.

35 P. Levitt, *The Transnational Villagers* (Berkeley: University of California Press, 2001); Levitt, "The Case of Dominicans," in Gutiérrez, op. cit., 229–57, at pp. 241–45.

36 Ibid., 252.

37 kff.org/kaiserpolls/upload/Immigration-in-America.

38 N. Stoltz Chinchilla and N. Hamilton, in Gutiérrez, op. cit., 219.

39 W. Frey, "Census 2000 Reveals New Native-Born and Foreign-Born Shifts Across U.S.," Report No. 02-520, Population Studies Center at the Institute for Social Research (University of Michigan, 2002); J. S. Passel and R. Suro, "Rise, Peak and Decline: Trends in U.S. Immigration, 1992–2004," Pew Hispanic Center Working Paper, 2005; V. Zuñiga and R. Hernández León, eds., *New Destinations: Mexican Immigration in the United States* (Washington, DC: Russell Sage Foundation, 2006); D. S. Massey, ed., *New Faces in New Places: The Changing Geography of American Immigration* (Washington, DC: Russell Sage Foundation 2008).

40 *Es Más*, August 3, 2011.

41 hispanichartford.org/community/history/.

42 *Seattle Times*, July 3, 2011.

43 E. Porter, "Flow of Immigrants' Money to Latin America Surges," *New York Times*, October 19, 2006.

44 imi.ox.ac.uk/pdfs/imi-working-papers/working-paper-18-crisis-and-remittances; *New York Times,* October 16, 2006.

45 A. M. Stevens-Arroyo, "From Barrios to Barricades: Religion and Religiosity in Latino Life," in Gutiérrez, op. cit., 303–54, at p. 323.

46 Ibid., 338.

47 Levitt, "The Case," Gutiérrez, op. cit., 246.

48 Stevens-Arroyo, in Gutiérrez, op. cit., 304.

49 Ibid., 348.

50 http://abcnews.go.com/ABC_Univision/latinos-save-american-catholicism/story?id=17491901#.UNkaQ6CRWrg.

51 Stevens-Arroyo, in Gutiérrez, op. cit., 325.

52 Kanellos et al., op. cit., 387.

53 Thomas, op. cit., 120.
54 O. J. Martínez, *Border People: Life and Society in the U.S.-Mexico Borderlands* (Tucson: University of Arizona Press, 1994), 97–101.
55 Kanellos et al., op. cit., 140–41.
56 Ibid., 447 (translation modified).
57 Ibid., 255.
58 T. R. Reid, "Spanish in School Leads to Suspension," *Washington Post*, December 9, 2005; http://www.washingtonpost.com/wp-dyn/content/article/2005/12/08/AR2005120802122.html.
59 G. Borjas, *Mexican Immigration to the United States* (Chicago: University of Chicago Press, 2007), 109.
60 Hayes-Bautista, op. cit., 137.
61 Ibid., 126.
62 Ibid., 132–33.
63 Ibid., 138–43.
64 Ibid., 129–32.
65 *New York Times*, September 4, 1998.
66 K. R. Johnson, "The Continuing Latino Quest for Full Membership and Equal Citizenship," in Gutiérrez, op. cit., 391–420, at p. 395.
67 Hayes-Bautista, op. cit., xvi, 10–11, 71–88.
68 Ibid., 170.
69 Interview with Bill O'Reilly, Fox TV, July 20, 2010.
70 http://thecaucus.blogs.nytimes.com/2011/10/15/cain-proposes-electrified-border-fence/; http://thecaucus.blogs.nytimes.com/2011/10/15/bachmann-goes-after-perry-on-immigration-pledges-border-fence/; nytimes.com/aponline/2012/08/26/us/ap-us-arizona-border-fence.html?ref=borderfenceusmexico.
71 C. Rhodenhaugh, "Thank you, Stephen Colbert," *The Observer*, October 1, 2010.
72 Hayes-Bautista, op. cit., 144.
73 *New York Times*, April 23, 2010.
74 *New York Times*, July 22, 2011.
75 Norwegian television documentary, posted by V. Duque at http://raciality.blogspot.co.uk/2009/06/videos-shawna-fordes-gang-of-killer.html on June 28, 2009; D. Neiwert, *And Hell Followed with Her: Crossing the Dark Side of the American Border* (New York: Nation, 2013).
76 *Washington Post*, March 18, 2011.
77 *News Taco*, March 21, 2011.
78 pewhispanic.org/2012/09/19/characteristics-of-the-60-largest-metropolitan-areas-by-hispanic-population/.

CHAPTER NINE: RETROSPECT AND PROSPECT

Epigraph: *El partido liberal*, January 30, 1891, in *Nuestra América* (Havana: Casa de las Américas, 1974), 39.
 1 S. Schama, *The Embarrassment of Riches: An Interpretation of Dutch Culture in the Golden Age* (New York: Knopf, 1987); H. R. Trevor-Roper, "Religion, the

Reformation, and Social Change," in *The Crisis of the Seventeenth Century: Religion, the Reformation and Social Change* (Indianapolis: Liberty Fund, 1967), 1–42; T. Zeldin, *France, 1848–1945*, vol. 1 (Oxford: Oxford University Press, 1973), 645.

2   G. Winstanley, "A New-year's Gift for the Parliament and Army (1650)," in *Winstanley: The Law of Freedom and Other Writings*, ed. C. Hill (Cambridge: Cambridge University Press, 1983), 185.

3   F. Fernández-Armesto and D. Wilson, *Reformations: A Radical Interpretation of Christianity and the World* (New York: Scribner, 1997).

4   S. de Madariaga, *Ingleses, franceses, españoles: Ensayo de psicología comparada* (Buenos Aires: Sudamericana, 1946).

5   J. H. Elliott, *Empires of the Atlantic World: Britain and Spain in North America, 1492–1830* (New Haven, CT: Yale University Press, 2006).

6   F. García Calderón, *Latin America: Its Rise and Progress* (London: Unwin, 1913).

7   F. Fernández-Armesto, "What Is History Now?," in D. Cannadine, ed., *What Is History Now?* (New York: Palgrave, 2002), 148–61.

8   D. Mallory, ed., *The Life and Speeches of the Honorable Henry Clay*, 2 vols. (New York, 1843), 357.

9   F. Fernández-Armesto, "Revoluciones atlánticas: consecuencias en los ámbitos anglosajón e hispano," in G. Anes and E. Garrigues, eds., *La ilustración española en la independencia de los Estados Unidos* (Madrid: Pons, 2007), 181–98.

10   G. L. Coil, "War Crimes of the American Revolution," *Military Law Review* 82 (Fall 1978): 171–98; A. Starkey, "War and Culture, a Case Study: The Enlightenment and the Conduct of the British Army in America, 1755–1781," *War and Society* 8 (1) (May 1990): 1–28; J. L. Van Buskirk, *Generous Enemies: Patriots and Loyalists in Revolutionary New York* (Philadelphia: University of Pennsylvania Press, 2002), chap. 3, esp. pp. 76–78; G. Best, *Humanity in Warfare* (New York: Columbia University Press, 1980), 44–45, 108–9; G. Best, *War and Society in Revolutionary Europe, 1770–1870* (1982; reprint, Montreal: McGill-Queen's University Press, 1998), 21–28.

11   D. F. O'Leary, *Bolívar and the War of Independence*, ed. R. F. McNerney (Austin: University of Texas Press, 1970), 65.

12   E. de Vattel, *The Law of Nations, or Principles of the Law of Nature Applied to Nations*, ed. B. Kapossy (Indianapolis: Liberty Fund, 2008), 280.

13   S. Bolívar, *Obras completas del Libertador*, ed. V. Lecuna, 3 vols. (Havana: Lex, 1950), 3: 423.

14   Ibid., 2; 537.

15   *Barbarities of the Enemy Exposed in a Report of the Committee of the House . . . Appointed to Enquire into the Spirit and Manner in Which the War Has Been Waged by the Enemy* (Troy, NY, 1813), 1.

16   T. G. Tancredo, *In Mortal Danger: The Battle for America's Border and Security* (Nashville, TN: WND Books, 2006); http://intelligencesquaredus.org/debates/past-debates/item/556-dont-give-us-your-tired-your-poor-your-huddled-masses.

17   pewhispanic.org/2012/04/23/net-migration-from-mexico-falls-to-zero-and-perhaps-less/.

PERMISSIONS

ART

Frontispiece: Maceo Montoya, *La Inmensidad*, 2007, acrylic on canvas.
Part One: The Granger Collection, NYC. All rights reserved.
Part Two: Prints and Photographs Division, Library of Congress, LC-USZC4 -3605.
Part Three: Prints and Photographs Division, Library of Congress, LC-USF33 -012432-M3.

TEXT CREDITS

Excerpt from *No Life for a Lady* by Agnes Morley Cleaveland. Copyright © 1941 by Agnes Morley Cleaveland; copyright © renewed 1969 by Loraine Lavender. Reprinted by permission of Houghton Mifflin Harcourt Publishing Company. All rights reserved.

"From Barrios to Barricades: Religion and Religiosity in Latino Life" by Anthony M. Stevens-Arroyo, from *The Columbia History of Latinos in the United States Since 1960*, edited by David G. Gutiérrez. Copyright © 2004 Columbia University Press. Reprinted with permission of the publisher.

"Late Victorians," from *Days of Obligation* by Richard Rodriguez, copyright © 1992 by Richard Rodriguez. Used by permission of Viking Penguin, a division of Penguin Group (USA) LLC.

The Mexican Side of the Texan Revolution [1836], by the Chief Mexican Participants, translated and edited by Carlos Eduard Castañeda (Dallas, TX: P. L. Turner Company, 1928). We have made diligent efforts to contact the copyright holder to obtain permission to reprint this selection. If you have information that would help us, please write to Permissions Department, W. W. Norton & Company, Inc., 500 Fifth Avenue, New York, NY 10110.

"The Other 'Other Hispanics': South American–Origin Latinos in the United States" by Marilyn Espitia, from *The Columbia History of Latinos in the United*

INDEX

Box, John C., 256
Boyuca, 18
braceros, 266–69
Brazil, 311, 333
Brewer, Jay, 326
British Empire:
  cultural legacy of, 75–76
  growth of, after Seven Years' War, 98–100
  as imitation of Spanish Empire, 84–85, 88
  as threat to Spanish Empire, 113, 117, 119
  see also Great Britain, British
Brown, John, 246
Brown: The Last Discovery of America
  (Rodriguez), 285
Bryce, James, 234
Bucareli, Antonio María, 113
Buenos Aires, 64, 157
buffalo, 40, 41, 60, 64, 65, 178–79, 216, 219,
  224, 225
Buffalo Bill's Wild West show, 284
Buffon, Georges-Louis, Count de, 102
Burleigh, Lord, 338
Burnett, Peter H., 177, 178
Burr, Aaron, 121, 122, 144, 344
Bush, George W., 323
Byers, William, 172–73
Byzantine Empire, 59–60

Cabet, Étienne, 205–6
Cabeza de Vaca, Alvar Núñez, 35–39, 41, 43
Cabot, John, 86
Cacapol, 64
Caddos, 62
Cadena Torres, Juana María, 276
Cádiz, 118
Cadodaquious, 62
Calafia, Queen, 112, 355
Calhoun, James S., 182
California, xxix, 71, 72, 109, 110, 112–19,
  145, 189, 208, 214, 261, 265, 334, 353
  entrance to Union of, 162
  gold rush in, xxii, 161–62, 172, 181, 226
  Land Commission, 158
  land grants in, 157–59, 160–61
  Land Law in, 157–58
  Mexican rebellions in, 166
  missions in, 114–17, 133
  Native Americans in, 176–77, 179–80
  rebellions in, 142
  segregation in, 269

  trade in, 139–40
  US immigrants in, 138–40
California, Gulf of, 52
Californios, 179–80
Calvin, Jean, 337
Camper, Petrus, 259
Canada, 23, 77, 96, 109, 111, 118, 129, 335,
  352, 353
Canadian River, 65
Canary Islands, 72
Cangapol, 64
cannibalism, 6, 8
Caparra, 15
capitalism, 331, 339–40
Carbajal, José-María Jesús, 137, 235
Caribbean, 98, 129, 248, 291, 311
Caribs, 12, 16, 22
Carleton, James H., 183
Carlisle Indian Industrial School, 184, 186,
  284
Carlos III, King of Spain, 96
Carlos IV, King of Spain, 125
Carpentier, Horace, 159
Carrasco, Roberto, 275
Carver, Jonathan, 101
cassava, 15
Castañeda Hotel, 189
Castaño de Sosa, Gaspar, 44
castizos, 118
Castro, Fidel, 303, 305
Catalonia, 341
Cather, Willa, 196
Catholic Church, Catholicism, 30, 55, 82,
  138, 163, 223, 252, 254–55, 311–13,
  333, 336–38, 342–43
cattle, 22, 25, 27, 64, 114, 216, 219, 228
caudillos, 344–45
Celler, Emmanuel, 290–91
Census Bureau, US, xxii
Central America, 24, 107, 286
Central American Republic, 130
Central American Union, 129
Central Pacific Railroad, 186–87
Cervantes, Miguel de, 46
Césaire, Aimé, 282
César, Julio, 117
Cézanne, Paul, xxi
Chacón, Eusebio, 165, 313
Chalaques, 34
Chama River, 51